BIBLICAL LANGUAGES: GREEK
2

Sheffield Academic Press

Idioms of the Greek New Testament

Second Edition

Stanley E. Porter

Biblical Languages: Greek
2

To Jeffrey T. Reed, John Wesley Reed,
and the memory of Granville Sharp

First published by JSOT Press 1992
Second edition with corrections 1994

Sheffield Academic Press Ltd
Mansion House
19 Kingfield Road
Sheffield S11 9AS
England

Typeset by Sheffield Academic Press
and
Printed on acid-free paper in Great Britain
by The Cromwell Press
Melksham, Wiltshire

British Library Cataloguing in Publication Data

Porter, Stanley E.
Idioms of the Greek New Testament.—
(Biblical Languages: Greek Series, ISSN
0309-0966-7407)
I. Title II. Series
487.4

ISBN 1-85075-357-1
ISBN 1-85075-379-2 pbk

CONTENTS

Preface

This book has been several years in the making and has undergone many revisions, encouraged by friends and colleagues. I do not even pretend that it is fully adequate, but it has apparently proved helpful in its various permutations to others who have endeavored to increase their knowledge of the Greek of the NT. In light of that I release it to the wider public, with the hope that it will continue to prove useful and instructive, and—if nothing else—to provoke further learning.

I wish to thank several years of second-year Greek students at Biola University (La Mirada, California, USA) for their many helpful comments while they endured reading and using this material in the form of photocopied pages. These years were some of my most enjoyable.

Several of my colleagues and former students have provided helpful suggestions as to how this text could be made more useful to a variety of students. Much of what accessibility it has comes as the result of their help. In particular I wish to thank Jeffrey T. Reed, John Wesley Reed, Scot Snyder, Ruth Anne Reese, Craig L. Blomberg, Philip Kern and my father.

I wish also to thank my editor at Sheffield Academic Press, Dr J. Webb Mealy, for his keen attention to details, larger concepts and their expression.

This book is dedicated to my students, current and former, in particular Jeff and John Reed, as well as to the memory of Granville Sharp (1735–1813). His memorial can be seen in Poets' Corner in Westminster Abbey, London, and well illustrates for me the greatness to which a grammarian can aspire.

Preface to the Second Edition

I wish to thank all of the reviewers and the numbers of teachers and students who have used and made helpful comments regarding this book. I especially wish to thank my own students and colleagues at Trinity Western University and the Associated Canadian Theological Schools, Langley, B.C., Canada, for their interest in this project. I have taken the occasion of this edition to correct several mistakes. That this book has warranted a second edition so soon is a testimony to the continuing vitality of study of the Greek of the New Testament. If this volume has played even a small role in that movement, I will have had my reward.

LIST OF ILLUSTRATIONS

ABBREVIATIONS

BAGD	W. Bauer, W.F. Arndt, F.W. Gingrich and F.W. Danker, *Greek–English Lexicon of the New Testament*
BDF	F. Blass, A. Debrunner and R.W. Funk, *A Greek Grammar of the New Testament*
Bib	*Biblica*
BT	*The Bible Translator*
CBQ	*Catholic Biblical Quarterly*
ExpTim	*Expository Times*
FN	*Filología Neotestamentaria*
GTJ	*Grace Theological Journal*
JBL	*Journal of Biblical Literature*
JSNT	*Journal for the Study of the New Testament*
JTS	*Journal of Theological Studies*
N–A	E. Nestle and K. Aland (eds.), *Novum Testamentum Graeca*
NASB	*New American Standard Bible*
NEB	*New English Bible*
NIDNTT	C. Brown (ed.), *The New International Dictionary of New Testament Theology*
NIV	New International Version
NovT	*Novum Testamentum*
NTS	*New Testament Studies*
RSV	Revised Standard Version
SJT	*Scottish Journal of Theology*
TDNT	G. Kittel and G. Friedrich (eds.), *Theological Dictionary of the New Testament*
TEV	Today's English Version
TynBul	*Tyndale Bulletin*
TZ	*Theologische Zeitschrift*
UBSGNT	United Bible Societies' *Greek New Testament*
WTJ	*Westminster Theological Journal*
ZNW	*Zeitschrift für die neutestamentliche Wissenschaft*

Introduction

Idioms of the Greek New Testament, the title of this volume, may arouse some curiosity. The term 'idiom' is not being used in the technical sense of set phrases in the language; rather, it is being used after the fashion established by C.F.D. Moule, in his extremely helpful work, *An Idiom Book of NT Greek*, to refer to the various patterns of usage of the Greek of the NT. At the outset, it is perhaps useful to state that the Greek of the NT, so far as this book is concerned, constitutes an established corpus suitable for linguistic analysis. Consequently, there is relatively little reference in this volume to standards of usage found in other bodies of Greek texts from various periods. This is a major departure from a number of other grammars, which assume knowledge of classical standards, for example, and simply comment on features of NT Greek as they reinforce or depart from these standards.

My own approach is to consider the Greek of the NT to be a collection of texts from the wider corpus of Greek texts available during the first century AD, i.e. Hellenistic Greek. Consequently, I enter into discussion of Semitic influence upon NT Greek only incidentally. First, my own studies have left me rather skeptical that sizeable and significant examples of Semitic influence on NT Greek can be established, apart possibly from use of certain vocabulary items, which is not a topic of discussion in this book. Secondly, from a linguistic standpoint, whether there is or is not Semitic influence is really beside the point, since the NT is here treated synchronically, that is, without regard for any hypothetical linguistic background of its authors, but with concentration on the NT as a body of analyzable linguistic examples. The Greek described in this book is of necessity a regularized form of even the language of the NT. Many generalizations and patterns are cited which do not capture all of the peculiar instances of usage by a given biblical author. This is done in order to formulate a general analysis of NT Greek.

My purpose for this book is modest. This book is designed for students who have completed approximately one year of Greek, and who would like an intermediate handbook to help them make a transition to using advanced grammars such as BDF, Robertson, Moulton and Turner. Although a number will come to this book, appropriately enough, with one year of classical Greek background, it is more likely that students who use it will have studied one year of NT Greek. My evidence indicates that first-year courses are taught in widely divergent ways and produce students of widely variant abilities and preparations. One of the struggles in producing this book was to find the right level at which to pitch it. I assume that the student who uses it will already know the basics of how to recognize and parse nouns, adjectives and verbs, and will have a basic understanding of phrase and clause structure.

For some, this book may seem too difficult and inaccessible. I apologize in advance for any difficulties. I would like to encourage you, however, to continue to work with it. Perhaps more background is needed before using it to its fullest, although I have endeavored to make it useful in several ways. First, I define important terms as the chapters proceed. I have also included a glossary of recurring terms. If this list does not answer all of your questions, dictionaries and grammar books may be helpful. The first four chapters may prove a little more difficult than the others, but they contain essential terminology used throughout the book. Secondly, in constructing this grammar book I have tried at significant junctures to include (usually in parantheses) the labels and categories often found in other, similar grammars. These terms are not always synonymous, but perhaps by including a variety of labels this book will be more accessible to students and teachers alike. Students may well find terms familiar from their first-year texts or from other tools which they find helpful. Similarly, teachers may find convenient labels with which they are familiar from using other grammars.

For some, this book may appear too easy. I must admit to have passed by more than a few very interesting linguistic and exegetical issues, ones which I would have liked to discuss and which would have found a place in a full-fledged reference grammar. I would like to encourage you, however, not to give up on this book either. I hope that you will make it a frequent reference tool, since I have included some things which are not readily found in other texts of this sort.

There are several areas in which I believe that this grammar book makes serious advances over other equivalent grammars. First, my analysis is based upon principles of modern linguistics, translated and adapted for students and teachers who may not have had any exposure to its technical language and method.[1] For example, I have taken a synchronic approach to the NT, treating it as consisting of representative Greek texts produced by actual language users of the first century AD. I have approached the language as a self-referring linguistic system, and consequently have avoided discussing Greek in terms of, for example, Latin. Of course, it is unavoidable that I have had to use English to describe Greek, and translations of most of the examples have been included, but these are not a substitute for understanding how the language itself works. The translations are not designed to be elegant renderings of Greek; they are meant to indicate my understanding of a particular point through a useful gloss. I also apologize in advance for any renderings that have come out non-inclusive in my efforts to be literal. In my version, I have attempted to maintain a distinction between form and function. This has resulted in some inevitable inconsistencies for a variety of reasons, not least because no language—having been a living tool in the mouths of its users—is completely tractable. But I have found myself repeatedly making distinctions between a given form and how that form is used (i.e. how it functions) in the Greek language.

The book is divided into two sections, the first dealing with the functions of individual words and their phrasal relations; the second dealing with clauses and larger units. Within a chapter, the formal and functional distinction is usually maintained, with major categories often based on formal features of the language, but with semantic, syntactical and functional distinctions made within these categories. It has not always been easy to differentiate these sub-categories, and there is some repetition which I hope is tolerable (e.g. particles, prepositions and dependent clauses). One must always recognize when discussing the use of individual words or forms that these items are used within larger linguistic contexts. The larger linguistic context must always be considered (see Chapter 21 on discourse analysis).

1. For those interested in this subject, see S.E. Porter, 'Studying Ancient Languages from a Modern Linguistic Perspective: Essential Terms and Terminology', *FN* 2 (1989), pp. 147-72; *idem*, *Verbal Aspect in the Greek of the NT, with Reference to Tense and Mood* (New York: Peter Lang, 1989), pp. 1-16.

Secondly, I have brought a new and sometimes distinctive perspective to several of the major topics for discussion in Greek grammar and linguistics. Although I am cognizant of the history of discussion of these topics over the last century or so, I believe that some of the positions I have arrived at are very important, though not necessarily definitively correct. In that sense this book is still in progress. The areas in which I have consciously tried to advance the discussion include tense and aspect (Chapter 1), mood and attitude (Chapter 2), cases and gender (Chapter 4), prepositions (Chapter 9), participles (Chapter 10), conditional clauses (Chapter 16), word order and clause structure (Chapter 20), and discourse analysis (Chapter 21). To facilitate discussion, even though I have a particular viewpoint on the topic, I attempt to place my discussion into the history of discussion, so that if a given student or teacher does not share my perspective this grammar can still prove useful on the given topic. The issue of tense and aspect is one of great current interest, and I strongly argue for verbal aspect over tense as the governing semantic category for Greek verbal usage. I recognize that this is a controversial position, but would ask that even those readers who do not share my perspective will give Chapter 1—and the book—a chance, nevertheless. I have tried to be as accommodating to various perspectives as I can, including not pushing verbal aspect overly hard in other areas of the book.

The reader will notice that there is some imbalance among the lengths of the various chapters. This is true of many grammars, and can only be explained along two lines: first, certain topics require greater discussion than others simply to provide comparable coverage; and secondly, certain topics are far more exciting and hold more interest for students than others, resulting in their greater length of treatment.

A third feature of this book is the rather extensive use of examples, as well as reference to pertinent secondary literature. The examples I cite may not be the ones a given reader is finding troublesome, but I have attempted to treat a range of topics and to include enough examples to illustrate any given point being made, without being redundant. The standard I have used is to try to include two good examples of any given grammatical phenomenon. Sometimes there are more, rarely are there less. The examples have been secured through a variety of means, including culling other grammars for examples that seem constantly to re-emerge as worthy of discussion, incorporating examples from my own research that illustrate my perspective on a given category, and citing a few problematic texts for which I may not have a definitive answer.

I trust that this handbook will be used in conjunction with widespread reading of the Greek text of the NT, enabling students of the original language to add significant examples of their own to those given here. There is, of course, no substitute for extensive and systematic study of the Greek language as it is used in its original context.

I am grateful to the many grammarians who have gone before me, and I have tried to acknowledge my debt through citations of secondary literature. I have for the most part confined myself to English language sources, especially standard grammars, except in those cases where works in other languages are unparalleled or precedent-setting. I have also included a few references to other recent secondary literature (commentaries, journal articles), but I have made no attempt to be exhaustive, only representative. Perhaps these references will aid students to undertake their own exegetical investigations by pointing them toward other literature. Also, I have included no paradigms and do not discuss accidence and word-formation, assuming that the student will already have access to suitable information in these areas.

At periodic intervals in the grammar I refer to the categories of slot and filler. This does not presuppose my adoption of this linguistic model for description of the Greek of the NT. But in the course of developing this book, students have often found these categories helpful. By the terms 'slot and filler', I mean that various syntactical structures (i.e. the arrangements of words) are made up of smaller structures. For example, a clause might have a subject, a predicate and a complement. Thus this clause has three slots which need to be filled with appropriate subject, predicate and complement fillers. To go further, the subject might be filled by a nominal phrase, that is, a group of words with a noun or other substantive as its head-term, along with its modifiers. Thus this nominal phrase has a structure with a number of slots which need to be filled with appropriate substantive and modifier fillers. Although not in a rigorous way, I draw upon this kind of analysis to aid in description, having found this model useful for differentiating form and function. For example, the participle in Greek is a word like many others which follows a particular formal paradigm; that is, this word is recognizable by certain recurring structural patterns. But the participle can fill several different kinds of slots. In one context it might fill a noun modifier slot, in the same way that an adjective might in relation to a noun. In another context it might fill a verb modifier slot, in the same way that an adverb might in relation to a verb. In another context it might fill a substantive slot, in the same way that a noun might as part of a nominal phrase. The list could go on, but the illustration is well enough made. The participle is still a participle—the form is the same. But the function of the participle may vary according to how it is used. The categories of slot and filler help draw out these distinctions.

The Greek of the NT provides an eminently worthwhile and worthy body of literature for serious academic study, and my hope is that this grammar will enable many to take further steps toward its mastery.

Part I

WORDS AND PHRASES

Chapter 1

TENSE AND ASPECT, AND PERIPHRASTIC CONSTRUCTIONS

Introduction

Since the days of the earliest grammarians of Greek, who happened to be Greek speakers themselves, it has been recognized that the verb occupies a very important place in the Greek language. This is not to say that other grammatical elements are not very important, or that there are not other languages which place similar importance on the verb, but the flexibility and range of usage of the verb in Greek commends it to further analysis. This is especially true with regard to what are traditionally called the verb tenses. Virtually every verb in Greek (a few exceptions, namely aspectually vague verbs, will be noted below) must be conjugated according to tense-form (i.e. the verb form must be an aorist, present or perfect), whatever else it may be, such as an imperative, indicative or subjunctive. In other words, in every slot which a verb form fills, a verb tense-form (and consequently a verbal aspect, as discussed in section 1 below) must be selected.

1. *Verbal Aspect: Definition*

The original function of the so-called 'tense stems' of the verb in Indo-European languages (of which Greek is one) was not levels of time (past, present or future), as many suppose, but one of verbal aspect (i.e. how the verbal action was perceived to unfold; see section 2 below on history of discussion).[1] In Greek, *verbal aspect is defined*

1. Cf. Hebrew, where a similar realization has been in force since the work of Ewald and Driver: H. Ewald, *Syntax of the Hebrew Language of the OT* (trans. J. Kennedy; Edinburgh: T. & T. Clark, 1881), pp. 1-13; S.R. Driver, *A Treatise on the Use of the Tenses in Hebrew: And Some Other Syntactical Questions* (Oxford: Clarendon Press, 3rd edn, 1892), pp. 1-6.

as a semantic (meaning) category by which a speaker or writer grammaticalizes (i.e. represents a meaning by choice of a word-form) a perspective on an action by the selection of a particular tense-form in the verbal system. The semantic features (the 'meanings') of the different verbal aspects are attached to the tense-forms. The verbal aspects are therefore morphologically based (i.e. form and function are matched). Verbal aspect is a semantic feature which attaches *directly* to use of a given tense-form in Greek. Other values—such as time—are established at the level of larger grammatical or conceptual units, such as the sentence, paragraph, proposition, or even discourse (see Chapter 21). The choice of the particular verbal aspect (expressed in the verb tense-form) resides with the language user, and it is from this perspective that grammatical interpretation of the verb must begin.[1]

1.1. *The Three Verbal Aspects*

There are three verbal aspects in Greek, linked to the three major tense-forms.[2] a. *Perfective aspect is the meaning ('semantics') of the aorist tense: the action is conceived of by the language user as a complete and undifferentiated process.* This is regardless of how in actual fact the action occurs, that is, whether it is momentary or lasts a significant length of time: ἡ ἀστραπὴ ἤστραψε (the lightning flashed),[3] or ἐβασίλευσεν ὁ θάνατος ἀπὸ 'Αδὰμ μέχρι Μωϋσέως (death reigned from Adam until Moses; Rom. 5.14). b. *Imperfective aspect is the meaning of the present tense, including the so-called imperfect form* (augmented present form with secondary endings)*: the action is conceived of by the language user as being in progress.* In other words, its internal structure is seen as unfolding. c. *Stative aspect is the meaning of the perfect tense, including the so-called pluperfect form* (not always augmented but with secondary endings)*: the action is*

1. Cf. Porter, *Verbal Aspect*, ch. 2.

2. The morphological categories of first (sigmatic, weak) and second (irregular, strong) aorists, various kinds of presents (with infixes, endings, and so forth) and strong and weak perfects, as well as the distinction between *mi* verbs and *omega* verbs, do not enter into discussion here. These are simply distinctions made in how the forms themselves are constructed and altered. The individual forms within the categories are described according to their paradigms as aorists, presents, and perfects respectively, and this categorization is the one of importance for the discussion of verbal aspect.

3. Cf. Lk. 17.24: ἡ ἀστραπὴ ἀστράπτουσα... (the lightning flashing...), which is presumably not a different kind of lightning.

conceived of by the language user as reflecting a given (often complex) state of affairs. This is regardless of whether this state of affairs has come about as the result of some antecedent action or whether any continued duration is implied.

The ways in which verbal aspect may be illustrated are several, but the significant concept is that the aspects are arranged in relation to each other. Several analogies may be helpful at this point (see Chapter 21 sections 1.2, 2.1, and 3.2).

1.1.1. *Verbal opposition.* Modern linguistics has made students of language aware that language production may usefully be discussed in terms of its opposing choices, so that it is seen in terms of a coordinated system. This implies that when one element is selected, other similar elements in the language are not selected. The perfective (aorist) aspect is the least heavily weighted of the Greek verbal aspects, and hence carries the least significant meaning attached to use of the form. In Greek the aorist is what some have called the 'default' tense; that is, it is the tense chosen when there is no reason to choose another. The imperfective (present/imperfect) aspect is more heavily weighted, and to use it in opposition to the perfective (aorist) implies greater semantic significance. The stative (perfect/pluperfect) aspect is most heavily weighted, and to use it in opposition to the perfective (aorist) and imperfective (present/imperfect) aspects implies the greatest semantic significance. In Rom. 6.7-10 the aorist, present and perfect verbs are used in coordination: 'For the one who dies (ἀποθανών) is justified (δεδικαίωται) from sin [an emphatic opening statement]; but if we die (ἀπεθάνομεν) with Christ, we believe (πιστεύομεν) that indeed we can expect to live (future—see section 2.4 below) with him, knowing (εἰδότες) that Christ, being raised (ἐγερθείς) from the dead, no longer dies (ἀποθνῄσκει); death no longer dominates (κυριεύει) him. For the death he died (ἀπέθανεν), he died (ἀπέθανεν) to sin once; but what he lives (ζῇ), he lives (ζῇ) to God.' The perfect verb form is used to introduce the section (δεδικαίωται), as well as to specify the content of the Christian's knowledge (εἰδότες). Repeated aorist tense-forms are used to lay down the fundamental events upon which the Christian's status depends. The more emphatic present tense then describes the events.

1.1.2. *Planes of discourse* (fig. 1). Recent work by linguists in the analysis of discourse differentiates the planes of discourse into three (see Chapter 21): background, foreground and frontground. These three planes are depicted below as a case of books (background), against which one shelf is featured (foreground), and a single book is selected (frontground). The aorist is the background tense, which forms the basis for the discourse; the present is the foreground tense, which introduces significant characters or makes appropriate climactic references to concrete situations; and the perfect is the frontground tense, which introduces elements in an even more discrete, defined, contoured and complex way. In Acts 16.1-5, aorist tense-forms are used for the narrative events, present tense-forms are used for selected or highlighted events, and the perfect tense-form is reserved for selective mention of a few very significant items, including the 'determined things' (τὰ κεκριμένα). The context and the tense-forms work together to create this picture of the world. A verbal aspectual analysis of tense usage applies not only to narrative but also to exposition. In Rom. 5.1-2, Paul begins with the assumption that, since his readers are justified (aorist), they are to enjoy (present) peace with God. The enjoyment of peace stands out against the backdrop of justification, his new topic of discussion building upon the old. In v. 2 Paul brings out more forcefully the status which his audience enjoys: they have access and stand in grace—both statements using perfect tense verb forms.

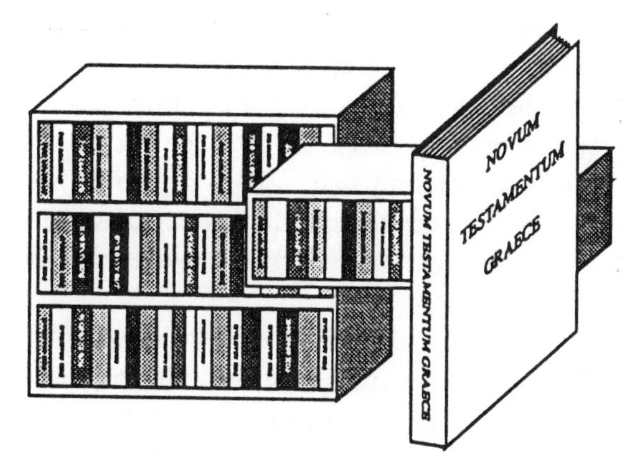

Figure 1. *Planes of Discourse*

1.1.3. *Visualization.* If each aspect represents the author's grammaticalized perspective on an event, it is logical to ask how that perspective might be visualized. The analogy of a parade proves useful. If I am a television correspondent in a helicopter flying over the parade, I view the parade in its immediacy from a vantage outside the action as 'perfective'; that is, in its entirety as a single and complete whole. If I am a spectator standing with others along the side of the road watching the parade pass by in front of me, I view the action immersed within it as 'imperfective'; that is, as an event in progress. And if I am the parade manager in corporate headquarters considering all of the conditions in existence at this parade, including not only all the arrangements that are coming to fruition but all the accompanying events that allow the parade to operate, I view the process not in its particulars or its immediacy but as 'stative'; that is, as a complex condition or state of affairs in existence. For example, in Rom. 8.11 with ἐγείραντος (aorist), 2 Cor. 1.9 with ἐγείροντι (present), 2 Tim. 2.8 with ἐγηγερμένον (perfect): each verse uses a different tense-form to refer to the same event, the raising of Christ. The use of each depends upon the author's contextual emphasis.

Several further categories may usefully be discussed at this point.

a. *The future form in Greek does not constitute either a time-based tense-form or a verbal aspect in its full sense as discussed above.* Morphologically the distinguishing feature of the *sigma* (λύω » λύσω) reflects its origins in the subjunctive.[1] Grammarians have been divided regarding the exact semantic value or meaning of the future form, although many are willing to concede that a temporal value is not paramount (see section 2.4 below).

b. The effect of prefixes (prepositions) upon the verb tenses has often been construed as perfectivizing the action, that is, making any tense-form equivalent to an aorist.[2] This judgment must now be abandoned,[3] with the recognition that *verbal aspect is not affected by attachment of a prefix*, even though the lexical sense of the item may be altered, e.g. ἔφαγεν (eat) and κατέφαγεν (devour) (see Chapter 9 section 2 on prepositions).

c. A very small number of verbs in Greek (all verbs of the -μι conjugation) never developed a full set of tense-forms, and hence do not participate in the aspectual system (this is not the same as defective

1. Porter, *Verbal Aspect*, p. 404.

2. BDF, §318; J.H. Moulton, *A Grammar of NT Greek*. I. *Prolegomena* (Edinburgh: T. & T. Clark, 3rd edn, 1908), pp. 111-15.

3. Porter, *Verbal Aspect*, appendix 1A.

verbs, which may display only a limited number of the three verbal paradigms). The result is that these verbs offer no meaningful choice between one aspect and another. These verbs, of which εἰμί is the primary example,[1] are called aspectually vague. *Aspectually vague verbs may be used in any verbal context since they do not carry the semantic weight of perfective, imperfective or stative verbal aspect.* Consequently, one must be cautious in giving interpretative significance to use of one of these verbs.[2] Discussion of periphrastic constructions below (section 3) depends upon this distinction.

1.2. *Time and the Tense-Forms*

Temporal values (past, present, future) are not established in Greek by use of the verbal aspects (or tense-forms) alone. This may come as a surprise to those who, like most students of Greek, were taught at an elementary level that certain tense-forms automatically refer to certain times when an action occurs. The usual equation, called 'absolute tense', states that the aorist, imperfect and pluperfect tenses convey the idea of past time; the present and perfect tenses that of present time; and the future tense that of future time. This is not the place to argue against the absolute tense conception in detail, although subsequent discussion in this and other chapters will illustrate some of the crucial issues in its refutation. I do not mean to say that Greeks did not have a means of conveying when an event might have occurred, however. A more viable category is 'relative tense'. This presupposes that in Greek the temporal ordering of events is not measured in relation to a fixed point (absolute time), but by the relations established among the involved events with regard to each other and to the context. This relating is achieved by a variety of indicators available in the language (e.g. use of temporal adverbs, such as νῦν, τότε). In other words, elements *other* than verbal aspect (context, for example) are the primary conveyors of temporal information in Greek. This applies in the case not only of the non-indicative mood forms, but of the indicative mood as well (see section 2 below, and Chapter 2 on moods).

A variety of contextual features (often called deictic indicators)

1. The paradigm of εἰμί in the Greek of the NT is different from that of some other, especially earlier, Greek dialects. The student may want to take note of these differences.

2. Porter, *Verbal Aspect*, ch. 10.

must be analyzed to establish temporal values: references to person, place and time, and discourse features.[1] The last of these appear to be the most significant, themselves conveying the very information most often attributed to the verb tense-forms, for example, in the generalization that the aorist tense-form means past time, the present tense-form means present time, and so on. For the Greeks, the perfective aspect (expressed by the aorist form), with its perspective of seeing actions in their entirety or as complete, was apparently felt to be most compatible with speaking about actions seen as complet*ed*; hence its frequent use in narrative. The imperfective aspect (expressed by the present form), with its perspective of seeing progressive development of an action, was apparently felt to be compatible with continuing examination; hence its frequent use in description or exposition. Consequently, the aorist is the tense which forms the backbone of narrative, while the present appears frequently in non-narrative contexts. Of course, this is only a generalization and not determinative, since any of the verbal aspects can (and may well) appear in any temporal context. The interpreter's task is to consider all of the relevant information—including verb tenses, discourse type and so forth—before deciding *when* an event is to be conceived of as occurring.

1.3. *History of Discussion of Verbs in Greek*

Understanding of the function of the Greek tense-forms has undergone several transformations in the last several centuries. It is widely agreed that the ancient Greek grammarians themselves were not able to formulate clearly the exact relations of the tense-forms (although they gave it a good try), but the fact that they began to discuss them provided a useful starting point for subsequent research.

1.3.1. *Rationalist period.* The first period of significance has been called the rationalist period (17th–early 19th century). It was characterized by belief that the Greek tense-forms should conform to some preconceived logical system derived from the European languages used for analysis (usually English or German, or possibly Latin). The result was a heavily time-based system, in which a one-to-one correlation was drawn between tense-form and time of action (i.e. absolute tense), thus present tense = present time. Consequently, these gram-

1. S.C. Levinson, *Pragmatics* (Cambridge: Cambridge University Press, 1983), pp. 54-96.

marians devised means to explain recognizable deviations from their absolute-time perspective, such as the so-called gnomic aorist (an aorist form which is not past in time reference, but is used of recurring natural events), and the so-called historic present (a present form which is used in narration). Whereas these grammarians had their greatest significance from an academic standpoint in the nineteenth century and before, their legacy remains, especially in elementary Greek grammars, where their influence is virtually unabated.

1.3.2. *Aktionsart*. The second significant period is characterized by reliance on the concept of *Aktionsart* (a German word apparently invented around 1885 by Brugmann and introduced into English in 1906 by Moulton in his *Prolegomena*). It is perhaps best described and defended in the classic grammar by Brugmann,[1] although many standard reference grammars use this approach. This framework was developed in the flush of discovery in the nineteenth century of the genetic relations among many Indo-European languages. *The theory of Aktionsart is the supposition that the verb tenses of Greek are used to convey how an action objectively occurs*. The result is a complex scheme whereby certain values are attached to the verb tense-forms, such as punctiliar to the aorist, durative or linear to the present. Thus one might find reference to inceptive (action at its beginning point), perfective (action brought to completion), or iterative (action occurring at intervals) action, and so on. The scheme varies with the individual author. A recognizable shortcoming of this perspective is its ambivalence toward the relation between tense-forms and their abilities to characterize action objectively. For example, Greek does not have an iterative tense-form, and often aorist action is not punctiliar.[2] The result is frequent, major alterations in the system to accommodate deviations, often explained in terms not of a given tense-form but of the underlying root of the verb as either punctiliar or durative. (The perfect tense-form was always problematic.) This analysis has difficulty explaining description of the same event using, for example, the aorist and the present tenses, since the objective measurement of kind of action cannot be defined solely in terms of

1. K. Brugmann, *Griechische Grammatik* (ed. A. Thumb; Munich: Beck, 4th edn, 1913 [1885]), pp. 538-41.

2. See F. Stagg, 'The Abused Aorist', *JBL* 91 (1972), pp. 222-31; C.R. Smith, 'Errant Aorist Interpreters', *GTJ* 2 (1981), pp. 205-26.

verbal usage. Furthermore, it is arbitrary to characterize all action as fitting into only three objective categories, punctiliar, linear and resultive. This view is promoted widely in many of the standard advanced Greek reference grammars (e.g. Robertson, BDF, Moulton), most of these tools being written at least fifty years ago.[1]

1.3.3. *Verbal aspect.* Although several significant precursors posited, for example, a distinction between subjective aspect and objective *Aktionsart*,[2] major work on verbal aspect first appeared after World War II.[3] In light of the advent of modern linguistics and its emphasis upon synchronic treatment of a given language's verbal system, more and more grammarians became content to examine the verbal system of Greek in terms of the verb forms available within the language itself, regardless of reconstructed genetic forebearers.[4] The result is the recognition that Greek verbal aspect centers upon use of the three major tense-forms and some consistent semantic features attached to them. Choice of a verbal aspect is seen to lie at the discretion of the speaker or writer, within certain well-established patterns of usage.

2. *Verbal Aspect and its Range of Functions*

Traditional grammatical discussions of tense-form usage, as found in many of the older grammars, make use of all sorts of rather complicated terminology.[5] Such terms as inceptive aorist, punctiliar present, and so forth, are common. However, this terminology is not used here. As seen in section 1 above, verbs function in Greek as indicators of the speaker or writer's view of a particular action, regardless of how that action might 'objectively' have transpired in the real world or 'when' it might have transpired. The verb tenses grammaticalize (i.e. represent a meaning by selection of a particular verb tense-form)

1. Cf. also B.M. Fanning, *Verbal Aspect in NT Greek* (Oxford: Clarendon Press, 1990), chs. 1 and 2.

2. H. Jacobsohn, Review of *Vorlesungen*, by J. Wackernagel, *Gnomon* 2 (1926), pp. 378-86; cf. G. Curtius, *Elucidations of the Student's Greek Grammar* (trans. E. Abbott; London: John Murray, 2nd edn, 1875), pp. 207-18.

3. J. Holt, *Etudes d'aspect* (Copenhagen: Universitetsforlaget i Aarhus, 1943).

4. See A.T. Robertson, *A Grammar of the Greek NT in the Light of Historical Research* (Nashville: Broadman, 4th edn, 1934), pp. 46-48; K.L. McKay, 'Syntax in Exegesis', *TynBul* 23 (1972), pp. 44-45.

5. See Fanning, *Verbal Aspect*, ch. 3.

this subjective viewpoint through the category of verbal aspect.[1] Greeks were still able to make reference to various times of the day or night and to distinguish kinds of action, but they did so by using a variety of indicators, *with verb tenses as only one factor in establishing the temporal context*. The discussion below is divided into five temporal categories, in which each of the verb tense-forms may be used—past, present, future (which are fairly self-explanatory), omnitemporal and timeless (which are explained in more detail below). Some grammarians—even if they recognize the non-temporal use of the tense-forms in the non-indicative moods (see Chapter 2)—insist on the tense-forms having time-based usage in the indicative mood.[2] The following instances show that this position cannot be sustained. There has been a tendency among some scholars simply to disregard usage which does not conform to some pre-established temporal scheme, whereas others recognize that so-called exceptions may in fact be part of a range of legitimate, even though not frequent, usage. The following examples thus not only illustrate the functions of the verbal aspects but exemplify their use in a range of temporal contexts using the indicative mood. Verbal aspect in the non-indicative moods is illustrated in subsequent chapters.

2.1. *The Present and Imperfect Tense-Forms*

The present and imperfect tense-forms occur in contexts where the user of Greek wishes to depict the action as in progress, regardless of whether this is an objective characterization. The imperfective verbal aspect grammaticalized by the present tense-form may be used in a variety of temporal contexts.[3]

2.1.1. *Present for present action* (descriptive, progressive, conative, iterative present).

This usage occurs with frequency, especially in descriptive or expository prose.

1. See McKay, 'Syntax', p. 136; Porter, *Verbal Aspect*, p. 88, and Chapter 2 below. See also B. Comrie, *Aspect: An Introduction to the Study of Verbal Aspect and Related Problems* (Cambridge: Cambridge University Press, 1976), pp. 1-6, esp. 4.
2. E.g. K.L. McKay, *Greek Grammar for Students: A Concise Grammar of Classical Attic with Special Reference to Aspect in the Verb* (Canberra: Australian National University, 1974), pp. 141-48; Fanning, *Verbal Aspect*, ch. 4.
3. Robertson, *Grammar*, pp. 880-82.

Acts 17.22-23: θεωρῶ...εὐσεβεῖτε...καταγγέλλω...(I see... you are religious...I am announcing...).

Rom. 1.8-13 *passim*: εὐχαριστῶ...καταγγέλλεται...λατρεύω ...ποιοῦμαι...ἐπιποθῶ...οὐ θέλω...(I give thanks...it is announced...I worship...I am making...I long...I do not want...).

2.1.2. *Present for past action* (historic present). The use of the present tense-form in narrative is widespread, and has been discussed repeatedly by grammarians. Its use is one of the reasons for recurrent discussion about its function, since it goes directly against one of the traditional views of how tense-forms function in Greek (i.e. in relation to time: present tense = present time). Although at one time some scholars thought that this use of the present tense-form was a sign of Semitic verbal influence upon the Greek of the NT, recent evidence—in which some secular Hellenistic Greek writers manifest this usage in greater proportion than NT writers—renders this view untenable.[1]

Among the several proposals for how to understand this use of the present tense-form, there are four worth considering here. a. Dramatic use of the present tense.[2] Many grammarians argue that this use occurs when the author wants to propel actions from the past into the present so that they gain vividness. Although this view is perpetuated in many commentaries, it must be rejected because of its outdated view of tense functions, the lack of indication in the text of such a perspectival shift, and the resulting clumsiness in perspective when tenses are seen as shifting so quickly. An example is Mk 5.35-42, where there are nine present verbs, three aorist verbs and one imperfect verb, unlikely evidence indeed that events are shifted temporally for vividness. b. Tense reduction.[3] Kiparsky argues that in repeated sequences of tenses in Greek some of the tense-forms are 'reduced' from a past to a present form. Besides the sheer speculation involved regarding the relation of this pattern to proto-Indo-European language usage, several

1. Porter, *Verbal Aspect*, pp. 134-36; K. Eriksson, *Das Präsens historicum in der nachklassischen griechischen Historiographie* (Lund: Håkan Ohlsson, 1943), pp. 8-24.

2. Fanning, *Verbal Aspect*, pp. 226-29; Brugmann, *Griechische Grammatik*, pp. 555, 556.

3. P. Kiparsky, 'Tense and Mood in Indo-European Syntax', *Foundations of Language* 4 (1968), pp. 30-57; cf. S.M. Reynolds, 'The Zero Tense in Greek: A Critical Note', *WTJ* 32 (1965), pp. 68-72.

relation of this pattern to proto-Indo-European language usage, several grammarians have pointed out that this hypothesis does not conform to the way in which the Greek verbal system is structured (the aorist is best considered the reduced form), and there are numerous passages where either there is no reduction or the present tense-form begins the sequence (e.g. Xenophon, *Anabasis* 1.1.1). c. Change of setting or character.[1] Some have argued that the historic present is used to mark significant changes in the narrative flow. Whereas this may well occur (e.g. Mk 1.12, 21; 3.31), and this category must be considered when formulating an explanation of this usage, the instances where it does not mark significant change are too manifest to endorse this scheme as a sufficient explanation. d. Verbal aspect.[2] Believing that too much previous analysis has been concerned with equating tense-forms with time, several recent grammarians rightly indicate that different tense-forms can obviously be used in similar temporal contexts, and that the imperfective verbal aspect (present tense-form) is used whenever one wishes to draw added attention to a given event. For example, in Mk 1.21, 30, 6.1, 9.2, Jn 1.29 a change of setting is indicated; in Mk 5.15, Mt. 26.40 a climactic turning point is selected; in Jn 19.9 dialogue is highlighted; and in Mk 15.29 the concluding events of a sequence are focused upon. (Mark is a relatively frequent user of the historic present.) Even though the historic present and other tense-forms may be used in past contexts, this does not mean that the historic present and, for example, the aorist mean the same thing—their sphere of temporal reference may overlap, but their verbal aspect is different. Whereas the aorist is merely used in its common narrative function, the present form draws added attention to the action to which it refers.[3]

Mk 1.21, 30: καὶ εἰσπορεύονται εἰς Καφαρναούμ...καὶ εὐθὺς λέγουσιν αὐτῷ περὶ αὐτῆς (and they entered into Capernaum ...and immediately they spoke to him concerning her)—at decisive junctures in the narrative.

Acts 10.11: καὶ θεωρεῖ τὸν οὐρανόν (and he saw heaven)—to highlight Peter's vision.

1. R. Buth, 'Mark's Use of the Historical Present', *Notes on Translation* 65 (1977), pp. 7-13.

2. K.L. McKay, 'Further Remarks on the "Historical" Present and Other Phenomena', *Foundations of Language* 11 (1974), pp. 247-51.

3. Porter, *Verbal Aspect*, pp. 189-98.

2.1.3. *Present for future action* (futuristic present). When a speaker sees an action as carrying over into the future, the present tense-form may be used. This usage is not frequent, indicating—along with the problematic nature of speaking about the future—to some grammarians that Greek is best analyzed as a bi-temporal language, that is, a language which focuses upon two spheres of temporal reference, past and present. This use of the present tense-form is known in classical Greek as well, especially in prophetic oracles (Herodotus 7.140-41), although use in oracles is not widespread in the Greek of the NT. Verbs of motion appear relatively frequently with this sense.

Mt. 17.11: Ἠλίας...ἔρχεται καὶ ἀποκαταστήσει πάντα (Elijah...is going to come and will restore all things).

Mt. 26.2: τὸ πάσχα γίνεται, καὶ ὁ υἱὸς τοῦ ἀνθρώπου παραδίδοται (the Passover is going to come about, and the son of man is going to be betrayed); Mt. 26.18: ποιῶ τὸ πάσχα (I am going to celebrate the Passover); and Mt. 26.45: ὁ υἱὸς τοῦ ἀνθρώπου παραδίδοται (the son of man is going to be betrayed).

Frequently present and future forms occur in sequence, the matter of greater emphasis occurring in the present tense-form.[1]

Mt. 26.2, above.

Mk 10.33: ἀναβαίνομεν εἰς Ἱεροσόλυμα, followed by καὶ ὁ υἱὸς τοῦ ἀνθρώπου παραδοθήσεται (we are going to go up into Jerusalem...and the son of man will be betrayed), followed by other future forms.

2.1.4. *Present for action occurring at any time (omnitemporal)* (gnomic present).[2] Perhaps because of the use of the simple English present tense to speak of processes which can occur at any time ('the sun comes up in the morning', implying that it always does), some grammarians have failed to recognize use of the present tense-form in Greek to speak of regularly recurring actions, especially those which recur in nature.

Mt. 6.26: birds οὐ σπείρουσιν οὐδὲ θερίζουσιν οὐδὲ συνάγουσιν (do not sow and do not reap and do not gather).

Mt. 7.17-18: πᾶν δένδρον ἀγαθὸν καρποὺς καλοὺς ποιεῖ τὸ δὲ σαπρὸν δένδρον καρποὺς πονηροὺς ποιεῖ· οὐ δύναται δένδρον ἀγαθὸν καρποὺς πονηροὺς ποιεῖν, οὐδὲ δένδρον σαπρὸν

1. Moulton, *Prolegomena*, p. 120.
2. See under aorist, section 2.2.4 below, for discussion of various views.

καρποὺς καλοὺς ποιεῖν (every good tree produces good fruit and the bad tree produces worthless fruit; a good tree is not able to produce worthless fruit, and the bad tree is not able to produce good fruit).

Mk 2.22: οὐδεὶς βάλλει οἶνον νέον εἰς ἀσκοὺς παλαιούς (no one puts new wine into old wineskins).

Jn 3.8: τὸ πνεῦμα ὅπου θέλει πνεῖ (the wind blows where it wills).

Jas 3.3-12, where an extended comparison is drawn between the tongue and processes found in nature.

2.1.5. *Present for timeless action.* The timeless use of the tenses is reserved for occasions where the question of time-reference simply does not occur. The event described is seen to be outside of temporal considerations. For example, this usage is particularly frequent in the kinds of statements which occur in theology and mathematical propositions.[1] Since verbal aspect is not a time-bound category, it could be argued that every use of a verb in Greek is timeless, since use of the verb form in and of itself specifies nothing regarding the time of an action. Despite the truth of this, and since in many contexts various indications of temporal reference are made, it is better to reserve this category for specific examples where time is seen not to be an issue. The parables contain numerous instances of timeless usage of the tense-forms, where despite the narrative progression the nature of the literary form renders the usage timeless. (This usage is often confused with the gnomic use, treated above.)

Mt. 5.14-15: οὐ δύναται πόλις κρυβῆναι ἐπάνω ὄρους κειμένη· οὐδὲ καίουσιν λύχνον καὶ τιθέασιν αὐτὸν ὑπὸ τὸν μόδιον ἀλλ' ἐπὶ τὴν λυχνίαν, καὶ λάμπει πᾶσιν τοῖς ἐν τῇ οἰκίᾳ (a city situated on a mountain is not able to be hidden; and they do not light a lamp and place it under the bushel but upon the lamp stand, and it burns for all in the house).

2 Cor. 9.7: ἱλαρὸν...δότην ἀγαπᾷ ὁ θεός (God loves a joyful giver).

Several extended Pauline passages should be included as well, such as Rom. 2.1-8.

2.1.6. *Imperfect. The imperfect form* (along with the pluperfect—see 2.3.2 below) *is the closest that the Greek language comes to a form*

1. J. Lyons, *Semantics* (Cambridge: Cambridge University Press, 1977), p. 680.

actually related to time (this does not mean that it is an absolute tense, however). Through a combination of features, including the added bulk of the augment and the secondary endings upon the present stem, Greek language users restricted its usage and meaning, often to past contexts.

a. *Past use* (progressive, descriptive, iterative). The past use of the imperfect is widespread in narrative, sharing this task with the aorist. The fact that both can appear in similar contexts raises the question of the nature of their distinction. On the basis of the imperfective aspect of the imperfect, it is the narrative form used when an action is selected to dwell upon.[1]

Mk 1.31-34 (*contra* Mt. 8.15-16; Lk. 4.39-41 with aorists), where the imperfect ἔφερον (they were bearing) is used in v. 32.

With verbs of saying an alternation is frequently found between the aorist and the imperfect.[2]

Jn 11.36, 37: ἔλεγον...οἱ Ἰουδαῖοι...τινὲς δὲ ἐξ αὐτῶν εἶπαν ...(the Jews were saying...but some of them said...).

Acts 2.13, 14: ἕτεροι...ἔλεγον ὅτι...δὲ ὁ Πέτρος...ἐπῆρεν καὶ...ἀπεφθέγξατο αὐτοῖς...(others...were saying that...but Peter...lifted...and declared to them...).

The imperfect is similar in function to the historic use of the present. Although they share the same verbal aspect, the present is used to draw even more attention to an action.

Mk 3.20, 21: καὶ ἔρχεται εἰς οἶκον· καὶ συνέρχεται...οἱ παρ' αὐτοῦ ἐξῆλθον...ἔλεγον γὰρ ὅτι ἐξέστη (and he went into a house; and [a crowd] gathered together...those around him went out ...for they were saying that he was crazy), where the present tense-form introduces the scene and establishes the situation, the aorist carries the narrative, and the imperfect records the thoughts of Jesus' followers.

b. *Non-past use* (conative). In a variety of instances the imperfect is used in contexts where its imperfective aspect (though not past reference) is brought to the fore. One of the most prominent uses is in the protasis of the so-called second class (contrary to fact) conditional (see Chapter 16 on conditional clauses). Another example includes what some grammarians call the 'conative' imperfect, in which

1. W.W. Goodwin, *A Greek Grammar* (London: St Martin's, 1894), p. 12.
2. BDF, §329.

contemplated but unbegun or unaccomplished action is referred to.

Lk. 23.54: σάββατον ἐπέφωσκεν (the Sabbath was about to dawn).

Jn 11.8: νῦν ἐζήτουν σε λιθάσαι οἱ Ἰουδαῖοι (the Jews are now seeking to stone you), where the adverb νῦν is to be taken seriously.

Phlm. 13: ἐγὼ ἐβουλόμην (I wish).

'Catenative' constructions (in which two verbs, each grammaticalizing verbal aspect, are joined in a close syntactical unit; Chapter 11 section 1.2.3) with imperfect verbs are frequently to be taken in this way.

Mt. 23.23: ἔδει ποιῆσαι (it is necessary to do).

2.2. *The Aorist Tense-Form*

The aorist tense-form is consistently the most widely used of the verb tenses in Greek. *The aorist tense-form occurs in contexts where the user of Greek wishes to depict an action as a complete and undifferentiated process.* Because of its augment, which is often thought of as a past-time indicator (it probably began simply as an adverb restricting its use to certain narrative contexts),[1] the aorist tense-form is often equated with past action.[2] The numerous examples in which this scheme is not true demand explanation.

2.2.1. *Aorist for past action* (narrative, constative, and even ingressive, effective and punctiliar aorists are categories found in other grammars; these categories are not employed here, as noted above). There is no disputing that the aorist tense-form frequently occurs in past-time contexts. It is the predominant narrative tense of Greek, in the sense that it is the tense which is relied upon to carry a narrative along when no attention is being drawn to the events being spoken of.

Acts 28.11-15: ἀνήχθημεν...ἐπεμείναμεν ἡμέρας τρεῖς... κατηντήσαμεν . . . ἤλθομεν . . . παρεκλήθημεν . . . ἤλθαμεν . . . ἦλθαν...ἔλαβε...(we set sail. ..we stayed three days. ..we met. .. we came...we were called upon...we went...[the brethren] came ... [Paul] took...).

Acts 28.30: ἐνέμεινεν...διετίαν ὅλην ἐν ἰδίῳ μισθώματι (he stayed for the entire two years in his own room).

1. McKay, *Greek Grammar*, p. 223.

2. That the augment cannot be seen as a past-time indicator is proved by examination of the Homeric writings, in which the so-called gnomic use virtually always has the augment, whereas the augment is often lacking in narrative contexts—cf. Porter, *Verbal Aspect*, pp. 208-209.

2 Cor. 11.24, 25: πεντάκις τεσσεράκοντα παρὰ μίαν ἔλαβον, τρὶς ἐραβδίσθην...τρὶς ἐναυάγησα (five times I received forty minus one lashes, three times I was beaten...three times I was shipwrecked), with numerical adverbs (a very difficult example for the 'punctiliar' view of the aorist tense-form).

2.2.2. *Aorist for present action* (dramatic aorist). In a number of contexts the aorist is used to refer to present action. Grammarians have long debated why this is possible, some of them finding it the result of phenomena in proto Indo-European.[1] Without needlessly speculating about the history of the language, however, it is best simply to acknowledge along with recent research that such a usage is not only possible but more widespread than once recognized.[2] (The apodoses of conditional constructions are not treated here, since they form part of a larger grammatical construction which is timeless by definition; see Chapter 16.) Several kinds of constructions seem to evidence this usage of the aorist more than others, including verbs of emotion or of action of short duration; sentences with particular adverbs, such as νῦν; as well as a variety of other single uses.

Mt. 23.23: ἀφήκατε τὰ βαρύτερα τοῦ νόμου (you neglect the heavier things of the law), parallel to a present tense verb, ἀποδεκατοῦτε (tithe).

Lk. 16.4: ἔγνων (I know), the unjust steward's reaction when an idea comes into his mind.

Jn 13.31: νῦν ἐδοξάσθη ὁ υἱὸς τοῦ ἀνθρώπου καὶ ὁ θεὸς ἐδοξάσθη ἐν αὐτῷ (now the son of man is glorified and God is glorified in him), with νῦν.

Rom. 5.11: νῦν τὴν καταλλαγὴν ἐλάβομεν (we now receive reconciliation).

The 'epistolary aorist' is often explained as a 'genuine' use of the aorist for past reference, with the proviso that the author is writing from the perspective of the reader.[3] There is another possible explanation of this phenomenon, however. In epistolary contexts,

1. Robertson, *Grammar*, p. 841.

2. A.E. Péristérakis, *Essai sur l'aoriste intemporel en grec* (Athens: n.p., 1962), esp. pp. 125-63.

3. E.g. E.D.W. Burton, *Syntax of the Moods and Tenses in NT Greek* (repr. Grand Rapids: Kregel, 1976 [3rd edn, 1898]), p. 21. See most recently Levinson, *Pragmatics*, pp. 73-74.

writers do not mix spheres of temporal reference between their own and their readers' time; rather, writers tend to compose their letters from their own temporal perspective, using the appropriate verbal aspects (tense-forms) to indicate their personal perspective on the events described.[1] Especially common is to find the aorist used to refer to the entire writing process. Examples of the epistolary aorist are abundant in the NT, and are found in extra-biblical literature as well (e.g. Thucydides 1.129.3; P.Oxy. 1156.12-14). NT examples include: Phlm. 12; 1 Pet. 5.12; Eph. 6.22.

1 Jn 2.12-14 (γράφω [I write] three times, ἔγραψα three times) can be explained at least in part by this analysis. Various theories regarding reference to other letters or to earlier parts of the letter, and so on,[2] are unnecessary if the present tense-forms are seen as making emphatic statements which are recapitulated by the aorist tenses, all referring to the entire epistle.

2.2.3. *Aorist for future action* (futuristic or proleptic aorist). This is a very infrequent use of the aorist tense-form. The reason for this probably lies in the fact that the Greek aorist carries the least semantic weight, so that when the realm of the non-existent was spoken of the aorist was not considered substantial enough.[3] There is no English equivalent for translational purposes, since the English future tense with 'will' is too strong. Thus the 'going to' phrase is used below. (The apodoses of conditional statements are not treated here, since they are part of a larger grammatical construction which is timeless by definition; see Chapter 16.)

Jn 17.18: κἀγὼ ἀπέστειλα αὐτοὺς εἰς τὸν κόσμον (and I am going to send them into the world).

Rom. 8.30: οὓς δὲ ἐδικαίωσεν, τούτους καὶ ἐδόξασεν (whom he justified, these he is also going to glorify), admittedly not the only explanation of this verse.

Jude 14: ἰδοὺ ἦλθεν κύριος ἐν ἁγίαις μυριάσιν αὐτοῦ (behold, the Lord is going to come with his countless saints).

Rev. 14.8: ἔπεσεν, ἔπεσεν Βαβυλὼν ἡ μεγάλη (great Babylon is

1. Porter, *Verbal Aspect*, pp. 228-30.

2. On the issues involved, see R.E. Brown, *The Epistles of John* (Garden City, NY: Doubleday, 1982), pp. 294-301, esp. 294-97.

3. Cf. B.G. Mandilaras, *The Verb in the Greek Non-Literary Papyri* (Athens: Hellenic Ministry of Culture and Sciences, 1973), p. 168 n. 1.

going to fall, is going to fall!); there may be many more examples in Revelation; cf. 15.1.

2.2.4. *Aorist for action occurring at any time (omnitemporal)* (gnomic aorist). The so-called 'gnomic aorist' has garnered much attention, even from traditional grammarians, because of its apparent departure from the standard use of the aorist tense-form to refer to past action. That it may be used to refer to actions which do not occur in the past is commonly acknowledged, but why this occurs is not agreed. There have been at least four proposed solutions. a. Denial of the phenomenon.[1] This explanation has struck most grammarians, however, as special pleading in light of a predisposition to equate the aorist tense-form with past time. b. Mythological basis. At least one grammarian has contended that the Greeks used the gnomic aorist to base their formative myths in the security of the past.[2] This outdated anthropology makes the Greeks into a unique people, while at the same time neglecting simple linguistic facts: other cultures less mythologically minded than the Greeks make gnomic statements in their languages as well. c. Specific past action. Many grammarians argue that behind the gnomic action lies a specific past action to which reference is being made. This perpetuates the equation of tense-form and time in an unnecessary search for a single past action.[3] d. Verbal aspect.[4] Once the time and tense linkage is rightly severed, the gnomic use of the tenses becomes understandable. One of the ways in which language users refer to events is to see them not simply as confined to one temporal sphere (past, present or future) but as occurring over time and perhaps as representative of the kind of thing which regularly occurs, especially in nature. In the NT, most of the examples of the gnomic aorist are used with reference to the processes of nature. The English present tense must suffice in translation, so long as one is not misled into thinking the Greek tense-form is equivalent to it.

Rom. 3.23: πάντες...ἥμαρτον καὶ ὑστεροῦνται τῆς δόξης τοῦ

1. G.B. Winer, *A Treatise on the Grammar of NT Greek* (trans. W.F. Moulton; Edinburgh: T. & T. Clark, 1882), p. 346.

2. B.A. van Gronigen, 'Quelques considérations sur l'aoriste gnomique', in *Studia Varia Carolo Guilielmo Vollgraff* (Amsterdam: North-Holland, 1948), pp. 49-61.

3. BDF, §333.

4. Porter, *Verbal Aspect*, pp. 221-25.

θεοῦ (all...sin and fall short of the glory of God), with aorist and present tense-forms.

Eph. 5.29: οὐδεὶς...ποτε τὴν ἑαυτοῦ σάρκα ἐμίσησεν (no one...ever hates his own flesh).

Jas 1.11: ἀνέτειλεν...ὁ ἥλιος σὺν τῷ καύσωνι καὶ ἐξήρανεν τὸν χόρτον, καὶ τὸ ἄνθος αὐτοῦ ἐξέπεσεν καὶ ἡ εὐπρέπεια τοῦ προσώπου αὐτοῦ ἀπώλετο (the sun comes up with its heat and withers the grass, and its flower falls away and the beauty of its appearance perishes).

1 Pet. 1.24-25: ἐξηράνθη ὁ χόρτος καὶ τὸ ἄνθος ἐξέπεσεν (the grass is withered and the flower falls away).

2.2.5. *Aorist for timeless action.* Timeless action has been defined above (section 2.1.5). The timeless aorist occurs frequently in parables. Sustained theological passages exemplify this usage as well.

Rom. 1.19-25: ἐφανέρωσεν...ἐδόξασαν...ηὐχαρίστησαν... ἐματαιώθησαν...ἐσκοτίσθη...ἐμωράνθησαν...ἤλλαξαν... παρέδωκεν...μετήλλαξαν...ἐσεβάσθησαν...ἐλάτρευσαν... ([God] makes clear...they glorify...give thanks...are made foolish...are darkened...are made foolish...exchange...[God] gives over...they exchange...worship...serve...). After beginning the section (v. 18) with an emphatic timeless present (ἀποκαλύπτεται), Paul continues with aorist verbs specifying details of human perversion. Cf. TEV translation, which implies this understanding.

Individual examples are to be considered also.

Mk 1.11 and parallels: σὺ εἶ ὁ υἱός μου ὁ ἀγαπητός, ἐν σοὶ εὐδόκησα (you are my beloved son, in you I am pleased), where the claim that this usage is dependent upon the Semitic verbal system can rightly be dismissed.[1]

Lk. 7.35: ἐδικαιώθη ἡ σοφία ἀπὸ πάντων τῶν τέκνων αὐτῆς (wisdom is justified by all her children); cf. Mt. 11.19: ἐδικαιώθη ἡ σοφία ἀπὸ τῶν ἔργων αὐτῆς (wisdom is justified by her works).

2.3. *The Perfect and Pluperfect Tense-Forms*

The perfect and pluperfect tense-forms occur in contexts where the user of Greek wishes to depict the action as reflecting a given (often complex) state of affairs. The stative aspect carries the most semantic

1. Porter, *Verbal Aspect*, pp. 126-29.

conveyed by the tense-form *by itself* (without reference to contextual factors) than by any other tense-form. This has long been recognized, but when it comes to defining what the meaning of the tense is, there has been disagreement. The definition enshrined for centuries regarding continuance of completed action[1] must now be replaced. This definition was never without problems, as an examination of the grammars shows, where various categories must be introduced to cope with major conceptual difficulties (e.g. discussions of so-called intensive, extensive and completed perfects). The force of the stative aspect is that the grammatical subject of the verb is the focus of the state of affairs.[2] Thus the perfect οἶδα means 'I know' or 'I am in a knowledgeable state', not 'I know and the fact remains known'; and ἤλπικα means 'I am in a hopeful state'. After competing with the aorist, the perfect eventually dropped out of use, but this did not occur until much later than the time of the writing of the NT documents (see the McKay articles).

2.3.1. *Perfect tense-form.* The uses of the perfect tense-form cover the range for the other tense-forms, including the spheres of past, present, future, omnitemporal ('gnomic'), and timeless usage.

a. *Past use.* In many contexts the perfect tense-form may be used in narrative, often in parallel with other narrative tense-forms.

Jn 1.15: John κέκραγεν (cried), parallel to the preceding past-referring present, μαρτυρεῖ (bore witness).

Jn 12.40: τετύφλωκεν αὐτῶν τοὺς ὀφθαλμούς (he blinded their eyes), parallel to the following past-referring aorist.

1. E.g. BDF, §340; Fanning, *Verbal Aspect*, pp. 103-20.

2. J.P. Louw, 'Die semantiese waarde van die perfektum in hellenistiese Grieks', *Acta Classica* 10 (1967), pp. 23-32; K.L. McKay, 'On the Perfect and Other Aspects in NT Greek', *NovT* 23 (1981), pp. 289-329; cf. *idem*, 'The Use of the Ancient Greek Perfect down to the End of the Second Century AD', *Bulletin of the Institute of Classical Studies* 12 (1965), pp. 1-21; *idem*, 'On the Perfect and Other Aspects in the Greek Non-Literary Papyri', *Bulletin of the Institute of Classical Studies* 27 (1980), pp. 23-49; *contra* Robertson, *Grammar*, pp. 895-96; BDF, §342(4); N. Turner, *A Grammar of NT Greek*. III. *Syntax* (Edinburgh: T. & T. Clark, 1963), pp. 83-84; Mandilaras, *The Verb*, p. 222, who argue for a shift to an object-oriented use of the perfect.

2 Cor. 2.13: οὐκ ἔσχηκα ἄνεσιν τῷ πνεύματί μου (I did not have rest in my spirit).

2 Cor. 12.17: ὧν ἀπέσταλκα πρὸς ὑμᾶς (of which things I sent to you).

Rev. 5.7: ἦλθεν καὶ εἴληφεν (he came and took), with aorist and perfect tense-forms.

b. *Present use*. This is a frequent use of the perfect tense-form, in light of its pronounced semantic weight.

Jn 1.26: μέσος ὑμῶν ἕστηκεν ὃν ὑμεῖς οὐκ οἴδατε (in your midst he stands whom you do not know), with two occurrences.

Jn 5.45: εἰς ὃν ὑμεῖς ἠλπίκατε (in whom you hope).

Jn 12.23: ἐλήλυθεν ἡ ὥρα (the hour is come).

Acts 4.10: οὗτος παρέστηκεν ἐνώπιον ὑμῶν ὑγιής (this one stands before you healthy).

c. *Future use*. This is a rare usage, since it requires an already infrequent form to be used with reference to an only anticipated temporal sphere.

Jas 5.2-3: ὁ πλοῦτος ὑμῶν σέσηπεν καὶ τὰ ἱμάτια ὑμῶν σητόβρωτα γέγονεν, ὁ χρυσὸς ὑμῶν καὶ ὁ ἄργυρος κατίωται καὶ ὁ ἰὸς αὐτῶν εἰς μαρτύριον ὑμῖν ἔσται καὶ φάγεται τὰς σάρκας ὑμῶν ὡς πῦρ (your riches are going to rot and your garments are going to become moth-eaten, your gold and silver are going to rust, and their rust will be for a testimony to you and it will eat your flesh as fire), describing the things to occur to the rich, with the perfect used parallel to future forms. It can be no accident that the author uses the semantically strongest tense-form available.

1 Jn 2.5: ἡ ἀγάπη τοῦ θεοῦ τετελείωται (the love of God is going to be complete).

d. *Omnitemporal use* (gnomic). In a few instances the perfect tense-form is used to refer to recurring processes of nature.

Lk. 12.7: αἱ τρίχες τῆς κεφαλῆς ὑμῶν πᾶσαι ἠρίθμηνται (all the hairs of your head are numbered).

Rom. 7.2: ἡ...ὕπανδρος γυνὴ τῷ ζῶντι ἀνδρὶ δέδεται νόμῳ (the...married woman is bound by law to [her] living husband); 1 Cor. 7.39: γυνὴ δέδεται ἐφ' ὅσον χρόνον ζῇ ὁ ἀνὴρ αὐτῆς (a woman is bound for such time her husband lives).

e. *Timeless use.* Whereas all usage of the tense-forms in Greek is in one sense timeless (since they do not carry any independent time-orienting information), there are several significant instances where the timeless nature of an action is focused upon.

Rom. 4.14: εἰ...οἱ ἐκ νόμου κληρονόμοι, κεκένωται ἡ πίστις καὶ κατήργηται ἡ ἐπαγγελία (if...they of the law are heirs, faith is empty and the promise is rendered inoperative), included because the protasis is verbless.

Rom. 13.8: ὁ...ἀγαπῶν τὸν ἕτερον νόμον πεπλήρωκεν (the one who loves the other [person] fulfils [the] law), where construal of the object does not affect interpretation of the verb.[1]

Jas 2.10, 11: ὅστις...ὅλον τὸν νόμον τηρήσῃ πταίσῃ δὲ ἐν ἑνί, γέγονεν πάντων ἔνοχος...εἰ δὲ οὐ μοιχεύεις φονεύεις δέ, γέγονας παραβάτης νόμου (whoever...keeps the whole law, but stumbles in one, becomes liable for all...but if you do not commit adultery but you murder, you become a transgressor of the law), where the conditional statement is parallel.

1 Jn 4.12: θεὸν οὐδεὶς πώποτε τεθέαται (no one has ever seen God).

2.3.2. *Pluperfect tense-form. Like the imperfect in relation to the present tense-form* (see section 2.1.6 above), *the pluperfect can be categorized as a form which tends to be used in past-time contexts.* The use of the pluperfect is restricted in the NT, probably due to its unwieldy morphological bulk, including reduplication, secondary endings, and occasionally even the augment. Periphrastic constructions (see section 3 below) are used in place of many pluperfects, with the augmented form of εἰμί (imperfect) and perfect participle.

Mk 1.34: ᾔδεισαν αὐτόν (they knew him).

Lk. 16.20: Λάζαρος ἐβέβλητο πρὸς τὸν πυλῶνα αὐτοῦ (Lazarus was cast at his door), an instance within a parable.

In many instances the pluperfect is not past-referring, especially in the protases of conditional constructions (see Chapter 16).

Mt. 12.7: εἰ...ἐγνώκειτε τί ἐστιν...(if...you knew what is...).

Jn 8.19: εἰ ἐμὲ ᾔδειτε (if you knew me).

1. See C.E.B. Cranfield, *A Critical and Exegetical Commentary on the Epistle to the Romans* (2 vols.; Edinburgh: T. & T. Clark, 1975, 1979), II, pp. 675-76.

2.4. *The Future Form*

2.4.1. *Introduction.* The future form raises important questions for grammarians and theologians alike, since the attempt is often made to ground theological questions in grammatical answers. The future form is morphologically related to the subjunctive, as seen in the use of the *sigma* and similar vowel configurations in earlier Greek. In recent discussion, however, there has been the increasing realization that there is more to consider regarding the future form than the name implies. Currently there are four major ways to analyze the use of the future verb form. a. One group of grammarians argue that the future form is an absolute tense-form used to describe events which are to take place in the future.[1] But as BDF's discussion well illustrates, this analysis must be qualified so radically, with such labels as the gnomic future and relative future, that the category becomes vacuous. b. Others suggest that the future form is both an indicative and a non-indicative (similar to the subjunctive) form, with functions ascribable to each category.[2] Categories such as the volitive, imperatival and deliberative can be explained in this way, although there remains a large degree of imprecision in the formulation. c. More convincing is the explanation that the future form is a modal form just like the subjunctive, and others.[3] This explanation, while holding promise for treating the various functions of the form, fails to deal with all of its formal and paradigmatic characteristics, such as the presence of infinitive and participle forms. d. A recent explanation recognizes a special and unique place in the Greek verbal system for the future form.[4] The form is aspectual in that it resembles an indicative form, but it is not fully aspectual in that it does not enter into a meaningful set of oppositions with the aorist, present and perfect tense-forms. Any attempt to read verbal aspect into the future form of Hellenistic Greek is bound to be frustrated, despite the fact that for a while in earlier Greek some verbs had two future forms (e.g.

1. E.g. BDF, §348.

2. E.g. Winer, *Treatise*, pp. 348-51; Robertson, *Grammar*, pp. 872-76; Mandilaras, *The Verb*, pp. 181-91; McKay, *Greek Grammar*, pp. 147-48.

3. E.g. E. Schwyzer, *Griechische Grammatik* (2 vols.; Munich: Beck, 1939, 1950), II, pp. 290-94; cf. C.F.D. Moule, *An Idiom Book of NT Greek* (Cambridge: Cambridge University Press, 2nd edn, 1959), pp. 21-23. See esp. V. Magnien, *Le futur grec* (Paris: Champion, 1912), II, pp. v-vii.

4. E.g. Porter, *Verbal Aspect*, ch. 9.

ἀχθήσομαι and ἄξομαι from ἄγω [lead]). Its uses, however, are compatible with those of the indicative and non-indicative moods. Rather than temporal values, *the future form grammaticalizes the semantic (meaning) feature of expectation.* This is related to the semantic feature of the non-indicative forms (projection), with a greater sense of certainty (see Chapter 2 section 2 on the non-indicative mood forms).

2.4.2. *Uses of the future form.* The future form may be used in a variety of contexts, many of them not future-time referring, as grammarians have long recognized.

a. *Prospective.* Rather than saying that the future verb form is future-referring, it is more precise to say that it is prospective or looking toward the future, a fairly common use in the NT.

Mt. 7.22: πολλοὶ ἐροῦσίν μοι ἐν ἐκείνῃ τῇ ἡμέρᾳ (many will say to me in that day).

b. *Commanding* (volitive). Although this use of the future form is frequently analyzed as the result of Semitic influence, classical Greek parallels indicate that the most that can be argued here is that Semitic usage enhanced an already possible Greek usage. This use is common in quotations from the OT.

Mt. 21.3: ἐρεῖτε (you say), following the protasis of a third class conditional (see Chapter 16).

Mt. 27.4: σὺ ὄψῃ (you see to it).

c. *Timeless.*

Mt. 6.33: ταῦτα πάντα προστεθήσεται ὑμῖν (all these things will be added to you), where the expectation is that they will be added.

Rom. 5.7: μόλις...ὑπὲρ δικαίου τις ἀποθανεῖται (hardly... will someone die for a just person), where it can hardly be expected.

d. *Omnitemporal* (gnomic).

Mk 2.22: ῥήξει ὁ οἶνος τοὺς ἀσκούς (the wine will tear the wine-skins), a legitimate expectation because of natural processes.

Rom. 7.3: μοιχαλὶς χρηματίσει (she will be named adultress), an expectation she could do without.

e. *Deliberative* (modal). Deliberative usage occurs when the writer or speaker wishes to ascribe intention directly to an agent.

Mt. 21.37: ἐντραπήσονται τὸν υἱόν μου (they will respect my son), that is, the expectation is that they will respect him.

Lk. 9.57: ἀκολουθήσω σοι (I will follow you), but this is only an intention.

Many of the grammarians mentioned above have noted that the future and the subjunctive verb forms often appear in similar environments, especially in conditional and relative clauses. The future form seems to carry with it a higher degree of expectation for fulfilment regarding the action.

Mt. 5.25: μήποτέ σε παραδῷ ὁ ἀντίδικος τῷ κριτῇ...καὶ εἰς φυλακὴν βληθήσῃ (lest the opponent hand you over to the judge...and you will be cast into prison), where once one falls into the hands of the judge, prison can be expected.

Lk. 8.17: οὐ...ἐστιν κρυπτὸν ὃ οὐ φανερὸν γενήσεται οὐδὲ ἀπόκρυφον ὃ οὐ μὴ γνωσθῇ καὶ εἰς φανερὸν ἔλθῃ (there is nothing hidden which will not become evident, and nothing concealed which might not be made known and become evident).

3. *Periphrastic Verbal Constructions*

3.1. *Elements of a Periphrastic Verbal Construction*

Periphrastic verbal constructions are formed by the grammatically appropriate combination of a form of the auxiliary verb εἰμί *and a participle.* The participle contributes the semantic (meaning) feature of verbal aspect to the construction (as well as voice; see Chapter 3 section 1). The form of εἰμί, which is aspectually vague (i.e. it does not provide a meaningful choice of aspect), is used to grammaticalize attitude (i.e. mood; see Chapter 2) of the action in its context, as well as person and number (see Chapter 3 section 2).

In determining whether a given instance of εἰμί and a participle is periphrastic, it is useful to keep in mind that no elements may intervene between the auxiliary verb and the participle except for those which complete or directly modify the participle (not the verb εἰμί). Hence 2 Cor. 2.17 (οὐ...ἐσμεν ὡς οἱ πολλοὶ καπηλεύοντες τὸν λόγον τοῦ θεοῦ [we are not like many, peddling the word of God; *not*: we are not peddling the word of God, as do many]) and Lk. 1.21 (ἦν ὁ λαὸς προσδοκῶν τὸν Ζαχαρίαν [the people were there, expecting Zacharias]) are not periphrastic constructions, since in each case the grammatical subject is placed between the auxiliary verb and the participle. Troublesome for determination of whether a construction is periphrastic are phrases which might indicate location (in, on, etc.) or time (when, at, etc.), if they appear between the auxiliary and the participle. If they limit the auxiliary, then the construction is not periphrastic. See, for example, Col. 3.1: ὁ Χριστός ἐστιν ἐν δεξιᾷ τοῦ θεοῦ καθήμενος, which could be understood as 'Christ is at the right hand of God, seated', or 'Christ is seated at the right hand of God'. The consequences of this differentiation can be important.[1] For example, if Mk 1.13 (ἦν ἐν τῇ ἐρήμῳ τεσσεράκοντα ἡμέρας πειραζόμενος) were periphrastic, it would be compatible with the view that Jesus was said to be in the desert and tempted by Satan for all forty days (he was being tempted in the desert for forty days). The non-periphrastic interpretation leaves it open that the temptations are seen to have occurred at the end of the period (he was in the desert forty days, being tempted). The interpretation here depends upon whether one sees the temporal phrase (forty days) as limiting the auxiliary or the participle.

Virtually every verb form in Greek may be substituted for by means of a periphrastic construction, although it is rare to find a periphrastic with the aorist participle (see section 3.2.3 below). Where a choice of the simple and periphrastic forms is available (i.e. in those places where the periphrastic has not replaced a little-used or cumbersome form, e.g. pluperfect), the periphrastic is considered to have the same general meaning as the simple form of the verb. They both grammaticalize the same verbal aspect (i.e. the participle and the finite form use the same tense-form), as well as the same mood (see Chapter 2). However, grammarians who wish to stress that the periphrastic is more emphatic or significant, or that it draws attention to the participle and its modifiers, are probably correct.[2]

3.2. *Examples of Periphrastic Constructions*

3.2.1. *Present participle.* The present participle often forms a part of a periphrastic verbal construction, in conjunction with a variety of forms of the auxiliary εἰμί.

1. Porter, *Verbal Aspect*, pp. 409-16.
2. J. Gonda, 'A Remark on "Periphrastic" Constructions in Greek', *Mnemosyne* Series 4, 12 (1959), pp. 97-112.

a. *Unaugmented form of* εἰμί (present). There is increased usage of this construction in Hellenistic Greek, although classical Greek already showed increased usage over previous periods.

Mt. 1.23; Mk 5.41; 15.22, 34; Acts 4.36: ὅ ἐστιν μεθερμηνευόμενον (which is interpreted).

Col. 2.5: εἰμι χαίρων καὶ βλέπων (I am rejoicing and seeing), although *UBSGNT*[3] and N–A[26] place a comma after εἰμί.

b. *Augmented form of* εἰμί (imperfect). Widespread use of this kind of periphrastic in the Lukan writings discounts any heavy Semitic influence upon its development.[1]

Mt. 7.29; Mk 1.22; Lk. 4.31; 5.17; 13.10; 19.47: ἦν διδάσκων (he was teaching).

Mk 9.4: ἦσαν συλλαλοῦντες (they were conversing).

Gal. 1.22: ἤμην...ἀγνοούμενος (I was...unknown).

2 Cor. 5.19: θεὸς ἦν ἐν Χριστῷ κόσμον καταλλάσσων ἑαυτῷ (in Christ, God was reconciling the world to himself), with periphrasis the best explanation, although there is much controversy among grammarians and commentators.[2]

c. *Future form of* εἰμί. This is a very rare usage in extra-biblical Greek.[3]

Mt. 10.22; 24.9; Mk 13.13; Lk. 21.17: ἔσεσθε μισούμενοι (you will be hated).

Lk. 5.10: ἀπὸ τοῦ νῦν ἀνθρώπους ἔσῃ ζωγρῶν (from now on you will be catching men).

d. *Subjunctive form of* εἰμί. This infrequent usage only occurs in a few *possible* examples in the NT.

Jas 1.4: ἦτε τέλειοι καὶ ὁλόκληροι ἐν μηδενὶ λειπόμενοι (you might be complete and whole and lacking in nothing), an example

1. Cf. G. Björck, *ΗΝ ΔΙΔΑΣΚΩΝ: Die periphrastischen Konstruktionen im Griechischen* (Uppsala: Almqvist & Wiksell, 1940).

2. See S.E. Porter, καταλλάσσω *in Ancient Greek Literature, with Reference to the Pauline Writings* (Córdoba, Spain: Ediciones El Almendro, 1994), ch. 6.

3. W.J. Aerts, *Periphrastica: An Investigation into the Use of* εἶναι *and* ἔχειν *as Auxiliaries or Pseudo-Auxiliaries in Greek from Homer up to the Present Day* (Amsterdam: Hakkert, 1965), p. 59.

rightly criticized because of separation of the participle from the auxiliary.

e. *Imperative form of* εἰμί.

Lk. 19.17: ἴσθι ἐξουσίαν ἔχων (have authority).

3.2.2. *Perfect participle.* Periphrastic constructions with the perfect participle are a long-recognized phenomenon in ancient Greek, especially in light of the cumbersome perfect and pluperfect forms, for which a periphrastic was a much to be preferred alternative.

a. *Unaugmented form of* εἰμί (present). This is a fairly common construction in ancient Greek from various periods, including the Hellenistic.

Mt. 10.30: ἠριθμημέναι εἰσίν (they are numbered).

Jn 2.17; 6.31, 45; 10.34; 12.14; 20.30: ἐστιν γεγραμμένον (it is written), or variations.

b. *Augmented form of* εἰμί (imperfect).

Lk. 4.16, 17: ἦν τεθραμμένος...ἦν γεγραμμένον (he was brought up...it was written).

Jn 19.11: ἦν δεδομένον (it was given).

Gal. 2.11: κατεγνωσμένος ἦν (he was condemned).

c. *Future form of* εἰμί.

Mt. 16.19: ὃ ἐὰν δήσῃς ἐπὶ τῆς γῆς ἔσται δεδεμένον ἐν τοῖς οὐρανοῖς, καὶ ὃ ἐὰν λύσῃς ἐπὶ τῆς γῆς ἔσται λελυμένον ἐν τοῖς οὐρανοῖς (whatever you bind upon the earth shall be bound in heaven, and whatever you loose upon the earth shall be loosed in heaven); cf. also Mt. 18.18. Few passages with periphrastic constructions have generated as much discussion as this one, with many of the grammatical issues having theological implications.[1]

Heb. 2.13: ἐγὼ ἔσομαι πεποιθὼς ἐπ' αὐτῷ (I will put my trust upon him).

d. *Subjunctive form of* εἰμί.

Jn 3.27: ᾖ δεδομένον (it might be given).

1. Porter, *Verbal Aspect*, pp. 471-74; for a fuller discussion of the issues, see *idem*, 'Vague Verbs, Periphrastics, and Mt. 16.19', *FN* 1 (1988), pp. 155-73.

2 Cor. 1.9: πεποιθότες ὦμεν (we might trust).

e. *Participle of* εἰμί.

Eph. 4.18: ὄντες ἀπηλλοτριωμένοι (being foreigners); Col. 1.21: ὄντας ἀπηλλοτριωμένους (being foreigners).

3.2.3. *Aorist participle.* For whatever reason (and grammarians have debated this),[1] periphrastic constructions with the aorist participle are exceedingly rare. There are only three examples worth considering from NT Greek, all with the augmented (imperfect) form of the auxiliary, but they are open to question.

Lk. 23.19: ὅστις ἦν διὰ στάσιν τινὰ γενομένην ἐν τῇ πόλει καὶ φόνον βληθεὶς ἐν τῇ φυλακῇ (who had, on account of a certain rebellion having arisen in the city and murder, been cast in prison), where there is plenty of material intervening between the auxiliary and the participle.

Acts 8.13: βαπτισθεὶς ἦν (he was baptized).

2 Cor. 5.19: ἦν...θέμενος ἐν ἡμῖν τὸν λόγον τῆς καταλλαγῆς (he...had placed in us the word of reconciliation), where the aorist participle must share the same auxiliary with at least one and possibly two other participles (see above [section 3.2.1.b] on this verse). This example is highly debatable.

1. See Porter, *Verbal Aspect*, pp. 476-77.

Chapter 2

MOOD AND ATTITUDE

Introduction

Whereas the tense-forms are used to grammaticalize verbal aspect, or the writer or speaker's perspective on the action, *the mood forms are used to grammaticalize the language user's perspective on the relation of the verbal action to reality*. In other words, the mood forms indicate the speaker's 'attitude' toward the event. The choice of attitude is probably the second most important semantic choice by a language user in selection of a verbal element in Greek, second only to verbal aspect. To use the language of slot and filler (see Introduction), whenever a finite verb[1] is selected to fill a slot, the element that fills the slot must contain an indication of attitude as grammaticalized by selection of a mood form. In the first stage of discussion, these mood forms can be divided into two distinct categories: indicative and non-indicative mood forms.

1. *Indicative Mood Form*

The traditional definition of the indicative mood is that it expresses the actual condition of reality. Some even call it the 'mood of fact'.[2] Recent work by several grammarians and linguists moves away from this perspective, with recognition that the indicative may be as subjective

1. A finite verb is one that takes grammatical person (i.e. first, second or third) as part of the information attached to the verb form itself.

2. E.g. Goodwin, *Greek Grammar*, p. 280; H.W. Smyth, *Greek Grammar* (rev. G.M. Messing; Cambridge, MA: Harvard University Press, 1956), p. 481; Winer, *Treatise*, pp. 351-52; Burton, *Syntax*, pp. 73-74; Moule, *Idiom Book*, p. 20; this is implied by Moulton, *Prolegomena*, pp. 164-65; see also J. Humbert, *Syntaxe grecque* (Paris: Klincksieck, 3rd edn, 1960), p. 111.

as any other mood (in that sense its title, 'indicative', is misleading, since it does not 'indicate' in any sense that the other mood forms do not). That the indicative mood is used in this way has long been recognized by a number of grammarians, especially those in the German tradition.[1]

The indicative mood form is selected in Greek to grammaticalize an assertion about what is put forward as the condition of reality.[2] The relation between use of the indicative (or any other mood form, for that matter) and reality is, therefore, a tenuous one at best (e.g. what mood is used for lying if there is an absolute correlation between the indicative mood and reality?). It is better to express the attitudes as subjective relations between the language user and his or her perception of reality, with the indicative mood form used to grammaticalize simple assertions about what the writer or speaker sees as reality, whether or not there is a factual basis for such an assertion.[3] To use linguistic terminology, the indicative is the 'unmarked' mood form. As Robertson states, the indicative 'is the normal mode to use when there is no special reason for employing another mode'.[4] Hence, it may be used with statements or questions (questions are treated in more detail in Chapter 18), truths and untruths.

Jn 13.21: Ἰησοῦς ἐταράχθη τῷ πνεύματι καὶ ἐμαρτύρησεν καὶ εἶπεν...(Jesus was troubled in spirit and bore witness and said...), where Jesus is asserted to have felt and acted a particular way.

Mk 1.21: καὶ εἰσπορεύονται εἰς Καφαρναούμ (and they entered into Capernaum).

Rom. 1.8: πρῶτον μὲν εὐχαριστῶ τῷ θεῷ μου (first, I give thanks to my God).

Jn 13.8: ἐὰν μὴ νίψω σε, οὐκ ἔχεις μέρος μετ' ἐμοῦ (if I do not

1. Schwyzer, *Griechische Grammatik*, II, p. 303; Robertson, *Grammar*, pp. 914-15; H.E. Dana and J.R. Mantey, *A Manual Grammar of the Greek NT* (N.p.: Macmillan, 1955), pp. 165-69; M. Zerwick, *Biblical Greek* (Rome: Pontifical Biblical Institute, 1963), pp. 100-101; Mandilaras, *The Verb*, p. 241; see also R. Kühner and B. Gerth, *Ausführliche Grammatik der griechischen Sprache* (2 vols.; repr. Leverkusen: Gottschalksche, 4th edn, 1955), I, p. 201.

2. See J. Gonda, *The Character of the Indo-European Moods, with Special Regard to Greek and Sanskrit* (Wiesbaden: Otto Harrassowitz, 1956), pp. 3, 6.

3. See F.R. Palmer, *Mood and Modality* (Cambridge: Cambridge University Press, 1986), esp. p. 16.

4. Robertson, *Grammar*, p. 915; cf. McKay, *Greek Grammar*, p. 148.

wash you, you do not have a portion with me), with the assertion made as the consequence of a condition (using the subjunctive, see section 2.2 below).

Mk 1.24: ἦλθες ἀπολέσαι ἡμᾶς; (did you come to destroy us?), with the question used to request information regarding the assertion.

Someone may assert things that are not true using the indicative, as well. As Robertson says, 'Most untruths are told in the indicative mode'.[1]

Mk 5.35, 39: ἡ θυγάτηρ σου ἀπέθανεν...τὸ παιδίον οὐκ ἀπέθανεν ἀλλὰ καθεύδει (your daughter is dead...the child is not dead but is sleeping), where both sides cannot be correct, but each statement is asserted with equal attitudinal force.

2. *Non-Indicative Mood Forms: Imperative, Subjunctive, Optative, Future*

A significant number of grammarians have long recognized that the non-indicative mood forms do not make any assertion about reality, whether past, present or future, and hence they are non-assertive.[2] This does not mean that these forms indicate a lack of belief in the reality of the actions spoken about, only that at the point of speaking or writing no assertion is made grammatically, that is, using grammatical means. *The semantic feature grammaticalized by the non-indicative mood forms is one of 'projection' in the mind of the speaker or writer.*[3] Each mood form can be used to project a world

1. Robertson, *Grammar*, p. 915.

2. Schwyzer, *Griechische Grammatik*, II, p. 304; Robertson, *Grammar*, *passim*; Moulton, *Prolegomena*, p. 164; Dana and Mantey, *Manual Grammar*, pp. 165-68, 170-71; Moule, *Idiom Book*, p. 20; Gonda, *Character*, p. 7. Unfortunately many seem to find a temporal basis in even the non-indicative mood forms: W.W. Goodwin, *Syntax of the Moods and Tenses of the Greek Verb* (London: Macmillan, 5th edn, 1892), pp. 23, 27; Kühner and Gerth, *Ausführliche Grammatik*, I, p. 217; J.A. Brooks and C.L. Winbery, *Syntax of NT Greek* (Washington, DC: University Press of America, 1979), pp. 103-104, 107-18.

3. The non-indicative mood forms pose a number of problems for rendering their equivalents in English. The words 'should', 'might' and 'may' are frequently used to convey the senses of the subjunctive and optative. One must realize that these words may well need to be deleted in creating a polished translation. Other translational difficulties are addressed below as they arise.

for consideration. The semantic feature of projection will be further defined when each of the forms is considered below. The close relation among the non-indicative mood forms is seen, however, in the fact that imperatives and subjunctives (as well as optatives) may appear in similar commanding and forbidding contexts.

The participle and infinitive could be placed in the same category as the non-indicative mood forms, since in fact they do not of themselves make an assertion about reality. But they are better treated separately (see Chapters 10 and 11), since they lack the formalized means of indicating attitude by way of selecting a specific mood form.

2.1. *The Imperative Form*

The imperative form is normally used to direct someone's action.[1] It is not a 'future' tense, even though the directed action may—if and only if it comes about—be future in relation to the time of speaking, since it refers to a realm projected in the mind of the speaker or writer (see Chapter 13 section 1).[2]

2.1.1. *Action and aspect* (see Chapter 13 section 2.1). It has been well established[3] that the traditional definitions of the present and aorist imperatives in relation to verbal action do not work. The traditional definition is that the aorist has something to do with performing an action instantaneously, once for all, especially an action which is not currently being done, while the present has something to do with continual, habitual, repeated or ongoing action. In his tabulations, Boyer shows that for present imperatives four of seven are general and give no indication of the time when an event may occur.[4] Examples which

1. See J.L. Boyer, 'A Classification of Imperatives: A Statistical Study', *GTJ* 8 (1987), pp. 35-54, who provides statistics concerning the various categories of the imperative.

2. Note that the forms of the third person plural imperative have changed from classical to Hellenistic Greek. To summarize, the -ντων and -σθων endings have been replaced by -ωσαν throughout the paradigm.

3. Moule, *Idiom Book*, pp. 20-21; Porter, *Verbal Aspect*, pp. 336-47, 351-60; Fanning, *Verbal Aspect*, ch. 5; see also K.L. McKay, 'Aspect in Imperatival Constructions in NT Greek', *NovT* 27 (1985), pp. 201-26; cf. *idem*, 'Aspect of the Imperative in Ancient Greek', *Antichthon* 20 (1986), pp. 41-58; *contra* J. Thorley, 'Aktionsart in NT Greek: Infinitive and Imperative', *NovT* 31 (1989), pp. 290-313.

4. Boyer, 'Classification of Imperatives', p. 43.

dispute the traditional analysis are not difficult to find.

Lk. 19.13: πραγματεύσασθε ἐν ᾧ ἔρχομαι (carry on doing business until I come), where the aorist imperative is used of ongoing action.

2 Cor. 13.11, 12: χαίρετε, καταρτίζεσθε, παρακαλεῖσθε, τὸ αὐτὸ φρονεῖτε, εἰρηνεύετε...ἀσπάσασθε ἀλλήλους ἐν ἁγίῳ φιλήματι (rejoice, be made complete, be comforted, think the same thing [= be unified], be at peace...greet each other with a holy kiss), followed by the present indicative. It is doubtful that the aorist imperative is telling the Corinthians to begin something they are not doing, while the present imperatives are instructing them to continue with something in which they are already engaged.

Eph. 5.18: μὴ μεθύσκεσθε οἴνῳ...ἀλλὰ πληροῦσθε ἐν πνεύματι (don't get drunk with wine...but be filled with the Spirit). The traditional scheme makes it difficult to see why the present imperatives are used, since it leaves open the possibility (a) that getting drunk once (with the aorist?) would be permissible and (b) that the Ephesians are already involved in drinking.

A verbal aspectual framework enables the difficulties of such analysis to be overcome (see Chapter 13 section 2.3).

1 Pet. 2.17: πάντας τιμήσατε, τὴν ἀδελφότητα ἀγαπᾶτε, τὸν θεὸν φοβεῖσθε, τὸν βασιλέα τιμᾶτε (honor all, love the brotherhood, fear God, honor the king), where the aorist imperative serves as a summary-term for the following specifying or particularizing present imperatives.

Mt. 5.44: ἀγαπᾶτε τοὺς ἐχθροὺς ὑμῶν καὶ προσεύχεσθε ὑπὲρ τῶν διωκόντων ὑμᾶς (love your enemies and pray for the ones persecuting you), where Jesus uses present imperatives to direct certain actions to begin. The Sermon on the Mount is full of these kinds of directive statements.

Jas 1.21: δέξασθε τὸν ἔμφυτον λόγον (receive the implanted word), which seems to imply an already begun action.

The imperative of the perfect tense-form is very rare, but it retains its stative aspectual value.

Mk 4.39: πεφίμωσο (be silent).

Acts 15.29: ἔρρωσθε (greetings), a standard Hellenistic letter closing.

Eph. 5.5 and Jas 1.19: ἴστε (know), where the form may be indicative.[1]

2.1.2. *Second and third person singular and plural.* Greek has imperative forms in the second and third person, singular and plural. Whereas the second person is similar to the English form when translated, the third person imperative requires what has sometimes been labeled a permissive sense (let...). However, any permissive sense is a phenomenon of English translation, not Greek.[2] The third person Greek imperative is as strongly directive as the second person.

Mt. 6.6: εἴσελθε εἰς τὸ ταμεῖόν σου καὶ...πρόσευξαι τῷ πατρί σου (go into your private room and...pray to your father), with second person singular imperatives.

Jas 1.2: πᾶσαν χαρὰν ἡγήσασθε (consider [it] all joy), with the second person plural imperative.

Rom. 6.12: μὴ οὖν βασιλευέτω ἡ ἁμαρτία ἐν τῷ θνητῷ ὑμῶν σώματι (therefore, sin is not to rule in your mortal body), with the third person singular imperative.

Lk. 16.29: ἀκουσάτωσαν αὐτῶν (they are to hear them), with the third person plural imperative, which only appears approximately 34 times in the NT, compared to about 200 third person singular forms.

There is potential ambiguity whether a present tense second person plural active or middle/passive form is indicative or imperative in mood, since they are identical forms. Context must be taken into account (except when the negative is present, since the imperative is negated by μή, and the indicative by οὐ).

Rom. 6.22: νυνὶ δέ, ἐλευθερωθέντες ἀπὸ τῆς ἁμαρτίας δουλωθέντες δὲ τῷ θεῷ, ἔχετε τὸν καρπὸν ὑμῶν εἰς ἁγιασμόν. Should this be translated, 'but now, being free from sin and enslaved to God, you have your fruit unto holiness', or 'but now, being free from sin and enslaved to God, have your fruit unto holiness'? Although virtually every commentator takes ἔχετε as indicative, in the context of Romans it could well be an imperative, with Paul exhorting his readers in his diatribal style to possess that which their condition

1. I have argued that the example in Eph. 5.5 is an imperative and believe the same is true for Jas 1.19; see S.E. Porter, 'ἴστε γινώσκοντες in Eph. 5.5: Does Chiasm Solve a Problem?', *ZNW* 81 (1990), pp. 270-76.

2. Brooks and Winbery, *Syntax*, p. 117.

warrants. Grammar alone cannot solve such an exegetical dispute.

The interjections ἴδε and ἰδού (e.g. Jn 1.29, 36; Mt. 26.46, 47 and approximately 200 other times in the NT) are actually the second person singular aorist active and middle imperatives of εἶδον, although they are set forms in the NT.

2.1.3. *Imperatives and subjunctives.* In Greek, whereas the present imperative may be used for commands and for prohibitions (with the negative μή; cf. P.Oxy. 744.4, where the negated present subjunctive is used in a prohibition), the aorist imperative is restricted in its usage in prohibitions. Instead, the negated (with μή) aorist subjunctive serves to express prohibition in the second person, even though the negated aorist imperative usually is used in the third person (except for a few instances where the negated subjunctive is used: e.g. 1 Cor. 16.11; 2 Cor. 11.16; 2 Thess. 2.3; see section 2.3 below). The use of the negated aorist subjunctive as a prohibition is very widespread, although there are a few exceptions in earlier extra-biblical Greek. The shared use of the imperative and subjunctive forms in prohibitions points to a common semantic feature.

Mk 9.25: ἔξελθε ἐξ αὐτοῦ καὶ μηκέτι εἰσέλθῃς εἰς αὐτόν (come out of him and no longer enter into him), with the aorist imperative and negated subjunctive.

Mt. 6.19: μὴ θησαυρίζετε ὑμῖν θησαυρούς (don't store up for yourselves treasures), with the negated present imperative.

Col. 2.21: μὴ ἅψῃ μηδὲ γεύσῃ μηδὲ θίγῃς (don't handle, don't taste, don't touch), with the negated aorist subjunctive used three times. This is a controversial verse regarding whether the author is giving his own commands or citing those of others.

Mt. 24.17-18: ὁ ἐπὶ τοῦ δώματος μὴ καταβάτω ἆραι τὰ ἐκ τῆς οἰκίας αὐτοῦ, καὶ ὁ ἐν τῷ ἀγρῷ μὴ ἐπιστρεψάτω ὀπίσω ἆραι τὸ ἱμάτιον αὐτοῦ (the one on the house should not come down to take the things out of his house, and the one in the field should not return to take his garment), with negated third person aorist imperatives.

2.2. *The Subjunctive Form*

The subjunctive form is used to refer to a realm not of assertion but of projection, hence it may be used in dependent purpose and result (see Chapter 14) and conditional (see Chapter 16) clauses. The subjunctive may function in independent clauses as well. *The subjunctive form is used to grammaticalize a projected realm which may at some time exist and may even now exist, but which is held up for examination simply as a projection of the writer or speaker's mind for consideration.* As Gonda says, 'The subjunctive...expresses visualization. A process in the subj. represents a mental image on the part of the speaker which, in his opinion is capable of realization, or even awaits realization.'[1]

2.2.1. *Verbal aspect.* The contrast between the aorist and present subjunctives is seen in their contrasting verbal aspects.[2]

Mk 9.37: ὃς ἂν ἓν τῶν τοιούτων παιδίων δέξηται ἐπὶ τῷ ὀνόματί μου, ἐμὲ δέχεται· καὶ ὃς ἂν ἐμὲ δέχηται, οὐκ ἐμὲ δέχεται ἀλλὰ τὸν ἀποστείλαντά με (whoever receives one of such children in my name, receives me; and whoever receives me, does not receive me but the one who sent me), with the shift from aorist subjunctive to present subjunctive in the two protases indicating a shift from simply receiving Jesus to receiving God himself.

2.2.2. *Negated aorist subjunctive.* In Greek, in the second person the negated aorist subjunctive serves as the prohibition instead of the negated aorist imperative.

Mt. 5.36: μήτε ἐν τῇ κεφαλῇ σου ὀμόσῃς (don't swear by your head).

1 Tim. 5.1: πρεσβυτέρῳ μὴ ἐπιπλήξῃς, ἀλλὰ παρακάλει (don't rebuke an elder, but exhort [him]), with the following present imperative used of the preferred action.

Mt. 5.17: μὴ νομίσητε ὅτι...(don't think that...).

Mt. 10.9: μὴ κτήσησθε χρυσόν (don't take gold).

2.2.3. *Commands and prohibitions* (hortatory, volitive, and deliberative subjunctives). *Commands and prohibitions (and similar kinds of directive statements) in the first person singular and plural are made by using what is often called the hortatory subjunctive.* Some grammarians differentiate a deliberative subjunctive from a hortatory

1. Gonda, *Character*, p. 70.

2. See Porter, *Verbal Aspect*, ch. 7, for numerous examples; cf. Fanning, *Verbal Aspect*, ch. 6. *Contra* J. Thorley, 'Subjunctive Aktionsart in NT Greek: A Reassessment', *NovT* 30 (1988), pp. 193-211.

subjunctive, especially in questions.[1] This is not necessary, however, since the semantic feature of projection is common to both. As Moule says, the deliberative subjunctive 'is merely the hortatory turned into a question: the hortatory says *let me do so-and-so*, the deliberative says *am I to do...?*'[2]

The singular form of the hortatory subjunctive is uncommon, and usually follows an imperative, as in other Hellenistic Greek.

Lk. 6.42 // Mt. 7.4: ἄφες ἐκβάλω τὸ κάρφος (permit me to remove the speck).

Jn 19.15: τὸν βασιλέα ὑμῶν σταυρώσω; (should I crucify your king?), possibly a future form.

Acts 7.34: νῦν δεῦρο ἀποστείλω σε εἰς Αἴγυπτον (now come, let me send you into Egypt).

The plural is more frequent (approximately 70 examples in the NT). The plural hortatory subjunctive is used to exhort an audience to participate in an action which the speaker believes should be considered or performed. The speaker does not necessarily include him- or herself among the participants, despite the use of the first person plural form.

Lk. 2.15: διέλθωμεν δὴ ἕως Βηθλέεμ καὶ ἴδωμεν τὸ ῥῆμα τοῦτο (let us go to Bethlehem and let us see this thing).

Lk. 15.23: φέρετε τὸν μόσχον τὸν σιτευτόν, θύσατε καὶ φαγόντες εὐφρανθῶμεν (bring the fatted calf, kill [it] and, eating, let us rejoice), where the father includes himself with the hortatory subjunctive, after directing others using second person imperatives.

Rom. 5.1: εἰρήνην ἔχωμεν πρὸς τὸν θεόν (let us have peace with God), where there is a textual variant with the indicative, although the external evidence is clearly for the subjunctive.[3]

Rom. 6.1: ἐπιμένωμεν τῇ ἁμαρτίᾳ (let us abide in sin), an example in which the author, Paul, does not actually include himself as one who might remain in sin, but uses the hortatory subjunctive as part of his rhetorical stance.

Heb. 4.1: φοβηθῶμεν...μήποτε...(let us fear...lest...), but cf. use

1. Moulton, *Prolegomena*, pp. 184-86; Robertson, *Grammar*, p. 927; Brooks and Winbery, *Syntax*, p. 108.

2. Moule, *Idiom Book*, p. 22.

3. See B.M. Metzger, *A Textual Commentary on the Greek NT* (London: United Bible Societies, rev. edn, 1975), p. 511.

of the second person plural imperative in Heb. 3.12, 13.

Heb. 6.1: ἐπὶ τὴν τελειότητα φερώμεθα (let us be brought to maturity).

Mt. 6.31: τί φάγωμεν; ἤ, τί πίωμεν; ἤ, τί περιβαλώμεθα; (what are we going to eat? or what are we going to drink? or what are we going to put on?).

Mk 12.14: δῶμεν ἢ μὴ δῶμεν; (should we give or should we not give [to Caesar]?).

Moulton suggests that the several examples of negated third person aorist subjunctives are used in a hortatory sense.[1]

1 Cor. 16.11: μή τις...αὐτὸν ἐξουθενήσῃ (let no one...treat him with contempt); 2 Cor. 11.16: μή τίς με δόξῃ ἄφρονα εἶναι (let no one consider me to be unwise); 2 Thess. 2.3: μή τις ὑμᾶς ἐξαπατήσῃ (let no one deceive you).

2.2.4. *Emphatic negation of the subjunctive*. Sometimes the subjunctive is emphatically negated (usually with οὐ μή). Some grammarians question whether the double negative is genuinely emphatic.[2]

Mt. 5.20, 26: οὐ μὴ εἰσέλθητε εἰς τὴν βασιλείαν...οὐ μὴ ἐξέλθῃς ἐκεῖθεν, where the emphatic sense may be 'under no circumstances will you enter into the kingdom...no way will you come out of there'.

Heb. 13.5: οὐδ' οὐ μή σε ἐγκαταλίπω (I will never ever leave you), with multiple negation.

2.3. *The Optative Form*

The optative form (negated by μή in NT Greek) was not as widely used by Hellenistic writers, except by a few writers who were trying to imitate their Attic forerunners (e.g. Arrian). The form probably was curtailed because speakers felt that they could do the same thing the optative did by using the subjunctive, but without having to worry about the rather awkward paradigm (the subjunctive was probably much easier to remember). As regards meaning, the optative, when compared with the subjunctive, appears to be very similar but slightly remoter, vaguer, less assured, or more contingent.[3] In other words,

1. Moulton, *Prolegomena*, p. 178.
2. See Moulton, *Prolegomena*, pp. 187-92; but cf. Moule, *Idiom Book*, p. 22.
3. So Moule, *Idiom Book*, p. 23.

like the subjunctive, *the optative mood grammaticalizes the semantic feature of projection but with an element of contingency.* The high overlap in meaning with the subjunctive also probably contributed to the optative falling into disuse in the Hellenistic period, although when it occurs its particular meaning should be noted.

A common distinction is made between the volitive, commanding or wishing (57% of all instances) and the deliberative or potential (with ἄν; 43% of all instances) uses of the optative.[1] This analysis might prove useful in some cases, but a firm distinction in functions on the basis of the presence or absence of the conditional particle ἄν does not hold.[2] In the NT the optative form only occurs about 65 times, with many of the instances in the clause μὴ γένοιτο (may it never be) in the Pauline literature (e.g. Rom. 6.2, and 14 other times).

2.3.1. *Volitive usage* (commanding, wishing).

Mk 11.14: μηκέτι εἰς τὸν αἰῶνα ἐκ σοῦ μηδεὶς καρπὸν φάγοι (may no one ever eat fruit from you forever).

Phlm. 20: ἐγώ σου ὀναίμην ἐν κυρίῳ (may I benefit from you in the Lord).

1 Pet. 1.2: χάρις ὑμῖν καὶ εἰρήνη πληθυνθείη (grace to you and may peace be multiplied).

2.3.2. *Deliberative usage* (potential).

Acts 8.31: πῶς...ἂν δυναίμην; (how...might I be able?), a relatively infrequent instance of first person usage.

Acts 26.29: εὐξαίμην ἂν τῷ θεῷ (might I pray to God), according to Turner the only example of deliberative usage that is not a question.[3]

2.3.3. πρὶν ἤ.

There are two examples in the NT of optatives following πρὶν ἤ, a classical construction.

1. See J.L. Boyer, 'The Classification of Optatives: A Statistical Study', *GTJ* 9 (1988), pp. 129-40, for statistics and analysis.

2. Cf. V. Bers, *Greek Poetic Syntax in the Classical Age* (New Haven: Yale University Press, 1984), pp. 125-26, who after surveying usage claims that 'the semantic role of ἄν is negligible in the Attic system' and that its distribution is conjoined to 'stereotyped expressions', as opposed to ἄν being a marker of 'verbal mood'.

3. Turner, *Syntax*, p. 123.

Acts 7.2: πρὶν ἢ κατοικῆσαι αὐτὸν ἐν Χαρράν (before he settled in Harran), although most take this as an instance of the infinitive.

Acts 25.16: πρὶν ἢ ὁ κατηγορούμενος κατὰ πρόσωπον ἔχοι τοὺς κατηγόρους τόπον τε ἀπολογίας λάβοι περὶ τοῦ ἐγκλήματος (before the one condemned has [his] accusers face to face and receives a chance for defense concerning the charge), quite possibly an instance where the optative is used for the subjunctive in indirect speech (see Chapter 17 section 2.2.2).

2.4. *The Future Form*

The future form could well be placed here for examination since its functions are in many ways similar to those of the non-indicative mood forms. See Chapter 1 (section 2.4) for treatment of the future form.

Chapter 3

VOICE, NUMBER AND PERSON

Introduction

This chapter discusses three topics of importance to Greek, but ones often neglected because in many ways they appear to be self-evident or so similar to English. With regard to voice, it will be seen below (section 1) that there are a number of significant grammatical and even theological issues at stake. Number (section 2.1) and person (section 2.2), while perhaps less spectacular, are themselves important and are introduced for more than simply the sake of completeness.

1. *Voice*

Voice is a form-based semantic category used to describe the role that the grammatical subject of a clause plays in relation to an action. Voice is grammaticalized in Greek through selection among two or three sets of voice endings. The history and development of the three voices of Greek—active, middle and passive—are complex and uncertain. Most grammarians are agreed that the active and middle forms preceded development of the passive form, as difficult as that may be to grasp for English speakers, who have no direct equivalent to the Greek middle.[1] There is room for much more work in areas related to Greek voice. One of those areas is deponent verbs, verbs where the paradigm does not include all three voices. In this situation, for example, one of the voice forms (e.g. the middle or passive) is

1. See Moulton, *Prolegomena*, pp. 152-53; see also J. Lyons, *Introduction to Theoretical Linguistics* (Cambridge: Cambridge University Press, 1968), pp. 371-78.

called upon to perform the function (e.g. the active function) of the form which is missing (see section 1.4 below on deponent verbs).

1.1. *The Active Voice*

With the active voice, the agent (the person or thing represented as performing the action) is the grammatical subject of the verb. The action expressed by the verb may pass from the agent to some other person or object (so-called transitive use of the verb), or it may not (so-called intransitive use of the verb).[1] The active voice is the least semantically weighted of the voices, and simply states that some agent acts in an event. BDF[2] and Robertson[3] give thorough lists of verbs in the NT which may be either transitive or intransitive. As Robertson points out,[4] transitivity has nothing per se to do with voice, but is a matter of the individual meanings of the words themselves. Thus examples of transitive verbs appear with all three voices, including the active voice.

Lk. 7.29: πᾶς ὁ λαὸς...καὶ οἱ τελῶναι ἐδικαίωσαν τὸν θεόν (all the people...and the tax collectors justified God), an example where the double agent acts toward the recipient of the action (transitive verb).

Lk. 11.47: οἰκοδομεῖτε τὰ μνημεῖα τῶν προφητῶν (you are building the tombs of the prophets), in which the Greek active verb does not need an explicit subject (i.e. a subject word such as ὑμεῖς is not necessary).

Lk. 17.16: ἔπεσεν ἐπὶ πρόσωπον παρὰ τοὺ πόδας αὐτοῦ (he fell upon [his] face at his feet), an example of intransitive use of an active verb.

a. Verbs of perception (knowing, speaking, thinking, and so forth) frequently have the recipient of the action expressed in a dependent

1. Lyons, *Introduction to Theoretical Linguistics*, p. 350. The notion of one, two and three place verbs—according to the number of nouns or noun phrases which can combine with the verb—is useful. To use the language of slot and filler, a one place verb has one noun-slot (subject), a two place verb has two noun-slots (subject, object), a three place verb has three noun-slots (subject, two objects [so-called direct and indirect objects]).

2. BDF, §308.

3. Robertson, *Grammar*, pp. 799-800.

4. Robertson, *Grammar*, p. 797.

clause, often introduced by ὅτι (see Chapter 17).

Phil. 1.12: γινώσκειν δὲ ὑμᾶς βούλομαι...ὅτι...(but I want you to know...that...).

Phil. 1.16: εἰδότες ὅτι...(knowing that...).

b. As in English, Greek verbs of motion are virtually always intransitive.

Mk 12.18: ἔρχονται Σαδδουκαῖοι πρὸς αὐτόν (Sadducees came to him).

Acts 16.1: κατήντησεν δὲ [καὶ] εἰς Δέρβην καὶ εἰς Λύστραν (and he arrived [both] at Derbe and at Lystra).

c. Some verbal modifiers in the accusative case are not the recipients of the action; they are performing an adverbial function of modifying the verb and are not to be considered objects as defined above (see Chapter 4 on cases and Chapter 7 on adverbs).

2 Cor. 13.1: τρίτον τοῦτο ἔρχομαι πρὸς ὑμᾶς (for this third time I am coming to you), where the temporal word (τρίτον) has its own modification.

2 Cor. 13.11: λοιπόν...χαίρετε (finally [with respect to the rest]...rejoice), a standard use of λοιπόν, an accusative of respect, as a sentence connective.

1.2. *The Passive Voice*

With the passive voice, the agent (the person or thing represented as performing the action) is no longer the grammatical subject of the clause. The object or recipient of the action takes the agent's place as grammatical subject. The verb appears in the passive voice form, and the agent or means may or may not be expressed.[1] The frequent result of use of the passive voice is that attention regarding the action is placed upon the grammatical subject (recipient) rather than the agent.

1.2.1. *Specified agency.* In cases where agency is expressed, primary (personal) agency is often expressed using ὑπό + genitive case,

1. To use the language of slot and filler, in the passive voice the recipient or object of the active-voice verb now fills the slot of the grammatical subject. There is the option of the former filler of the subject slot filling a new slot as part of an agent phrase (often using a preposition).

secondary (intermediate) agency using διά + genitive (also ἐκ, frequently in Paul), and instrumental or impersonal agency using ἐν + dative or the simple dative case.

Mk 1.9: Ἰησοῦς...ἐβαπτίσθη εἰς τὸν Ἰορδάνην ὑπὸ Ἰωάννου (Jesus...was baptized into the Jordan by John). The active statement would be 'John baptized Jesus', but the passive is used to single out Jesus as the point of emphasis, rather than John, who would be the point of focus if the active verb were used.

Mt. 1.22: πληρωθῇ τὸ ῥηθὲν ὑπὸ κυρίου διὰ τοῦ προφήτου (the thing spoken by the Lord through the prophet might be fulfilled). The primary agent is the Lord, but the secondary or intermediate agent is the human author (both modifying the passive participle). The agent of the passive subjunctive πληρωθῇ must be inferred, but is probably understood to be the same Lord who is seen as the agent producing the Scripture (see section 1.2.2 below).

Rom. 5.1: δικαιωθέντες...ἐκ πίστεως (being justified...by faith).

Acts 11.16: ὑμεῖς...βαπτισθήσεσθε ἐν πνεύματι ἁγίῳ (you... will be baptized by the Holy Spirit), with ἐν used 'instrumentally' (see the Glossary). This function of ἐν is also fairly common with active verbs: Lk. 22.49: πατάξομεν ἐν μαχαίρῃ; (shall we strike with a sword?).

Mk 5.4: αὐτὸν πολλάκις πέδαις καὶ ἁλύσεσιν δεδέσθαι (he was often bound by shackles and chains), followed by an instance of primary agency.

1.2.2. *Unspecified agency*. In instances where the agent is not specified, the interpreter occasionally must speculate regarding agency. However, it is not always necessary to engage in such speculation.

Mk 1.15: πεπλήρωται ὁ καιρός (the time is fulfilled), where no agent is specified.

Some posit that there are instances, especially in the Gospels, where the unspecified agent is implied to be God. This is referred to as the 'divine or theological passive'. Scholarly speculation is that direct reference to God was avoided out of reverence and respect, although the relatively frequent mention of God in the Gospels minimizes this rationale.[1]

Mt. 5.4, 6, 7, 9: παρακληθήσονται...χορτασθήσονται...

1. See Zerwick, *Biblical Greek*, p. 76.

ἐλεηθήσονται...κληθήσονται (they shall be comforted...fed... given mercy...called).

Mt. 16.19 (cf. 18.18): ἔσται δεδεμένον ἐν τοῖς οὐρανοῖς...ἔσται λελυμένον ἐν τοῖς οὐρανοῖς (it shall be bound 'by' heaven...it shall be loosed 'by' heaven), where Jeremias speculates that the dative prepositional phrase is a roundabout way of referring to God.[1]

1.2.3. *Passive with accusative case object.* In a few instances the Greek passive verb form may take an object, what might best be labeled an accusative of respect (see Chapter 4 section 2.3.3). Whereas this is unusual for English (though not impossible—'he was given the rights to the land' and 'I was thrown the book'), it appears that Greek verbs with two accusative case objects in the active voice often retain one of the objects in the accusative when transformed into a passive construction.[2]

Lk. 7.29: βαπτισθέντες τὸ βάπτισμα Ἰωάννου (being baptized with respect to the baptism of John).

Phil. 1.11: πεπληρωμένοι καρπὸν δικαιοσύνης (being filled with respect to the fruit of righteousness); cf. Col. 1.9: πληρωθῆτε τὴν ἐπίγνωσιν (you might be filled with respect to knowledge).

Phil. 3.8: τὰ πάντα ἐζημιώθην (I was made to suffer loss with respect to all things).

1 Tim. 6.5: διεφθαρμένων ἀνθρώπων τὸν νοῦν (people depraved with respect to the mind).

1.3. *The Middle Voice*

The Greek middle voice is the most difficult for English speakers, since there does not appear to be an exact grammatical equivalent. English speakers can do approximately the same things with their language as the middle form does in Greek, but various syntactical means rather than a single expression are required. The translation of the Greek middle voice will often be the same as the translation of the English active voice. (The Greek middle-voice verb can be transitive or intransitive, an issue which apparently does not have direct bearing on voice.) Even if a reflexive pronoun (e.g. himself, herself) is used

1. J. Jeremias, *NT Theology: The Proclamation of Jesus* (trans. J. Bowden; London: SCM Press, 1971), p. 9.

2. See BDF, §159; Goodwin, *Greek Grammar*, pp. 265-66.

in English, this does not mean that the English rendering and the Greek middle form convey the exact same meaning.

1.3.1. *Meaning of the Greek middle voice.* Grammarians are undecided how exactly to characterize the Greek middle voice, but most are agreed that a reflexive middle sense ('he washed himself'), in which the agent (subject) and recipient (object) of the action are the same, is *not* the predominant one in the Hellenistic period.[1] Moulton (perhaps a bit extremely), after surveying the evidence in the NT, believes that the middle voice is 'quite inaccurately' described as reflexive.[2] Of all the possible examples, he concedes only Mt. 27.5 (ἀπήγξατο), but even here not without question, suggesting the translation 'choke' rather than the reflexive 'hang oneself'. Moulton points out the humor in taking the middle reflexively in 2 Pet. 2.22: ὗς λουσαμένη (a pig washes itself [?]). This analysis weakens interpretations which rely heavily on the reflexive sense, although it certainly does not demonstrate that such a sense is impossible.

Lk. 11.21: ὁ ἰσχυρὸς καθωπλισμένος φυλάσσῃ τὴν ἑαυτοῦ αὐλήν (the strong man, having armed himself, guards his own courtyard), an example of a reflexive use of the middle voice.

A better and more comprehensive description is that *the Greek middle voice expresses more direct participation, specific involvement, or even some form of benefit of the subject doing the action.* Thus it could be reflexive in some contexts (these are probably best confined to intransitive uses), or it could simply draw attention to the subject, even if the subject is not the only participant (i.e. where an object is involved). On the basis of formal, statistical and semantic criteria, the Greek middle voice carries the most semantic weight of the Greek voices. The features of participation, involvement or benefit are not meant to convey only positive connotations, but to describe the heightened involvement of the subject in the event. Thus Moule's definition says that the middle voice 'calls attention to the whole

1. Robertson, *Grammar*, p. 806; Moulton, *Prolegomena*, pp. 155-56; Moule, *Idiom Book*, p. 24; Turner, *Syntax*, p. 54; Winer, *Treatise*, p. 316; Dana and Mantey, *Manual Grammar*, p. 158. In light of this consistent opinion among reputable grammarians, it is difficult to accept Black's unqualified statement that 'The basic function of the middle voice is reflexive' (D.A. Black, 'Some Dissenting Notes on R. Stein's *The Synoptic Problem* and Markan "Errors"', *FN* 1 [1988], p. 96).

2. Moulton, *Prolegomena*, p. 155.

subject being concerned with the action',[1] and Moulton's says that the middle voice emphasizes 'the part taken by the subject in the action'.[2]

Mk 7.4: βαπτίσωνται (they participate in washing), here for the beneficial purpose of preparation for eating.

Lk. 2.5: ἀπογράψασθαι (to participate in registering), for the benefit of fulfilling the royal edict, even if Mary and Joseph are not the only ones involved in the process of registering.

In a few instances the middle voice and a pronoun are both found. This is apparently an emphatic construction.

Jn 19.24: διεμερίσαντο τὰ ἱμάτιά μου ἑαυτοῖς (they divided up for themselves my garments).

Acts 7.58: οἱ μάρτυρες ἀπέθεντο τὰ ἱμάτια αὐτῶν (the witnesses placed their garments), with the intensive pronoun (αὐτῶν), probably unnecessary except for emphatic purposes.

Acts 20.24: οὐδενὸς λόγου ποιοῦμαι τὴν ψυχὴν τιμίαν ἐμαυτῷ ('I do not consider my life of any account as dear to myself' [NASB]).

1.3.2. *Translation of the Greek middle voice.* The participatory or involved sense of the Greek middle voice may need to be rendered *in English* by a variety of means. These include at least the following.

a. Reflexive pronoun: 2 Tim. 4.15: σὺ φυλάσσου (guard yourself); Mk 14.41: ἀναπαύεσθε; (are you resting yourself?).

b. Reciprocal pronoun: Mt. 26.4: συνεβουλεύσαντο (they counselled one another); Jn 9.22: συνετέθειντο οἱ Ἰουδαῖοι (the Jews had agreed with one another).

c. Prepositional phrase: Lk. 14.7: τὰς πρωτοκλισίας ἐξελέγοντο (they picked out for themselves the places of honor); Mt. 16.22: προσλαβόμενος αὐτὸν ὁ Πέτρος (Peter, having taken him to himself).

1.3.3. *Important uses of the Greek middle voice.* Three examples illustrate well the importance of sorting out the Greek middle voice.

1 Cor. 13.8: εἴτε...προφητεῖαι, καταργηθήσονται· εἴτε γλῶσ-

1. Moule, *Idiom Book*, p. 24.

2. Moulton, *Prolegomena*, p. 158; cf. Robertson, *Grammar*, p. 804; BDF, §307; Brooks and Winbery, *Syntax*, p. 111; Goodwin, *Greek Grammar*, p. 264. See also B.L. Gildersleeve, *Syntax of Classical Greek* (repr. Groningen: Bouma, 1980), I, p. 64.

σαι, παύσονται· εἴτε γνῶσις, καταργηθήσεται (if...prophecies, they will be eliminated; if tongues, they will cease; if knowledge, it will be eliminated). A frequently heard interpretation of this verse understands the middle voice to say that tongues will cease on their own (with no external agent), while prophecy and knowledge will be abolished by direct agency (using the passive verb).[1] Carson finds fault with this understanding on several counts:[2] (1) the reflexive sense is not the most common or usual understanding of the middle voice; (2) no contextual indicators point to the reflexive sense here; (3) other clear uses of παύω in the NT do not have a reflexive sense: Lk. 8.24: after Jesus rebukes the wind and the waves ἐπαύσαντο καὶ ἐγένετο γαλήνη (they ceased and it became calm), but not on their own; Acts 21.32: οἱ...ἰδόντες τὸν χιλίαρχον καὶ τοὺς στρατιώτας ἐπαύσαντο (they...seeing the chiliarch and soldiers, ceased). If one wants to argue the case that 'tongues' have ceased on their own (reflexive middle sense) at a particular point, it will have to be made apart from reliance upon the use of the middle voice here.

Col. 2.15: ἀπεκδυσάμενος τὰς ἀρχὰς καὶ τὰς ἐξουσίας ἐδειγμάτισεν ἐν παρρησίᾳ (stripping the powers and authorities, he displayed [them] in boldness). Some interpreters and translators have taken this usage as reflexive: Jesus Christ stripped off from himself the powers and authorities (as if he were wearing them) and displayed them in triumph.[3] Understanding the passage as speaking of Jesus Christ's beneficial or participatory stripping of the defeated demonic enemies of their power makes better sense of the imagery, especially in this transitive context.[4]

Jas 4.2-3: οὐκ ἔχετε διὰ τὸ μὴ αἰτεῖσθαι ὑμᾶς, αἰτεῖτε καὶ οὐ

1. Brooks and Winbery, *Syntax*, p. 101.

2. D.A. Carson, *Exegetical Fallacies* (Grand Rapids: Baker, 1984), pp. 77-79.

3. See e.g. J.B. Lightfoot, *St Paul's Epistles to the Colossians and to Philemon* (repr. Grand Rapids: Zondervan, 1959), pp. 190-91. Confusion over understanding the middle voice is evident in P.T. O'Brien's treatment. Because he evidently believes that the active English translation means that the Greek middle force cannot be present (and he wants to reject Lightfoot's interpretation), he argues for a Greek active sense: *Colossians, Philemon* (Waco, TX: Word Books, 1982), pp. 127-28.

4. See F.F. Bruce, *The Epistles to the Ephesians and Colossians* (with E.K. Simpson; Grand Rapids: Eerdmans, 1957), pp. 239-40 n. 68. There is also the issue of whether Jesus Christ or God is the subject, but that is beside the point here.

λαμβάνετε διότι κακῶς αἰτεῖσθε (you do not have because you do not ask, you ask and you do not receive because you ask badly). Scholars differ regarding this verse. Moulton surveys opinion and rejects solutions which claim that there is no difference between the active and middle/passive forms of αἰτέω. He says, 'If the middle is really the stronger word, we can understand its being brought in just where an effect of contrast can be secured, while in ordinary passages the active would carry as much weight as was needed'.[1] See also 1 Jn 5.15; Mk 6.2-25; 10.35, 38; Mt. 20.20, 22; all with similar usage.

1.4. *Deponent Verbs*

A significant factor which must be taken into account is that not all individual verbs have all verbal forms of voice, even though the verbs may have active, middle and/or passive meanings connected with them. Complicating the situation is the fact that, for the present and the perfect tense-forms, the middle and the passive voice forms are the same. But the aorist and future forms have distinctive passive forms.[2] For a number of verbs, however, one or more of the voice forms in a given tense-form were not created by users of the language. The result is usually called deponency. This is a term which has not commended itself to all grammarians, however, primarily because of the difficulty in finding stable criteria by which one can determine how deponency works.[3]

1.4.1. *Definition of deponency. Deponency is the phenomenon whereby for a given verb one voice form (or more) is not found and the semantics (meaning) of this voice are grammaticalized by substitution of another voice form of the verb.*[4] A very common pattern is for the middle (or middle/passive) form to have active meaning when an active voice form is not found. For example, the verb ἔρχομαι

1. Moulton, *Prolegomena*, p. 160.

2. This situation is perhaps further complicated by the fact that the -(θ)ην endings of the passive are later developments from the active endings.

3. Robertson, *Grammar*, pp. 811-13; Moulton, *Prolegomena*, p. 153.

4. This category is to be distinguished (so far as one is able) from the notion of defective verbs, in which one or more of the tense, mood or voice forms is lacking but there is no semantic shift to fill in the missing sense. Suppletive verbs (in which verbs from more than one root are placed in the same paradigm, e.g. ἔρχομαι with ἦλθον) often result from the combination of verbs defective for an entire tense-form.

does not have a present active form, but the present middle/passive form is used with active meaning (or so it seems—see section 1.4.2 below). A fairly common pattern is for some verbs to have deponent future forms, even though they are not deponent in other tense-forms: e.g. λαμβάνω (present), ἔλαβον (aorist), λήμψομαι (future).

The majority of middle voice forms in the Greek of the NT may well be deponent, although there is a surprisingly large number of ambiguous instances. *A general rule is that presence of an active form eliminates a verb from being considered deponent, although it is not necessarily deponent even if there is no active form.* Deponency may also be different for each tense-form (e.g. a verb may be deponent in the aorist but not in the present tense-form).[1]

1.4.2. *Instances requiring further analysis.* For some verbs there is little apparent difficulty in determining deponency, but there are a number of verbs where the determination is not so clear. In some instances it is a matter of deciding whether a given verb is in fact deponent. In other instances it is a matter of deciding whether the meaning of a given form is active, middle or passive, especially in cases where the middle and passive forms are the same.

a. *The question of deponency.* Robertson provides a list of verbs which by formal criteria might be considered deponent (i.e. the verb has a middle or passive form and no active form), but which apparently retain their middle sense. These verbs are used in both present and aorist tense-forms. Robertson's list includes verbs of mental action and verbs peculiar in their forms.

Verbs of mental action:[2] αἰσθάνομαι (Lk. 9.45), ἀρνέομαι (Lk. 12.9), προαιτιάομαι (Rom. 3.9), ἀσπάζομαι (Acts 25.13), διαβεβαιόομαι (Tit. 3.8), ἐντέλλομαι (Heb. 11.22), ἐπιλανθάνομαι (Mt. 16.5), εὔχομαι (Rom. 9.3), ἡγέομαι (Phil. 3.8), λογίζομαι (Phil. 4.8), μαίνομαι (Acts 26.25), μέμφομαι (Rom. 9.19), φείδομαι (Rom. 8.32).

1. For a helpful discussion of deponency, see B. Friberg and T. Friberg (eds.), *Analytical Greek NT* (Grand Rapids: Baker, 1981), pp. 811-16. They are inaccurate, however, to categorize verbs on such a strict individual basis that prefixed forms are treated separately from unprefixed (e.g. 2 Cor. 4.8, where ἀπορούμενοι [perplexed] is considered middle but the following ἐξαπορούμενοι [despairing] is considered deponent).

2. Robertson, *Grammar*, p. 812.

Verbs peculiar in their forms:[1] there are also a number of verbs where it is difficult to determine why the verb has a middle form unless it is middle in sense, especially if there is also a passive form. Consequently, it must be questioned whether these verbs should be considered deponent: γίνομαι, where there are both middle (ἐγενόμην) and passive (ἐγενήθην) aorist forms and an active perfect tense-form (γέγονα); ἅλλομαι, βούλομαι, δύναμαι, ἐργάζομαι, κάθημαι, πορεύομαι, φοβέομαι, and the like, where the aorist is passive in form; as well as ἀποκρίνομαι, where the aorist usually has the passive form, and appears approximately 200 times in the NT.

One must be cautious before abandoning too quickly the semantic feature usually grammaticalized by a particular voice form. On the basis of this evidence, and evidence above regarding the middle voice, one might be justified in seeing some middle sense with virtually all verbs with middle-voice form, regardless of whether they can be analyzed as deponent.

b. *The question of meaning.* A second set of examples concerns instances where determination of meaning is clearly ambiguous. For example, having decided that a given form is middle or deponent, one must still decide whether the given form has active, middle or passive sense. This issue is complicated by the difficulty in the present and perfect tense-forms of determining whether a middle/passive form is middle or passive in sense, or whether such a distinction can be made in a given instance.

Lk. 15.6: συγχάρητε (rejoice). The aorist passive imperative is apparently used with active or middle sense, there being no active or middle aorist form of this verb.

Mk 3.24, 25, 26: σταθῆναι...σταθῆναι...ἀνέστη...στῆναι (stand). The aorist active and passive infinitives and active indicative of the root στα- appear in close proximity. The temptation is to see the active and passive forms as active in sense. Cf. e.g. Mt. 2.9 or 27.11 with ἐστάθη: is it to be translated 'it stood' or 'it was made to stand' with understood agent?

Eph. 5.14: φανερούμενον, with the middle or passive participle.[2] If it is middle, the meaning might be captured in English translation

1. Robertson, *Grammar*, p. 813, supplemented.

2. Moule, *Idiom Book*, p. 25.

with the phrase 'everything which *illuminates* is light'. If it is passive the rendering would be 'everything which *is illuminated* is light'. The consequences of such an understanding are potentially significant.

2. *Number and Person*

2.1. *Number*

The Greek of the NT, like most Hellenistic Greek, has two possible numbers, singular and plural.[1] These are grammatical categories which often are correlative with actual numbers, though this is not required. Although the majority of singular subjects take singular verb forms and plural subjects take plural verb forms, this is not always the case.

2.1.1. *Neuter plural subjects and singular verbs.*

a. *Examples.* Grammarians are not decided why but it is frequently the case that neuter plural subjects take singular verb forms. Some suggest that neuter items are by nature collective, while others suggest that (in earlier times) the neuter plural ending was identical with a singular collective ending.[2] Regardless of the reasons, this is a persistent, although perhaps weakening, tendency in the Greek of the NT (as opposed to earlier Attic Greek).

Jn 9.3: φανερωθῇ τὰ ἔργα (the works might be manifest).

Jn 10.21: ταῦτα τὰ ῥήματα οὐκ ἔστιν δαιμονιζομένου (these are not the words of one demon-possessed); Jn 10.25: τὰ ἔργα... μαρτυρεῖ περὶ ἐμοῦ (the works...bear witness concerning me).

Acts 1.18: ἐξεχύθη πάντα τὰ σπλάγχνα αὐτοῦ (all his entrails were poured out).

2 Pet. 2.20: γέγονεν αὐτοῖς τὰ ἔσχατα χείρονα τῶν πρώτων (the last things became worse to them than the first).

b. *Exceptions.* Plural subjects with plural verbs are also to be found.

Mt. 6.32: πάντα...ταῦτα τὰ ἔθνη ἐπιζητοῦσιν (the nations seek all these things).

Mk 3.11: τὰ πνεύματα τὰ ἀκάθαρτα, ὅταν αὐτὸν ἐθεώρουν, προσέπιπτον αὐτῷ καὶ ἔκραζον λέγοντες ὅτι...(the unclean

1. The dual number was already restricted in use during classical times.
2. Schwyzer, *Griechische Grammatik*, II, p. 607.

spirits, whenever they saw him, fell before him and cried, saying that...).

Lk. 24.11: ἐφάνησαν ἐνώπιον αὐτῶν ὡσεὶ λῆρος τὰ ῥήματα ταῦτα (these words appeared to them as nonsense).

Jn 19.31: κατεαγῶσιν αὐτῶν τὰ σκέλη καὶ ἀρθῶσιν (their legs might be broken and they might be taken away).

Jas 2.19: τὰ δαιμόνια πιστεύουσιν καὶ φρίσσουσιν (the demons believe and shudder).

Both singular and plural verbs with the same substantive are to be found.

Lk. 4.41: ἐξήρχετο...δαιμόνια ἀπὸ πολλῶν, κραυγάζοντα καὶ λέγοντα...ὅτι ᾔδεισαν τὸν Χριστὸν αὐτὸν εἶναι (demons came out [singular] from many, crying and saying [both plural]... because they knew [plural] him to be the Christ).

Lk. 8.30-31: εἰσῆλθεν δαιμόνια πολλὰ εἰς αὐτόν. καὶ παρεκάλουν αὐτόν (many demons entered [singular] into him. And they were beseeching [plural] him).

Various proposals for these exceptions have been suggested. Some grammarians posit that the subjects involved are animated, especially when they are spirits or demons,[1] but not all grammarians are convinced.[2] The evidence above shows that this is at best a tendency.

2.1.2. *Collective nouns with plural verbs.* Frequently a collective noun (in which a distinct plurality of items is referred to with a substantive singular in form) will not take a singular verb but will take a plural verb.

Mt. 21.8: ὁ...πλεῖστος ὄχλος ἔστρωσαν ἑαυτῶν τὰ ἱμάτια (most of the crowd spread their own garments).

Lk. 19.37: ἤρξαντο ἅπαν τὸ πλῆθος τῶν μαθητῶν χαίροντες αἰνεῖν τὸν θεόν (all the crowd of the disciples, rejoicing, began to praise God).

Both singular and plural verbs with the same substantive are also to be found.

Mk 3.32: ἐκάθητο περὶ αὐτὸν ὄχλος καὶ λέγουσιν αὐτῷ (a crowd sat [singular] around him and said [plural] to him).

Lk. 1.21: ἦν ὁ λαὸς προσδοκῶν τὸν Ζαχαρίαν, καὶ ἐθαύμαζον

1. Winer, *Treatise*, pp. 645-49; BDF, §133.
2. Robertson, *Grammar*, pp. 403-404.

(the crowd was there [singular], expecting [singular] Zacharias, and they were marveling [plural]).

Acts 21.36: ἠκολούθει...τὸ πλῆθος τοῦ λαοῦ κράζοντες (the crowd of people was following [singular], crying [plural]).

1 Cor. 16.15: οἴδατε τὴν οἰκίαν Στεφανᾶ, ὅτι ἐστὶν ἀπαρχὴ τῆς Ἀχαΐας καὶ εἰς διακονίαν τοῖς ἁγίοις ἔταξαν ἑαυτούς (you know the house of Stephanus, that it is [singular] the firstfruit of Achaia and they appointed [plural] themselves for service to the saints).

2.1.3. *Failure of concord. Concord in number refers to the normal pattern of singular subject with singular verb and plural subject with plural verb.* Besides the examples treated above (sections 2.1.1 and 2.1.2), there are a number of other instances where concord is not found in the Greek of the NT. There are various explanations of this, but no single explanation covers all of the instances. A frequent pattern is to find a singular element closest to the singular verb.[1]

Jn 2.2: ἐκλήθη...καὶ ὁ Ἰησοῦς καὶ οἱ μαθηταὶ αὐτοῦ (both Jesus was called and his disciples).

Jn 8.52: Ἀβραὰμ ἀπέθανεν καὶ οἱ προφῆται (Abraham died and the prophets).

Acts 16.31: σωθήσῃ σὺ καὶ ὁ οἶκός σου (you will be saved and your house), an example of failed concord of person as well (see section 2.2.5 below).

1 Tim. 6.4-5: γίνεται φθόνος, ἔρις, βλασφημίαι, ὑπόνοιαι πονηραί, διαπαρατριβαί (envy, strife, blasphemies, evil suspicions, constant arguments come about).

Jas 2.15: ἐὰν ἀδελφὸς ἢ ἀδελφὴ γυμνοὶ ὑπάρχωσιν (if brother or sister are naked).

There are several examples where a verb is in the singular with an unexpressed singular subject, but a plural nominative case phrase is added.

Mt. 12.3: ἐπείνασεν καὶ οἱ μετ' αὐτοῦ (he hungered and those with him); Lk. 22.14; Jn 4.53.

1. S.G. Green, *Handbook to the Grammar of the Greek Testament* (London: Religious Tract Society, n.d.), p. 183.

2.2. *Person*

Every finite verb in Greek by definition grammaticalizes person, in which a given form of the verb takes appropriate endings indicating a grammatical relation between the subject and the participants in the action. The traditional labels are first, second and third person, but these terms are not as descriptive and useful as they might be. For example, they mask the fact that there is a closer semantic relation between first and second persons than there is with third person. The reason for this is that first person and second person imply that the participants be present, whereas third person does not.[1]

2.2.1. *First person.* First person is used when the participant is included either actively or conceptually in the action. First person singular refers to the speaker, but first person plural is not simply the multiplication of speakers. It may be used to refer to many speakers, it may refer to the speaker and those whom the speaker wishes to include with him- or herself, and it may simply refer in a more inclusive fashion to those whom the speaker wishes to address. A common problem in the use of the first person plural in the Pauline epistles is the determination of who is included and to what degree others are included by Paul.[2] Notoriously difficult is Paul's use of the first person singular in Rom. 7.7-25: does Paul mean himself, the Jewish people (probably excluding Paul as an individual), a generic human, or what?[3] There is a variety of rhetorical reasons why Paul might use the first person singular and plural, some of them possibly tied to his use of the diatribe style.

2 Cor. 10.1 (αὐτὸς...ἐγὼ Παῦλος παρακαλῶ ὑμᾶς [I, Paul, beseech you]) is a very clear use of the emphatic first person singular referring to the speaker. First person verbs through to 2 Cor. 11.3 continue to refer to Paul himself even when plural verbs are used,[4] apart from 10.8, 9, 22. These verbs probably refer to his readers alone. Cf. Phil. 1.3–4.20, where, after beginning with a salutation from

1. See Lyons, *Introduction to Theoretical Linguistics*, pp. 276-78.

2. Robertson, *Grammar*, pp. 406-407; Moulton, *Prolegomena*, p. 86; BDF, §280; and most commentaries.

3. Theological issues are unavoidable here. See Cranfield, *Romans*, I, pp. 342-47; and the bibliography in J.D.G. Dunn, *Romans 1–8* (Dallas: Word Books, 1988), pp. 374-75.

4. Robertson, *Grammar*, p. 407.

Timothy and Paul, the body of the epistle is in the first person singular. This is in contrast, for example, to Colossians, where in 1.3-23 and *passim* the plural is used, certainly with reference to Paul, and also possibly to Timothy.

2.2.2. *Second person.* Second person is used by the speaker to refer to the hearer (or hearers), whether the person is real or imagined (for the sake of discussion).

Rom. 2.21: ὁ...διδάσκων ἕτερον σεαυτὸν οὐ διδάσκεις; ὁ κηρύσσων μὴ κλέπτειν κλέπτεις; (do you, who teach another, not teach yourself? Do you, who preach not to steal, steal?). The second person singular as part of Paul's diatribe style addresses a hypothetical discussion partner.

2 Cor. 13.5: ἑαυτοὺς πειράζετε εἰ ἐστὲ ἐν τῇ πίστει (test yourselves if you are in the faith), with the second person plural referring to Paul's actual hearers.

2.2.3. *Third person.* Third person is used by the speaker to refer to people and things other than the speaker and hearer. Consequently, the remoteness of the third person is conducive to impersonal uses of the third person verb form (see section 2.2.4 below).

Gal. 6.1: ἐὰν καὶ προλημφθῇ ἄνθρωπος ἔν τινι παραπτώματι (if a man should be caught in any trespass), Paul says before shifting to second person plural to address his hearers.

Jn 7.32: ἤκουσαν οἱ Φαρισαῖοι τοῦ ὄχλου (the Pharisees heard the crowd), a common use of third person in narrative.

2.2.4. *Impersonal verbs. An impersonal verb is one in which the subject is not specified either explicitly or implicitly.* Impersonal verbs are generally confined to the third person singular, although some have posited that under Semitic influence the plural could be used in this way as well.[1] The following verbs are generally considered

1. See M. Black, *An Aramaic Approach to the Gospels and Acts* (Oxford: Clarendon Press, 3rd edn, 1967), pp. 126-28; *contra* L. Rydbeck, *Fachprosa, vermeintliche Volkssprache und Neues Testament: Zur Beurteilung der sprachlichen Niveauunterschiede im nachklassischen Griechisch* (Uppsala: n.p., 1967), pp. 27-45. Even though 'they' might be an appropriate translation, besides the fact that a subject can often be found for the third person plural verb, the use of the third person plural verb in extra-biblical writers (e.g. Teles) minimizes the possible Semitic influence.

impersonal:[1] δεῖ (it is necessary), χρή (it is expedient), πρέπει (it is fitting), δοκεῖ (it seems), μέλει (it is of concern); and some forms of εἰμί, including ἔξεστι (it is lawful).

Mk 12.14: οὐ μέλει σοι περὶ οὐδενός (it is not a concern to you concerning anyone), but cf. the following ἔξεστιν with an infinitive subject.

There are several precautions to observe regarding impersonal verbs. The first is that the interpreter must be careful that some substantive is not the actual subject of the verb. Each one of the verbs cited above has instances in the NT where a subject can be implied. For example, in Acts 15.5, δεῖ περιτέμνειν αὐτοὺς παραγγέλλειν τε τηρεῖν τὸν νόμον Μωϋσέως (to circumcise them and to command them to keep the law of Moses is necessary), the double infinitive phrase is the subject, a fairly common occurrence with this kind of verb.[2] The same holds for such verbs as ἐγένετο (referring to an event) and γέγραπται (usually followed by the quotation which stands written).

The second precaution is that the interpreter must be aware of certain verbs which take conventionally-understood subjects:[3] 1 Cor. 15.52: σαλπίσει (he will sound the trumpet), with an understood trumpeter; Jas 5.17: οὐκ ἔβρεξεν (it did not rain), where Greeks may well have understood God or the gods as bringing rain (cf. Mt. 5.45).

2.2.5. *Failure of concord. Concord in person refers to the normal pattern of agreement with regard to person* (first person subject with first person verb, and so forth). There are a number of instances where concord is not found in the Greek of the NT. There are various explanations of this, but no single explanation covers all of the instances. A common pattern is for the person of the first element to be in concord with the verb.[4]

Acts 16.31: σωθήσῃ σὺ καὶ ὁ οἶκός σου (you will be saved and your house), an example of failed concord of number as well (see section 2.1.3 above).

1. Cf. Moule, *Idiom Book*, pp. 27-29, who differentiates useful categories.
2. Moule, *Idiom Book*, p. 27.
3. Green, *Handbook*, p. 180.
4. Green, *Handbook*, p. 183.

Gal. 1.8: ἡμεῖς ἢ ἄγγελος ἐξ οὐρανοῦ εὐαγγελίζηται (we or a messenger from heaven might bring good news), where the second element is in concord.

Chapter 4

CASES AND GENDER

Introduction

Greek is an inflected or (to use the language of some modern linguists) a 'fusional' language. This means that words within the same class, in particular nouns, adjectives and pronouns, as well as participles, have inseparable formal elements (endings) attached or fused to them, which differentiate formal characteristics such as case, number and gender.[1] Virtually all grammarians are agreed that, according to the inflectional endings on nouns, adjectives and so on, Greek has a four- or five-case system (depending on whether one treats the vocative as a distinct case—see sections 2.1 and 2.2 below). The cases have been labeled as the nominative, accusative, genitive, dative and vocative. The genders of Greek are three: masculine, feminine and neuter. This is the formal evidence.

1. *Points of Clarification Regarding Cases*

While it is relatively easy to learn the formal endings that indicate the cases in Greek, understanding their meanings has proved much more difficult. Discussion of the Greek cases has proceeded along several different lines.[2] Some grammarians begin with an original or primitive local meaning of each case, and attempt to find some trace of this original meaning in each use.[3] Others treat cases as a means of syntactical differentiation, to describe the use of a word in a particular word

1. Verbs are also inflected words in Greek. See Chapters 1–3 for discussion of the meanings of their various inflectional endings.

2. See J.P. Louw, 'Linguistic Theory and the Greek Case System', *Acta Classica* 9 (1966), pp. 73-88.

3. E.g. Robertson, *Grammar*, pp. 453-54; Dana and Mantey, *Manual Grammar*, pp. 68-69 and *passim*.

arrangement.[1] Others define the cases by means of a set of functional criteria gleaned from instances of contextual usage.[2] And still others do not bother to define the cases at all, but simply treat individual categories of usage (e.g. BDF, Turner, Zerwick, Moule). There is little recent evidence—at least in study of the Greek of the NT—that Robertson's statement needs to be modified: 'Perhaps nowhere has confusion been worse confounded than in the study of the Greek cases'.[3] As a result, several preliminary points must be made and a groundwork laid before the cases may be discussed in detail.

1.1. *The Five-Case System*

Several grammarians still assert that the Greek of the NT maintains an eight-case system. Their argument rests on two criteria. First is the supposition that Greek originally had ablative, locative and instrumental case forms. Second is their supposed ability to differentiate legitimate functions of these cases. Regardless of the proto-history of the Greek language, by the time of the earliest extant remains of Greek these cases as formally distinct are at best only barely traceable. By the time of Hellenistic Greek the formal categories are restricted to four or five distinct inflected cases. Semantic or functional criteria provide a dubious argument for eight cases, since by this standard one might well cite a far larger number of cases than eight, as will be explored below. *Formal synchronic criteria (i.e. treatment of the Greek language as used during the Hellenistic period, especially as it is found in the Greek of the NT) dictate that analysis begin with at most five cases.*

1.2. *Determining the Meanings of the Cases*

Competing factors are apparently involved in analysis of the cases. These include the meaning contributed by context in a given instance (e.g. Paul's use of ἐκ πίστεως Ἰησοῦ in Rom. 3), the meaning contributed by particular syntactical features (e.g. Ἰησοῦ is in the genitive case and apparently related to πίστεως, also in the genitive following the preposition ἐκ), and the meaning contributed by the fundamental semantics of a case as part of the Greek case system (e.g.

1. E.g. Brooks and Winbery, *Syntax*, p. 2.
2. E.g. Brugmann, *Griechische Grammatik*, pp. 427-28.
3. E.g. Robertson, *Grammar*, p. 446.

the fact that a genitive and not a dative is used). As a result,[1] *Greek cases are subject to a three-tiered analysis, including the meaning of the form, syntax and context* (see fig. 2 below). The formal level (the meaning of the case itself) is essential to what the case does. Its fundamental meaning is then restricted or refined by how it appears in relation to other words in its immediate vicinity (syntax), and how this association of meanings may apply in a larger linguistic context. All three levels apply at any given time, requiring the interpreter to weigh a number of meaningful factors at once.

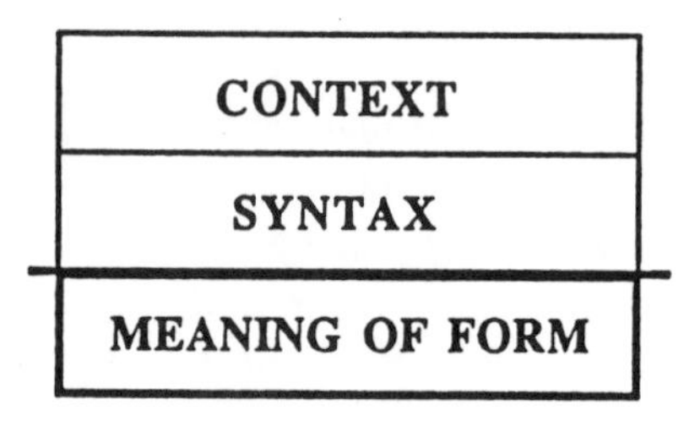

Figure 2. *Levels of Greek Case Analysis*

1.3. *Hierarchy of Greek Cases*

The Greek case system can be arranged hierarchically as well, indicating particular internal relations among the cases. Recent research indicates that the nominative case is the fundamental or foundational case in the Greek case system. The so-called oblique cases (accusative, genitive and dative) are to be distinguished from the nominative case. But the oblique cases maintain a set of relations as well. The accusative case is the foundational case of these three, followed by the genitive and then dative cases.[2]

This analysis accounts for several other factors often noted by grammarians. One is the encroachment of the more fundamental cases (e.g. nominative and accusative) on the less fundamental, resulting in the eventual squeezing out of the dative case begun during the Hellenistic period. Another is the apparent overlap in usage of the

1. Following Louw, 'Linguistic Theory', pp. 75-78.

2. See Louw, 'Linguistic Theory', pp. 78-87; A.C. Moorhouse, 'The Role of the Accusative Case', in A. Rijksbaron, H.A. Mulder and G.C. Wakker (eds.), *In the Steps of R. Kühner* (Amsterdam: Gieben, 1988), pp. 209-12; A. Kenny, *A Stylometric Study of the NT* (Oxford: Clarendon Press, 1986), pp. 50-61, on statistics for the cases.

cases. Often the meaning of one of the less fundamental cases (e.g. genitive or dative) may be included in the broader meaning of the more fundamental cases, at least on one or two of the levels of analysis. For example, all three of the oblique cases may function syntactically as objects of verbs, and may in a given context be translated similarly, but this overlap does not mean that they are completely synonymous in meaning. Each case maintains its semantic (meaning) features.[1]

2. *The Greek Cases*

In the following discussion the semantics (meaning) of each case form are briefly established. Then these semantic categories are analyzed in light of varying syntactical patterns and in light of contextual usage. What is said about the semantics of the cases applies to any given use of the case form, that is, whether the item treated is a noun or is another inflected word (e.g. adjective, participle), even though nouns constitute the majority of examples. The case system is at work regardless of the particular morphological features of the individual words. For example, a noun of the first, second or third declension in the nominative has the same semantic features of case as any other noun in the nominative. In other words, no particular semantic weight attaches to the declensions.

2.1. *The Nominative Case*

Grammarians have debated the essential semantics of the nominative case, suggesting it variously as the case of the subject (a syntactical category of restricted applicability),[2] as the naming case (a functional category, again somewhat restricted in use),[3] or as the 'unmarked' or purely nominal case, in other words, as the case that simply designates. This is similar to seeing the nominative case as the naming case, but without the implication of specificity.[4] *The semantic designation of*

1. See Winer, *Treatise*, p. 225.

2. Dana and Mantey, *Manual Grammar*, p. 66.

3. Moulton, *Prolegomena*, p. 69; Brooks and Winbery, *Syntax*, p. 4; W.D. Chamberlain, *An Exegetical Grammar of the Greek NT* (repr. Grand Rapids: Baker, 1979), p. 27.

4. Louw, 'Linguistic Theory', pp. 78-79; cf. Winer, *Treatise*, p. 226; Green, *Handbook*, p. 16.

the nominative case as purely nominal circumscribes the fundamental meaning which allows the various syntactical and contextual configurations in which it is used. These include its frequent use as subject or as an independent clause, as well as other independent uses.

2.1.1. *Subject*. Other cases may serve as subjects in various constructions (for example the accusative with the infinitive, or the genitive with the participle in a genitive absolute construction; see section 2.3.3 below and Chapter 9), but one of the primary syntactical uses of the nominative case is as the grammatical subject of a clause.

Mt. 8.18: ἰδὼν...ὁ Ἰησοῦς ὄχλον περὶ αὐτὸν ἐκέλευσεν ἀπελθεῖν εἰς τὸ πέραν (Jesus, seeing a crowd around him, commanded to go to the other side).

Rom. 8.2: ὁ γὰρ νόμος...(for the law...).

The nominative case item may function as its own clause (see section 2.1.4 below), in which the nominative item simply designates the nominal idea.

2.1.2. *Predicate*. With certain verbs—such as εἰμί, ὑπάρχω, γίνομαι (sometimes called linking verbs, because they link or equate two items), and some others, such as εὑρίσκω—the completive of the verb appears in the nominative case, like the subject (this is often called a predicate nominative).[1] On rules for determining the subject in linking-verb constructions, see Chapter 5 section 2.5.

Lk. 8.41: οὗτος ἄρχων τῆς συναγωγῆς ὑπῆρχεν (this one was a leader of the synagogue).

Jn 1.14: ὁ λόγος σὰρξ ἐγένετο (the word became flesh).

1 Jn 4.8: ὁ θεὸς ἀγάπη ἐστίν (God is love).

1 Cor. 4.2: πιστός τις εὑρεθῇ (someone might be found faithful).

2.1.3. *Apposition*. The nominative case item may be used to specify or restate a substantive. This is commonly though not exclusively found in the salutations of the epistles.

Rom. 1.1: Παῦλος δοῦλος Χριστοῦ Ἰησοῦ κλητὸς ἀπόστολος ἀφωρισμένος εἰς εὐαγγέλιον θεοῦ (Paul, a servant of Christ Jesus,

1. It must be remembered that with these verbs there is agreement in the cases of the subject and object, and that the subject, e.g. with the infinitive, is not always in the nominative case: Phil. 1.13: ὥστε τοὺς δεσμούς μου φανεροὺς ἐν Χριστῷ γενέσθαι (so that my chains have become known in Christ).

a called apostle, designated for the gospel of God), where there are two appositive nouns and an appositive participle, all in the nominative case.[1]

2.1.4. *Nominal clause* (absolute). The simple nominative case item may form its own clause in Greek. The fact that translations will often use a form of the verb 'to be' has led to the supposition that this verb is elided or omitted in Greek. Another interpretation—and the one adopted here—is that the 'unmarked' case could be used on its own to form a clause, that is, simply to specify the nominal idea.

Rom. 1.7: χάρις ὑμῖν καὶ εἰρήνη ἀπὸ θεοῦ πατρὸς ἡμῶν (grace to you and peace from God our father); cf. 1 Cor. 1.3; 2 Cor. 1.2; Gal. 1.3; Eph. 1.2; Phil. 1.2; Col. 1.2; 1 Thess. 1.1; 2 Thess. 1.2; Tit. 1.4; Phlm. 3; 1 Tim. 1.2 and 2 Tim. 1.2. In support of the understood verb is 2 Jn 3 (ἔσται [will be]), but cf. 1 Pet. 1.2; 2 Pet. 1.2; and Jude 2 with forms of πληθύνω (fulfil).

Rom. 6.17; 7.25: χάρις...τῷ θεῷ...(thanks...to God...).

Rom. 7.16: καλός ([it is] good).

Rom. 11.33: ὦ βάθος πλούτου καὶ σοφίας καὶ γνώσεως θεοῦ (oh, the depth of the riches and wisdom and knowledge of God).

Col. 3.17: πᾶν ὅ τι ἐὰν ποιῆτε ἐν λόγῳ ἢ ἐν ἔργῳ, πάντα ἐν ὀνόματι κυρίου Ἰησοῦ (everything which you might do in word or in deed, all things in the name of the Lord Jesus).

2 Pet. 2.22: κύων ἐπιστρέψας...ὗς λουσαμένη (a dog, returning...a pig, washing), unless these are predicate uses of the participle (see Chapter 10 section 2).

2.1.5. *Independent clause* (hanging). This construction occurs when a substantive (noun or noun substitute), such as a participle, in the nominative case lacks 'proper' grammatical agreement with a clause to which it is to be linked. The independent nominative appears in a range of biblical and extra-biblical Greek, and has taxed many a grammarian for an explanation. For example, some argue that it evidences the influence of the Semitic languages on the Greek of the NT.[2] Others claim that it reveals a discontinued construction where the author either lost the train of thought or changed the construction

1. Cf. 1 Cor. 1.1; 2 Cor. 1.1; Gal. 1.1; Eph. 1.1; Phil. 1.1; Col. 1.1; 1 Tim. 1.1; 2 Tim. 1.1; Tit. 1.1; Phlm. 1; Jas 1.1; 1 Pet. 1.1; 2 Pet. 1.1; Jude 1.

2. See Zerwick, *Biblical Greek*, p. 10.

of the sentence (i.e. anacoluthon).[1] Still others argue that it reveals a legitimate use of the nominative case in Greek, reflecting its unmarked or merely nominal character.[2] There is also debate about how the independent nominative functions. Since the independent nominative is in sense, though not in grammar, linked to an element in another clause, this construction quite possibly is used to draw attention to an item in the main clause which would be otherwise overlooked. The independent nominative may also serve as a topic marker or shifter which does not become grammatically entangled in the main construction.

Mt. 12.36: πᾶν ῥῆμα ἀργὸν ὃ λαλήσουσιν (every useless word which [they] will speak), linked to a clause where the subject is in the third person plural.

Jn 7.38: ὁ πιστεύων εἰς ἐμέ (the one who believes in me), where there is a punctuation variant in which this nominative could be the subject of the preceding imperative, πινέτω (let [someone] drink, i.e., the one who believes in me).

Acts 7.40: ὁ...Μωϋσῆς οὗτος, ὃς ἐξήγαγεν ἡμᾶς ἐκ γῆς Αἰγύπτου (this Moses, who led us out of the land of Egypt), where reference to Moses is resumed with a dative case pronoun in a subsequent clause.

Phil. 1.30: τὸν αὐτὸν ἀγῶνα ἔχοντες (having the same struggle), referring to ὑμῖν in v. 29.

Col. 3.16: ἐν πάσῃ σοφίᾳ διδάσκοντες καὶ νουθετοῦντες ἑαυτούς, ψαλμοῖς ὕμνοις ᾠδαῖς πνευματικαῖς ἐν [τῇ] χάριτι ᾄδοντες ἐν ταῖς καρδίαις ὑμῶν τῷ θεῷ (teaching in all wisdom and admonishing yourselves, singing psalms, hymns, spiritual songs in thanksgiving in your hearts to God), where the nominative plural participles probably resume the ὑμῖν in the first part of the verse.

2.1.6. *Direct address and names*. There are two syntactical configurations treated here, united by their use of names or titles.

a. The first usage has been described variously: use of the nominative in place of the vocative;[3] use interchangeably of two cases which often share the same endings;[4] or use of the unmarked case for address, a

1. Moulton, *Prolegomena*, p. 69.
2. Louw, 'Linguistic Theory', p. 79.
3. Moulton, *Prolegomena*, p. 71; Winer, *Treatise*, pp. 227-28.
4. Robertson, *Grammar*, p. 461; Dana and Mantey, *Manual Grammar*, p. 71.

function the nominative case shares with the vocative and accusative cases. As Louw says, 'The nominative, in contradistinction to the vocative, is less exclamative, less direct, more reserved and formal because it merely states the nominative idea'.[1]

Lk. 8.54: ἡ παῖς, ἔγειρε (child, rise).

Mk 3.34: ἴδε ἡ μήτηρ μου καὶ οἱ ἀδελφοί μου (behold, my mother and my brothers). ἴδε and ἰδού are always followed by items in the nominative case.

Jn 13.13: ὁ διδάσκαλος καὶ ὁ κύριος (teacher and lord).

Jn 19.3: χαῖρε, ὁ βασιλεὺς τῶν Ἰουδαίων (greetings, the king of the Jews); cf. Mt. 27.29; Mk 15.18, both with the vocative.

b. Some phrases list names in the nominative case, regardless of whether another case might have been expected.

Lk. 19.29: ἤγγισεν εἰς Βηθφαγὴ καὶ Βηθανία[ν] (he was near to Bethphage and Bethany), with textual variants for Bethany.

Jn 1.6: ὄνομα αὐτῷ Ἰωάννης (his name was John).

Jn 18.10: ἦν...ὄνομα τῷ δούλῳ Μάλχος (the servant's name was Malchus).

2.1.7. *Time*. Use of the nominative case for temporal reference is rare. Although it resembles the use of the accusative case for extension of time, it is far less well-coordinated syntactically and even less semantically precise.

Mk 8.2: ἡμέραι τρεῖς προσμένουσιν (for the extent of three days they have waited).

Lk. 9.28: μετὰ τοὺς λόγους τούτους ὡσεὶ ἡμέραι ὀκτώ (after these words, about the extent of eight days).

2.2. *The Vocative Case*

The vocative case is used in the Greek of the NT for direct address, even though the nominative case may be used in this way also (see section 2.1.6.a above). In many instances there is no formal distinction between the nominative and vocative, which suggests that the vocative is not a true case.[2] The vocative is formally distinguished only in the masculine singular nouns of the first declension, the masculine and feminine singular nouns of the second declension, and in a few instances

1. Louw, 'Linguistic Theory', p. 80.
2. Robertson, *Grammar*, p. 461.

of the masculine and feminine singular nouns of the third declension. There is no distinction in the plural form in any declension. At the most the case is formally restricted, and when used it should be noted.[1]

Mt. 11.25: πάτερ, κύριε τοῦ οὐρανοῦ καὶ τῆς γῆς (Father, Lord of heaven and earth), with the nominative case in v. 26; Jn 6.68: κύριε (Lord).

Mt. 27.46: θεέ μου θεέ μου (my God, my God); cf. Lk. 18.11: ὁ θεός (God).

Rom. 2.1: ὦ ἄνθρωπε πᾶς ὁ κρίνων (every person who judges); Jas 2.20: ὦ ἄνθρωπε κενέ (foolish person), with the vocative adjective. The exclamatory particle ὦ occasionally, though not always, is used with the vocative form (it occurs 17 times in the NT): Mt. 15.28: ὦ γύναι (woman).

Jn 17.25: πάτερ δίκαιε (just father), with the vocative adjective.

2.3. *The Accusative Case*

The accusative case—the most widely used of the oblique (or non-nominative) cases in all of ancient Greek—has been described by Moorhouse as the 'oblique case *par excellence*'.[2] From this basis he derives its unmarked character (least semantic distinction) in relation to the other oblique cases. The accusative case has been variously characterized by others as the case of the goal,[3] the case of limitation,[4] the case of extension,[5] or the indefinite case.[6] This range of characterizations came about by observance of the wide range of usage of the accusative case. Like the nominative case, which simply expresses the nominal idea, *the accusative case in syntactically restricted (oblique) contexts expresses an idea without defining it. This fundamental meaning accounts for its several syntactical and contextual uses.*

2.3.1. *Object.* The accusative case is widely used as the so-called 'direct

1. See Winer, *Treatise*, p. 228.

2. Moorhouse, 'The Role of the Accusative Case', p. 209.

3. H. Mulder, 'Non-Accusative Second Arguments of Two-Place Verbs in Ancient Greek', in A. Rijksbaron, H.A. Mulder and G.C. Wakker (eds.), *In the Footsteps of R. Kühner*, pp. 219ff.

4. Dana and Mantey, *Manual Grammar*, p. 92.

5. Robertson, *Grammar*, p. 468; Brooks and Winbery, *Syntax*, p. 45, who posit the previous two.

6. Louw, 'Linguistic Theory', pp. 80-81; cf. Robertson, *Grammar*, p. 468; Dana and Mantey, *Manual Grammar*, p. 91.

object' of a transitive verb, although all of the oblique cases may serve in this way. There is no need here for extensive exemplification.

Mt. 7.9, 10: μὴ λίθον ἐπιδώσει αὐτῷ...μὴ ὄφιν ἐπιδώσει αὐτῷ; (he will not give a stone to him...he will not give a serpent to him, will he?), where the dative of advantage/disadvantage is also used.

Lk. 11.46: φορτίζετε τοὺς ἀνθρώπους φορτία δυσβάστακτα (you burden people with difficult burdens), an example of the cognate accusative, in which the root of the main verb and of the object are the same (this is also an example of the double accusative—see section 2.3.2 below).

Eph. 4.3: τηρεῖν τὴν ἑνότητα (to keep the unity), completing an infinitive.

Col. 2.19: κρατῶν τὴν κεφαλήν (holding fast to the head), completing a participle.

2 Tim. 4.7: τὸν καλὸν ἀγῶνα ἠγώνισμαι, τὸν δρόμον τετέλεκα, τὴν πίστιν τετήρηκα (I fought the good fight, completed the course, kept the faith), with the first a cognate accusative.

2.3.2. *Double*. There are occasions when a verb takes several objects in the accusative case, rather than using the accusative and one of the other cases. *When the two objects are related, it is an instance of the predicate double accusative, where the quality or attribute of one accusative is given to the other.*[1] The primary object of the verb is, generally speaking, the item which (a) is a proper name, (b) has the article, (c) is a pronoun, or (if the above are indecisive) (d) occurs first; the other is the predicate.[2]

Jas 5.10: ὑπόδειγμα λάβετε...τοὺς προφήτας (receive the prophets as a sign).

2 Pet. 3.15: τὴν τοῦ κυρίου ἡμῶν μακροθυμίαν σωτηρίαν ἡγεῖσθε (consider the patience of our Lord as salvation).

2 Cor. 4.5: οὐ...ἑαυτοὺς κηρύσσομεν ἀλλὰ Ἰησοῦν Χριστὸν κύριον, ἑαυτοὺς δὲ δούλους ὑμῶν (we are not proclaiming ourselves but Jesus Christ as Lord, and ourselves as your servants), a double example.

The other use of the double accusative occurs when two different

1. Winer, *Treatise*, p. 285; Robertson, *Grammar*, p. 480; BDF, §157; Turner, *Syntax*, p. 246.

2. See D.B. Wallace, 'The Semantics and Exegetical Significance of the Object-Complement Construction in the NT', *GTJ* 6 (1985), pp. 91-112.

objects limit the verb, without relation to each other. In many instances one of the objects is a person and the other a thing.

Mk 9.41: ὃς...ἂν ποτίσῃ ὑμᾶς ποτήριον ὕδατος (whoever... gives you a cup of water to drink).

Lk. 11.46: φορτίζετε τοὺς ἀνθρώπους φορτία δυσβάστακτα (you burden people with difficult burdens).

2.3.3. *Respect* (manner, adverbial). This usage is very flexible, encompassing what is variously called the accusative of manner and the adverbial accusative. Although many grammars consider NT usage to be restricted in comparison with classical usage,[1] *the accusative of respect reflects in many ways the essential semantics of the accusative case* (*i.e. all accusatives might be considered accusatives of respect in that an action is performed with respect to some person or thing*). Some grammarians classify the use of the accusative as 'subject' of an infinitive as an accusative of respect.[2]

Eph. 4.15: αὐξήσωμεν εἰς αὐτὸν τὰ πάντα (let us grow into him with respect to all things).

Jn 6.10: ἀνέπεσαν...οἱ ἄνδρες τὸν ἀριθμὸν ὡς πεντακισχίλιοι (the men sat, with respect to number about five thousand).

Heb. 2.17: γένηται καὶ πιστὸς ἀρχιερεὺς τὰ πρὸς τὸν θεόν (he might become a faithful high priest with respect to the things directed toward God).

The passive verb with an object in the accusative case is probably best classified as an accusative of respect (see Chapter 3 section 1.2.3).

Lk. 7.29: βαπτισθέντες τὸ βάπτισμα (being baptized with respect to the baptism).

1 Thess. 2.4: πιστευθῆναι τὸ εὐαγγέλιον (to be entrusted with respect to the gospel).

2.3.4. *Time or space*. The accusative case, like the other cases, may be used temporally or spatially. This could be considered a specific contextual application of the accusative of respect, where words of time or spatial location denote an extent of time or space, without specifying its range. Louw thinks that the lack of specificity of the case itself accounts for the relatively frequent use of quantifiers with the

1. BDF, §160.
2. See Chapter 11 section 4; Brooks and Winbery, *Syntax*, p. 51.

accusative element (numerals, pronouns, and the like).[1]

Mt. 26.39: προελθὼν μικρόν (going before a little ways), where the accusative is adverbial in force.

Lk. 15.29: τοσαῦτα ἔτη δουλεύω σοι (so many years I served you).

Lk. 22.41: αὐτὸς ἀπεσπάσθη...ὡσεὶ λίθου βολήν (he was led away...about a stone's throw).

Jn 2.12: ἔμειναν οὐ πολλὰς ἡμέρας (they remained for not many days).

2.3.5. *Apposition* (independent). The appositional accusative is an instance where an item in the accusative case, with its modifiers, restates or defines a clause or some item in it. The appositional element normally is in proximity to the thing it defines, even though it is grammatically independent.

Rom. 8.3: τὸ γὰρ ἀδύνατον τοῦ νόμου...ὁ θεὸς τὸν ἑαυτοῦ υἱὸν πέμψας ἐν ὁμοιώματι σαρκὸς ἁμαρτίας καὶ περὶ ἁμαρτίας κατέκρινεν τὴν ἁμαρτίαν ἐν τῇ σαρκί (for the thing impossible for the law...God, sending his own son in likeness of sinful flesh and concerning sin, condemned sin in the flesh),[2] with the appositional element preceding the item it defines.

2 Pet. 2.12: οὗτοι δέ, ὡς ἄλογα ζῷα γεγεννημένα φυσικὰ εἰς ἅλωσιν καὶ φθοράν (but they, as unreasoning creatures born wild for capture and destruction), introduced by ὡς.

2.3.6. *Absolute*. The accusative absolute consists of a participle in the accusative case in suitable grammatical relation with a substantive in the accusative case, forming a clause not syntactically linked to the surrounding clauses. There is disagreement among grammarians concerning how many genuine examples of the accusative absolute there are in the NT (see also Chapter 10 section 2.1).

Acts 26.3: μάλιστα γνώστην ὄντα σε πάντων τῶν...ἐθῶν (you are exceedingly knowledgeable of all the...customs), designated by some grammarians as an instance of anacoluthon (broken or irregular syntactical construction),[3] but endorsed by others as an instance of the accusative absolute.[4]

1. Louw, 'Linguistic Theory', p. 83.
2. Paraphrasing Moule, *Idiom Book*, p. 35.
3. E.g. Winer, *Treatise*, p. 290.
4. Dana and Mantey, *Manual Grammar*, p. 95.

Eph. 1.18: πεφωτισμένους τοὺς ὀφθαλμοὺς τῆς καρδίας (the eyes of the heart are enlightened).

In classical Greek, certain verbs are commonly found in the accusative case in absolute constructions (ἐξόν, ὑπάρχον, δέον). In the NT only τυχόν is used.

1 Cor. 16.6: τυχόν (perchance); cf. Lk. 20.13; Acts 12.15 in MS D.

2.4. *The Genitive Case*

The genitive case has been variously described as the case of origin,[1] definition or description,[2] specification,[3] or restriction.[4] Louw goes further and specifies two broad contextual applications: 'the notion of restriction can be applied with reference to the object *itself* (partitive) or to its *adjunct* (pertaining to)'.[5] In other words, the item restricted might be that which is placed in the genitive case, or the item in the genitive case might restrict something else. In either instance *the essential semantic feature of the genitive case is restriction.*[6] The number of classificatory schemes of the genitive are almost as many as the various classifications themselves. The following list provides an essential minimum number of categories.[7]

2.4.1. *Quality, definition or description.* This might well be considered the essential use of the genitive case; consequently, *some grammarians consider the defining or describing function of the genitive pervasive in all uses* (see the paragraph above). Often in translation an English adjective may be used, although the translation might be glossed with

1. Winer, *Treatise*, p. 230.

2. Brooks and Winbery, *Syntax*, p. 7; Dana and Mantey, *Manual Grammar*, p. 72, although they treat the ablative separately.

3. Robertson, *Grammar*, p. 493.

4. Louw, 'Linguistic Theory', pp. 83-84.

5. Louw, 'Linguistic Theory', p. 85.

6. The formulation in BDF (§§83-100) appears similar but is developed around a set of mixed syntactical and contextual criteria. Louw treats the ablative case as one of separation but as a sub-category under discussion of the genitive form. He must admit that separation and restriction may have synonymous contextual applications. It is better to see the subjective or possessive genitive as doing everything the so-called ablative case can do, since the single form does not require positing another distinct case. Separation is often indicated in the Greek of the NT with the genitive case and the prepositions ἐκ and ἀπό (BDF, §180).

7. See Chapter 10 section 2.1 on the genitive absolute.

a word making the idea of restriction explicit.

Mt. 13.18: τὴν παραβολὴν τοῦ σπείραντος (the parable of the sower).

Mk 1.4: κηρύσσων βάπτισμα μετανοίας (preaching baptism of repentance, i.e. restricted to repentance).

Lk. 4.22: τοῖς λόγοις τῆς χάριτος (the words of grace, or gracious words).

Rom. 2.5: ἡμέρᾳ ὀργῆς (day of wrath); Rom. 6.6: τὸ σῶμα τῆς ἁμαρτίας (body of sin).

2.4.2. *Partitive use.* The partitive genitive restricts the governing (head) term to a portion of a larger body denoted by the item in the genitive. The restrictive sense of the genitive is clearly evident in this usage.

Lk. 16.24: τὸ ἄκρον τοῦ δακτύλου αὐτοῦ (the tip of his finger).

Rom. 16.5: ὅς ἐστιν ἀπαρχὴ τῆς Ἀσίας (who is the firstfruit of Asia); cf. Jas 1.18: ἀπαρχήν τινα τῶν αὐτοῦ κτισμάτων (a certain firstfruit of his creations).

2.4.3. *Possession, ownership, origin or source.* Each of these classificatory terms reveals some sort of dependent or derivative status for the governing (head) term in relation to the word in the genitive. Pronouns are often used in this construction.

Mt. 26.51: ἀπέσπασεν τὴν μάχαιραν αὐτοῦ καὶ πατάξας τὸν δοῦλον τοῦ ἀρχιερέως ἀφεῖλεν αὐτοῦ τὸ ὠτίον (he drew his sword and, striking the servant of the chief priest, struck off his ear), with reference to one of Jesus' followers and the servant.

Mk 1.6: περὶ τὴν ὀσφὺν αὐτοῦ (around his waist).

Rom. 1.1: δοῦλος Χριστοῦ Ἰησοῦ (servant of Christ Jesus); cf. 1 Cor. 1.1; 2 Cor. 1.1; Eph. 1.1; Phil. 1.1; Col. 1.1; 1 Tim. 1.1; 2 Tim. 1.1; Tit. 1.1; Phlm. 1; Jas 1.1; 1 Pet. 1.1; 2 Pet. 1.1.

Phil. 4.7: ἡ εἰρήνη τοῦ θεοῦ (the peace of God).

1 Pet. 1.1: ἐκλεκτοῖς παρεπιδήμοις διασπορᾶς (elect, refugees of the dispersion).

Mt. 4.21: Ἰάκωβον τὸν τοῦ Ζεβεδαίου καὶ Ἰωάννην τὸν ἀδελφὸν αὐτοῦ (James the son of Zebedee and John his brother); Acts 13.22: Δαυὶδ τὸν τοῦ Ἰεσσαί (David the son of Jesse). These examples employ a common construction to denote familial relationship. Some grammarians[1] take the word of relation as elided or omitted (e.g. 'son'), but this is unnecessary. The genitive element establishes the relationship.[2]

2.4.4. *Apposition*. When the genitive case is used to restate the governing term, often restricting it so as to make it more specific or to define it, the appositional genitive is being employed.

Jn 2.21: ἔλεγεν περὶ τοῦ ναοῦ τοῦ σώματος αὐτοῦ (he was speaking concerning the temple of [which is] his body).

2 Cor. 1.22: δοὺς τὸν ἀρραβῶνα τοῦ πνεύματος (giving the pledge of [which is] the Spirit), a usage which could be interpreted as partitive or descriptive.

2 Pet. 2.6: πόλεις Σοδόμων καὶ Γομόρρας (the cities of [which are] Sodom and Gomorrah).

2.4.5. *Objective genitive*. The objective and subjective genitives are provocative (see section 2.4.6 below). The construction consists of two terms, the governing term and the term (or word) in the genitive case modifying it. A helpful way to understand the objective genitive is to think of the words in the construction as rewritten into an English sentence. *If the term (or word) in the genitive would serve as the direct object if the governing term were a verb, or if the term in the genitive would limit or receive the action in some way, then it may be an objective genitive.*

Mt. 12.31: ἡ...τοῦ πνεύματος βλασφημία (the...blasphemy of the Spirit), i.e. 'blaspheme the Spirit'.

Acts 9.31: τῷ φόβῳ τοῦ κυρίου (the fear of the Lord), but cf. the following sentence with the subjective genitive: τῇ παρακλήσει τοῦ ἁγίου πνεύματος (the comfort of the Holy Spirit).

Rom. 10.2: ζῆλον θεοῦ ἔχουσιν (they have zeal for God).

1 Cor. 1.6: τὸ μαρτύριον τοῦ Χριστοῦ ἐβεβαιώθη ἐν ὑμῖν (the witness toward Christ was confirmed in you).

Col. 3.14: σύνδεσμος τῆς τελειότητος (bond of perfection); cf. Eph. 4.3 below in section 2.4.6.

2.4.6. *Subjective genitive*. In contrast to section 2.4.5 above, *if the term (or word) in the genitive would serve as the subject if the*

1. E.g. Dana and Mantey, *Manual Grammar*, pp. 76-77.
2. Cf. BDF, §162.

governing term were a verb, or if the term in the genitive would be the initiator of the action in some way, then it may be a subjective genitive. Many instances of the subjective genitive cannot be distinguished from the possessive genitive.

Rom. 8.35: τίς ἡμᾶς χωρίσει ἀπὸ τῆς ἀγάπης τοῦ Χριστοῦ; (who will separate us from Christ's love?).

2 Cor. 5.14: ἡ...ἀγάπη τοῦ Χριστοῦ (the...love of Christ), i.e. Christ's love, as opposed to love for Christ; cf. Rom. 5.5: ἡ ἀγάπη τοῦ θεοῦ ἐκκέχυται ἐν ταῖς καρδίαις ἡμῶν διὰ πνεύματος ἁγίου (the love of God is poured out in our hearts through the Holy Spirit).

Eph. 4.3: τῷ συνδέσμῳ τῆς εἰρήνης (the bond of peace); cf. Col. 3.14 above in section 2.4.5.

1 Thess. 1.3: μνημονεύοντες ὑμῶν τοῦ ἔργου τῆς πίστεως καὶ τοῦ κόπου τῆς ἀγάπης καὶ τῆς ὑπομονῆς τῆς ἐλπίδος (remembering your work of [produced by] faith and labor of [produced by] love and endurance of [produced by] hope).

1 Jn 2.16: ἡ ἐπιθυμία τῆς σαρκὸς καὶ ἡ ἐπιθυμία τῶν ὀφθαλμῶν καὶ ἡ ἀλαζονεία τοῦ βίου (the fleshly desire and eyes-originated desire and life-originated boasting).

Rom. 3.22: πίστεως Ἰησοῦ Χριστοῦ, which has been an item of recurring debate. The debate is often put in terms of whether the genitive is (a) subjective (or source or origin) and rendered 'faith of Jesus Christ', 'faith given by Jesus Christ', or even 'Jesus Christ's faithfulness', or (b) objective and rendered 'faith in Jesus Christ', or (c) both. Semantic or syntactical analysis alone will not solve the problem; context must decide. Commentators weigh such factors as whether suitable parallels are found in Romans 4 with reference to Abraham's faith, whether reference to 'to all who believe' (v. 22) is redundant, whether Christ's faithfulness is an issue for Paul in Romans, and whether and in what way Paul's emphasis is on God's righteousness.[1]

2.4.7. *Comparison.* An item in the genitive case is frequently used restrictively to draw a comparison with something else. The comparative adjective is normally found in the construction.

1. For recent statements for the subjective and objective positions respectively, see M.D. Hooker, 'ΠΙΣΤΙΣ ΧΡΙΣΤΟΥ', *NTS* 35 (1989), pp. 321-42; Dunn, *Romans 1–8*, pp. 166-67. D.A. Campbell (*The Rhetoric of Righteousness in Romans 3.21-26* [Sheffield: JSOT Press, 1992]) attempts to break the impasse by appeal to the rhetorical structure of Rom. 3.21-26 (a contextual approach).

Mt. 5.20: πλεῖον τῶν γραμματέων καὶ Φαρισαίων (more than the scribes and Pharisees); Mt. 5.37: τὸ...περισσὸν τούτων (the... thing that is more than these).

Jn 5.36: τὴν μαρτυρίαν μείζω τοῦ Ἰωάννου (the witness greater than John).

1 Jn 3.20: μείζων ἐστὶν ὁ θεὸς τῆς καρδίας ἡμῶν (God is greater than our heart).

2.4.8. *Value or price.* The genitive can be used to restrict the value or price of something. This might be considered a sub-category of the genitive of quality or description, limited to particular kinds of vocabulary items.

Mt. 10.29: οὐχὶ δύο στρουθία ἀσσαρίου πωλεῖται; (are not two sparrows sold for an assarion?).

Lk. 12.7: πολλῶν στρουθίων διαφέρετε (you are worth more than many sparrows).

Acts 5.8: τοσούτου τὸ χωρίον ἀπέδοσθε;...ναί, τοσούτου (were you paid such for the land?...Yes, such [a price]).

1 Cor. 6.20: ἠγοράσθητε...τιμῆς (you were bought...for a price).

2.4.9. *Time or space.* All of the cases may be used with a temporal or spatial sense. The genitive restricts the time or location within which something occurs. This is not to be confused with the kind of genitive found in Rom. 2.5 (ἡμέρᾳ ὀργῆς [day of wrath]), which is descriptive.

Mt. 24.20: μὴ γένηται ἡ φυγὴ ὑμῶν χειμῶνος μηδὲ σαββάτῳ (your flight might not come about during the winter or on the Sabbath), where the dative of time is also used.

Lk. 18.7: τῶν ἐκλεκτῶν αὐτοῦ τῶν βοώντων αὐτῷ ἡμέρας καὶ νυκτός (his elect calling to him day and night).

Lk. 19.4: ἐκείνης ἤμελλεν διέρχεσθαι (he was going to pass through that place), with reference to Jericho in Lk. 19.1.

2.4.10. *Object.* Some verbs are completed by elements (objects) in the genitive case.[1] Even though the English translation may resemble use of other oblique cases, the semantic feature of restriction is still present with the use of the genitive case. It is not infrequent for the

1. See BDF, §§169-78.

verb in these instances to have a prefixed preposition that is used with the genitive case.

Acts 19.40: ἐγκαλεῖσθαι στάσεως (being accused of a riot).

Rom. 7.1: ὁ νόμος κυριεύει τοῦ ἀνθρώπου (the law has control over the person); Rom. 6.9: θάνατος αὐτοῦ οὐκέτι κυριεύει (death no longer has control over him).

Eph. 2.12: ἀπηλλοτριωμένοι τῆς πολιτείας (being excluded from citizenship).

Jas 2.13: κατακαυχᾶται ἔλεος κρίσεως (mercy triumphs over judgment).

An interesting item of dispute is the object of the verb ἀκούω with the genitive or the accusative case. This is important for discussion of Acts 9.7 and 22.9. In Acts 9.7 Paul says that his companions ἀκούοντες ...τῆς φωνῆς (heard...the voice), while in 22.9 it says τὴν...φωνὴν οὐκ ἤκουσαν (they did not hear the voice). The traditional understanding is that with the genitive ἀκούω means to hear but *not* understand, while with the accusative ἀκούω means to hear *and* understand; or that the genitive is concerned with the form of speech but the accusative with the content. It is also possible that the genitive in Acts 9.7 refers to Paul's voice.[1]

2.5. *The Dative Case*

The dative case has been variously described. The problem of labeling is compounded by whether one treats the dative (or so-called 'true' dative) as one of three cases (the others being the locative and instrumental) with the same form (see introduction to this chapter), or whether one posits a single dative case (the view endorsed here). Whereas most grammarians want to assert that the dative case may be used in a wide-ranging variety of contexts,[2] this does not determine its semantics. In many ways *the dative case is the most explicit and particular of the cases in meaning and function, grammaticalizing the semantic feature of relation.*[3]

2.5.1. *Respect* (association, possession, sphere). The dative of respect

1. See F.F. Bruce, *The Acts of the Apostles* (Grand Rapids: Eerdmans, 1959), p. 199.

2. E.g. Winer, *Treatise*, pp. 260-61.

3. See Louw, 'Linguistic Theory', pp. 81, 83. See Chapter 10 section 2.1 on the dative absolute.

is labeled by some grammarians as the associative dative, dative of possession or dative of sphere (locative). Sometimes it resembles the instrumental dative as well (see section 2.5.3 below). *The dative of respect is perhaps the usage of the dative which brings out most clearly its fundamental semantic feature: a relationship is specified.* Writers of the Greek of the NT seem to prefer the dative to the accusative of respect, perhaps reflecting the colloquial language's preference for the more expressive form.[1]

Jn 1.6: ὄνομα αὐτῷ Ἰωάννης (his name was John), i.e. the name with respect to him was John.

Rom. 6.2, 6, 10: οἵτινες απεθάνομεν τῇ ἁμαρτίᾳ...τοῦ μηκέτι δουλεύειν ἡμᾶς τῇ ἁμαρτίᾳ...τῇ ἁμαρτίᾳ ἀπέθανεν ἐφάπαξ (we who died to sin...we no longer are servants to sin...he died to sin once).

2 Cor. 6.14: τίς γὰρ μετοχὴ δικαιοσύνῃ καὶ ἀνομίᾳ ἢ τίς κοινωνία φωτὶ πρὸς σκότος; (for what is the partnership with respect to righteousness and lawlessness, or what is the fellowship with respect to light with darkness?).

Heb. 5.11: νωθροὶ γεγόνατε ταῖς ἀκοαῖς (you became lazy with respect to hearing).

2.5.2. *Advantage or disadvantage*. This is a more circumscribed relationship, in which some action is directed toward someone either to his or her benefit or detriment. The so-called 'indirect object' may often be categorized as the dative of advantage or disadvantage, terminology which combines syntactical and contextual designations.

Mt. 7.6: μὴ δῶτε τὸ ἅγιον τοῖς κυσίν (don't give the holy thing to dogs).

Mt. 23.31: μαρτυρεῖτε ἑαυτοῖς (you testify against yourselves).

Mt. 18.12: ἐὰν γένηταί τινι ἀνθρώπῳ (if it might happen to a certain person), where the parable of the lost sheep follows.

2 Cor. 5.13: εἴτε γὰρ ἐξέστημεν θεῷ· εἴτε σωφρονοῦμεν ὑμῖν (for either we are out of our minds for God, or we are wise for you), a verse with punctuation variants.

2.5.3. *Instrument, agent, cause, means or manner*. Many grammarians separate these categories, but it is difficult to establish a specific

1. See Louw, 'Linguistic Theory', p. 88.

difference in most instances. They all label a relationship by which (normally) a thing (and occasionally a person) brings about or enters into an action with respect to something else. The preposition ἐν + dative case is often used similarly, giving good evidence that the dative case may have already been weakening in force during the Hellenistic period.[1]

Lk. 15.17: ἐγὼ δὲ λιμῷ ὧδε ἀπόλλυμαι (but I am being destroyed here by famine).

Lk. 23.15: οὐδὲν ἄξιον θανάτου ἐστὶν πεπραγμένον αὐτῷ (nothing worthy of death is done by him), which BDF considers the only dative of direct agency in the NT.[2]

Jn 21.8: τῷ πλοιαρίῳ ἦλθον (they came by small boat).

Acts 16.37: λάθρᾳ ἡμᾶς ἐκβάλλουσιν; (in secret are they casting us out?).

Rom. 8.14: ὅσοι...πνεύματι θεοῦ ἄγονται (whoever...are led by the Spirit of God).

Rom. 15.27: εἰ...τοῖς πνευματικοῖς αὐτῶν ἐκοινώνησαν τὰ ἔθνη (if...the nations shared in their spiritual things).

1 Cor. 11.5: πᾶσα...γυνὴ προσευχομένη ἢ προφητεύουσα ἀκατακαλύπτῳ (every...woman praying or prophesying uncovered), i.e. her manner of praying is that she is uncovered.

Eph. 2.8: τῇ γὰρ χάριτί ἐστε σεσῳσμένοι διὰ πίστεως (for by grace you are saved through faith).

1 Pet. 1.18, 19: οὐ φθαρτοῖς, ἀργυρίῳ ἢ χρυσίῳ ἐλυτρώθητε ...ἀλλὰ τιμίῳ αἵματι (not by corrupt things, silver or gold were you redeemed...but by valuable blood).

2.5.4. *Time or space* (locative). The dative case may be used to designate temporal or spatial relations, specifying a particular spot or time (even if it is extended in actual duration) in which something occurs. The spatial dative is very limited in the NT.

Mt. 20.19: τῇ τρίτῃ ἡμέρᾳ ἐγερθήσεται (on the third day he will be raised).

Lk. 24.1: τῇ...μιᾷ τῶν σαββάτων (on the...first [day] of the Sabbath), with the use of the temporal genitive as well.

Rom. 16.25: κατὰ ἀποκάλυψιν μυστηρίου χρόνοις αἰωνίοις

1. See BDF, §100.
2. BDF, §191.

σεσιγημένου (according to the revelation of the mystery silent for aeons of time).

Rom. 4.12: τοῖς στοιχοῦσιν τοῖς ἴχνεσιν (those who walk in the footsteps), and in stereotyped phrases: Rom. 15.19 with κύκλῳ (circle).

2.5.5. *Object*. Some verbs are completed by elements (objects) in the dative case. Even though the English translation may resemble use of other oblique cases, the semantic feature of relation is still present with the use of the dative case.[1]

Lk. 24.11: ἠπίστουν αὐταῖς (they were not believing them).

Rom. 7.25: αὐτὸς ἐγὼ...δουλεύω νόμῳ θεοῦ...νόμῳ ἁμαρτίας (I myself...serve the law of God...the law of sin), with several objects in the dative case.

3. *Gender*

Gender is a grammatical category in Greek used to designate certain inflected words (e.g. nouns, adjectives, participles) as masculine, feminine or neuter. When it was first used gender may have been related to sex (e.g. 'woman', γυνή, is feminine in gender), and there are still some correlations between gender and sex in Greek (see below). But as a grammatical term gender in ancient Greek is little more than one of the inflectional categories applied to the Greek noun, adjective, article, and the like.[2] Whereas the gender of adjectives, participles and so forth varies according to function, every noun has a designated grammatical gender. This gender often will not correlate with gender in English, not least because English does not formally grammaticalize gender. For example, πλοῖον (boat) is neuter in Greek, but ships are often considered feminine in English; παιδίον is neuter in Greek, but small children are usually considered masculine or feminine in English depending upon the sex of the child, just as παῖς in Greek can be either masculine or feminine (cf. German where *das Mädchen* [young girl] is neuter). Concord or agreement in this category may be broken on occasion, however.

1. See Robertson, *Grammar*, p. 539.

2. On the issue of gender in language, see Lyons, *Introduction to Theoretical Linguistics*, pp. 283-88.

3.1. *Patterns of Gender Designation*

Although gender is a grammatical category, there are several noteworthy patterns.[1]

3.1.1. *Nouns of masculine gender.* In Greek, some general classes of nouns tend to be masculine, including the names of males, as well as rivers (ὁ Ἰορδάνης; and the word for river: ὁ ποταμός) and winds (ὁ ἄνεμος). This is possibly because these natural phenomena were considered gods by early Greeks.

3.1.2. *Nouns of feminine gender.* In Greek, some general classes of nouns tend to be feminine, including the names of females, as well as trees (ἡ συκῆ), countries (ἡ Αἴγυπτος), islands (ἡ Κρήτη), most towns (ἡ Ῥώμη) and many abstract terms (ἡ ἀγάπη).

3.1.3. *Nouns of neuter gender.* In Greek, some nouns are considered neuter, including diminutive forms (τὸ παιδίον), and substantivized abstract items (e.g. when the article is used with an adverb, prepositional phrase, infinitive, or the like).

3.2. *Exceptional Patterns*

There are several patterns which appear to be exceptions to the above rules, but which can be described for sake of reference.

3.2.1. *Nouns of common gender.* There are a number of Greek nouns which may take masculine or feminine gender, depending upon whether the item referred to is male or female: θεός, παῖς, ὄνος, ἄρκτος.

3.2.2. *Nouns of fixed gender regardless of sex.* There are a number of Greek nouns in which one gender is used for reference to creatures of either sex. For example, ἡ ἀλώπηξ (fox) is feminine, even when used in Lk. 13.32 with metaphorical application to Herod.

3.2.3. *Nouns and the declensions.* Although the correlation is far from an absolute one, it is noteworthy that the majority of Greek nouns of the first declension are feminine, and the majority of the second declension are masculine. Some grammarians have thought that at an

1. Green, *Handbook*, p. 18.

earlier time in the history of Greek any noun of the first declension was feminine and any noun of the second declension was masculine.[1] This was not the case by classical and Hellenistic or NT times.

1. See Robertson, *Grammar*, pp. 254, 257-59.

Chapter 5

The Article

Introduction

Use of the article in Greek is not like use of the definite article in English, not least because Greek does not have the same choice of forms.[1] Consequently, the Greek article is best not called the 'definite article', since this implies a non-existent indefinite article. Once a Greek speaker or writer chose to use the article, there was not a choice whether an indefinite or definite one would be used. Therefore, the presence or absence of an article does not make a substantive definite or indefinite.[2] These considerations regarding the article have led to a number of peculiarities for interpreters. Below are presented several significant features about use of the Greek article. The discussion is not exhaustive, but should prove helpful in establishing contextual guidelines. In translation, one may well have to supply the English articles 'the' or 'a' to render the presence or absence of the Greek article (but there is not a one-to-one correlation). This more often than not will reflect the conventions of English rather than Greek usage.

1. *A Scheme for the Article*

One of the difficulties in understanding the article is the tendency to want to make the Greek article do the same things as the English article. Try as one might, there are persistent ways in which they cannot

1. The most thorough treatment of the Greek article to date is T.F. Middleton, *The Doctrine of the Greek Article Applied to the Criticism and Illustration of the NT* (London: Rivington, 2nd edn, 1841).

2. When Greek users wish to make an item 'indefinite', they can use the indefinite pronoun τις (see Chapter 8 section 2.8).

be correlated. The following table is a schematic arrangement for interpretation of substantives with and without the article.[1]

Substantive	*Use 1*	*Use 2*
Articular (with article)	(a) particular	(c) categorical
Anarthrous (without article)	(b) non-particular (qualitative)	(d) individual

When the article is used, the substantive may refer to a particular item, or it may represent a category of items. When the article is not used, the substantive may refer to the non-particular or qualitative character of an item, or it may refer to an individual item. One immediately notices that the presence or absence of the article may affect the sense of the substantive in two related ways. Uses (a) and (d) are similar in meaning, as are uses (b) and (c) (translations may well reflect this similarity). Matters of particularity and individuality are established not on the basis of whether the article is present, but on the basis of the wider context.

1.1. *Usage with the Article (Articular or Arthrous)*

1.1.1. *'Particular' use of the article.* The article may particularize a substantive. This usage frequently occurs with abstract substantives (see section 2.3 below).

1 Cor. 13.13: μείζων δὲ τούτων ἡ ἀγάπη (but the greater of these is love), i.e. the particular love spoken of in the chapter.

Jn 1.17: ὁ νόμος διὰ Μωϋσέως ἐδόθη, ἡ χάρις καὶ ἡ ἀλήθεια διὰ Ἰησοῦ Χριστοῦ ἐγένετο (the law was given through Moses, grace and truth came through Jesus Christ).

Rom. 13.7: ἀπόδοτε πᾶσιν τὰς ὀφειλάς, τῷ τὸν φόρον τὸν φόρον, τῷ τὸ τέλος τὸ τέλος, τῷ τὸν φόβον τὸν φόβον, τῷ τὴν τιμὴν τὴν τιμήν (give to all their due, tax to whom tax, duty to whom duty, fear to whom fear, honor to whom honor).

1.1.2. *'Categorical' use of the article.* The article may make a substantive representative of a category of items.

Lk. 10.7: ἄξιος...ὁ ἐργάτης τοῦ μισθοῦ αὐτοῦ (the worker is worthy of his wage), where English would probably say 'a worker'.

1. This is adapted from Carson, *Exegetical Fallacies*, pp. 82-84. See also Brooks and Winbery, *Syntax*, p. 67.

An analogy might be drawn to the idea that trade unions represent 'the worker'.

Mt. 12.35: ὁ ἀγαθὸς ἄνθρωπος...καὶ ὁ πονηρὸς ἄνθρωπος (the good person...and the evil person), in the context of a parable.

Jn 10.11: ὁ ποιμὴν ὁ καλὸς τὴν ψυχὴν αὐτοῦ τίθησιν ὑπὲρ τῶν προβάτων (the good shepherd gives his life for the sheep).

Rom. 7.1, 2: τοῦ ἀνθρώπου...ἡ γὰρ ὕπανδρος γυνὴ τῷ ζῶντι ἀνδρὶ δέδεται (the husband...for the married woman is bound to the living husband), with three instances.

1 Tim. 3.2: δεῖ...τὸν ἐπίσκοπον (it is necessary...for the overseer).

1.2. *Usage without the Article (Anarthrous)*

1.2.1. *'Non-particular' (qualitative) use without the article.* The quality rather than particularity of a substantive may be referred to in structures without the article.

1 Cor. 5.1: ἀκούεται ἐν ὑμῖν πορνεία (sexual infidelity is heard of among you), i.e. 'some kind of sexual infidelity'.

Jn 1.14: πλήρης χάριτος καὶ ἀληθείας (full of grace and truth), the qualities of grace and truth.

Rom. 8.3: ὁ θεὸς τὸν ἑαυτοῦ υἱὸν πέμψας ἐν ὁμοιώματι σαρκὸς ἁμαρτίας καὶ περὶ ἁμαρτίας (God, sending his own son in [a qualitative] likeness of sinful flesh and concerning sin), along with the particular use of the article with 'God' and 'son'.

1.2.2. *'Individual' use without the article.* Individual items may be specified without use of the article.

Jn 4.27: μετὰ γυναικὸς ἐλάλει (he was speaking with [the] woman).

Col. 2.20: ἐν κόσμῳ (in [the] world); Jn 1.1: ἐν ἀρχῇ (in [the] beginning); 1 Jn 1.1: ἀπ' ἀρχῆς (from [the] beginning). See section 2.8.4 below.

This formulation illustrates that in Greek the presence or the absence of the article does not determine whether the substantive is particular or non-particular, categorical or individual. For example, ὁ ἄνθρωπος may mean a particular individual (Jn 4.50) or it may mean a representative of the human race (Mt. 5.13 in the plural). In Rom. 15.22 τὰ πολλά may mean either 'the many' (categorical) or 'the large number referred to' (particular). Context of usage must decide.

2. *Distinctive Uses of the Article*

If it is true that the presence or absence of the article does not of itself determine the particular or categorical use of a substantive, one might legitimately ask, why did Greek have the article at all? This is a very good question. Most grammarians answer it by citing the historical origins of the article in the demonstrative pronoun, as if that alone forms the basis for understanding the article. It is used like a demonstrative in Acts 17.28, in Paul's quotation of Aratus, *Phaenomena* 5: τοῦ γὰρ καὶ γένος ἐσμέν (for of this one we are offspring). A synchronic perspective (i.e. examination of how the article is used in the Greek of the NT), however, provides the general guidelines laid out above in section 1. There appear to be several other ways in which the article is used in Greek, however, which further help to explain its use in a given context. This group of uses is illustrative and not exhaustive. More than one reason for a usage may appear to be in force, complicating the interpretative situation.

2.1. *Anaphoric Usage*

Anaphoric usage of the article is its backward-looking use. The Greek article may occur with subsequent instances of a substantive to refer back to or 'resume' the substantive's initial use. The initial reference may or may not appear with the article, depending upon what kind of substantive it is and how it is used. The anaphoric use of the article is similar to what many believe was the original use of the article as a demonstrative pronoun. Some translations may even use 'this' or 'that' to translate the article with the substantive.

Mt. 2.7: Ἡρῴδης...καλέσας τοὺς μάγους (Herod...calling the magi [referred to in v. 1]).

Jn 4.43: μετὰ...τὰς δύο ἡμέρας ἐξῆλθεν ἐκεῖθεν (after...the two days [mentioned in v. 40] he went away from there).

Jas 2.3: τῷ πτωχῷ εἴπητε (you might say to the poor one [referred to in v. 2]).

1 Pet. 2.7: ὑμῖν οὖν ἡ τιμὴ τοῖς πιστεύουσιν (the honor therefore [is] to you who believe), where ἡ τιμή does not have a specific previous referent (antecedent), but one implied in the previous verse which speaks of 'the elect, precious cornerstone'.

2.2. *Usage with Names of Places and People*

Proper names often do not appear with the article, since as seen above in section 1 it is not necessary for an item to have the article to be specific, especially when it is a particular individual known to the reader. But in some contexts a name has the article. It is difficult to regularize all usage, but *several reasons for use of the article with names seem prevalent: (a) emphasis, i.e. calling attention to the name; (b) designation of case, especially for names that are indeclinable; (c) designation of title (ὁ κύριος, ὁ Χριστός), and (d) anaphora* (see section 2.1 above).[1]

Acts 15.19: τοῖς ἀπὸ τῶν ἐθνῶν ἐπιστρέφουσιν ἐπὶ τὸν θεόν (those from the Gentiles turning to [the] God), possibly expressing the speaker's surprise that any Gentiles are turning to God (the speaker is James, a Jew).

Jn 1.45: εὑρίσκει Φίλιππος τὸν Ναθαναήλ (Philip found Nathaniel), otherwise it could be Nathaniel finding Philip (Nathaniel is indeclinable, although Philip is declinable). Use of τοῦ for τόν would indicate Philip as the son of Nathaniel: cf. Lk. 3.23-38, the genealogy.

Rom. 15.3: ὁ Χριστὸς οὐχ ἑαυτῷ ἤρεσεν (the Christ did not please himself).

Mt. 3.5: πᾶσα ἡ Ἰουδαία καὶ πᾶσα ἡ περίχωρος τοῦ Ἰορδάνου (all Judea and all the surrounding region of the Jordan), two examples with place names.

2.3. *Usage with Abstract Substantives*

Abstract substantives in Greek often appear with the article, probably performing its particularizing function. The article's appearance is not a universal rule, however: e.g. Jn 1.16: χάριν ἀντὶ χάριτος (grace in place of grace). Moule treats exceptions and inconsistencies: e.g. Jn 8.44: ἐν τῇ ἀληθείᾳ οὐκ ἔστηκεν ὅτι οὐκ ἔστιν ἀλήθεια ἐν αὐτῷ (he does not stand in the truth because truth is not in him).[2] There are several frequently occurring words which regularly take the article in NT Greek: νόμος, πνεῦνα, θάνατος, νεκροί, ἔθνη. English does not translate the article in many instances.

1. See G.D. Fee, 'The Use of the Definite Article with Personal Names in the Gospel of John', *NTS* 17 (1970–71), pp. 168-83, who differentiates contexts in which the names appear with and without the article. He is convinced that anaphoric use of the article is rare with names in John's Gospel.

2. Moule, *Idiom Book*, pp. 111-14.

Acts 28.4: ἡ δίκη ζῆν οὐκ εἴασεν (justice did not permit [him] to live).

Rom. 13.7: ἀπόδοτε πᾶσιν τὰς ὀφειλάς, τῷ τὸν φόρον τὸν φόρον, τῷ τὸ τέλος τὸ τέλος, τῷ τὸν φόβον τὸν φόβον, τῷ τὴν τιμὴν τὴν τιμήν (give to all their due, tax to whom tax, duty to whom duty, fear to whom fear, honor to whom honor).

1 Cor. 11.14: ἡ φύσις αὐτὴ διδάσκει (nature itself teaches).

In Romans, there has been much controversy over use of the article with νόμος (law). Sanday and Headlam[1] in their commentary represent a tradition which makes significant exegetical decisions on the basis of presence or absence of the article: ὁ νόμος is law of Moses; νόμος is law in general, or Mosaic law in its quality as law. That this distinction cannot be sustained in Romans has been well illustrated of late.[2]

2.4. *Usage with Adjectives, Participles and Phrases*
In Greek almost any word or group of words can be made into a substantive, including adjectives (see Chapter 6), participles (see Chapter 10), infinitives (see Chapter 11), adverbs (see Chapter 7) and prepositional phrases (see Chapter 9). In other words, many words can be made to function in the way that a noun does. One of the easiest ways to do this is to place an article before the word. Adjectives and participles, as well as various phrases, are the most common classes of items used in this way (the infinitive is reserved for treatment in Chapter 11). *The article with adjectives, participles and various phrases normally particularizes—although it may also categorize—the meaning of the item used as a substantive.* The neuter article is often used to make particular some inanimate or abstract item.

Mt. 6.13: ἀπὸ τοῦ πονηροῦ, which may be rendered 'from evil', or more likely 'from the evil one', depending upon whether it is a categorical or particular use; 1 Cor. 1.27: καταισχύνῃ τοὺς σοφούς (he might shame the wise [people]), both examples with adjectives.

Mt. 5.6: οἱ πεινῶντες καὶ διψῶντες (those hungering and thirsting); Gal. 6.13: οἱ περιτεμνόμενοι (the circumcised), all with participles.

Acts 13.13: οἱ περὶ Παῦλον (those with Paul); 2 Cor. 10.7: τὰ κατὰ πρόσωπον βλέπετε (you are observing the superficial things),

1. W. Sanday and A. Headlam, *A Critical and Exegetical Commentary on the Epistle to the Romans* (Edinburgh: T. & T. Clark, 5th edn, 1902), p. 58.

2. See esp. D.J. Moo, '"Law", "Works of the Law", and Legalism in Paul', *WTJ* 45 (1983), pp. 73-100.

i.e. the things based on appearance, both examples with prepositional phrases.

Acts 20.32: τὰ νῦν (the present things), with an adverb.

Rom. 8.26: τὸ...τί προσευξώμεθα (what we might pray), with an entire clause.

2.5. *Usage with Linking Verbs*

Work by E.C. Colwell and more recently by L. McGaughy[1] has devised a thorough and generally consistent method for determining which of two Greek substantives is the subject with a linking verb. According to McGaughy, if two substantives stand in appropriate grammatical concord (agreement in number and person with the verb, and so forth), there are three possibilities for determining which is the subject. If one substantive is a demonstrative or relative pronoun, it is the subject. If one of the substantives has an article, it is the subject. If both have articles, the one first in order is the subject. Colwell specified that with a definite predicate substantive (he determined in advance what a definite predicate substantive was), if it precedes the linking verb, in approximately 87% of the cases it occurs without the article (anarthrous). If it follows, in approximately 90% of the cases it occurs with the article (articular). There are obvious problems with Colwell's scheme: it predetermines what is definite (it cannot establish definiteness of the predicate),[2] it is only a generality, and it does not apply to relative clauses or proper nouns.[3]

Mk 6.3: οὐχ οὗτός ἐστιν ὁ τέκτων (is this one not the carpenter?), where the predicate has the article, but the demonstrative pronoun is the subject; Acts 9.20: οὗτός ἐστιν ὁ υἱὸς τοῦ θεοῦ (this one is the son of God).

Jn 8.12: ἐγώ εἰμι τὸ φῶς τοῦ κόσμου (I am the light of the world).

Jn 20.31: Ἰησοῦς ἐστιν ὁ Χριστός (the Christ is Jesus), an example which McGaughy considered an exception, but probably

1. E.C. Colwell, 'A Definite Rule for the Use of the Article in the Greek NT', *JBL* 52 (1933), pp. 12-21; L.C. McGaughy, *A Descriptive Analysis of EINAI as a Linking Verb in NT Greek* (Missoula, MT: Scholars Press, 1972).

2. According to Carson (*Exegetical Fallacies*, p. 87), some recent studies indicate that definite and indefinite nouns with linking verbs are approximately equal in number in the Greek of the NT. Of course this still begs the question of what a definite noun is.

3. Turner, *Syntax*, p. 184.

more because of his traditional understanding of the passage than because of his own rules; cf. also 1 Jn 2.22; 4.15; 5.1, 5.[1]

Jn 1.1: καὶ θεὸς ἦν ὁ λόγος (and the word was God), a legitimate translation of the passage according to Colwell's work, *if* the predicate is definite.

Rom. 1.9: μάρτυς...μού ἐστιν ὁ θεός (God is my witness).

2.6. *The Granville Sharp Rule*

In the early nineteenth century, Granville Sharp developed a rule (one of several) regarding use of the article with substantives in NT Greek. Unfortunately, this rule has been widely misunderstood. Granville Sharp's rule states simply that *if a single article links two or more singular substantives (excluding personal names), the second and subsequent substantives are related to or further describe the first.*[2]

Eph. 3.18: τὸ πλάτος καὶ μῆκος καὶ ὕψος καὶ βάθος (the breadth and length and height and depth), with four units of measure joined together.

Acts 26.30: ὁ βασιλεὺς καὶ ὁ ἡγεμών (the king and the governor), where the king and the governor are separate people.

There are some examples which are not covered by Sharp's rule.

Jn 20.28: ὁ κύριός μου καὶ ὁ θεός μου (my lord and my God), where the article is repeated for the same individual. Sharp's rule does not address instances where items with individual articles may be equated.

Mt. 17.1: τὸν Πέτρον καὶ Ἰάκωβον καὶ Ἰωάννην τὸν ἀδελφὸν αὐτοῦ (Peter and James and John his brother), where one article covers several personal names; cf. Mk 9.2, where an article precedes each name. Sharp's rule does not apply to personal names.

Several significant difficulties with Sharp's rule have arisen. One difficulty is the resistance by some to the implications of his analysis for treatment of certain passages.

Tit. 2.13: τῆς δόξης τοῦ μεγάλου θεοῦ καὶ σωτῆρος ἡμῶν Ἰησοῦ Χριστοῦ; cf. also 2 Pet. 1.1, 11; 2.20; 3.18; Eph. 5.20. Should

1. This was perceptively pointed out in E.V.N. Goetchius, Review of *A Descriptive Analysis of EINAI*, by L.C. McGaughy, *JBL* 95 (1976), p. 148.

2. The rule is cited in Winer, *Treatise*, pp. 162-63 n. 3. See also D.B. Wallace, 'The Semantic Range of the Article-Noun-Kai-Noun Plural Construction in the NT', *GTJ* 4 (1983), pp. 59-84, citing Sharp on p. 62. His study is used for discussion of the plural below.

this passage be translated 'the glory of our great God and Saviour, Jesus Christ' (a statement with christological implications), or 'the glory of the great God and of our saviour, Jesus Christ,' or 'the glory of our great God, namely our saviour Jesus Christ'? Grammarians and commentators have differed in opinion, with Moulton[1] and Robertson[2] opting for the first on the basis of parallels in the papyri, as well as the application of Sharp's rule, and with Winer[3] arguing for the second on theological grounds.[4]

A further difficulty is misapplication of this rule to plural substantives. When plural elements are involved, the possible kinds of correlation of the items are increased. Wallace has provided a helpful framework for differentiating five sub-classes of usage for plural substantives linked by a single article.

1. Entirely distinct though united groups: Mt. 3.7: πολλοὺς τῶν Φαρισαίων καὶ Σαδδουκαίων (many of the Pharisees and Sadducees).
2. Overlapping groups: Lk. 14.21: τοὺς πτωχοὺς καὶ ἀναπείρους καὶ τυφλοὺς καὶ χωλούς (the poor and crippled and blind and lame), all considered together though no one person may have had all of these afflictions.
3. First group contained within the second: Mt. 12.38: τινες τῶν γραμματέων καὶ Φαρισαίων (certain of the scribes and Pharisees); cf. Mt. 5.20 also.
4. Second group contained within the first: 1 Cor. 5.10: τοῖς πλεονέκταις καὶ ἅρπαξιν (with the greedy and swindlers), within a larger list connected by ἤ.[5]
5. Identical groups: Jn 1.40: εἷς ἐκ τῶν δύο τῶν ἀκουσάντων παρὰ Ἰωάννου καὶ ἀκολουθησάντων αὐτῷ (one of the two hearing John and following him).

2.7. *Apollonius's Canon*

This grammatical generality (formulated by the second-century Greek

1. Moulton, *Prolegomena*, p. 84.
2. Robertson, *Grammar*, pp. 785-86.
3. Winer, *Treatise*, p. 162.
4. For a review of the various positions, see J.N.D. Kelly, *A Commentary on the Pastoral Epistles* (London: A. & C. Black, 1963), pp. 245-46.
5. Wallace ('Semantic Range', pp. 74-75) notes that this is the most infrequent category, with all of the examples having textual variants.

grammarian Apollonius Dyscolus) states that *two syntactically joined nouns are either both articular or both anarthrous.*[1] But there are numerous, noteworthy exceptions to this rule for balance of articles (400 or so by Hull's reckoning). These often can be explained by other criteria. These criteria include the following uses: personal names in any environment, nouns governed by prepositions, predicate nominatives, modifying use of κύριος (perhaps indicating a proper name), the vocative, modification by various adjectives, including τις, numbers, πᾶς, πολύς, ἱκανός and πόσος, and instances of apposition.

2.7.1. *The rule maintained.*

2 Cor. 6.7: ἐν λόγῳ ἀληθείας (in word of truth).

Col. 1.5: ἐν τῷ λόγῳ τῆς ἀληθείας (in the word of the truth).

These examples conform to the rule, with the nouns in regimen both either without the article (anarthrous) or with the article (articular).

2.7.2. *The rule violated.* The following examples do not conform to the rule, and are not included among the explainable exceptions listed above. Instances of this sort total over 30 in the NT.

Heb. 1.3: καθαρισμὸν τῶν ἁμαρτιῶν ποιησάμενος (making purification of the sins), unless one of the other grammatical tendencies noted above is in effect.

Lk. 4.17: βιβλίον τοῦ προφήτου Ἠσαΐου (book of the prophet Isaiah), where use of the name should render the noun specific without the article.

2.8. *Special Constructions*

There are still some uses of the Greek article which stand out, either because they are unusual or because they cause some peculiar ambiguity.

2.8.1. *Article functioning pronominally.* It was noted above (section 2.1) that the article in some instances may function by pointing out or resuming a previous usage (as if it were a demonstrative pronoun). A common use of the article is its pronominal function, in which it functions as if it were a personal pronoun.

Mt. 13.28, 29: ὁ δὲ ἔφη...ὁ δέ φησιν (but he said...but he said).

Lk. 15.12: ὁ δὲ διεῖλεν αὐτοῖς τὸν βίον (and he divided [his] possessions among them).

1. See S.D. Hull, 'Exceptions to Apollonius' Canon in the NT: A Grammatical Study', *Trinity Journal* NS 7 (1986), pp. 3-16, for analysis, statistics and examples.

2.8.2. μέν...δέ. The particles μέν...δέ are often coordinated with the article to function much like a pronoun. There are two major uses: anaphoric and partitive.

Acts 14.4: οἱ μὲν ἦσαν...οἱ δέ (some were...but others), where the use is anaphoric to πλῆθος above.

Eph. 4.11: αὐτὸς ἔδωκεν τοὺς μὲν ἀποστόλους, τοὺς δὲ προφήτας, τοὺς δὲ εὐαγγελιστάς, τοὺς δὲ ποιμένας καὶ διδασκάλους (he gave some apostles, some prophets, some evangelists, some pastors and teachers), where there is a partitive sense.

It is not uncommon for one of the two members to be missing.

Mt. 26.67: οἱ δὲ ἐράπισαν (and they struck), with no οἱ μέν clause.

Acts 15.30: οἱ μὲν οὖν ἀπολυθέντες κατῆλθον (therefore, they, having been released, went down), with no οἱ δέ clause.

A controversial instance is Mt. 28.17: οἱ δὲ ἐδίστασαν (but they doubted). The question is whether the phrase indicates a partitive sense (some doubted), continuity (all of the disciples doubted), or a change of subject (others doubted). Each of the three is possible for this construction, but in this context the partitive sense is probably correct.[1]

2.8.3. *Ambiguous constructions*. The use of the article in place of a personal pronoun can lead to some constructions being potentially ambiguous.

Acts 2.41: οἱ μὲν οὖν ἀποδεξάμενοι τὸν λόγον αὐτοῦ ἐβαπτίσθησαν. Does this mean 'those who accepted his word were baptized', or 'they, having accepted his word, were baptized'? It depends upon how the article is seen in relation to the participle.

Mt. 2.9: οἱ δὲ ἀκούσαντες τοῦ βασιλέως ἐπορεύθησαν. In grammatical terms, this could mean either that 'they who heard the king departed', or that 'they, having heard the king, departed'. Interpreters have usually opted for the latter.

2.8.4. *Omission of the article in prepositional phrases*. The article of a substantive in a prepositional phrase is often omitted. Moulton describes this use as entirely normal, stating further, 'There is nothing *indefinite* about the anarthrous noun there'.[2]

Mk 2.1: ἐν οἴκῳ ἐστίν (he is at home), literally 'in house'.

1. See P.W. van der Horst, 'Once More: The Translation of οἱ δέ in Mt. 28.17', *JSNT* 27 (1986), pp. 27-30, who surveys previous opinions as well as the options.

2. Moulton, *Prolegomena*, p. 82.

1 Pet. 1.5: τοὺς ἐν δυνάμει θεοῦ φρουρουμένους διὰ πίστεως εἰς σωτηρίαν ἑτοίμην ἀποκαλυφθῆναι ἐν καιρῷ ἐσχάτῳ (those being guarded in [the] power of God through [the] faith for [the] prepared salvation to be revealed in [the] last time), where English articles are demanded for the sense.

Chapter 6

ADJECTIVES

Introduction

The five-case system of Greek is discussed in Chapter 4, in which it is seen that Greek—an inflected language—indicates a number of important semantic and syntactical features using inflectional endings. The system of usage of these endings is important for the structure of the language, as will be seen even more significantly in discussion of word order (Chapter 20). The inflectional system is important not only for nouns, which are the center of attention regarding the cases, but also for a number of other words, including especially adjectives and participles. No matter what the origin, whether in the noun or not (opinions vary), Greek developed two special classes of modifying words, that is, of words used to modify other words: adjectives and adverbs (see Chapter 7 on adverbs).

Adjectives are words used primarily to modify nouns. This is not to say that other words cannot be used in the same way (e.g. participles), nor is it to say that this is the only way in which this class of word can be used (it is not; see below). Greek language users developed the adjective as a special class of modifier to help them in the task. One of the distinctives of adjectives is their having a complete paradigm of forms, including masculine, feminine and neuter genders, singular and plural number, as well as cases. It is readily apparent that not all adjectives are morphologically regular. There are some adjectives, of course, which are very regular, including distinct forms for all three genders. But there are also adjectives which only grammaticalize two sets of forms: one for masculine and feminine genders, and the other for neuter gender. Some adjective forms follow the pattern of first or second declension nouns, while some follow third declension, with all of the attendant formal differences (including contraction of vowels). But for all of their differences, their function is similar. Treatment below will not distinguish the paradigmatic features, since these are accidental features in relation to the semantics of the adjective. (This chapter concentrates upon adjectives, but other words used similarly are mentioned and discussed as well.)

1. *Syntax of the Adjective*

The syntax of the Greek adjective involves five general categories of usage. The syntactical relations are important in deciding the semantic force of the adjective (or, better, modifier) in a given instance.

1.1. *Attributive Structure*

Attributive structure in Greek involves the direct attribution of qualities or characteristics to a substantive. An English example is 'the large book', where the attribute of 'largeness' is given directly to the book. This can be usefully described with the categories of slot and filler (see the table of positions below). In a given Greek clause one might find a group of words (phrase) in which a substantive (often a noun) is the main word. This group of words may serve, for example, as a subject, in which instance it may well be in the nominative case (except, for example, if it is the subject of an infinitive), or it may serve another function and take another case. The point is that this group of words has a syntactical structure, which may be seen as consisting of a number of slots. One of the slots must be filled with a substantive (this may be sufficient in a given instance to render the group of words complete). But there are other *potential* slots to be filled, including those to be filled by modifying words and the article. *'Attributive structure' observes that the tendency in Greek (though not the absolute rule) is that, when a substantive is in a group where a modifier (often an adjective) is also filling a slot, either they both have the article of the governing (or head) term (substantive) or they both do not.* If they both do have the article, they may share the same article, with the adjective falling between the article and the substantive (article–adjective–substantive) (position 1), or the adjective may have its own article (article–substantive–article–adjective) (position 2). The substantive without an article may also be followed by an adjective with the article (position 3). Examples of this are fairly common where names are used: e.g. Rom. 16.7, 8, 9, 10, 11, 12, 13. It is also possible for attributive structure where neither item has the article (adjective–substantive or vice versa) (position 4).[1] The substantive and its modifier agree in case, gender and number.

Position 1: article–adjective–substantive
Position 2: article–substantive–article–adjective
Position 3: substantive–article–adjective
Position 4: adjective–substantive *or* substantive–adjective

Acts 1.1: τὸν...πρῶτον λόγον ἐποιησάμην (I completed the first word), position 1.

Col. 1.2: τοῖς ἐν Κολοσσαῖς ἁγίοις καὶ πιστοῖς ἀδελφοῖς ἐν Χριστῷ (to the holy and faithful brothers in Christ in Colossae), position 1. Some interpreters take ἁγίοις as a substantival use of the adjective, while others take it as an attributive adjective along with πιστοῖς, which the translation reflects.

Mt. 6.14: ἀφήσει καὶ ὑμῖν ὁ πατὴρ ὑμῶν ὁ οὐράνιος (your heavenly father will also forgive you), position 2.

Jn 1.9: ἦν τὸ φῶς τὸ ἀληθινόν (he was the true light), position 2.

Jn 14.27: εἰρήνην τὴν ἐμήν (my peace), position 3.

Acts 7.35: ἀγγέλου τοῦ ὀφθέντος αὐτῷ (the angel who was seen by him), position 3 with a participle as modifier.

Mk 4.32: ποιεῖ κλάδους μεγάλους ([a mustard plant] produces large branches), position 4.

Jn 20.30: πολλὰ...καὶ ἄλλα σημεῖα ἐποίησεν ὁ Ἰησοῦς (Jesus did many and other signs), position 4.

Prepositional phrases or adverbs may also be used in attributive structure (as can participles—see Chapter 10 section 3.1).[2]

Rom. 9.11: ἡ κατ' ἐκλογὴν πρόθεσις (the purpose according to election).

Phil. 3.14: τῆς ἄνω κλήσεως (the 'upward' calling).

A word in the genitive (frequently not an adjective) may be used in attributive position with a substantive (attributive genitive). A substantive modified attributively by a following articular word in the genitive case regularly does not repeat the article of the substantive.[3]

1. See D.B. Wallace, 'The Relation of Adjective to Noun in Anarthrous Constructions in the NT', *NovT* 26 (1984), pp. 128-67, esp. 150-59.

2. See R.L. Mowery, 'The Articular Prepositional Attributes in the Pauline Corpus', *Bib* 71 (1990), pp. 85-90.

3. See S.E. Porter, 'The Adjectival Attributive Genitive in the NT: A Grammatical Study', *Trinity Journal* NS 4 (1983) pp. 3-17, for various examples

Rom. 5.15, 17: τῷ τοῦ ἑνὸς παραπτώματι (the transgression of the one).

1 Cor. 1.17: ὁ σταυρὸς τοῦ Χριστοῦ (the cross of Christ), but cf. v. 18: ὁ λόγος...ὁ τοῦ σταυροῦ (the word of the cross).

1.2. *Predicate Structure*

Predicate structure in Greek is a means of adding something to the qualities or characteristics of a substantive, not by entering into a direct modifying relationship, but *by ascribing or predicating something to a substantive*. An English example is 'the book is large', in which 'largeness' is ascribed to the book. In Greek, the fact that these words are linked in this way is marked by the modifying word, often an adjective, *not* having an article, whether or not the substantive does. One immediately notices the potential ambiguity in instances where the substantive does not have an article either—is this an attributive or predicate relationship (see section 1.1 regarding position 4 above)? Sometimes not even context will be decisive. Perhaps one of the most common examples of predicate structure is the sentence which in English is translated with the linking verb 'to be', regardless of whether a form of εἰμί appears in Greek. The substantive and the adjective (or similar word) agree in case, gender and number.

Mt. 5.3: μακάριοι οἱ πτωχοὶ τῷ πνεύματι...(the poor in spirit [are] blessed...), in which beatitudes a number of predications are made.

Mt. 6.22: ἐὰν οὖν ᾖ ὁ ὀφθαλμός σου ἁπλοῦς, ὅλον τὸ σῶμά σου φωτεινὸν ἔσται (if therefore your eye is sound, your whole body will be filled with light), with two examples of predicate structure.

Mt. 9.37: ὁ μὲν θερισμὸς πολὺς οἱ δὲ ἐργάται ὀλίγοι (the harvest [is] great but the workers [are] few), with two nominal (verbless) predicate clauses.

Jn 4.11: τὸ φρέαρ ἐστὶν βαθύ (the well is deep).

1.3. *Exceptional Adjectives and Other Modifying Words*

1.3.1. *Predicate structure and attributive meaning. Some words always appear in predicate structure in relation to a substantive, even if they are modifying directly and might be said to have attributive force* (see also Chapter 7). These include, for example, the demonstrative words.

and analysis. This pattern was found often in classical Greek as well, contrary to the comments of a number of NT Greek grammarians (Turner, *Syntax*, p. 217; cf. BDF, §271).

Lk. 15.3: εἶπεν δὲ πρὸς αὐτοὺς τὴν παραβολὴν ταύτην (and he spoke to them this parable).

Certain adjectives tend to take predicate structure. These include πολύς occasionally (but cf. Mk 12.37: [ὁ] πολὺς ὄχλος [the great crowd]) and ὅλος always in the Greek of the NT.

Mk 15.41: ἄλλαι πολλαὶ αἱ συναναβᾶσαι αὐτῷ (many other women coming up with him). The predicate and attributive distinction with πολύς is difficult to insist upon when the substantive is anarthrous, which it often is: e.g. Mt. 24.11: πολλοὶ ψευδοπροφῆται (many false prophets).

Mt. 22.14: πολλοὶ...εἰσιν κλητοὶ ὀλίγοι δὲ ἐκλεκτοί (many... are called but few chosen).

Mt. 22.40: ὅλος ὁ νόμος (the whole law).

Acts 21.30: ἡ πόλις ὅλη (the entire city).

1 Thess. 4.10: ἐν ὅλῃ τῇ Μακεδονίᾳ (in all Macedonia).

1.3.2. *Adjectives in attributive and predicate structure. Some adjectives have a different meaning depending upon whether they appear in predicate or attributive structure.*

a. πᾶς. The adjective πᾶς denotes the concept of completeness, whether it specifies a conglomeration of individual parts (each, every) or an undifferentiated whole. When it occurs in predicate structure, it specifies the items as considered together, and is often translated 'all' (*extensive* use). When it occurs in attributive structure it specifies completeness and is often translated 'whole' or 'entire' (*intensive* use). When it occurs in attributive structure without the articular substantive it is often translated 'each' or 'every' (it may be *intensive or extensive*). It is often difficult to differentiate this last structure from the two structures above, illustrating that the above schema is not a definitive guide to translation and understanding.[1]

Acts 20.18: πῶς μεθ' ὑμῶν τὸν πάντα χρόνον ἐγενόμην (how I was with you the entire time); cf. Acts 19.7: ἦσαν...οἱ πάντες ἄνδρες ὡσεὶ δώδεκα (the entire group of men were about twelve).

Phil. 1.3-4: εὐχαριστῶ τῷ θεῷ μου ἐπὶ πάσῃ τῇ μνείᾳ ὑμῶν... ἐν πάσῃ δεήσει μου (I give thanks to my God upon all remembrance of you...in my every prayer).

1. See Moule, *Idiom Book*, pp. 94-95.

Col. 1.10: περιπατῆσαι ἀξίως τοῦ κυρίου εἰς πᾶσαν ἀρεσκείαν, ἐν παντὶ ἔργῳ ἀγαθῷ καρποφοροῦντες (to walk worthily of the Lord in every pleasing thing, bearing fruit in every good work); cf. Col. 1.28: διδάσκοντες πάντα ἄνθρωπον ἐν πάσῃ σοφίᾳ (teaching every man in every wisdom [or all wisdom]).

1 Tim. 1.15: πάσης ἀποδοχῆς ἄξιος (worthy of entire acceptance).[1]

2 Tim. 3.16: πᾶσα γραφὴ θεόπνευστος, in which one must decide if this is predicate or attributive structure. If it is predicate usage, it may be rendered 'all Scripture is inspired' (or 'all inspired Scripture'). If it is attributive usage, it may be rendered 'the whole of Scripture is inspired' or 'every inspired Scripture'. Moule believes that the second translation of attributive usage is unlikely.[2]

Rom. 16.15: τοὺς σὺν αὐτοῖς πάντας ἁγίους (the entirety of the saints with them, or 'all the saints who are with them' [NASB]?).

b. αὐτός (see Chapter 8 section 2.2). The intensive pronoun (αὐτός, αὐτή, αὐτό), when it is used in attributive structure, serves as a modifier, often translated 'same'; when it is used in predicate structure, it serves as an intensive pronoun, often translated '-self'.

Mk 6.17: αὐτὸς...ὁ Ἡρῴδης (Herod himself).

Rom. 8.16, 26: αὐτὸ τὸ πνεῦμα (the Spirit itself).

1 Thess. 2.1: αὐτοὶ γὰρ οἴδατε...(for you yourselves know...), a frequent use to intensify grammatical person.

Rom. 7.25: αὐτὸς ἐγὼ...δουλεύω (I myself...serve), a frequent use to intensify another pronoun.

Mt. 26.44: τὸν αὐτὸν λόγον (the same word).

2 Cor. 4.13: τὸ αὐτὸ πνεῦμα (the same spirit).

Phil. 1.30: τὸν αὐτὸν ἀγῶνα (the same struggle).

1.4. *Substantival Usage*

In some cases *an adjective* (*or another modifying word*, such as a participle—see Chapter 10 section 3.1) *will occupy the position of the substantive in a phrase. This is known as the substantival use of the adjective (or another word).* Some claim that there is an understood substantive with the adjective, but this is unnecessary or even impos-

1. See G.W. Knight III, *The Faithful Sayings in the Pastoral Letters* (repr. Grand Rapids: Baker, 1979), pp. 25-29, who argues for intensive use, reflected in the translation.

2. Moule, *Idiom Book*, p. 95.

sible to posit in many cases, as Moule admits.[1] The adjective could be used in many instances in the same way as other substantives such as nouns, so that in some instances it is almost impossible to tell if the word is a noun or an adjective. The substantival use of the adjective normally occurs with the article.

Acts 17.21: οἱ ἐπιδημοῦντες ξένοι (the visiting foreigners), where the substantival adjective takes its own modifying participle.

Rom. 1.17: ὁ δὲ δίκαιος ἐκ πίστεως ζήσεται (but the just person by faith will live).

Rom. 3.8: ποιήσωμεν τὰ κακὰ ἵνα ἔλθῃ τὰ ἀγαθά; (should we do the evil things so that the good things might come?), reflecting a frequent use of the substantival neuter adjective with the article.

Rom. 5.7: μόλις γὰρ ὑπὲρ δικαίου τις ἀποθανεῖται· ὑπὲρ γὰρ τοῦ ἀγαθοῦ τάχα τις καὶ τολμᾷ ἀποθανεῖν (for hardly will someone die for a just person; for on behalf of a good person someone perhaps might indeed dare to die).

Rom. 9.22: γνωρίσαι τὸ δυνατὸν αὐτοῦ (to make known his power).

Occasionally the article is not present, even though the adjective is substantival.

Mt. 11.5: τυφλοὶ ἀναβλέπουσιν καὶ χωλοὶ περιπατοῦσιν, λεπροὶ καθαρίζονται καὶ κωφοὶ ἀκούουσιν, καὶ νεκροὶ ἐγείρονται καὶ πτωχοὶ εὐαγγελίζονται (blind are seeing and crippled are walking, lepers are cleansed and deaf are hearing, and dead are raised and poor are preached to).

Mt. 5.45: τὸν ἥλιον αὐτοῦ ἀνατέλλει ἐπὶ πονηροὺς καὶ ἀγαθοὺς καὶ βρέχει ἐπὶ δικαίους καὶ ἀδίκους ([God] brings up his sun upon evil and good people and brings rain upon just and unjust people).

Rom. 1.14: Ἕλλησίν τε καὶ βαρβάροις, σοφοῖς τε καὶ ἀνοήτοις ὀφειλέτης εἰμί (I am a debtor to both Greeks [noun] and barbarians, and wise and ignorant people).

1.5. *Adverbial Usage*

In some instances *an adjective may be used—often in the accusative case—as a modifier of a verbal rather than a substantival element.* These examples are confined to a relatively small group of words, and

1. Moule, *Idiom Book*, p. 96.

appear to have been treated by users of Greek as adverbial in function, even though they might be called accusatives of respect or accusatives of time (see Chapter 4 sections 2.3.3 and 2.3.4).

Mk 6.31: ἀναπαύσασθε ὀλίγον (rest for a little while).

Jn 13.9: μὴ τοὺς πόδας μου μόνον (not my feet only).

Jn 16.19: μικρὸν καὶ οὐ θεωρεῖτέ με, καὶ πάλιν μικρὸν καὶ ὄψεσθέ με; (in a little while and you are not going to see me, and again in a little while and you will see me?).

Acts 7.12: ἐξαπέστειλεν τοὺς πατέρας ἡμῶν πρῶτον (he sent out our fathers first).

Phil. 3.1: τὸ λοιπόν, ἀδελφοί μου, χαίρετε ἐν κυρίῳ (finally, my brothers, rejoice in the Lord), with a connective sense. τὸ λοιπόν is translated variously, including 'furthermore', 'finally' and 'henceforth'.[1] The genitive of this word is also used as a connective: Gal. 6.17: τοῦ λοιποῦ (therefore).[2]

2. *Comparative and Superlative Adjectives*

There is a range of discussion about what happened in the development of Greek adjectives from the classical to the Hellenistic periods. *One formal feature which distinguishes adjectives from nouns in Greek is that adjectives can take not only a positive form (the simple adjective) but a comparative ('more') and superlative ('most') form.*[3] Grammarians are not in firm agreement regarding the status of the three forms of the adjective in the Greek of the NT. Some argue that the comparative and superlative forms can be shifted down a category each, so that the superlative form is sometimes comparative in force and the comparative is sometimes positive in force.[4] Others claim that the superlative is disappearing, forcing the comparative to serve both comparative and superlative functions.[5] There are even a few instances of the positive form having superlative force. In any event, the use of

1. See M.E. Thrall, *Greek Particles in the NT: Linguistic and Exegetical Studies* (Leiden: Brill, 1962), pp. 25-30.

2. See Moule, *Idiom Book*, pp. 161-62.

3. The forms of the adjectives are not all created in the same way, with so-called regular (-τερ-, -τατ-) and irregular (-ων, -ιστ-) forms. There are even some variations within these formal categories. Their function is the point of discussion here.

4. Moule, *Idiom Book*, p. 97.

5. Chamberlain, *Exegetical Grammar*, p. 43.

a comparative or superlative form requires that the interpreter weigh the contextual factors carefully in deciding the force of the adjective, as well as rendering an English translation. The item of comparison with the comparative adjective is expressed by the genitive or by ἤ + same case substantive (e.g. Jn 4.1, 2).

Jn 15.20: οὐκ ἔστιν δοῦλος μείζων τοῦ κυρίου αὐτοῦ (a servant is not greater than his lord).

Mk 5.7: Ἰησοῦ υἱὲ τοῦ θεοῦ τοῦ ὑψίστου (Jesus, son of the highest God). Chamberlain notes that the word ὕψιστος seems to have its superlative force whenever it is used of God in the NT:[1] e.g. Mt. 21.9; Mk 11.10; Lk. 1.32, 35, 76; 2.14; 6.35; 8.28; 19.38; Acts 7.48; 16.17; Heb. 7.1.

Mt. 22.36: ποία ἐντολὴ μεγάλη ἐν τῷ νόμῳ; (which is the great commandment in the law?), where the positive may be used with superlative ('greatest') sense.[2]

Mk 4.1: συνάγεται πρὸς αὐτὸν ὄχλος πλεῖστος (the greatest crowd gathered around him), where the superlative sense is hard to establish, probably requiring a translation like 'a great crowd'.

Mk 4.31, 32: μικρότερον ὂν πάντων τῶν σπερμάτων τῶν ἐπὶ τῆς γῆς...γίνεται μεῖζον πάντων τῶν λαχάνων (being smaller than all the seeds upon the ground...it becomes greater than all the green plants), referring to the mustard plant. One might want to argue here for the superlative ('smallest,' 'greatest') sense for the comparative forms (see RSV).

Lk. 7.28: μείζων ἐν γεννητοῖς γυναικῶν Ἰωάννου οὐδείς ἐστιν· ὁ δὲ μικρότερος ἐν τῇ βασιλείᾳ τοῦ θεοῦ μείζων αὐτοῦ ἐστιν (no one is greater among the offspring of women than John; but the smaller in the kingdom of God is greater than he), where the comparative forms may be used comparatively in the first and third instances but superlatively ('smallest') in the second.

Acts 17.21: Ἀθηναῖοι δὲ πάντες...εἰς οὐδὲν ἕτερον ηὐκαίρουν ἢ λέγειν τι ἢ ἀκούειν τι καινότερον. Is this to be translated 'All Athenians...enjoyed nothing else than to speak about or to listen to something new' (the rough sense of the RSV), 'to speak about or listen to the newest thing' (the NIV), or 'to speak about or listen to something newer' (implying something newer than the thing previous)?

1. Chamberlain, *Exegetical Grammar*, p. 43.
2. BDF, §245; Winer, *Treatise*, p. 308.

1 Cor. 13.13: πίστις ἐλπὶς ἀγάπη, τὰ τρία ταῦτα· μεῖζων δὲ τούτων ἡ ἀγάπη (faith, hope, love, these three things; but the greater of these is love), where three items are being evaluated, so that the superlative sense in English ('greatest') is probably justified.

Eph. 3.8: ἐμοὶ τῷ ἐλαχιστοτέρῳ πάντων ἁγίων ἐδόθη ἡ χάρις αὕτη (to me the 'less least' of all saints, this grace was given), where the superlative form (ἐλάχιστος) has a comparative ending (-τερ-) as well, probably to be seen as having an emphatically full force.[1]

Phil. 1.23: πολλῷ μᾶλλον κρεῖσσον (far, far better), where Paul is comparing whether he wants to be with Christ or to remain in the flesh.

3 Jn 4: μειζοτέραν τούτων οὐκ ἔχω χαράν (I have no greater joy than these), where the double comparative (μείζων + -τερ-) may serve as a reminder that irregular adjectives were troublesome to Greek writers themselves.

1. See J.H. Moulton and W.F. Howard, *A Grammar of NT Greek*. II. *Accidence and Word-Formation* (Edinburgh: T. & T. Clark, 1929), p. 166, who cite a parallel from Aristotle.

Chapter 7

ADVERBS

Introduction

Adverbs are a class of particles or indeclinable forms often used to modify verbs and other modifying words. The adverb is a neglected class of words in Greek grammatical discussion. It forms the second class of modifying words to be considered (see Chapter 6 on adjectives).

1. *Forms of the Adverb*

There are a number of different formal factors which distinguish the adverb. The ending -ως is very common, but other frequently occurring adverbial endings are -θεν and the *iota* vowel (-ει, -ῳ). Adjectives are also used adverbially, but they are discussed in the chapter above under the adverbial usage of the adjective (Chapter 6 section 1.5). Comparative and superlative adverbs (which formally resemble comparative and superlative adjectives) may be formed as well.[1]

Since almost any adjective can be transformed into an adverb with an -ως ending, it is impossible to list all of the adverbs here. The following is a small list of some adverbs (most not formed by affixing -ως), placed in broad categories according to their general sense:

> time: αὔριον, νῦν, πέρυσι, πρωΐ, σήμερον, τότε;
> location: ἄνω, ἐκεῖ, ἐκεῖθεν, ἐνθάδε, ἐντεῦθεν, κάτω, πόρρω, ὧδε;
> manner: ἅπαξ, εἰκῇ, ἐξαίφνης, ἡδέως, οὕτω(ς), παραχρῆμα, ταχέως.

Numerical adverbs ending in -ις may also be used. Nouns and adjectives in the accusative, genitive and dative cases which may be used like adverbs (e.g. δωρεάν, ἀκμήν, λοιποῦ, πέραν, χάριν, αὐτοῦ, ἰδίᾳ, πεζῇ) are not listed above, but must be considered as well.

1. See Dana and Mantey, *Manual Grammar*, p. 239.

So-called improper prepositions, which are generally considered adverbs, are listed at the end of Chapter 9 (section 5).

2. *Functions of the Adverb*

For a word which evidences little formal variation, the adverb may be used in a surprisingly large number of ways. *The adverb's primary function is to modify verbs, verbal phrases or other modifying words and to establish such factors as time, frequency, place or location, and manner.* The adverb may also be used to modify substantives, especially in prepositional phrases. Adverbial uses of the participle and infinitive are treated in their respective chapters (10 and 11).

2.1. *Modifying a Verb*

A common function of the adverb is to modify a verb or a verbal phrase (it is often difficult, and usually unnecessary, to specify how particular the modification is). These are categorized together here as modifications of a verb.

Mt. 6.11: δὸς ἡμῖν σήμερον (give to us today).

Mt. 17.15: πολλάκις...πίπτει εἰς τὸ πῦρ (many times...he falls into the fire).

Mt. 27.55: ἦσαν...ἐκεῖ γυναῖκες πολλαὶ ἀπὸ μακρόθεν θεωροῦσαι (many women were there, observing from afar), with two uses of adverbs. The first is used absolutely for location (ἐκεῖ), and the second for location in a prepositional phrase (μακρόθεν; as a substantive—see section 2.2 below).

Lk. 7.4: παρεκάλουν αὐτὸν σπουδαίως (they were calling out to him eagerly).

Rom. 5.7: μόλις γὰρ ὑπὲρ δικαίου τις ἀποθανεῖται· ὑπὲρ γὰρ τοῦ ἀγαθοῦ τάχα τις καὶ τολμᾷ ἀποθανεῖν (for hardly will someone die for a just person; for on behalf of a good person someone perhaps might indeed dare to die), with two adverbs of manner, μόλις and τάχα.

Mt. 14.35: πάντας τοὺς κακῶς ἔχοντας (all those having bad health), an expression used to speak of ill health, perhaps similar to the English 'I am poorly'.[1]

1. See Moule, *Idiom Book*, p. 161.

2.2. *Modifying or Functioning as a Substantive*

In some instances the adverb is used in ways very similar to the ways in which adjectives or other modifiers of nouns function, including substantival use.

Rom. 3.26: ἐν τῷ νῦν καιρῷ (in the 'now' time), with an adverb used in attributive structure to modify a noun.

1 Thess. 2.10: ὡς ὁσίως καὶ δικαίως καὶ ἀμέμπτως ὑμῖν τοῖς πιστεύουσιν ἐγενήθημεν (as we became holy and just and without blame to you who believe), where three adverbs are used with a linking verb, ἐγενήθημεν, in predicate structure.[1]

Col. 3.1, 2: τὰ ἄνω ζητεῖτε...τὰ ἄνω φρονεῖτε, μὴ τὰ ἐπὶ τῆς γῆς (seek the things above...think on the things above, not the things upon the earth), where adverbs function as substantives with the neuter article.

Mt. 11.12: ἕως ἄρτι (until now), with an adverb serving as the object of another adverb used as a preposition.[2]

2.3. *Modifying Another Modifier*

The adverb may be used to modify another modifier, often an adjective.

Mk 7.36: αὐτοὶ μᾶλλον περισσότερον ἐκήρυσσον (they themselves were proclaiming even more abundantly), with μᾶλλον modifying the comparative adjective used adverbially.

1 Tim. 3.16: ὁμολογουμένως μέγα ἐστὶν τὸ τῆς εὐσεβείας μυστήριον (confessedly great is the mystery of godliness), with an adverb modifying a predicate nominative adjective.

1. See Chamberlain, *Exegetical Grammar*, p. 110.
2. See Green, *Handbook*, p. 369.

Chapter 8

PRONOUNS

Introduction

Pronouns are a class of inflected words used for a variety of substitutionary referential purposes. Much of the information regarding the function of the pronouns is specified above where cases (Chapter 4) and use of the article (Chapter 5) are discussed. Therefore, when such categories as the semantics of the cases, and attributive and predicate structures are referred to, the above chapters should be consulted. This chapter is reserved for specifying the pronouns used in the Greek of the NT, along with making particular observations regarding usage. All of the pronouns listed below, except for the personal, reflexive and reciprocal pronouns, may be used as modifiers, not merely as substantives.

1. *Pronouns and Substitution*

It is often stated in grammar books that a pronoun 'is a word which stands for or in the place of or instead of a noun'.[1] This is one of many substitutionary roles which the pronoun plays, but as a definition this is insufficient. For example, in Mk 15.32, αὐτῷ in the last clause of the verse does not refer to a single noun but to the several words (ὁ Χριστὸς ὁ βασιλεὺς Ἰσραήλ) at the beginning of the verse. In Mk 16.3, ἑαυτάς refers to Μαρία ἡ Μαγδαληνὴ καὶ Μαρία ἡ [τοῦ] Ἰακώβου καὶ Σαλώμη (16.1), several people described with several nouns and other words. In Jas 1.27, the author says that pure and undefiled religion is 'this' (αὕτη): ἐπισκέπτεσθαι ὀρφανοὺς καὶ χήρας ἐν τῇ θλίψει αὐτῶν, ἄσπιλον ἑαυτὸν τηρεῖν ἀπὸ τοῦ κόσμου, a structure with two verbal phrases. In Rom. 5.12, most commentators agree that διὰ τοῦτο refers at least to

1. Brooks and Winbery, *Syntax*, p. 74.

vv. 9-11, quite possibly to vv. 1-11, and perhaps even further back.[1] Relative pronouns may have no referent (see section 2.6 below). Thus, to speak generally, *a pronoun may substitute for a variety of syntactical units, from a word to a much larger segment.*

2. *The Pronouns of the Greek of the NT*

2.1. *Personal Pronouns*

The personal pronouns of the first and second person (e.g. ἐγώ, σύ, ἡμεῖς, ὑμεῖς) occur in the Greek of the NT. The Attic third person pronoun (οὗ, σφεῖς) is not found, this function being performed by the intensive pronoun αὐτός (see section 2.2 below).

2.1.1. *Specification.* The usual debate regarding use of the personal pronoun is whether it is emphatic, with some grammarians arguing that it is,[2] and others that it is not.[3] But the term 'emphatic', while useful, is not as descriptive as it might be. Since the verb in Greek limits the subject (person), the pronoun may function in a variety of ways to specify the subject.

a. *Antithetical specification.*

2 Cor. 11.29: τίς...καὶ οὐκ ἐγὼ πυροῦμαι; (who...and am I not enflamed?), with the antithesis between the third and first persons.

b. *Selective or restrictive specification.*

Jn 2.10: πᾶς ἄνθρωπος...σὺ τετήρηκας τὸν καλὸν οἶνον (every person...you keep the good wine), with 'you' a member of all humanity.

1 Thess. 2.18: ἠθελήσαμεν...ἐγὼ μὲν Παῦλος (we wanted... indeed, I Paul).[4]

c. *Descriptive specification.*

Jn 5.44: πῶς δύνασθε ὑμεῖς πιστεῦσαι (how are you [as described above] able to believe), with reference to the characterization in vv. 42-43.

1. See Sanday and Headlam, *Romans*, p. 131.
2. Winer, *Treatise*, p. 190.
3. Robertson, *Grammar*, p. 676; Moulton, *Prolegomena*, p. 85.
4. See Moule, *Idiom Book*, p. 119.

2.1.2. *Possessive use*. The genitive form of the personal pronoun is often used in predicate position for possession or origin. It is used more widely than the possessive pronoun (see Chapter 4 section 2.4.3).

Mt. 6.6, 8: ὁ πατήρ σου...ὁ πατὴρ ὑμῶν (your father).

2 Cor. 1.18: ὁ λόγος ἡμῶν (our word).

2.1.3. *Reflexive use*. Dana and Mantey claim that there are at least two clear instances of the reflexive use of the personal pronoun in the NT.[1] This appears to be an issue of English translation.

Mt. 6.19, 20: [μὴ] θησαυρίζετε [δὲ] ὑμῖν θησαυρούς ([don't] store for yourselves treasures). Eph. 1.9 is a doubtful instance.

2.2. *Intensive Pronoun*

The intensive pronoun (αὐτός, αὐτή, αὐτό) is the most frequently found pronoun in the NT. It has replaced the third person personal pronoun. Besides its pronominal function (discussed below), it may function as a modifier or retain its intensive force, depending on whether it is used in attributive ('same') or predicate ('self') structure (see Chapter 6 section 1.3.2.b).

2.2.1. *Designation of subject, complement (object), or completive.*

Lk. 5.1: αὐτὸς ἦν ἑστώς (he was standing), designating the subject.

Jn 12.17: ἤγειρεν αὐτόν (he raised him), designating the object.

Acts 15.7: Πέτρος εἶπεν πρὸς αὐτούς (Peter said to them), completing the preposition.

Mt. 25.21: ἔφη αὐτῷ ὁ κύριος...(the lord said to him...), designating the so-called indirect object.

2.2.2. *Possessive use*. One of the most frequent uses of the genitive of the intensive pronoun is as an indicator of possession. It functions in place of the third person possessive pronoun, and is usually used in predicate position (see Chapter 4 section 2.4.3).

Lk. 1.36: ἐν γήρει αὐτῆς (in her old age).

Acts 16.32: ἐν τῇ οἰκίᾳ αὐτοῦ (in his house).

Lk. 5.20: τὴν πίστιν αὐτῶν (their faith).

Tit. 3.5: κατὰ τὸ αὐτοῦ ἔλεος (according to his mercy), an emphatic use of attributive structure.

1. Dana and Mantey, *Manual Grammar*, p. 124.

2.2.3. *Collective use*. The plural intensive pronoun may be used to refer to a collective singular item.

2 Cor. 5.19: θεὸς ἦν ἐν Χριστῷ κόσμον καταλλάσσων ἑαυτῷ, μὴ λογιζόμενος αὐτοῖς τὰ παραπτώματα αὐτῶν (in Christ, God was reconciling the world to himself, not counting their sins against them), where the collective members of the world are specified with the plural pronouns αὐτοῖς and αὐτῶν.

Acts 8.5: κατελθὼν εἰς [τὴν] πόλιν...ἐκήρυσσεν αὐτοῖς (having gone down into the city...he preached to them).

2.2.4. *Demonstrative function*. Most grammarians recognize a limited use of the intensive pronoun with demonstrative force.

Lk. 10.7: ἐν αὐτῇ...τῇ οἰκίᾳ; Lk. 10.21 and 12.12: ἐν αὐτῇ τῇ ὥρᾳ; Lk. 13.1: ἐν αὐτῷ τῷ καιρῷ; Acts 16.18 and 22.13: αὐτῇ τῷ ὥρᾳ. These examples are probably best translated 'in that house, hour, time, and the like', rather than 'in the same...'[1]

2.3. *Possessive Pronoun*

The possessive pronoun (ἐμός, σός, ἡμέτερος, ὑμέτερος) may be classified as an adjective, since it is used like an adjective (see Chapters 5 and 6). The possessive pronoun is not found in the third person, its function being taken by the genitive of the intensive pronoun. The genitive personal pronoun may replace the possessive pronoun in the first and second persons, as well. The use of the possessive pronoun (except for ἐμός in John) is greatly reduced in frequency from its usage in earlier Greek. The possessive pronoun usually appears in attributive position.

Rom. 10.1: ἡ...εὐδοκία τῆς ἐμῆς καρδίας (the...desire of my heart), in attributive position.

Mk 10.40: τὸ...καθίσαι ἐκ δεξιῶν μου ἢ ἐξ εὐωνύμων οὐκ ἔστιν ἐμὸν δοῦναι (to sit at my right or left hand is not mine to give), a relatively unusual instance of predicate structure.

2.4. *Reflexive Pronoun*

The reflexive pronoun (ἐμαυτοῦ, σεαυτοῦ, ἑαυτοῦ, and plural ἑαυτῶν for all persons) has reduced scope in NT Greek. In most instances the pronoun is an object (complement) of the verb.

1. See Moulton, *Prolegomena*, p. 91; Dana and Mantey, *Manual Grammar*, p. 130; Moule, *Idiom Book*, p. 120.

Jn 14.21: ἐμφανίσω αὐτῷ ἐμαυτόν (I will show myself to him).

Acts 16.28: μηδὲν πράξῃς σεαυτῷ κακόν (do nothing evil to yourself).

2 Cor. 13.5: ἑαυτοὺς πειράζετε (test yourselves), where the third person plural form serves the second person plural function.

There is potential confusion between the shortened or contracted form of the third person reflexive pronoun (αὑτόν) and αὐτόν. The genitive αὑτοῦ is not found in the NT and the shortened second person form is only found with textual variants (e.g. Jas 2.8 with σαυτόν). Moule suggests that the following examples require a reflexive form (but not all editors agree).[1]

Lk. 23.12: προϋπῆρχον γὰρ ἐν ἔχθρᾳ ὄντες πρὸς αὑτούς (for they were previously enemies, being against each other). At Lk. 24.12, *UBSGNT*[3] and N–A[26] print the uncontracted reflexive pronoun; cf. 1 Jn 5.18 with textual variants.

Jn 2.24: οὐκ ἐπίστευεν αὑτὸν αὐτοῖς (he did not entrust himself to them).

Col. 1.20: δι' αὐτοῦ ἀποκαταλλάξαι τὰ πάντα εἰς αὑτόν (through him to reconcile all things to himself), although most editors and commentators do not accept the reading of the reflexive pronoun here.[2]

2.5. *Reciprocal Pronoun*

The reciprocal pronoun (ἀλλήλων), which does not occur in the nominative case, is used when a mutual relationship is to be expressed between or among elements in a group, and hence only occurs in the plural.

Rom. 12.5: ἀλλήλων μέλη (members of one another).

Gal. 5.13: δουλεύετε ἀλλήλοις (serve one another).

1 Jn 4.7: ἀγαπῶμεν ἀλλήλους (let us love one another).

2.6. *Relative Pronouns*

Relative pronouns are widely used to bring clauses into relation to each other (see Chapter 14 for examples). Usually the relative pronoun follows its referent, with which it agrees in number and gender, while taking the case which accords with its function in its own clause.

1. Moule, *Idiom Book*, p. 119.

2. Cf. Lightfoot, *St Paul's Epistles to the Colossians and to Philemon*, p. 160, who suggests the reflexive form for the genitive pronoun.

There are several kinds of exceptions to this grammatical concord: e.g. attraction, where the pronoun (or its referent) changes its case to conform to the element in relation with it; and independent use, such as the protasis of a conditional-like statement (Mt. 18.6: ὃς...ἂν σκανδαλίσῃ [whoever causes to stumble]); cf. also 1 Jn 1.1, 3: ὃ ἦν ἀπ' ἀρχῆς, ὃ ἀκηκόαμεν, ὃ ἑωράκαμεν τοῖς ὀφθαλμοῖς ἡμῶν, ὃ ἐθεασάμεθα καὶ αἱ χεῖρες ἡμῶν ἐψηλάφησαν...ὃ ἑωράκαμεν καὶ ἀκηκόαμεν ἀπαγγέλλομεν καὶ ὑμῖν (what was from the beginning, what we have heard, what we have seen with our eyes, what we have seen and our hands have touched...what we have seen and have heard we are announcing also to you); Jude 22, 23: οὓς... οὓς...οὓς (some...others...).

2.6.1. ὅς *and* ὅστις. Since the indefinite relative pronoun (ὅστις, ἥτις, ὅτι) is limited in the Greek of the NT to use in the nominative case (except for the phrase ἕως ὅτου in, for example, Jn 9.18 and other places), many grammarians believe that any distinction between the relative and indefinite relative pronouns is lost.[1] That opinion is not shared by all, however.[2] There are sufficiently large numbers of examples where the *generic* ('which, as other like things') and *essential* ('which by its very nature') senses of the indefinite relative pronoun are discernible to warrant distinction (see also Mt. 7.24; Acts 10.47; 17.11; Rom. 6.2; 9.4; 2 Cor. 8.10; Jas 4.14) (see Chapter 15 introduction).

Mt. 7.24: πᾶς...ὅστις ἀκούει μου τοὺς λόγους τούτους... ὁμοιωθήσεται ἀνδρὶ φρονίμῳ, ὅστις ᾠκοδόμησεν αὐτοῦ τὴν οἰκίαν (everyone...who is of the type who hears these words of mine...is like a wise man, who is of the type who builds his house), generic use.

Jas 4.14: οἵτινες οὐκ ἐπίστασθε (you by your very nature do not know), essential use.

2.6.2. *Other forms*. There are several other forms of relative pronoun, most of which are used as indirect interrogative pronouns as well.[3]

1. BDF, §293.
2. Moulton, *Prolegomena*, pp. 91-92; Moule, *Idiom Book*, pp. 123-25.
3. See Chapter 18; Moulton, *Prolegomena*, p. 93.

a. ὅς γε *and* ὅσπερ (relative pronoun combined with intensive particle).

Rom. 8.32: ὅς γε τοῦ ἰδίου υἱοῦ οὐκ ἐφείσατο (who did not spare his own son).

b. οἷος, οἵα, οἷον (qualitative correlative relative pronoun).

2 Tim. 3.11: οἷά μοι ἐγένετο ἐν 'Αντιοχείᾳ (which things [sufferings] came to me in Antioch). This relative pronoun sometimes follows τοιοῦτος, or even precedes it (e.g. 1 Cor. 15.48).

c. ὁποῖος, ὁποία, ὁποῖον (qualitative relative pronoun).

Acts 26.29: ὁποῖος καὶ ἐγώ εἰμι (such as even I am).

d. ὅσος, ὅση, ὅσον (quantitative correlative relative pronoun).

Mk 3.8: ἀκούοντες ὅσα ἐποίει (hearing such things he was doing).

e. ἡλίκος, ἡλίκη, ἡλίκον (quantitative relative pronoun).

Col. 2.1: εἰδέναι ἡλίκον ἀγῶνα ἔχω ὑπὲρ ὑμῶν (to know how great a struggle I have for you).

2.7. *Demonstrative Pronouns*

All three demonstrative pronouns (οὗτος, ἐκεῖνος, ὅδε) are found in the NT. The third is greatly reduced (ten instances), however, only occurring once modifying a noun: Jas 4.13: τήνδε τὴν πόλιν (this city). When used as modifiers, demonstratives usually occur in predicate position. An exception is 2 Cor. 8.14 (τὸ ἐκείνων ὑστέρημα ...τὸ ἐκείνων περίσσευμα [their lack...their abundance]), where the alteration of normal order draws attention to the pronoun. In the NT, demonstrative pronouns have demonstrative force, that is, they are used to indicate nearness and remoteness, whether in time, space (location) or even narrative proximity, from the perspective of the language user. Usually they refer to something mentioned previously (*anaphoric* usage), although they may refer to something not yet mentioned (*cataphoric* usage). English translations will vary, depending upon the emphatic force of the demonstrative in a given context. As a result, translation as 'he, she' may be used, without implying that the demonstrative pronoun has lost its demonstrative sense.

2.7.1. οὗτος *and* ὅδε, *the near demonstrative pronouns ('this').*

Mt. 10.22: ὁ δὲ ὑπομείνας εἰς τέλος οὗτος σωθήσεται (but the one who remains to the end, this one will be saved), referring to the preceding verbal phrase (anaphoric usage).

Lk. 23.41: οὗτος δὲ οὐδὲν ἄτοπον ἔπραξεν (but this one did nothing wrong), referring to Jesus, who is located nearby.

Acts 21.11: τάδε λέγει τὸ πνεῦμα τὸ ἅγιον (the Holy Spirit says these things), followed by a statement, a common use of this pronoun in the NT and in extra-biblical Greek (cataphoric usage).

Jas 1.27: θρησκεία καθαρὰ καὶ ἀμίαντος...αὕτη ἐστίν, ἐπισκέπτεσθαι ὀρφανοὺς καὶ χήρας ἐν τῇ θλίψει αὐτῶν, ἄσπιλον ἑαυτὸν τηρεῖν ἀπὸ τοῦ κόσμου (pure and undefiled religion...is this: to care for orphans and widows in their distress, to keep oneself spotless from the world), where the pronoun refers forward (cataphoric usage). But see Chapter 11 section 2.1.

2.7.2. ἐκεῖνος, *the remote demonstrative pronoun ('that').*

Mt. 7.22: πολλοὶ ἐροῦσίν μοι ἐν ἐκείνῃ τῇ ἡμέρᾳ (many will say to me in that day), with reference to a remote day.

Acts 3.13: κρίναντος ἐκείνου ἀπολύειν ([Pilate] determined to release that one), with reference to Jesus, who was mentioned above, but with another statement intervening.

Jn 10.6: ἐκεῖνοι δὲ οὐκ ἔγνωσαν (but those [they] did not understand), in contrast to Jesus.

2.7.3. *Correlative adjectives.* Correlative adjectives such as τοιοῦτος, τοσοῦτος, τοιόσδε, τηλικοῦτος may be used like demonstrative pronouns, and are so categorized by some grammarians.

1 Cor. 11.16: ἡμεῖς τοιαύτην συνήθειαν οὐκ ἔχομεν (we do not have such a practice).

Heb. 2.3: πῶς ἡμεῖς ἐκφευξόμεθα τηλικαύτης ἀμελήσαντες σωτηρίας; (how shall we flee, neglecting so great a salvation?).

2.8. *Indefinite Pronoun*

2.8.1. The enclitic indefinite pronoun (τις, τι), not to be confused with the interrogative pronoun (τίς, τί; see section 2.9.1 below), may be used as a substantive or as a modifier (Acts 3.2: τις ἀνήρ [a certain man]). The sense of the indefinite pronoun is of an item which is representative or unspecified.

Lk. 22.35: μή τινος ὑστερήσατε; (you didn't lack anything, did you?).

Acts 17.18: τινὲς...καὶ τῶν Ἐπικουρείων καὶ Στοϊκῶν φιλοσόφων συνέβαλλον αὐτῷ (certain ones...of the Epicurean and Stoic philosophers gathered around him).

Phil. 1.15: τινὲς μὲν καὶ διὰ φθόνον καὶ ἔριν, τινὲς δὲ καὶ δι' εὐδοκίαν τὸν Χριστὸν κηρύσσουσιν (certain ones on account of envy and strife, and certain ones on account of good will preach Christ), with the pronouns used of contrasting representative groups.

2.8.2. εἷς. There are a few occasions when εἷς is used similarly to the indefinite pronoun.

Mt. 19.16: εἷς προσελθὼν αὐτῷ εἶπεν (someone, having come to him, said).

2.9. *Interrogative Pronouns*

The Greek of the NT uses several different interrogative pronouns. They usually occur first in a question.

2.9.1. τίς, τί. This is the most common interrogative pronoun, and it is used in direct and indirect questions (see Chapter 18).

Mt. 18.1: τίς...μείζων ἐστίν; (who...is greater?), an example of a direct question.

Mt. 20.22: οὐκ οἴδατε τί αἰτεῖσθε (you do not know what you are asking), an example of an indirect question.

Mt. 22.18: τί με πειράζετε; (why do you test me?), a use of τί with its common translation 'why'. This is probably best understood as an accusative of respect ('with respect to what').

Jn 18.29: τίνα κατηγορίαν φέρετε [κατὰ] τοῦ ἀνθρώπου τούτου; (what sort of accusation do you bear [against] this man?), where the interrogative pronoun is used as a modifier as well.

1 Tim. 1.7: μὴ νοοῦντες μήτε ἃ λέγουσιν μήτε περὶ τίνων διαβεβαιοῦνται (neither understanding which things they say nor concerning which things they assert), where the relative and interrogative pronouns are both used in one sentence.[1]

1. Winer, *Treatise*, p. 211.

2.9.2. *Other forms*. There are several other interrogative pronouns worth mentioning.

a. ποῖος, ποία, ποῖον (qualitative interrogative pronoun).

Rom. 3.27: διὰ ποίου νόμου; (through what sort of law?), in a direct question.

Jn 12.33: σημαίνων ποίῳ θανάτῳ ἤμελλεν ἀποθνῄσκειν (indicating by what kind of death he was going to die), in an indirect question.

Many grammarians posit that there is a loss of distinction between ποῖος and τίς in Hellenistic Greek.[1] The following verses are affected by this discussion.

Mt. 19.18: λέγει αὐτῷ, ποίας; (he said to him, which one?), with reference to the commandments.

1 Pet. 1.11: ἐραυνῶντες εἰς τίνα ἢ ποῖον καιρόν. The use of τίνα with ποῖον has resulted in at least three understandings of this verse: (a) 'what person or time' (RSV, NASB), (b) 'what time and circumstances' (NIV), or (c) 'what time'.[2] Several issues must be considered. If the two interrogative pronouns are synonymous, one can conclude that the phrase is redundant or tautologous (view c), or that τίνα does not modify καιρόν but is independent. If it is independent, it may have a personal referent while ποῖον modifies καιρόν (view a). If the two interrogatives are not synonymous, one can conclude that both are modifying καιρόν and that there is a distinction in sense (so view b). Most commentators select view b because they find the discussion of a person foreign to the context and hold that, even though the pronouns may be synonymous in other contexts, the use of the two together here calls for a distinction.

1. E.g. BDF, §298(2).

2. Among commentators and grammarians, there is division as well: (a) G.D. Kilpatrick, '1 Pet. 1.11 ΤΙΝΑ 'Η ΠΟΙΟΝ ΚΑΙΡΟΝ', *NovT* 28 (1986), pp. 91-92; W. Grudem, *The First Epistle of Peter* (Grand Rapids: Eerdmans, 1988), pp. 74-75; (b) BAGD, *s.v.*; E.G. Selwyn, *The First Epistle of St Peter* (repr. Grand Rapids: Baker, 2nd edn, 1981), p. 135; J.N.D. Kelly, *A Commentary on the Epistles of Peter and Jude* (repr. Grand Rapids: Baker, 1981), p. 60; J.R. Michaels, *1 Peter* (Waco, TX: Word Books, 1988), pp. 41-43; P. Davids, *The First Epistle of Peter* (Grand Rapids: Eerdmans, 1990), pp. 60-62; (c) BDF, §298(2).

b. πόσος (quantitative interrogative pronoun).

Mk 6.38: πόσους ἄρτους ἔχετε; (how many loaves do you have?).

This pronoun occurs nine times with μᾶλλον with a quantitative sense: Rom. 11.12: πόσῳ μᾶλλον τὸ πλήρωμα αὐτῶν (how much more their fullness).

c. ποταπός (qualitative interrogative pronoun).

Mt. 8.27: ποταπός ἐστιν οὗτος; (what sort is this one?).

d. πηλίκος (quantitative interrogative pronoun).

Heb. 7.4: θεωρεῖτε...πηλίκος οὗτος (see...how great this one is); the other occurrence of this pronoun in the NT has a textual variant (Gal. 6.11).

2.10. *Negative Pronouns*

The negatives οὐδείς and μηδείς may be classified as pronouns or adjectives. (The alternative form οὐθείς is also found in the Greek of the NT: e.g. Lk. 22.35; Acts 15.9; 1 Cor. 13.2.) These negatives are related in the same way as are οὐ and μή (see Chapter 19 on negation): οὐδείς tends to be used with the indicative, and μηδείς with the non-indicative moods.

Mt. 6.24: οὐδεὶς δύναται δυσὶ κυρίοις δουλεύειν (no one is able to serve two masters).

Lk. 4.26: πρὸς οὐδεμίαν αὐτῶν ἐπέμφθη Ἠλίας (Elijah was sent to none of them).

Rom. 13.8: μηδενὶ μηδὲν ὀφείλετε (owe nothing to anyone), with double negation (see Chapter 19 section 2.2).

Mk 5.43: ἵνα μηδεὶς γνοῖ τοῦτο (so that no one might know this).

οὐδείς functions often as a modifier in attributive structure.

Lk. 4.24: οὐδεὶς προφήτης δεκτός ἐστιν ἐν τῇ πατρίδι αὐτοῦ (no prophet is received in his homeland).

Jn 10.41: Ἰωάννης...σημεῖον ἐποίησεν οὐδέν (John...made no sign).

Chapter 9

PREPOSITIONS

Introduction

Prepositions are indeclinable fixed forms or particles used to enhance the force of the cases when words or groups of words are linked together. They have proved to be both interesting and challenging to grammarians of Greek, because although they are small, unchanging words, they are often made to perform a number of different functions. This causes much potential difficulty for discussing the prepositions, since it is often hard to capture the balance between English translations that draw out the differences among the prepositions and consequently sound stilted, and translations that use the best idiomatic renderings but make it difficult to appreciate Greek usage.

Many grammarians note that there is a relationship between adverbs (Chapter 7) and prepositions.[1] In fact, it is widely thought that prepositions developed from adverbs. Particular adverbs were selected by users of Greek to specify relations between one word or phrase and other words in the sentence, such as a substantive, a verb or a verb phrase. These adverbs became prepositions. The fact that prepositions precede their objects or take the pre-position accounts for their name (there are exceptions to this syntactical order, especially in Greek poetry). An example reflecting the early adverbial function of the preposition occurs in 2 Cor. 11.23: διάκονοι Χριστοῦ εἰσιν; παραφρονῶν λαλῶ, ὑπὲρ ἐγώ (are they servants of Christ? I am speaking madly, I more), where ὑπέρ appears to be modifying ἐγώ, with a number of adverbs (περισσοτέρως, ὑπερβαλλόντως, πολλάκις) following.

1. See M.J. Harris, 'Appendix: Prepositions and Theology in the Greek NT', *NIDNTT* (ed. C. Brown; vol. 3; Grand Rapids: Zondervan, 1978), p. 1172.

1. *Prepositions and Cases*

Analysis of prepositions has led many grammarians to say that prepositions govern particular cases. It is true that prepositions are related to cases. For example, ἐπί appears to have a dative case ending with the *iota*. But it is probably better to say that *a preposition is governed by its case, in some way helping the case to manifest its meaning and to perform more precisely its various functions.*[1] The Hellenistic period reveals increased use of the prepositions in relation to earlier Greek, because there was pressure beginning to be exerted upon the cases. The dative case was the first eventually to be squeezed out, as the accusative case grew in importance. Hence prepositions were found necessary by writers and speakers to clarify case meanings and relationships.

2. *Independent and Prefixed Prepositions*

Prepositions may be used in several different ways. The first is the simple use of the preposition in its own prepositional phrase. In all there are approximately 60 words used in this way in the NT, called proper and improper prepositions. Some grammarians distinguish between the proper prepositions—those which may be prefixed to verbs—and improper prepositions—those which are not prefixed to verbs. This distinction is important in the sense that 'proper' prepositions are used much more than improper prepositions, and are the ones most worth discussing below. But so far as the ways in which proper and improper prepositions function in prepositional phrases, there is no major distinction between the two.

The second way in which a preposition may be used is as a prefix to a verb (or to other words, such as nouns). (This use is restricted to certain prepositions—see the paragraph above.) Eighteen prepositions are used in this way. When a preposition is prefixed to a verb, it may function in one of three ways. First, it may *preserve but intensify* the meaning of the verb. This intensification is often times difficult to quantify, but there appears to be a reason in the writer or speaker's mind why the prefixed form should be used. For example, ἔφαγον is

1. See Louw, 'Linguistic Theory', p. 82; Winer, *Treatise*, pp. 449-50; Harris, 'Prepositions', p. 1173.

normally translated 'eat', while κατέφαγον is often translated 'devour'. A more pertinent example is ἀποκαταλλάσσω ('reconcile'), used in Eph. 2.16 and Col. 1.20, 22, whereas καταλλάσσω (also translated 'reconcile') is used in 1 Cor. 7.11, Rom. 5.10 and 2 Cor. 5.18, 19, 20. (Note that καταλλάσσω is itself a prefixed form, but it seems to fall under a different category, that of altering the meaning; see below.) The question arises as to why the author used (or possibly even coined) this rare prefixed form if the other form was available (the instances in Ephesians and Colossians are the first recorded occurrences of this word). Perhaps in light of the author's discussion of the work of Christ it was felt that a particular intensification of the action was called for. That this kind of process is at work is seen in use of the verb ἀποθνῄσκω ('die') in the NT. In classical Greek, the form of the verb in the present tense was θνῄσκω, but the simple unprefixed form was forced out by the prefixed form, which is used in NT Greek. The emphatic form thus became the only form, and as a consequence lost its emphatic contrast as well.

Secondly, the prefix may *transform* the meaning of the verb into a new meaning. Instances of this might include καταλλάσσω, cited above. ἀλλάσσω in Greek frequently has the meaning of 'exchange', as in Rom. 1.23: ἤλλαξαν τὴν δόξαν τοῦ ἀφθάρτου θεοῦ ἐν ὁμοιώματι εἰκόνος φθαρτοῦ ἀνθρώπου (they exchanged the glory of the incorruptible God in a likeness of an image of corruptible humanity). For Paul, the addition of the prefixed κατά (or διά) apparently brought out the verb's more specialized meaning of 'reconcile'. Another example is προσκυνέω, often translated 'worship', from the verb 'to kiss' with the preposition πρός. The meaning 'kiss toward' may in some way lie behind the act of worship and may be its meaning in some extra-biblical Greek. But an attempt to see this in its usage in the NT is often farfetched. The acts of worship recorded in the NT probably involved falling down at another's feet.

Thirdly, the prefix may *retain* its basic or local (some might say literal) meaning. For example, with verbs of movement, such as ἔρχομαι, the prefixing of a preposition simply adds the meaning of the prefix. Thus εἰσέρχομαι means 'go into' or 'enter'. The author of the First Gospel uses προσκυλίω ('roll toward') in Mt. 27.60 and ἀποκυλίω ('roll away') in 28.2.

3. *Visual Representation*

The following discussion of the 'proper' prepositions relies upon a series of visual representations to help get the fundamental or 'local' semantic feature of the particular form firmly in mind. The diagrams use two common shapes, a cube and a sphere, to aid in grasping and retaining the fundamental sense. Admittedly, some of the diagrams are more successful than others; in no case are they to be taken overly literalistically so that they restrict understanding. The subsequent analysis also draws upon the threefold analysis introduced in Chapter 4 regarding cases (see fig. 2, section 1.2). The meaning of the given preposition (represented by the diagram) is considered on two further levels: syntax (case) and context. The result is that the basic meaning of the form is used to discuss other, metaphorical extensions of this fundamental meaning, as they are manifested through syntactical and contextual features. Although the correlation is far from exact, most prepositions have a fundamental sense related to being situated in, moving toward or moving away from a location. Prepositions used with the accusative case often carry a sense of motion or direction toward a location; prepositions with the genitive case often carry a sense of motion or direction away from a location; and prepositions with the dative case often carry a sense of rest. This framework in no way implies that a Greek speaker or writer began by thinking of the basic sense of the preposition each time it was used. To the contrary, most usage was second nature to the native speaker, any connection between the two being long ago severed. But twentieth-century interpreters, who do not have native competence in the language, often find it useful to begin from a basic sense of the preposition. This provides a line of continuity among the various extensions of meaning. Many of these extensions are far removed from the basic sense, since their usage is based upon syntax and context. But this framework is designed to help bring more order to a potentially chaotic discussion by not multiplying categories unnecessarily. The translations attempt to capture the sense of each preposition, but too much weight should not be given to these at the expense of getting a feel for how the prepositions function to connect words or groups of words in particular contexts. All of the 18 classical 'proper' prepositions except ἀμφί are used as free-standing forms in the Greek of the NT.

4. *The Prepositions Discussed*[1]

4.1. ἀμφί *with the Accusative, Genitive and Dative Cases*

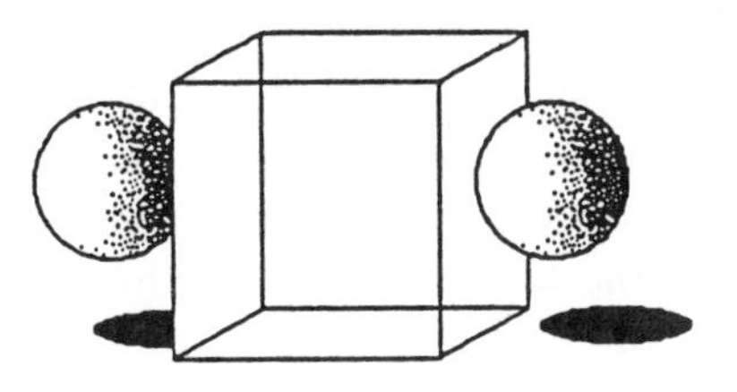

Figure 3. ἀμφί

The preposition ἀμφί does not occur independently in the NT or Hellenistic Greek as a whole, but only as a prefix to a verb. Its basic sense, as the diagram indicates (fig. 3), is 'on both sides'. This is illustrated in several examples of the prefixed form: e.g. Mk 1.16: ἀμφιβάλλω (I cast on both sides). The preposition is included here for the sake of completeness.

4.2. ἀνά *with the Accusative Case*[2]

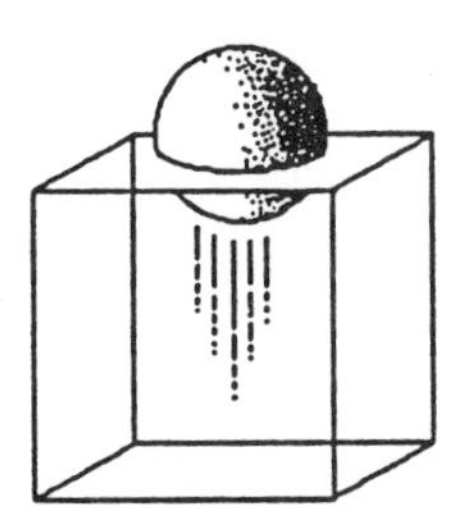

Figure 4. ἀνά

The preposition ἀνά, possibly related to the adverb ἄνω meaning 'up', as the diagram conveys (fig. 4), has a basic meaning of 'direction upward', probably with the sense of reaching a limit (here depicted as the top plane of the cube). There is one exception in the NT to ἀνά with the accusative case: Rev. 21.21: ἀνὰ εἷς (each one), where the

1. The prepositions are discussed in alphabetical order to ease in reference. Using Moulton's statistics (*Prolegomena*, p. 98), and using the frequency of ἐν as 1, for every preposition a ratio of frequency will be given for comparative purposes.

2. This is the most infrequently used preposition in the NT, with a ratio of .0045 to ἐν.

adverbial sense may still be present (up to one). In the NT, the sense of 'up' is most clearly seen in the use of ἀνά as a prefix to a verb: e.g. ἀνάγω (lead or bring up), although a distributive sense is also found in the prefixed instances (e.g. Mk 6.40; Lk. 10.1). The preposition ἀνά is an antonym of κατά (see under κατά, section 4.10 below), although several grammarians have noted that some of the applications are parallel. This may be because each is conveying the idea of direction upward or downward toward a limit. Use of this preposition is limited in the NT, being confined to approximately 13 instances (cf. Lk. 9.3 with a textual variant).

4.2.1. *Directional* (motion upward). This local use of the preposition appears in several formulaic phrases. But the fundamental sense of the preposition is clear.

Mt. 13.25: ἀνὰ μέσον (in the midst); cf. Mk 7.31.

4.2.2. *Distributive*. Although several grammarians note this as an exceptional usage, it is understandable in light of the sense of ἀνά as 'up to a limit'.

1 Cor. 14.27: ἀνὰ μέρος (one at a time).

4.3. ἀντί *with the Genitive Case*[1]

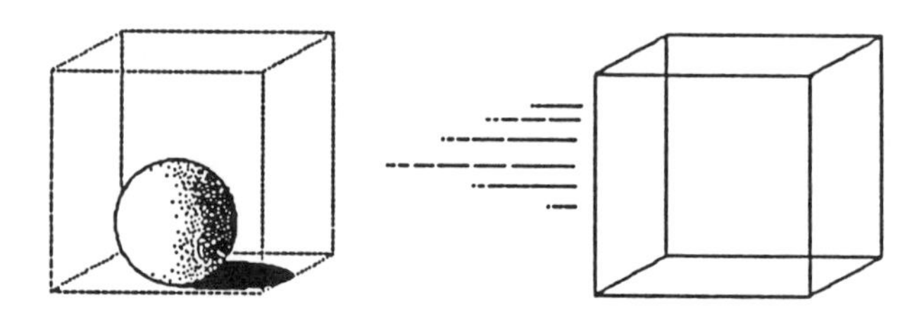

Figure 5. ἀντί

Although the basic sense of ἀντί is 'facing, against, opposite' (fig. 5), the most widely applied sense in the NT, and well-known in classical and other Hellenistic Greek, is substitutionary ('in place of'). This preposition occurs with the genitive case. Although not as controversial in its substitutionary sense as ὑπέρ (see ὑπέρ, section 4.17 below), there are several noteworthy passages where this preposition has

1. This is the second (only to ἀνά) most infrequently used preposition in the NT, with a ratio of .008 to ἐν.

added to the exegetical discussion. The substitutionary sense is maintained when the preposition is prefixed as well: e.g. Col. 1.24: ἀνταναπληρῶ τὰ ὑστερήματα τῶν θλίψεων τοῦ Χριστοῦ ἐν τῇ σαρκί μου ὑπὲρ τοῦ σώματος αὐτοῦ (I fill up [in place of] the lackings of the sufferings of Christ in my flesh on behalf of his body).

Mk 10.45: ὁ υἱὸς τοῦ ἀνθρώπου οὐκ ἦλθεν διακονηθῆναι ἀλλὰ διακονῆσαι καὶ δοῦναι τὴν ψυχὴν αὐτοῦ λύτρον ἀντὶ πολλῶν (the son of man did not come to be served but to serve and to give his soul a ransom in place of many). This is a well-known passage used to argue for the theological concept of substitutionary atonement, and Mark's only instance of ἀντί;[1] cf. also Mt. 20.28: λύτρον ἀντὶ πολλῶν (a ransom in place of many).

Jn 1.16: ἡμεῖς πάντες ἐλάβομεν καὶ χάριν ἀντὶ χάριτος (we all received even grace in place of grace). Instead of taking the preposition with most commentators as meaning 'in addition' (or 'upon', better rendered with ἐπί), the sense of replacement, possibly with reference to Gospel replacing law, is to be preferred.[2] This is the only instance of ἀντί in the Johannine writings.

1 Cor. 11.15: ἡ κόμη ἀντὶ περιβολαίου δέδοται [αὐτῇ] ([her] hair instead of a covering is given [to her]). The role of the female headcovering has been an item of dispute in some theological circles. This passage seems to indicate that the hair can serve as a substitute for it, but there are larger contextual difficulties.[3]

Heb. 12.2: Ἰησοῦν, ὃς ἀντὶ τῆς προκειμένης αὐτῷ χαρᾶς ὑπέμεινεν σταυρόν (Jesus, who instead of the joy lying before him endured a cross); cf. Heb. 12.16.

1. For a discussion of some of the issues, see V. Taylor, *The Gospel according to St Mark* (London: Macmillan, 1952), pp. 445-46.

2. For a survey of interpretations of this verse, see R.B. Edwards, 'χάριν ἀντὶ χάριτος (Jn 1.16): Grace and the Law in the Johannine Prologue', *JSNT* 32 (1988), pp. 3-15.

3. See G.D. Fee, *The First Epistle to the Corinthians* (Grand Rapids: Eerdmans, 1987), pp. 528-29, who adopts a sense of equivalence for ἀντί on the recommendation of BAGD (endorsed by Harris, 'Prepositions', p. 1179 as well). The evidence for this sense in the NT (Mt. 5.38; Rom. 12.17; 1 Thess. 5.15; 1 Pet. 3.9) is weak, the substitutionary sense proving satisfactory.

4.4. ἀπό *with the Genitive Case*[1]

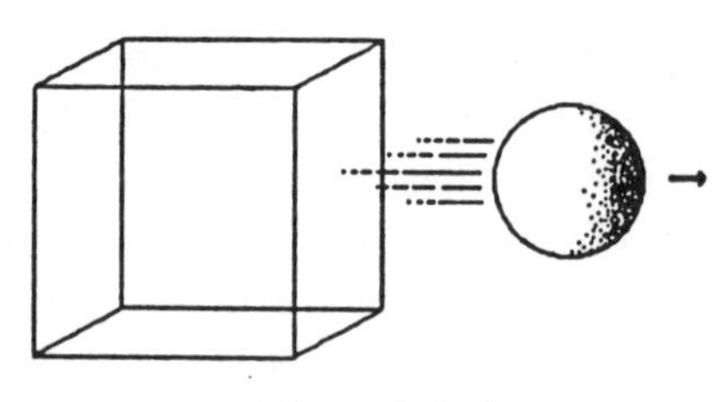

Figure 6. ἀπό

The prepositions ἀπό and ἐκ enjoy a great deal of semantic overlap (see under ἐκ, section 4.7 below). Consequently many of the same categories may be used. This is not to say that the two are complete synonyms, but their common use with the genitive case must play a significant role in their semantic overlap. Although later ἀπό seems to have forced out ἐκ, in Hellenistic Greek including the Greek of the NT a distinction is still applicable. One way to think of it is that ἐκ is more restricted, perhaps best translated in its basic sense as 'out of', as opposed to ἀπό meaning 'from' or 'away from' in a more general sense, implying separation (fig. 6). The preposition ἀπό is also an antonym of the prepositions πρός and ἐπί (accusative), in the same way that ἐκ is an antonym of εἰς.

A significant exception to the regular pattern of ἀπό with the genitive case is Rev. 1.4: χάρις ὑμῖν καὶ εἰρήνη ἀπὸ ὁ ὢν καὶ ὁ ἦν καὶ ὁ ἐρχόμενος (grace to you and peace from the one who is and who was and who is coming), where ἀπό with the nominative case is found, when the author (cf. vv. 4b and 5) clearly knows that ἀπό is used with the genitive. Note also the grammatically impossible ὁ ἦν ('the was'). Perhaps the entire phrase, rather than being solecistic, reflects a conscious use of poetic license: cf. 'from the Is, the Was and the Coming One'.

4.4.1. *Locative* (movement away from). This usage encompasses a number of senses, sometimes given separate categories by other grammarians (e.g. ablative). For example, this usage entails actual movement as well as movement extended to its completion, along with a partitive sense.

Mt. 5.29: ἔξελε αὐτὸν καὶ βάλε ἀπὸ σοῦ (take it out and cast [it]

1. This preposition is fairly frequent in the NT, with a ratio of .24 to ἐν.

away from you), where ἀπό is contrasted with ἐκ; Lk. 4.35: ἔξελθε ἀπ' αὐτοῦ (come out from him), probably a formula in exorcism.[1]

2 Thess. 1.9: οἵτινες δίκην τίσουσιν ὄλεθρον αἰώνιον ἀπὸ προσώπου τοῦ κυρίου καὶ ἀπὸ τῆς δόξης τῆς ἰσχύος αὐτοῦ (who will pay the penalty, an eternal destruction away from the face of the Lord and away from the glory of his strength).

Lk. 6.13: ἐκλεξάμενος ἀπ' αὐτῶν δώδεκα (electing from them twelve), a partitive use.

Lk. 12.4: μὴ φοβηθῆτε ἀπὸ τῶν ἀποκτεινόντων τὸ σῶμα (do not have fear from those who kill the body). Chamberlain considers this a Hebraism.[2]

4.4.2. *Temporal* (time from which). This usage specifies a time from which some event has occurred.

Lk. 16.16: ἀπὸ τότε ἡ βασιλεία τοῦ θεοῦ εὐαγγελίζεται (from then the kingdom of God is proclaimed), with an adverb functioning as object of the preposition.

Jn 13.19: ἀπ' ἄρτι λέγω ὑμῖν (from now I say to you).

Heb. 11.15: ἀφ' ἧς ἐξέβησαν (when they went out), where the set phrase ἀφ' ἧς may be used temporally, although the relative pronoun may be understood as referring back to τῆς γῆς in v. 13.

4.4.3. *Instrumental* (causal, agentive). Like several of the other prepositions, ἀπό may be used instrumentally. The connection with its fundamental meaning is probably related to the idea that moving away from some place explains the means by which this movement is effected.

Lk. 7.35: ἐδικαιώθη ἡ σοφία ἀπὸ πάντων τῶν τέκνων αὐτῆς (wisdom is justified by all her children), or 'gets justification from all her children'.

Lk. 24.41: ἔτι...ἀπιστούντων αὐτῶν ἀπὸ τῆς χαρᾶς (while they still were not believing because of joy).

Jas 1.13: ἀπὸ θεοῦ πειράζομαι (I am tempted by God), with the idea that 'temptation comes from God'.

1. See C.K. Barrett, *The NT Background: Selected Documents* (San Francisco: Harper and Row, rev. edn, 1989), p. 36, citing the Paris Magical Papyrus line 3013.

2. Chamberlain, *Exegetical Grammar*, p. 117.

4.5. διά *with the Genitive and Accusative Cases*[1]

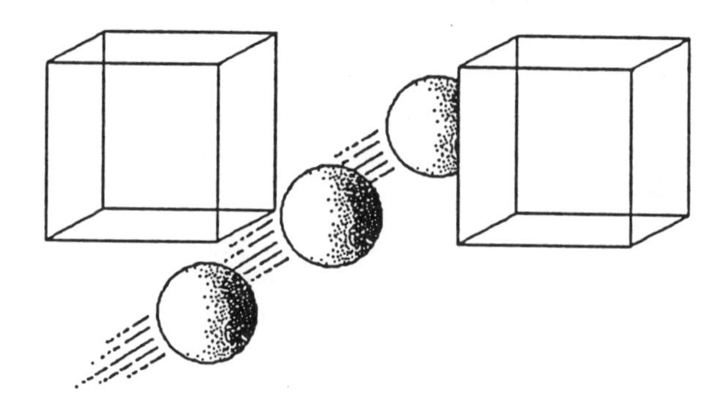

Figure 7. διά

The preposition διά may be related to the word δύο, 'two', and perhaps had the original meaning of 'between' (fig. 7). The sense captured by the translation 'through' perhaps originated in the idea of moving between two objects, or passing through between them. The causal sense seems to have been a further metaphorical extension, in that the conveyance through implies the cause of passing through, or the means by which passage is obtained. The preposition occurs with the genitive and accusative cases.

4.5.1. *Locative* (through) (genitive). This local sense of διά with the genitive is frequent.

Mk 9.30: παρεπορεύοντο διὰ τῆς Γαλιλαίας (they passed through Galilee); Jn 4.4: διέρχεσθαι διὰ τῆς Samare¤aw (to pass through Samaria), where the preposition is also prefixed to the verb.

Rom. 15.28: ἀπελεύσομαι δι' ὑμῶν εἰς Σπανίαν (I will go through you into Spain), where the sense of passing through the midst is clear.

2 Pet. 3.5: γῆ ἐξ ὕδατος καὶ δι' ὕδατος συνεστῶσα τῷ τοῦ θεοῦ λόγῳ (earth from water and through water, held together by the word of God). Moule suggests that the use of διά may be of waters above and below the earth.[2] The sense of extension through the seas to form

1. This preposition is fairly frequent in the NT, with a ratio of .24 to ἐν.
2. Moule, *Idiom Book*, p. 55.

dry land, however, is a more likely understanding. Cf. Heb. 11.29: διὰ ξηρᾶς γῆς (through dry land).

4.5.2. *Temporal* (genitive). Just as διά may be used of physical passing through, it may be used of temporal passage as well.

Lk. 5.5: δι' ὅλης νυκτὸς κοπιάσαντες (working through the entire night).

Acts 1.3: δι' ἡμερῶν τεσσεράκοντα (through forty days).

Acts 16.9: ὅραμα διὰ [τῆς] νυκτὸς τῷ Παύλῳ ὤφθη (visions were seen by Paul through [the] night).

Mt. 26.61: δύναμαι καταλῦσαι τὸν ναὸν τοῦ θεοῦ καὶ διὰ τριῶν ἡμερῶν οἰκοδομῆσαι (I am able to destroy the temple of God and through [the length of] three days to build [it]). 'Through' makes better interpretative sense of the preposition than 'after', if it is remembered that the idea of working through the period of time seems to be in mind.

4.5.3. *Instrumental* (secondary or intermediate agency or means) (genitive). Instrumental use of διά is similar to instrumental use of the dative (often with ἐν), and even causal use of διά with the accusative; that is, some person or thing serves as the device or means by which some action is performed.

Mt. 1.22: πληρωθῇ τὸ ῥηθὲν ὑπὸ κυρίου διὰ τοῦ προφήτου (the thing spoken by the Lord through the prophet might be fulfilled), where primary agency with ὑπό is also stated; Acts 1.2: ἐντειλάμενος τοῖς ἀποστόλοις διὰ πνεύματος ἁγίου (commanded the apostles through the Holy Spirit), with Jesus understood as primary agent.

Lk. 8.4: εἶπεν διὰ παραβολῆς (he spoke through a parable); Acts 15.32: διὰ λόγου πολλοῦ παρεκάλεσαν τοὺς ἀδελφούς (through many a word they comforted the brothers).

Rom. 2.27: τὸν διὰ γράμματος καὶ περιτομῆς παραβάτην νόμου (the transgressor of the law through letter and circumcision), where the prepositional phrase states the means.

Rom. 5.12: ὥσπερ δι' ἑνὸς ἀνθρώπου ἡ ἁμαρτία εἰς τόν κόσμον εἰσῆλθεν καὶ διὰ τῆς ἁμαρτίας ὁ θάνατος (as through one man sin entered into the world and through σιν, death); Col. 1.22: ἀποκατήλλαξεν ἐν τῷ σώματι τῆς σαρκὸς αὐτοῦ διὰ τοῦ θανάτου (he reconciled in the body of his flesh through death).

Eph. 2.8: τῇ...χάριτί ἐστε σεσῳσμένοι διὰ πίστεως (by...grace you are saved through faith); Rom. 8.25: δι' ὑπομονῆς (through perseverance).

1 Thess. 4.14: ὁ θεὸς τοὺς κοιμηθέντας διὰ τοῦ Ἰησοῦ ἄξει σὺν αὐτῷ (God will lead with him those sleeping through Jesus).

1 Tim. 2.15: σωθήσεται...διὰ τῆς τεκνογονίας (she will be saved ...through childbirth). This verse has aroused considerable discussion. The question is whether the author means that childbirth in some way provides a means of salvation for the woman (instrumental), or that the woman is brought safely through childbirth (locative).

1 Pet. 3.20: διεσώθησαν δι' ὕδατος (they were saved through water), an example of secondary agency, especially in light of v. 21, with δι' ἀναστάσεως (through resurrection).[1]

Some of these uses take on a nearly adverbial sense in translation, although it is clear that this meaning is derived from the instrumental sense.

Heb. 13.22: διὰ βραχέων ἐπέστειλα ὑμῖν, where the phrase means 'in a few words, I have written to you' (lit. through short things).

4.5.4. *Causal* (accusative). The causal use of the preposition διά is related to its instrumental sense, although an emphasis on the direct cause of the action is often conveyed.

Mt. 27.18: διὰ φθόνον παρέδωκαν αὐτόν (because of envy they betrayed him); Acts 28.2: διὰ τὸν ὑετὸν τὸν ἐφεστῶτα καὶ διὰ τὸ ψῦχος (because of the impending rain and because of the cold).

Mk 6.26: ὁ βασιλεὺς διὰ τοὺς ὅρκους καὶ τοὺς ἀνακειμένους οὐκ ἠθέλησεν ἀθετῆσαι αὐτήν (the king, because of the oaths and those sitting around, did not want to deny her).

Rom. 3.25: προέθετο ὁ θεὸς ἱλαστήριον διὰ [τῆς] πίστεως ἐν τῷ αὐτοῦ αἵματι εἰς ἔνδειξιν τῆς δικαιοσύνης αὐτοῦ διὰ τὴν πάρεσιν τῶν προγεγονότων ἁμαρτημάτων (God put forward a propitiation through faith in his blood for a showing of his righteousness because of the passing over of previous sins), with the instrumental use of the preposition with the genitive as well.

Rom. 4.25: ὃς παρεδόθη διὰ τὰ παραπτώματα ἡμῶν καὶ ἠγέρθη διὰ τὴν δικαίωσιν ἡμῶν (who was betrayed because of our transgressions and raised because of our righteousness). Many commentators

1. Cf. D. Cook, '1 Pet. 3.20: An Unnecessary Problem', *JTS* NS 31 (1980), pp. 75-76.

suggest that the two uses of διά must be taken in different senses,[1] usually causal and final,[2] or retrospective and prospective ('with a view to, for the sake of').[3] Barrett sees both as prospective.[4] Many of these interpretations appear to rely too much on establishing a temporal progression along theological lines, rather than relying upon a grammatical sense.

4.6. εἰς *with the Accusative Case*[5]

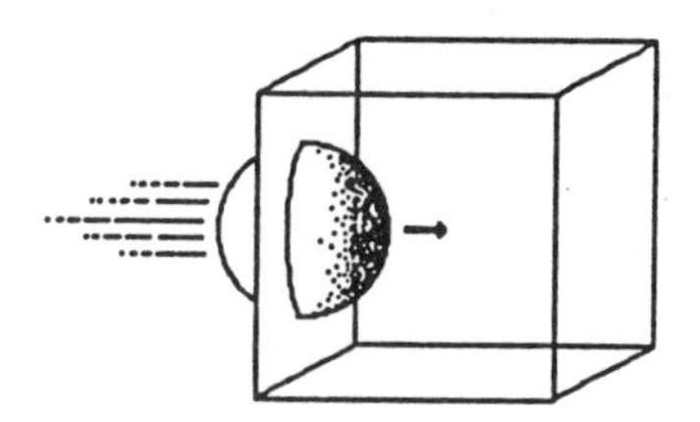

Figure 8. εἰς

The preposition efiw, which occurs only with the accusative case, may have been formally derived from the preposition ἐν, through the process of adding a final *sigma* (ἐνς), the *nu* dropping out, and compensatory lengthening of the vowel from ε to ει (not found in all dialects of Greek, however). This historical reconstruction is not as important as two other observations. First, because of the etymological relation, many grammarians argue that there is frequent confusion in the NT between εἰς and ἐν, as if they conveyed identical meanings because they had *similar* meanings. Secondly, as the diagram illustrates (fig. 8), εἰς in its basic meaning is concerned with the movement of the sphere toward and into the cube, as if this were the action that resulted in the condition of ἐν. Rather than seeing the two as synonymous, however, the historical and contextual evidence indicates that they overlap in meaning, while remaining distinct. Usage in the NT confirms this.

1. See Harris, 'Prepositions', p. 1184.
2. Cranfield, *Romans*, I, p. 252; Dunn, *Romans 1–8*, p. 225.
3. Sanday and Headlam, *Romans*, p. 116; Moule, *Idiom Book*, p. 55.
4. C.K. Barrett, *A Commentary on the Epistle to the Romans* (London: A. & C. Black, 1957), p. 100.
5. This preposition is the second most frequent in the NT, with a ratio of .64 to ἐν.

4.6.1. *Directional* (movement toward). The fundamental idea of 'movement toward' using εἰς may be applied to physical motion, including the passage of time.

Mt. 2.11: ἐλθόντες εἰς τὴν οἰκίαν (coming into the house).

Mt. 26.10: ἔργον γὰρ καλὸν ἠργάσατο εἰς ἐμέ (for she performed a good work toward me).

Rom. 15.16: λειτουργὸν Χριστοῦ 'Ιησοῦ εἰς τὰ ἔθνη (a minister of Christ Jesus toward the nations), with the direction extending not simply to a point but a people: 'as far as the nations'.

2 Tim. 1.12: μου φυλάξαι εἰς ἐκείνην τὴν ἡμέραν (to guard me until that day), possibly an example of extensive use (see section 4.6.2 below).

4.6.2. *Extensive*. A primary application of the meaning of the preposition εἰς is with reference to a figurative goal or state. This is a very frequent use of the preposition, encompassing a variety of contextual nuances.

Mt. 6.13: μὴ εἰσενέγκῃς ἡμᾶς εἰς πειρασμόν (don't lead us toward temptation).

Rom. 1.17: δικαιοσύνη γὰρ θεοῦ...ἀποκαλύπτεται ἐκ πίστεως εἰς πίστιν (for righteousness of God...is revealed from faith into faith), where a directional though not literal sense is intended.[1]

Rom. 6.3: ὅσοι ἐβαπτίσθημεν εἰς Χριστὸν'Ιησοῦν εἰς τὸν θάνατον αὐτοῦ ἐβαπτίσθημεν (as many of us as were baptized into Christ Jesus were baptized into his death).

4.6.3. *Purpose or resultive* (final/telic, ecbatic/consecutive). This metaphorical use of the preposition εἰς captures the relation between motion and intention. This preposition, which can be used to refer to a directed action, can also describe the purpose or result of that action.[2]

Rom. 5.18: ὡς δι' ἑνὸς παραπτώματος...εἰς κατάκριμα (as

1. The several various interpretations of the prepositional phrases and their referents are discussed by Cranfield, *Romans*, I, p. 99.

2. A separate category of causal εἰς is probably to be rejected. It was proposed by J.R. Mantey, 'The Causal Use of *Eis* in the NT', *JBL* 70 (1951), pp. 45-48; 'On Causal *Eis* Again', *JBL* 70 (1951), pp. 309-11; and responded to by R. Marcus, *JBL* 70 (1951), pp. 129-30; 71 (1952), pp. 43-44. It is tempting for some theologically problematic passages: see F.H. Agnew, '1 Pet. 1.2—An Alternative Translation', *CBQ* 45 (1983), pp. 68-73.

through one man's transgression...for the purpose [or with the result] of condemnation), an interpretation requiring theological analysis.

Col. 3.10: ἐνδυσάμενοι τὸν νέον...εἰς ἐπίγνωσιν (putting on the new [person]...for the purpose of knowledge); Rom. 12.3: φρονεῖν εἰς τὸ σωφρονεῖν (to set one's mind toward sound thinking).

Rom. 10.1: ἡ μὲν εὐδοκία...καὶ ἡ δέησις πρὸς τὸν θεὸν ὑπὲρ αὐτῶν εἰς σωτηρίαν (my desire...and prayer to God for them [is] for salvation), probably seen as result ('to result in salvation').

4.6.4. εἰς *synonymous with* ἐν. Several grammarians contend that εἰς and ἐν are used synonymously in NT as well as Hellenistic Greek.[1] The significant overlap in their meanings does not necessarily mean confusion or complete lack of distinction in their uses, however.

Mk 1.9: ἐβαπτίσθη εἰς τὸν Ἰορδάνην ὑπὸ Ἰωάννου (he was baptized into the Jordan by John), an example frequently cited as exemplifying this confusion.[2] But does this make the best sense of the passage? The preposition εἰς, with its wide range of uses, can indicate a sense of direction, including the resting place of a movement.[3] This makes good sense of the passage in Mark, where in v. 10 the author goes on to say that Jesus came up out of the water (ἀναβαίνων ἐκ τοῦ ὕδατος).

Jn 1.18: μονογενὴς θεὸς ὁ ὢν εἰς τὸν κόλπον τοῦ πατρός (only begotten God who is directed toward the bosom of the father), a highly significant theological statement of relation between the Father and the Son (cf. Jn 13.23: ἐν τῷ κόλπῳ τοῦ Ἰησοῦ [located in the bosom of Jesus]).[4]

Mk 13.16: ὁ εἰς τὸν ἀγρὸν μὴ ἐπιστρεψάτω...ἆραι τὸ ἱμάτιον αὐτοῦ (don't let the one in the field return...to take his garment), where Mt. 24.18, a parallel passage, has ἐν. Or does Mark mean 'the one who has gone into his field'?[5]

1. E.g. Turner, *Syntax*, p. 254.

2. See C.E.B. Cranfield, *The Gospel according to St Mark* (Cambridge: Cambridge University Press, 1977), p. 52, who does not substantiate his opinion.

3. See Moule, *Idiom Book*, p. 68, who cites Mk 1.9 as a use of the preposition εἰς combining motion and rest.

4. See Harris, 'Prepositions', pp. 1185-86, for a survey of the issues.

5. See Green, *Handbook*, p. 267.

4.7. ἐκ *with the Genitive Case*[1]

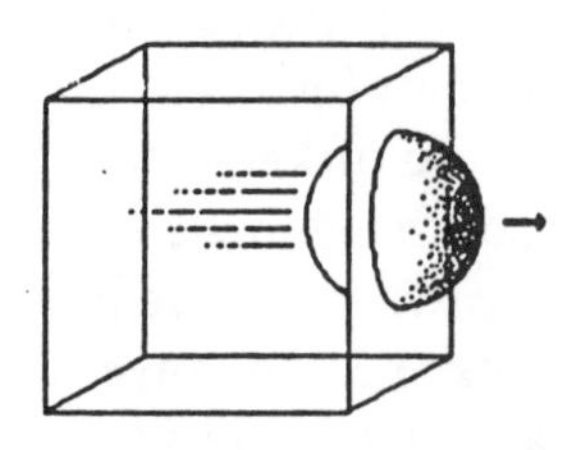

Figure 9. ἐκ

The preposition ἐκ, seen in the diagram above (fig. 9), occurs with the genitive case alone, and enjoys relationships especially with ἀπό, with which it is a partial synonym, and efiw, with which it is an antonym. The relationship with ἀπό has been described in various ways. One way to think of it is that ἐκ is more restricted, perhaps best translated in its basic sense as 'out of', as opposed to ἀπό meaning 'from' or 'away from' in a more general sense. Cf. Mk 1.35: ἐξῆλθεν καὶ ἀπῆλθεν εἰς ἔρημον τόπον (he went out and away into a deserted place), which may well indicate the distinction between the two prepositions. In fact, it well illustrates the relation among all three prepositions.[2] Moule is unnecessarily troubled over hard and fast distinctions between ἐκ and ἀπό because he neglects to see their clear overlap (e.g. Lk. 5.8: ἔξελθε ἀπ' ἐμοῦ [come out from me]).[3] There is also semantic overlap with the preposition ἐν, in the sense that ἐν may be used of the realm out of which (ἐκ) something originates.

4.7.1. *Locative* (movement out of). This usage illustrates the basic sense of the preposition, the one of which others are metaphorical extensions. This sense has several applications, sometimes labeled source, origin or partitive senses. All have the idea of 'movement out of'.

Mt. 3.17: φωνὴ ἐκ τῶν οὐρανῶν (a voice out of the heavens); Jn 7.40: ἐκ τοῦ ὄχλου (out of the crowd); Acts 8.39: ἀνέβησαν ἐκ τοῦ ὕδατος (they came up out of the water); cf. Mt. 3.16 with ἀπό.

Mk 7.21: ἐκ τῆς καρδίας τῶν ἀνθρώπων οἱ διαλογισμοὶ οἱ κακοὶ

1. This is the third most frequent preposition in the NT, with a ratio of .34 to ἐν.
2. Robertson, *Grammar*, pp. 577-78.
3. Moule, *Idiom Book*, p. 72.

ἐκπορεύονται (out of the heart of human beings evil disputes come out), with the preposition used twice with the same sense.

Jn 17.14: οὐκ εἰσὶν ἐκ τοῦ κόσμου καθὼς ἐγὼ οὐκ εἰμὶ ἐκ τοῦ κόσμου (they are not from the world as I am not from the world), a sense of origin.

2 Cor. 5.18: τὰ...πάντα ἐκ τοῦ θεοῦ τοῦ καταλλάξαντος ἡμᾶς (all things from the God who reconciles us), a sense of source.

Mt. 20.21, 23: εἷς ἐκ δεξιῶν σου καὶ εἷς ἐξ εὐωνύμων σου...τὸ δὲ καθίσαι ἐκ δεξιῶν μου καὶ ἐξ εὐωνύμων οὐκ ἔστιν ἐμὸν δοῦναι (one on your right and one on your left...to sit on my right and on the left is not mine to give). As Dana and Mantey say,[1] here the preposition should be translated 'on' (rather than 'from'). But this use, in which the idea is that one comes from the right hand and the other from the left, is understandably locative, no matter how the English is rendered.

1 Cor. 9.19: ἐλεύθερος...ὢν ἐκ πάντων (being free from all), a partitive sense.

4.7.2. *Temporal* (time from which). One of the specific applications of physical or spatial movement is temporal. The preposition ἐκ may be used of a restricted time from which someone or something has moved.

Mk 9.21: ἐκ παιδιόθεν (from youth), with a redundant affix (-θεν) on the adverb.

Jn 9.32: ἐκ τοῦ αἰῶνος οὐκ ἠκούσθη (from eternity it was not heard), in comparison to extensive use of εἰς with αἰῶνον.

Rom. 1.4: τοῦ ὁρισθέντος υἱοῦ θεοῦ ἐν δυνάμει κατὰ πνεῦμα ἁγιωσύνης ἐξ ἀναστάσεως νεκρῶν (designated Son of God in power according to the Spirit of Holiness from the time of the resurrection of the dead). The use may be instrumental (by the resurrection).[2]

4.7.3. *Instrumental* (causal, agentive). The instrumental use of ἐκ overlaps with the locative use of ἐκ to indicate origin or source. If something is the origin or source of something, it may often be possible to say that it is the instrument, cause or agent by which something comes about.

Mt. 27.7: ἠγόρασαν ἐξ αὐτῶν τὸν ἀγρόν (with them they bought

1. Dana and Mantey, *Manual Grammar*, p. 102.
2. See Cranfield, *Romans*, I, p. 62.

the field), with reference to Judas's returned pieces of silver.

2 Cor. 9.7: ἕκαστος καθὼς προῄρηται τῇ καρδίᾳ, μὴ ἐκ λύπης ἢ ἐξ ἀνάγκης (as each one decided in his heart, not out of [an attitude of] reluctance or out of obligation).

Rom. 5.1: δικαιωθέντες...ἐκ πίστεως (being justified...by faith), a frequent pattern of Pauline usage.

4.8. ἐν *with the Dative Case*[1]

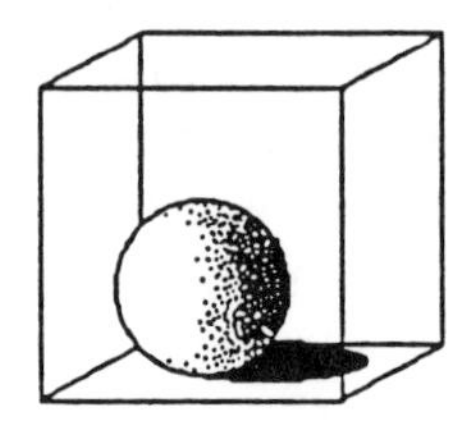

Figure 10. ἐν

The preposition ἐν is a very important preposition in NT Greek, not least because it seems to have been widely used to reinforce the function of the dative case, the only case with which it occurs. Its basic meaning is 'in' or 'in the realm of', hence the diagram indicates the sphere as statically located within the cube (fig. 10). There are many related senses which this preposition may take depending upon its use in a particular context, but the following seem to be the major or at least the more important ones.

4.8.1. *Locative*. This and the next usage are by far the most common and most closely related to the basic sense of the preposition ἐν. The locative use conveys the sense of location 'in', with location defined broadly.

Mt. 20.3: εἶδεν ἄλλους ἑστῶτας ἐν τῇ ἀγορᾷ (he saw others standing in the market); Mt. 2.5: ἐν Βηθλέεμ τῆς Ἰουδαίας (in Bethlehem of Judea).

Acts 9.17: Ἰησοῦς ὁ ὀφθείς σοι ἐν τῇ ὁδῷ (Jesus who was seen by you in the road), where English would probably use 'on' for physical location.

1 Cor. 15.28: ᾖ ὁ θεὸς [τὰ] πάντα ἐν πᾶσιν (God might be all

1. This preposition is the most frequent in the NT.

things in all things), with extension of location beyond a single place; Col. 3.11: [τὰ] πάντα καὶ ἐν πᾶσιν (all [races] and in all [races]), said of Christ.

4.8.2. *Distributional.* A question is sometimes raised in some interpreters minds regarding when 'within' or 'among' is called for in translation of ἐν (note that the examples usually cited involve plural objects of the preposition). But this is more of a problem with how the English rendering must be made than a problem in Greek, since the place of location in Greek does not need to be confined to a particular point.

Mk 2.6, 8: διαλογιζόμενοι ἐν ταῖς καρδίαις αὐτῶν... διαλογίζονται ἐν ἑαυτοῖς (reasoning in their hearts...they are reasoning among themselves), where the verse goes on to say τί ταῦτα διαλογίζεσθε ἐν ταῖς καρδίαις ὑμῶν; (why are you thinking [= reasoning] these things in your hearts?). These examples indicate that the locative sense is still at the center of the preposition's use.

Lk. 22.24: ἐγένετο...φιλονεικία ἐν αὐτοῖς (a dispute came about among them), where the English 'among' means that, 'within' them as a group, a dispute arose.

Col. 3.16: ὁ λόγος τοῦ Χριστοῦ ἐνοικείτω ἐν ὑμῖν πλουσίως (let the word of Christ dwell in/among you richly), an ambiguous example, as Moule notes.[1] This is more of a problem of English translation, which necessitates a choice between 'in' and 'among'.

4.8.3. *Spherical.* Something or someone may be located within the sphere of influence, control or domain of another or larger group ('in'), in the same way that one object or person may be within the confines of another (see section 4.8.6 below on ἐν Χριστῷ). The spherical use is therefore a direct extension of the locative sense.

Jn 3.35: πάντα δέδωκεν ἐν τῇ χειρὶ αὐτοῦ (he has placed all things in his hand).

1 Cor. 16.13, 14: στήκετε ἐν τῇ πίστει...πάντα ὑμῶν ἐν ἀγάπῃ γινέσθω (stand in the faith...let all your [actions] come about in love).

Eph. 2.15: τὸν νόμον τῶν ἐντολῶν ἐν δόγμασιν καταργήσας (nullifying the law of commandments in [the sphere of its] ordinances). An instrumental sense ('by') is also possible.

1. Moule, *Idiom Book*, p. 75.

4.8.4. *Temporal.* Just as location in a place may be specified with the preposition ἐν, so specification of location in time may also be indicated.

Jn 1.1: ἐν ἀρχῇ ἦν ὁ λόγος (in the beginning was the word), probably the most well-known use of this preposition in the NT where temporal location is designated.

Jn 6.44: κἀγὼ ἀναστήσω αὐτὸν ἐν τῇ ἐσχάτῃ ἡμέρᾳ (and I will raise him up in [= on] the last day). There is a textual variant for omission of ἐν to harmonize it with Jn 6.54, without the preposition; in v. 54 there is a very weak textual variant for its inclusion.

Acts 1.15: ἐν ταῖς ἡμέραις ταύταις ἀναστὰς Πέτρος ἐν μέσῳ τῶν ἀδελφῶν εἶπεν...(in these days, Peter, standing in the midst of the brothers, said...), where locative ἐν is also used.

4.8.5. *Instrumental* (manner, accompaniment, cause). The label 'instrumental' is given to a range of metaphorical extensions of the locative sense of ἐν. Temporal location can and often does imply the idea of accompaniment, control, agency, cause and even means (price).

Rev. 7.14: ἔπλυναν τὰς στολὰς αὐτῶν καὶ ἐλεύκαναν αὐτὰς ἐν τῷ αἵματι τοῦ ἀρνίου (they washed their robes and whitened them in/with/by the blood of the lamb), illustrating a logical relationship. Being placed in the blood makes the blood the instrument by which the whitening takes place. Rom. 5.9: δικαιωθέντες...ἐν τῷ αἵματι αὐτοῦ (being justified...by his blood); Rev. 1.5: ἐν τῷ αἵματι αὐτοῦ (by his blood), with reference to Christ's blood.

1 Cor. 4.21: ἐν ῥάβδῳ ἔλθω πρὸς ὑμᾶς (with a rod I might come to you), where the idea is that the instrument of the power with which Paul comes is the rod; Rev. 6.8: ἀποκτεῖναι ἐν ῥομφαίᾳ καὶ ἐν λιμῷ καὶ ἐν θανάτῳ (to kill by sword and by famine and by death [= plague]), followed by ὑπό + genitive; Lk. 22.49: πατάξομεν ἐν μαχαίρῃ; (shall we strike with a sword?).

Acts 11.16: Ἰωάννης μὲν ἐβάπτισεν ὕδατι, ὑμεῖς δὲ βαπτισθήσεσθε ἐν πνεύματι ἁγίῳ (John baptized in water, but you will be baptized with the Holy Spirit), where the instrumental use is shown to be an extension of the locative sense, illustrated by the dative without the preposition.

Mt. 13.3: ἐλάλησεν αὐτοῖς πολλὰ ἐν παραβολαῖς (he spoke to them many things in parables), describing the means of communication.

Acts 7.29: ἔφυγεν...Μωϋσῆς ἐν τῷ λόγῳ τούτῳ (Moses fled under the influence of this word), where the agentive or causal force of the word is illustrated.

4.8.6. ἐν Χριστῷ.[1] Most of the uses of the preposition ἐν which the interpreter will encounter should fit comfortably within the categories suggested above. One use, however, cannot avoid being mentioned, and that is with the phrase ἐν Χριστῷ. It is especially important in Paul's writings, although the Johannine writings use it as well. Some have interpreted it as a physical locative metaphor for some sort of corporate mystical union between the believer and Christ.[2] Another explanation, however, and one which appears to make better sense of Paul's language, is a spherical use, according to which it is said that one is in the sphere of Christ's control. A significant example is 1 Cor. 15.22: ὥσπερ γὰρ ἐν τῷ 'Αδὰμ πάντες ἀποθνῄσκουσιν, οὕτως καὶ ἐν τῷ Χριστῷ πάντες ζῳοποιηθήσονται (for as in Adam all die, so also in Christ all will be made alive). Those who take the preposition §n in a materialist sense here will see evidence from this verse for the realist view of original sin, in which humans in some way physically pre-existed in Adam. But the spherical sense appears more likely, according to which it is said that humans belong to particular realms, the one controlled by Adam and his actions and the one controlled by Christ and his.[3] This view then makes sense of such usage as Gal. 1.22: ἤμην...ἀγνοούμενος τῷ προσώπῳ ταῖς ἐκκλησίαις τῆς 'Ιουδαίας ταῖς ἐν Χριστῷ (I was...unknown by face to the churches in Christ of Judea).

1. See A.J.M. Wedderburn, 'Some Observations on Paul's Use of the Phrases "in Christ" and "with Christ"', *JSNT* 25 (1985), pp. 83-97, for a survey of research; and Harris, 'Prepositions', p. 1192, for various categories.

2. See C.F.D. Moule, *The Phenomenon of the NT* (London: SCM Press, 1967), pp. 21-42; cf. S.E. Porter, 'Two Myths: Corporate Personality and Language/Mentality Determinism', *SJT* 43 (1990), pp. 289-307.

3. See S.E. Porter, 'The Pauline Concept of Original Sin in Light of Rabbinic Background', *TynBul* 41.1 (1990), esp. pp. 13-18.

4.9. ἐπί *with the Accusative, Genitive and Dative Cases*[1]

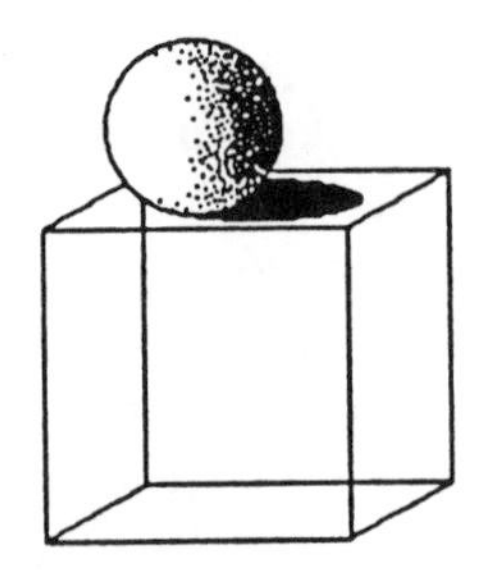

Figure 11. ἐπί

The preposition ἐπί, as the diagram illustrates (fig. 11), has a basic sense of 'location upon', perhaps implying actual resting upon (and not simply position over as with ὑπέρ, to which it is semantically related). A notable feature of this preposition is that, even though its fundamental meaning comes through fairly clearly in the vast majority of its uses, ἐπί occurs with all three oblique cases. This is more understandable when the function of the preposition is seen in terms of aiding the individual cases to be more precise in their expression.

4.9.1. *Directional* (movement upon or onto) (accusative). ἐπί with the accusative is often used in terms of movement, but there are extensions into temporal and figurative senses.

Mt. 26.55: ὡς ἐπὶ λῃστὴν ἐξήλθατε; (as upon a thief have you come out?); Lk. 14.31: ἐπ' αὐτόν (upon him).

Mk 16.2: ἔρχονται ἐπὶ τὸ μνημεῖον (they came to the tomb).

Rom. 4.24: τοῖς πιστεύουσιν ἐπὶ τὸν ἐγείραντα 'Ιησοῦν (to those who believe upon the one who raised Jesus); cf. Mt. 27.42; Acts 9.42; 11.17; 16.31; 22.19, all with similar phrasing; 1 Pet. 1.13: ἐλπίσατε ἐπὶ τὴν φερομένην ὑμῖν χάριν (hope upon the grace brought to you).

Mt. 3.7: ἐρχομένους ἐπὶ τὸ βάπτισμα αὐτοῦ ([Pharisees and Sadducees] coming to his baptism). Is there a sense of purpose here, in which location gives way to intention?

1. This preposition is used fairly often in the NT, only behind ἐν, εἰς and ἐκ, with a ratio of .32 to ἐν.

Mt. 15.32: σπλαγχνίζομαι ἐπὶ τὸν ὄχλον (I have compassion on the crowd).

Mt. 6.27: προσθεῖναι ἐπὶ τὴν ἡλικίαν αὐτοῦ πῆχυν ἕνα (to add one length onto his age), with the sense of addition.

Acts 16.18: τοῦτο δὲ ἐποίει ἐπὶ πολλὰς ἡμέρας (and she was doing this for many days). A temporal extent is implied, although, as Moule states, movement may still be the underlying idea.[1]

4.9.2. *Positional* (genitive). Physical position is still its basic sense, but ἐπί with the genitive can be figuratively extended to include temporal reference, among other uses.

Mt. 9.2: παραλυτικὸν ἐπὶ κλίνης βεβλημένον (a paralytic lying upon a bed); Mk 2.10: ἐπὶ τῆς γῆς (upon the earth).

Rom. 9.5: ὁ ὢν ἐπὶ πάντων θεός (the God who is over all), with a figurative extension of the positional sense.

Jn 21.1: ἐφανέρωσεν ἑαυτὸν πάλιν ὁ Ἰησοῦς τοῖς μαθηταῖς ἐπὶ τῆς θαλάσσης τῆς Τιβεριάδος (Jesus revealed himself again to the disciples on [the shore of] the sea of Tiberius). Cf. Mt. 21.19: ἰδὼν συκῆν μίαν ἐπὶ τῆς ὁδοῦ (seeing one fig tree on, i.e. alongside, the road); Mt. 14.26: ἰδόντες αὐτὸν ἐπὶ τῆς θαλάσσης (seeing him upon the sea), where Jesus is most likely depicted as walking upon the water.

Lk. 4.25: ἐπ' ἀληθείας...λέγω ὑμῖν (on [the basis of] the truth...I speak to you), with a figurative use in which truth is the basis (location upon).

4.9.3. *Locative* (dative). The translation that is often used with ἐπί and the dative is 'at'; this may include a variety of more and less literal senses.

Jn 4.6: ἐκαθέζετο...ἐπὶ τῇ πηγῇ (he was sitting...at the well).

Acts 5.9: οἱ πόδες τῶν θαψάντων τὸν ἄνδρα σου ἐπὶ τῇ θύρᾳ (the feet of the ones who buried your husband [are] at the door).

Lk. 4.22: ἐθαύμαζον ἐπὶ τοῖς λόγοις (they were marveling at the words).

2 Cor. 9.14: διὰ τὴν ὑπερβάλλουσαν χάριν τοῦ θεοῦ ἐφ' ὑμῖν (because of the surpassing grace of God upon you); Mt. 18.13: χαίρει ἐπ' αὐτῷ μᾶλλον ἢ ἐπὶ τοῖς ἐνενήκοντα ἐννέα τοῖς μὴ πεπλανημένοις

1. Moule, *Idiom Book*, p. 49.

(he rejoices more over it than over the 99 that have not strayed).

Heb. 9.26: ἅπαξ ἐπὶ συντελείᾳ τῶν αἰώνων (once at completion of the ages), where a temporal sense is retained.

Eph. 2.10: κτισθέντες ἐν Χριστῷ Ἰησοῦ ἐπὶ ἔργοις ἀγαθοῖς (created by Christ Jesus for good works), with a sense of purpose.

Acts 14.3: παρρησιαζόμενοι ἐπὶ τῷ κυρίῳ τῷ μαρτυροῦντι [ἐπὶ] τῷ λόγῳ τῆς χάριτος αὐτοῦ (being bold for the Lord who bears witness [for] the word of his grace). Note not only the textual variant with the second preposition, but that the sense of location is fundamental to Paul and Barnabas's boldness.

4.10. κατά *with the Genitive and Accusative Cases*[1]

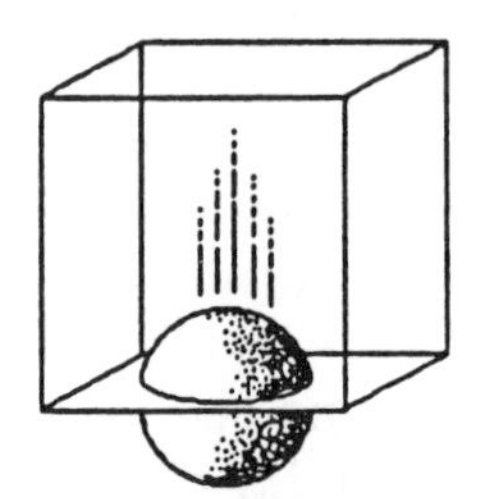

Figure 12. κατά

The preposition κατά occurs with two cases, the genitive and the accusative. Perhaps related etymologically to the adverb κάτω (down), its basic sense is 'direction downward', possibly to its deepest limit (here depicted as the bottom plane of the cube) (fig. 12). It is an antonym of the preposition ἀνά. Since κατά and ἀνά may refer to the furthest reaches of their respective directional movements, there is some overlap in their translations. They are not to be thought of as complete synonyms, however.

4.10.1. *Positional* (location or direction) (genitive and accusative). This is the basic sense of the preposition, and it appears with this meaning in both genitive and accusative cases. The difference is often between the genitive restricting the position to one of movement away

1. This preposition is used with moderate frequency in the NT, with a ratio of .17 to ἐν.

from ('down from') and the accusative simply giving the preposition's basic sense of position ('down upon').

a. *Genitive.*

Mt. 8.32: ὥρμησεν πᾶσα ἡ ἀγέλη κατὰ τοῦ κρημνοῦ (the entire herd rushed down from the cliff); Acts 27.14: ἔβαλεν κατ' αὐτῆς ἄνεμος τυφωνικός (a typhoon-like wind came down from it [Crete]).

Mt. 12.30: ὁ μὴ ὢν μετ' ἐμοῦ κατ' ἐμοῦ ἐστιν (the one who is not with me is against me), with the sense that the person is positionally located away from Jesus.

2 Cor. 8.2: ἡ κατὰ βάθους πτωχεία αὐτῶν, translated by Moule: '*their profound* (perhaps = *down to the depths*) *poverty*',[1] a figurative extension of the positional sense.

b. *Accusative.*

Lk. 10.4: μηδένα κατὰ τὴν ὁδὸν ἀσπάσησθε (greet no one on the road), with the sense of one being limited in one's response to those encountered on the trip.

Eph. 1.15: ἀκούσας τὴν καθ' ὑμᾶς πίστιν (hearing of your faith), i.e. the faith which belongs to or is 'located upon' the Ephesians.

4.10.2. *Standard* (genitive and accusative). This metaphorical extension seems derived from the fundamental sense of the preposition. An item with the preposition can be used to refer to the thing which is the ground or basis of something, and hence the item provides a standard for evaluation.

a. *Genitive.*

Mt. 26.63: ἐξορκίζω σε κατὰ τοῦ θεοῦ τοῦ ζῶντος (I put you under oath on the basis of the living God).

1 Cor. 15.15: ἐμαρτυρήσαμεν κατὰ τοῦ θεοῦ (we bear witness on the basis of God).

b. *Accusative.*

Lk. 2.22: ἐπλήσθησαν αἱ ἡμέραι...κατὰ τὸν νόμον Μωϋσέως (the days were fulfilled...according to the law of Moses).

Rom. 1.3: ἐκ σπέρματος Δαυὶδ κατὰ σάρκα (from the seed of David according to the flesh); Rom. 9.5: τὸ κατὰ σάρκα (the thing according to the flesh).

Rom. 4.4: ὁ μισθὸς οὐ λογίζεται κατὰ χάριν ἀλλὰ κατὰ ὀφείλημα

1. Moule, *Idiom Book*, p. 60.

(the wage is not counted on the basis of grace but on the basis of obligation); Acts 25.14: τὰ κατὰ τὸν Παῦλον (the things against Paul), with the sense of the 'things' forming the accusation against Paul.

Rom. 11.21: ὁ θεὸς τῶν κατὰ φύσιν κλάδων οὐκ ἐφείσατο (God did not spare the branches [grounded] according to nature), i.e. 'the natural branches'.

1 Cor. 15.3: Χριστὸς ἀπέθανεν...κατὰ τὰς γραφάς (Christ died... according to the Scriptures); Rom. 16.25: κατὰ ἀποκάλυψιν (on the basis of revelation).

2 Cor. 10.7: τὰ κατὰ πρόσωπον βλέπετε (you are looking at the superficial [according to appearance] things), i.e. the Corinthians are accused of dwelling on superficial things.

4.10.3. *Temporal* (accusative).

Mt. 27.15: κατὰ...ἑορτὴν εἰώθει ὁ ἡγεμών...(at...the feast the leader was accustomed...). The sense may also be distributive, 'at each feast', but this is probably due more to the verb, εἰώθει; Lk. 2.41: κατ' ἔτος (each year), a distributive temporal use; Lk. 11.3: τὸ καθ' ἡμέραν (that which is daily); Heb. 7.27; 9.25.

Acts 12.1: κατ' ἐκεῖνον...τὸν καιρόν (at that...time).

4.10.4. *Distributive* (accusative).

Mk 6.40: κατὰ ἑκατὸν καὶ κατὰ πεντήκοντα (by 100's and by 50's).

Acts 22.19: δέρων κατὰ τὰς συναγωγάς (beating in each of the synagogues).

4.11. μετά *with the Genitive and Accusative Cases*[1]

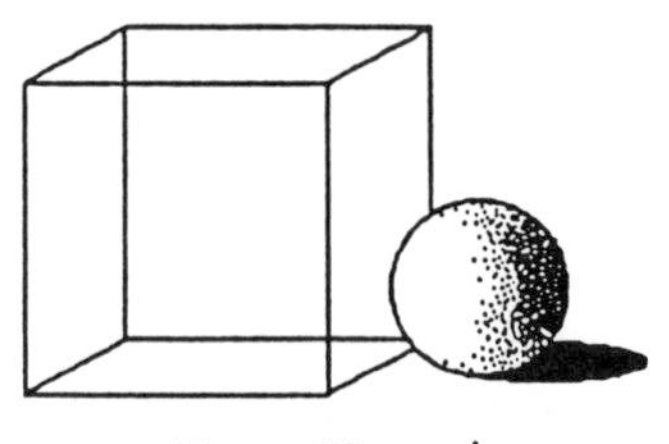

Figure 13. μετά

1. This preposition is used with moderate frequency in the NT, with a ratio of .17 to ἐν.

The preposition μετά, as its diagram suggests (fig. 13), conveys the idea of 'accompaniment', and enjoys a close relationship with σύν (see section 4.16 below for further discussion). The preposition occurs with the genitive and accusative cases.

4.11.1. *Accompanimental* (genitive). This meaning is most closely related to the basic sense, and is often translated as 'with'. Whereas σύν may convey the sense of accompaniment regarding similarly viewed items, μετά can sometimes convey the sense of accompaniment regarding dissimilarly viewed items. Cf. 1 Cor. 6.6: ἀδελφὸς μετὰ ἀδελφοῦ κρίνεται (brother goes to law with brother), where the litigants are depicted as at odds. There are a number of (a) literal and (b) figurative senses of accompaniment with μετά. These include an instrumental-like sense, in which presence implies participation.

a. *Literal.*

Mt. 12.30: ὁ μὴ ὢν μετ' ἐμοῦ κατ' ἐμοῦ ἐστιν, καὶ ὁ μὴ συνάγων μετ' ἐμοῦ σκορπίζει (the one who is not with me is against me, and the one who is not joined with me scatters), where both prepositions σύν and μετά are used, the prefixed verb with σύν perhaps used of the ideal (unity) but μετά used of the reality (disunity); Lk. 9.49: οὐκ ἀκολουθεῖ μεθ' ἡμῶν (he was not following with us).

Jn 4.27: μετὰ γυναικὸς ἐλάλει (he was speaking with the woman); Jn 11.56: μετ' ἀλλήλων (with each other); Rom. 12.18: μετὰ πάντων ἀνθρώπων (with all people).

b. *Figurative.*

Mt. 14.7: μεθ' ὅρκου ὡμολόγησεν (he swore with an oath), with an instrumental sense.

Mk 6.25: εἰσελθοῦσα εὐθὺς μετὰ σπουδῆς (entering immediately with haste), with an instrumental-like sense; Heb. 12.17: μετὰ δακρύων (with tears).

1 Tim. 4.14: ἐδόθη σοι διὰ προφητείας μετὰ ἐπιθέσεως τῶν χειρῶν τοῦ πρεσβυτερίου (it was given to you through prophecy with laying on of the hands of the eldership), with an instrumental-like sense, derived from the idea that if the hands are present they in some way participate in the action.

4.11.2. *Temporal* (succession) (accusative). Chamberlain claims that the meaning of μετά with the accusative, often translated 'after', derives from the sense of one passing through a series of events and then looking back on them.[1]

Mt. 26.2: μετὰ δύο ἡμέρας τὸ πάσχα γίνεται (after two days the Passover is going to come about), or perhaps 'with the passing of two days'.

Lk. 5.27: καὶ μετὰ ταῦτα ἐξῆλθεν (and after these things he went out).

Heb. 9.3: μετὰ...τὸ δεύτερον καταπέτασμα (after...the second curtain), although Chamberlain contends that this is an exception.[2] The sense that in one's movement through the temple one passes beyond the second veil, and now stands after or behind it, keeps this example within the semantic range of the use of the preposition.

4.12. παρά *with the Accusative, Genitive and Dative Cases*[3]

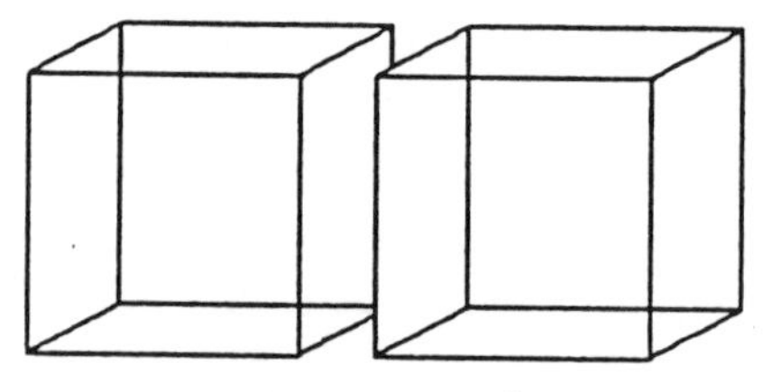

Figure 14. παρά

The preposition παρά, as the diagram indicates (fig. 14), has as its basic sense one of position 'alongside, parallel to or beside'. From this fundamental meaning various others are figuratively derived, although they seem to share this common sense. The preposition occurs with all three oblique cases.

4.12.1. *Locative* (accusative). This sense is found either with verbs of motion or with static verbs to specify an undefined location. παρά and the accusative do not occur in the NT with a person as the object of the preposition.

1. Chamberlain, *Exegetical Grammar*, p. 125.
2. Chamberlain, *Exegetical Grammar*, p. 125.
3. This preposition is used fairly infrequently in the NT, with a ratio of .07 to ἐν.

Mt. 13.1: ἐκάθητο παρὰ τὴν θάλασσαν (he sat alongside the sea).

Mk 1.16: παράγων παρὰ τὴν θάλασσαν τῆς Γαλιλαίας (passing along [the shore of] the sea of Galilee), where the preposition, used twice, locates the movement; Acts 10.6, where the location of a house is spoken of as παρὰ θάλασσαν (alongside the sea).

Mk 4.1, 4: διδάσκειν παρὰ τὴν θάλασσαν...ἔπεσεν παρὰ τὴν ὁδόν (to teach alongside the sea...it fell alongside the road), where a static verb and a verb of motion are used.

In some instances the locative sense is extended to mean that one thing placed alongside another replaces the other in some way.

Gal. 1.8: ἐὰν...ἄγγελος ἐξ οὐρανοῦ εὐαγγελίζηται [ὑμῖν] παρ' ὃ εὐηγγελισάμεθα ὑμῖν (if...an angel from heaven might proclaim [to you] alongside what we proclaimed to you), referring to a gospel that is being preached alongside the one Paul has preached in order to take its place.

Rom. 1.25: ἐλάτρευσαν τῇ κτίσει παρὰ τὸν κτίσαντα (they worshiped the creature in place of the creator), where the idea is that they worshiped the creature in a place alongside and hence usurping the place of the creator.

Rom. 12.3: μὴ ὑπερφρονεῖν παρ' ὃ δεῖ φρονεῖν (not to think more highly than [in place of] what it is necessary to think).

4.12.2. *Directional* (away from) (genitive). παρά with the genitive always has a personal object in NT Greek.

Jn 16.27: ἐγὼ παρὰ [τοῦ] θεοῦ ἐξῆλθον (I went out from alongside God).

Phil. 4.18: δεξάμενος παρὰ 'Επαφροδίτου (receiving from Epaphroditus).

Lk. 10.7: ἐσθίοντες καὶ πίνοντες τὰ παρῷ αὐτῶν (eating and drinking the things from them), where the sense of coming from them is maintained, even though an English translation may contain words of possession ('their things').

Jn 1.6: ἀπεσταλμένος παρὰ θεοῦ (sent from God), where a sense of agency is an extension of movement from beside; Lk. 1.45: παρὰ κυρίου (from the Lord).

4.12.3. *Positional* (alongside) (dative). This relational usage of the preposition is virtually always with a personal object. Cf. Jn 19.25: εἱστήκεισαν...παρὰ τῷ σταυρῷ τοῦ 'Ιησοῦ (they stood...alongside the cross of Jesus), where the cross is the object of the preposition, an unusual instance of an impersonal object.

Lk. 9.47: ἔστησεν αὐτὸ παρ' ἑαυτῷ (he stood it beside himself).

Acts 10.6: οὗτος ξενίζεται παρά τινι Σίμωνι βυρσεῖ (this person is lodging with a certain Simon the tanner), where being alongside implies 'with'.

Rom. 2.11: οὐ...ἐστιν προσωπολημψία παρὰ τῷ θεῷ (there is no favoritism with God), where the idea of resting alongside may be extended to include the sense of being in one's presence; Lk. 1.30: παρὰ τῷ θεῷ (alongside God), i.e. 'with'; 1 Cor. 3.19: ἡ γὰρ σοφία τοῦ κόσμου τούτου μωρία παρὰ τῷ θεῷ ἐστιν (for the wisdom of this world is foolishness alongside God), with almost a comparative sense.

4.13. περί *with the Accusative and Genitive Cases*[1]

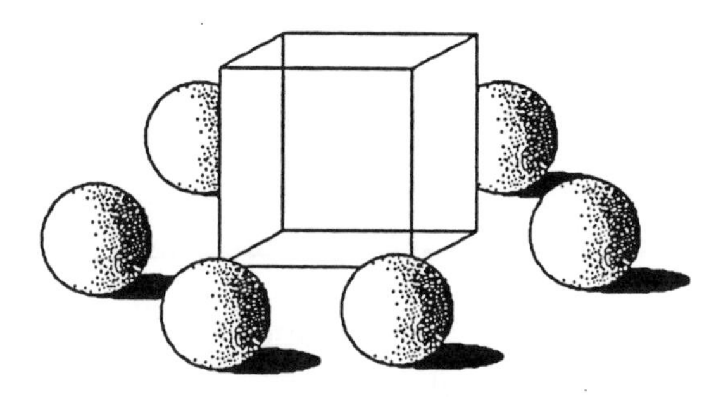

Figure 15. περί

The preposition περί, as the diagram illustrates (fig. 15), has a basic meaning of encirclement (often rendered with the words 'around, about'). Thus the spheres surround the cube. The preposition occurs with the accusative and genitive cases.

4.13.1. *Locative* (accusative). This is the sense closest to the preposition's fundamental sense. It often describes physical location.

Mk 3.8: ἀπὸ Ἱεροσολύμων καὶ ἀπὸ τῆς Ἰδουμαίας καὶ πέραν τοῦ Ἰορδάνου καὶ περὶ Τύρον καὶ Σιδῶνα (from Jerusalem and from

1. This preposition is used with moderate frequency in the NT, with a ratio of .12 to ἐν.

Idumea and the other side of the Jordan and around Tyre and Sidon), with the sense of 'the area around'.

Lk. 13.8: σκάψω περὶ αὐτήν (I might dig around it [a grape vine]); Mt. 3.4: περὶ τὴν ὀσφὺν αὐτοῦ (around his waist).

An extension of the local sense can be seen in usage which is understood as 'personal' location, in other words, someone is concerned with something (see section 4.13.3 below).

Acts 19.25: συναθροίσας καὶ τοὺς περὶ τὰ τοιαῦτα ἐργάτας (gathering also the workers concerned with such things), or as Moule says, 'in that line of business'.[1]

Acts 13.13: οἱ περὶ Παῦλον (those around Paul), meaning his companions; Lk. 22.49: οἱ περὶ αὐτόν (those around him); Phil. 2.23: ὡς ἂν ἀφίδω τὰ περὶ ἐμέ (as I might examine the things concerning me), i.e. the things awaiting my attention.

4.13.2. *Temporal* (accusative). The preposition may be used to designate an undefined point of time 'around' which something happened.

Mt. 20.3: ἐξελθὼν περὶ τρίτην ὥραν (going out around the third hour).

Acts 22.6: ἐγγίζοντι τῇ Δαμασκῷ περὶ μεσημβρίαν (being near to Damascus around noon).

4.13.3. *Focal, i.e. about, concerning* (genitive). This metaphorical extension of the basic meaning appears derived from the sense that if one thing surrounds another it has this other thing as its concern or is restricted to it.

Jn 9.17: τί σὺ λέγεις περὶ αὐτοῦ; (what are you saying about him?); Jn 19.24: λάχωμεν περὶ αὐτοῦ (let us draw lots about it).

Rom. 8.3: περὶ ἁμαρτίας κατέκρινεν τὴν ἁμαρτίαν ἐν τῇ σαρκί (concerning sin he condemned sin in the flesh).

1 Cor. 7.1: περὶ δὲ ὧν ἐγράψατε (about which things you wrote);[2] Phil. 2.19, 20: γνοὺς τὰ περὶ ὑμῶν...τὰ περὶ ὑμῶν (knowing the

1. Moule, *Idiom Book*, p. 62.

2. There has been widespread discussion of the περὶ δέ construction in 1 Cor. 7.1, 25; 8.1; 12.1; 16.1, 12. Recent opinion sees it as a topic marker introducing the next topic of discussion, an almost absolute use. See M.M. Mitchell, 'Concerning περὶ δέ in 1 Corinthians', *NovT* 31 (1989), pp. 229-56. On the use of περὶ μὲν γάρ, especially as it bears on text-critical issues in 2 Corinthians, see S.K. Stowers, '*Peri Men Gar* and the Integrity of 2 Cor. 8 and 9', *NovT* 32 (1990), pp. 340-48.

things concerning you...the things concerning you); Eph. 6.18: περὶ πάντων τῶν ἁγίων (concerning all the saints).

1 Jn 2.2: αὐτὸς ἱλασμός ἐστιν περὶ τῶν ἁμαρτιῶν ἡμῶν, οὐ περὶ τῶν ἡμετέρων δὲ μόνον ἀλλὰ καὶ περὶ ὅλου τοῦ κόσμου (he himself is the propitiation concerning our sins, and not concerning ours only but concerning the whole world), in the sense of 'surrounding or encompassing' and hence 'focusing upon'. This verse perhaps alludes to the OT sacrificial ritual (the atoning sacrifice) with its surrounding or encompassing smoke.

Mt. 26.28: τὸ αἷμά μου...τὸ περὶ πολλῶν ἐκχυννόμενον (my blood...poured out concerning many), where there is similarity to use of ὑπέρ in Mk 14.24; 1 Cor. 11.24; Lk. 22.20 (see section 4.17 below).

4.14. πρό *with the Genitive Case*[1]

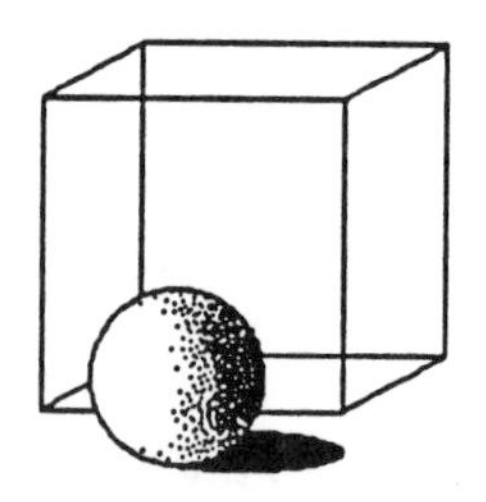

Figure 16. πρό

The preposition πρό, as the diagram conveys (fig. 16), has the basic meaning of 'before' or 'in front of' something else. This may have several applications, including temporal, positional and metaphorical senses. The preposition occurs with the genitive case.

4.14.1. *Locative* (before).

Acts 12.6: ὅτε δὲ ἤμελλεν προαγαγεῖν αὐτὸν ὁ Ἡρῴδης... φύλακές τε πρὸ τῆς θύρας ἐτήρουν τὴν φυλακήν (and when Herod was going to bring [Peter] forward...and guards were keeping the watch before the door), where the preposition πρό is used twice, once prefixed to a verb and once in a prepositional phrase, each with the sense of physical location.

1. This preposition is used fairly infrequently in the NT, with a ratio of .018 to ἐν.

Acts 14.13: ὅ...ἱερεὺς τοῦ Διὸς τοῦ ὄντος πρὸ τῆς πόλεως (the... priest of the Zeus who is before the city), referring to the location of the god's temple.

Jas 5.9: ὁ κριτὴς πρὸ τῶν θυρῶν ἕστηκεν (the judge stands before the gates).

4.14.2. *Temporal* (antecedent). This usage is very frequent in the NT.

Mt. 8.29: ἦλθες ὧδε πρὸ καιροῦ βασανίσαι ἡμᾶς; (you came here before the time to torment us?), where the demons address Jesus regarding the timing of his mission; Mt. 24.38: πρὸ τοῦ κατακλυσμοῦ (before the flood).

Jn 5.7: ἄλλος πρὸ ἐμοῦ καταβαίνει (another goes down before me), where the relation of the temporal and locative senses is clear; that is, position before implies time before.

Jn 12.1: ὁ...Ἰησοῦς πρὸ ἓξ ἡμερῶν τοῦ πάσχα ἦλθεν εἰς Βηθανίαν (Jesus, before six days of the Passover, went into Bethany), probably better translated in English as 'six days before the Passover'. The preposition indicates the relation of the time specified to the main event, not the length of the Passover itself. 2 Cor. 12.2: πρὸ ἐτῶν δεκατεσσάρων (fourteen years before).

1 Cor. 2.7: προώρισεν ὁ θεὸς πρὸ τῶν αἰώνων εἰς δόξαν ἡμῶν (God marked out ahead of time before the ages for our glory), where the preposition is both prefixed to the verb and used independently, each with temporal sense.

4.14.3. *Positional* (antecedent).

Jas 5.12: πρὸ πάντων...μὴ ὀμνύετε (above all...don't swear), where the sense of physical location before is extended to priority; 1 Pet. 4.8: πρὸ πάντων (before all), or 'above all'.

Col. 1.17: καὶ αὐτός ἐστιν πρὸ πάντων καὶ τὰ πάντα ἐν αὐτῷ συνέστηκεν (and he himself is before all things and all things in him hold together). The locative use is possible, but the sense seems to be one of positional precedence.

4.15. πρός *with the Accusative, Genitive and Dative Cases*[1]

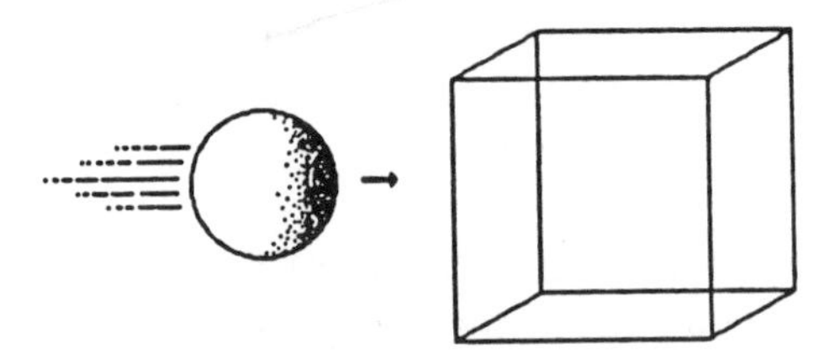

Figure 17. πρός

The preposition πρός, as the diagram illustrates (fig. 17), has a basic sense of position face-to-face toward something or someone.[2] This sense is often connected with movement. The preposition πρός is related to εἰς in much the same way as ἀπό is related to ἐκ, with πρός perhaps more extensive than εἰς. πρός is therefore an antonym of ἀπό. The preposition occurs with all three oblique cases.

4.15.1. *Directional* (toward) (accusative). The directional sense dominates use of this preposition in the NT. This is so much so that, with few exceptions, this preposition is only used in the NT with the accusative case, where it has varied nuances of meaning.

Mt. 7.15: ἔρχονται πρὸς ὑμᾶς (they are coming toward you).

Mk 1.33: ἦν ὅλη ἡ πόλις ἐπισυνηγμένη πρὸς τὴν θύραν (the entire city was there, gathered at the door), with the sense of facing the door.

Mk 4.1: συνάγεται πρὸς αὐτὸν ὄχλος πλεῖστος (a large crowd gathered in front of ['facing toward'] him), where seeing πρός as implying 'facing toward' is justified by two factors. The first is its contrast to παρά in the lines above. The second is the fact that Jesus has entered into a boat, warranting the crowd directing its attention toward him floating on the sea.

Eph. 6.12: οὐκ ἔστιν ἡμῖν ἡ πάλη πρὸς αἷμα καὶ σάρκα ἀλλὰ πρὸς τὰς ἀρχάς, πρὸς τὰς ἐξουσίας, πρὸς τοὺς κοσμοκράτορας τοῦ σκότους τούτου, πρὸς τὰ πνευματικὰ τῆς πονηρίας ἐν τοῖς ἐπουρανίοις (the struggle for us is not with blood and flesh but with the powers, with the authorities, with the world forces of this darkness,

1. This preposition is the fifth most frequent in the NT, with a ratio of .25 to ἐν.
2. Robertson, *Grammar*, p. 625.

with the spirits of evil in the heavenlies), with several instances, all related to facing off with adversaries.

Jn 1.1: ὁ λόγος ἦν πρὸς τὸν θεόν (and the word was with God), where the translation which has been institutionalized, 'with', does not do full justice to this use of the preposition to mean face-to-face presence;[1] cf. 1 Thess. 3.4; Mk 14.49; and 2 Cor. 5.8: μᾶλλον ἐκδημῆσαι ἐκ τοῦ σώματος καὶ ἐνδημῆσαι πρὸς τὸν κύριον (rather to be away from the body and to be at home with [standing before] the Lord).

Acts 5.10: ἔπεσεν...παραχρῆμα πρὸς τοὺς πόδας αὐτοῦ (he fell... immediately at his feet), a directional use.

Rom. 8.18: οὐκ ἄξια τὰ παθήματα τοῦ νῦν καιροῦ πρὸς τὴν μέλλουσαν δόξαν (the sufferings of the present time are not worthy to face the coming glory). The basic sense of face-to-face competition is evident, with the sufferings of this present age not standing up to the scrutiny of the glory about to be revealed.

This preposition is fairly common with verbs of speaking, the sense being that the words spoken are confronting the speaker or an issue.

Lk. 24.14: αὐτοὶ ὡμίλουν πρὸς ἀλλήλους (they swore to each other).

Rom. 8.31: τί οὖν ἐροῦμεν πρὸς ταῦτα; (what shall we say to [in the face of] these things?).

In expressions of time, πρός is used with the accusative as well. The sense is one of confronting an unspecified time.

Lk. 8.13: οἳ πρὸς καιρὸν πιστεύουσιν (some believed for a time).

Gal. 2.5: οὐδὲ πρὸς ὥραν εἴξαμεν τῇ ὑποταγῇ (not even for an hour did we yield in subjection).

4.15.2. *Directional* (away from) (genitive). There is only one example of πρός with the genitive in the NT. The function apparently was taken over by ἀπό and possibly ἐκ in Hellenistic Greek.

Acts 27.34: τοῦτο γὰρ πρὸς τῆς ὑμετέρας σωτηρίας ὑπάρχει (for this [nourishment] is for your salvation), which may be interpreted variously.[2] The sense seems best described as one of direction from or origin, that is, this is the source out of which arises your salvation.

1. See Harris, 'Prepositions', pp. 1204-1205.
2. See BDF, §240.

4.15.3. *Positional* (dative). There are only six or seven uses of the preposition πρός with the dative case in the NT. All of them convey a positional sense.

Mk 5.11: ἦν...ἐκεῖ πρὸς τῷ ὄρει ἀγέλη χοίρων μεγάλη (a large herd of swine were there at the mountain).

Lk. 19.37: ἐγγίζοντος...αὐτοῦ ἤδη πρὸς τῇ καταβάσει τοῦ ὄρους τῶν ἐλαιῶν (when he was already at the descent of the Mount of Olives).

Jn 18.16: ὁ...Πέτρος εἱστήκει πρὸς τῇ θύρᾳ ἔξω (Peter stood at the door outside); Jn 20.11, 12: πρὸς τῷ μνημείῳ...πρὸς τῇ κεφαλῇ ...πρὸς τοῖς ποσίν (at the tomb...at the head...at the feet).

Rev. 1.13: περιεζωσμένον πρὸς τοῖς μαστοῖς (being girded around [his] breast), with the preposition indicating position.

4.16. σύν *with the Dative Case*[1]

Figure 18. σύν

The preposition σύν enjoys a close relationship with μετά (see section 4.11 above). In many instances they seem to convey similar senses of accompaniment ('with'), whether this be physical or metaphorical togetherness. But, as the diagrams for each indicate, σύν seems to imply at least in its fundamental sense the idea of like things being 'with' each other (fig. 18). This does not mean that they are exactly the same thing, but that the way they are being characterized by the author implies points of similarity. This is not a hard and fast principle, however. The preposition occurs with the dative case.

Mt. 26.35: κἂν δέῃ με σὺν σοὶ ἀποθανεῖν (and even if it requires me to die with you); cf. Jn 12.2; Phil. 1.23; 1 Thess. 4.17.

Lk. 9.32: ὁ...Πέτρος καὶ οἱ σὺν αὐτῷ (Peter and those with him), implying by use of the preposition that they are in the same group; Acts 14.4: οἱ μὲν...σὺν τοῖς Ἰουδαίοις οἱ δὲ σὺν τοῖς ἀποστόλοις (those...with the Jews and those with the apostles).

Lk. 24.21: ἀλλά γε καὶ σὺν πᾶσιν τούτοις τρίτην ταύτην ἡμέραν

1. This preposition is used fairly infrequently in the NT, with a ratio of .048 to ἐν.

ἄγει ἀφ' οὗ ταῦτα ἐγένετο (but along with all these things it is the third day from when these things happened), where the travelers have just recounted the events surrounding Jesus' life and death.

1 Cor. 5.4: συναχθέντων ὑμῶν καὶ τοῦ ἐμοῦ πνεύματος σὺν τῇ δυνάμει τοῦ κυρίου ἡμῶν Ἰησοῦ (you and my spirit were gathered with the power of our Lord Jesus), where the power is joined to the person. The prefixed and independent prepositions are used.

4.17. ὑπέρ *with the Accusative and Genitive Cases*[1]

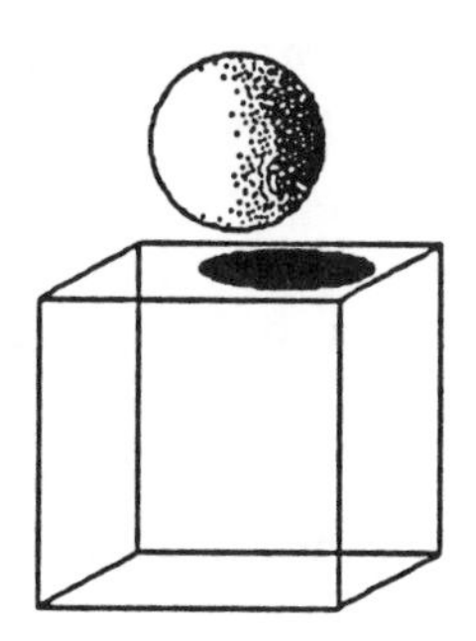

Figure 19. ὑπέρ

The preposition ὑπέρ, possibly related etymologically to ὑπό, serves in Greek as the antonym of ὑπό. Its basic meaning is normally understood as 'location above' (fig. 19). This has several applications, even though the literal physical sense apparently is not found in the NT or other Hellenistic Greek. The preposition occurs with the accusative and genitive cases.

4.17.1. *Positional* (above) (accusative). This use is an extension of the local, physical sense. The general usage is that something (in an undefined way) exceeds another, as if the former were located above or in a superior position to the latter.[2]

Mt. 10.24: οὐκ ἔστιν μαθητὴς ὑπὲρ τὸν διδάσκαλον οὐδὲ δοῦλος ὑπὲρ τὸν κύριον αὐτοῦ (a disciple is not above the teacher, and neither [is] a servant above his master); Mt. 10.37: ὁ φιλῶν πατέρα ἢ

1. This preposition is used fairly infrequently in the NT, with a ratio of .094 to ἐν.

2. Riesenfeld's idea of the comparative sense of ὑπέρ with the accusative is probably to be rejected. The positional sense is sufficient. See H. Riesenfeld, 'ὑπέρ', *TDNT*, VIII, p. 515.

μητέρα ὑπὲρ ἐμέ (the one who loves father or mother above me), that is, puts parents above me.

Acts 26.13: ὑπὲρ τὴν λαμπρότητα τοῦ ἡλίου περιλάμψαν με φῶς (a light shone around me greater than the brightness of the sun).

2 Cor. 1.8: καθ' ὑπερβολὴν ὑπὲρ δύναμιν ἐβαρήθημεν (we were burdened to excess, beyond [our] power). ὑπέρ with the genitive is used in the phrase above in this passage as well.

4.17.2. *Beneficial* (genitive). Robertson claims that the sense of benefit easily grows out of the local idea of 'over'.[1] The relation is that one thing is located positionally over another and is restricted to some interest in its well-being. The translation might use the wording 'on behalf of' or 'for one's benefit'.

Mk 9.40: ὃς...οὐκ ἔστιν καθ' ἡμῶν, ὑπὲρ ἡμῶν ἐστιν (who...is not against us is for us); Acts 8.24: δεήθητε ὑμεῖς ὑπὲρ ἐμοῦ (pray for me).

Jn 11.4: αὕτη ἡ ἀσθένεια οὐκ ἔστιν πρὸς θάνατον ἀλλ' ὑπὲρ τῆς δόξης τοῦ θεοῦ (this weakness is not toward death but for the glory of God).

Rom. 15.8: Χριστὸν διάκονον γεγενῆσθαι περιτομῆς ὑπὲρ ἀληθείας θεοῦ (Christ became a servant of the circumcision for the truth of God).

2 Cor. 1.6: εἴτε...θλιβόμεθα, ὑπὲρ τῆς ὑμῶν παρακλήσεως καὶ σωτηρίας· εἴτε παρακαλούμεθα, ὑπὲρ τῆς ὑμῶν παρακλήσεως (if ...we are afflicted, [it is] for your comfort and salvation; if we are comforted, [it is] for your comfort).

4.17.3. *Substitutionary*. Use of the prepositions in theologically loaded passages often raises very important grammatical issues. In this instance, the question is whether ὑπέρ can be used in a substitutionary sense similar to ἀντί, meaning 'instead of'. Winer states that there is an intrinsic connection between the idea of doing something for someone's benefit and doing it in place of someone.[2] The use of ὑπέρ in a substitutionary sense is not unknown in classical Greek and is in fact fairly widespread in the Hellenistic papyri, especially when a literate scribe writes for (in place of—ὑπέρ) another who is illiterate (e.g.

1. Robertson, *Grammar*, p. 631.
2. Winer, *Treatise*, pp. 478-80.

P.Teb. 104.39-40; P.Hamb. 4.14-15).[1] There is no reason apart from theological bias to exclude this usage in the NT. Many of the following examples can be taken in the beneficial or substitutionary sense, the latter especially being worth weighing when the death of Christ is spoken of.

Mk 14.24: τὸ αἷμά μου...τὸ ἐκχυννόμενον ὑπὲρ πολλῶν (my blood...poured out for many); cf. 1 Cor. 11.24; Lk. 22.20. See also Mt. 26.28 with περί (section 4.13.3 above).

Jn 11.50: εἷς ἄνθρωπος ἀποθάνῃ ὑπὲρ τοῦ λαοῦ (one person might die for the people).

Rom. 5.7, 8: μόλις γὰρ ὑπὲρ δικαίου τις ἀποθανεῖται· ὑπὲρ... τοῦ ἀγαθοῦ τάχα τις καὶ τολμᾷ ἀποθανεῖν...ἔτι ἁμαρτωλῶν ὄντων ἡμῶν Χριστὸς ὑπὲρ ἡμῶν ἀπέθανεν (for hardly will someone die for a just person; for...a good person perhaps someone might indeed dare to die...while we were still sinners Christ died for us).

2 Cor. 5.14, 15: εἷς ὑπὲρ πάντων ἀπέθανεν...καὶ ὑπὲρ πάντων ἀπέθανεν...τῷ ὑπὲρ αὐτῶν ἀποθανόντι καὶ ἐγερθέντι (one died for all...and for all he died...to the one who died for all and was raised).

Gal. 3.13: γενόμενος ὑπὲρ ἡμῶν κατάρα (becoming a curse for us).

1 Tim. 2.6: ὁ δοὺς ἑαυτὸν ἀντίλυτρον ὑπὲρ πάντων (the one who gave himself a ransom for all), with the preposition ἀντί prefixed to the noun, reinforcing the substitutionary sense.

Phlm. 13: ὑπὲρ σοῦ μοι διακονῇ (in your place he might serve me), where the substitutionary sense appears clear in a non-theological context.

1 Cor. 15.29: τί ποιήσουσιν οἱ βαπτιζόμενοι ὑπὲρ τῶν νεκρῶν; (what will they do, those who are baptized for the dead?). Does it make a difference whether these people were being baptized for the benefit of or in place of the dead?

1. See A.T. Robertson, 'The Use of ΥΠΕΡ in Business Documents in the Papyri', *Expositor* 8th Series, 18 (1919), pp. 321-27; Harris, 'Prepositions', pp. 1196-97.

4.18. ὑπό *with the Accusative and Genitive Cases*[1]

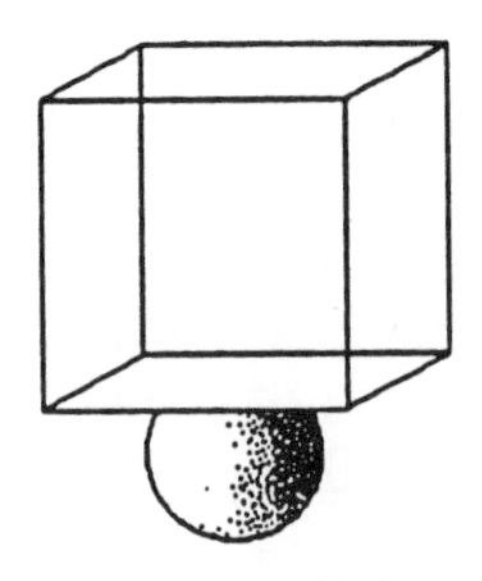

Figure 20. ὑπό

The preposition ὑπό, an antonym of ὑπέρ even though the two are possibly related etymologically, has the basic sense of 'location under' (fig. 20) with the positional extension of movement to or away from a place under. The preposition occurs with the accusative and genitive cases.

4.18.1. *Locative* (beneath) (accusative). The local sense, and its positional extension, are both present in the Greek of the NT. One time ὑπό is used in relation to place in time: Acts 5.21: εἰσῆλθον ὑπὸ τὸν ὄρθρον εἰς τὸ ἱερόν (they entered at sunrise into the temple), where a literal translation might be 'under the sunrise'.

Mt. 5.15: οὐδὲ...τιθέασιν αὐτὸν ὑπὸ τὸν μόδιον ἀλλ' ἐπὶ τὴν λυχνίαν (they do not place [a lamp] under the bushel but upon the lamp stand); Jn 1.48: ὑπὸ τὴν συκῆν (under the fig tree); Mk 4.32: ὑπὸ τὴν σκιὰν αὐτοῦ (under its shadow), with reference to the birds under the shadow of the mustard tree.

Mt. 8.8, 9: οὐκ εἰμὶ ἱκανὸς ἵνα μου ὑπὸ τὴν στέγην εἰσέλθῃς... ἐγὼ ἄνθρωπός εἰμι ὑπὸ ἐξουσίαν, ἔχων ὑπ' ἐμαυτὸν στρατιώτας (I am not worthy so that you might enter under my roof...I am a man under authority, having soldiers under me), where both locative (first instance) and positional (second and third instances) senses of the preposition are found.

Acts 4.12: οὐδὲ γὰρ ὄνομά ἐστιν ἕτερον ὑπὸ τὸν οὐρανόν (for there is not another name under heaven).

1 Pet. 5.6: ταπεινώθητε οὖν ὑπὸ τὴν κραταιὰν χεῖρα τοῦ θεοῦ (be humble therefore under the powerful hand of God).

1. This preposition is used fairly moderately in the NT, with a ratio of .08 to ἐν.

4.18.2. *Instrumental* (primary, personal or direct agency) (genitive). This very common use of the preposition often, though not always, occurs with a passive voice verb to denote primary (personal) agency. This is in distinction to the frequent uses of διά for secondary (intermediate) agency and ἐν for instrumental or impersonal agency. The relation of the instrumental sense of ὑπό to its basic or fundamental meaning is difficult to understand. Perhaps it is related to the idea of something underneath comprising a foundational cause of action (see κατά, section 4.10 above). See Chapter 3 section 1.2 on the passive voice.

Mt. 1.22: τὸ ῥηθὲν ὑπὸ κυρίου διὰ τοῦ προφήτου (the thing spoken by the Lord through the prophet), with primary and secondary agency expressed.

Mt. 3.6: ἐβαπτίζοντο...ὑπ' αὐτοῦ (they were baptized...by him).

Rev. 6.8: ἀποκτεῖναι ἐν ῥομφαίᾳ καὶ ἐν λιμῷ καὶ ἐν θανάτῳ καὶ ὑπὸ τῶν θηρίων τῆς γῆς (to kill by sword and by famine and by death [= plague] and by the beasts of the earth), where instrumental ἐν with natural processes is apparently contrasted with ὑπό for direct animate agency.

5. *Improper Prepositions*

The following is a list of all 42 of the so-called improper prepositions which appear in the Greek of the NT, with a representative example listed. Many of these are considered adverbs, particles or forms of nouns as well.

ἅμα + dative (together with): Mt. 13.29; ἄνευ + genitive (without): Mt. 10.29; ἄντικρυς + genitive (opposite): Acts 20.15; ἀντιπέρα + genitive (opposite): Lk. 8.26; ἀπέναντι + genitive (before): Acts 3.16; ἄτερ + genitive (without): Lk. 22.6, 35; ἄχρι(ς) + genitive (until): Gal. 3.19; ἐγγύς + genitive (near): Jn 11.54, ἐγγύς + dative (near): Acts 9.38; ἐκτός + genitive (outside): Acts 26.22; ἔμπροσθεν + genitive (before): Mt. 10.32; ἔναντι + genitive (before): Acts 8.21; ἐναντίον + genitive (before): Lk. 20.26; ἕνεκα and its various forms + genitive (on account of): Acts 19.32 (but usually before its object); ἐντός + genitive (within): Lk. 17.21, a widely disputed verse; ἐνώπιον + genitive (before): Lk. 1.19; ἔξω + genitive (outside): Mt. 10.14; ἔξωθεν + genitive (from outside): Rev. 14.20; ἐπάνω + genitive (above): Mk 14.5; ἐπέκεινα + genitive (beyond): Acts 7.43; ἔσω + genitive (within): Mk 15.16; ἕως + genitive (until): Mt. 1.17; κατέναντι + genitive (opposite): Mk 11.2; κατενώπιον + genitive (before): Col. 1.22; κυκλόθεν + genitive (around): Rev. 4.3, 4; κύκλῳ (the dative of κύκλος) + genitive (around): Rev. 4.6; μέσον (the accusative of μέσος) + genitive (in the midst): Phil. 2.15; μεταξύ + genitive (between): Mt. 23.35; μέχρι(ς) + genitive (until): Rom. 15.19; ὄπισθεν + genitive (behind): Mt. 15.23; ὀπίσω + genitive (after): Mt. 10.38; ὀψέ + genitive (after): Mt. 28.1, although this is disputed; παραπλήσιον + dative (near): Phil. 2.27; παρεκτός + genitive (apart from): Mt. 5.32; πέραν + genitive (on the other side): Mk 3.8; πλήν + genitive (except): Acts 8.1; πλησίον + genitive (near): Jn 4.5; ὑπεράνω + genitive (above): Eph. 4.10; ὑπερέκεινα + genitive (beyond): 2 Cor. 10.16; ὑπερεκπερισσοῦ + genitive (far more than): Eph. 3.20; ὑποκάτω + genitive (beneath): Mk 6.11; χάριν (the accusative of χάρις) + genitive (almost always following its object) (for the sake of): 1 Jn 3.12; χωρίς + genitive (without): Heb. 12.14.

Chapter 10

PARTICIPLES

Introduction

The participle (often called a verbal adjective)—a very important form in the Greek language—has similarities both to the adjective (noun) and to the verb. Its similarity to the verb includes its grammaticalizing of verbal aspect (tense) and voice, as well as its ability to take objects and verbal modifiers. Its similarity to the adjective (noun) includes designation of gender, case and number, as well as the ability to take the same modifiers as nouns. The participle, like the infinitive, does not grammaticalize mood or person. These features contribute to its ability to be used in a variety of contexts.

The use of the participle in the Greek of the NT, like its use in classical and other Hellenistic Greek, is widespread in the major tense forms (aorist, present and perfect) and the three voices. The only form of the participle with somewhat diminished use is the future. In NT Greek, the participle is virtually always negated by μή (some exceptions are noted in Chapter 19 on negation). This chapter gives details of the major patterns of syntactical usage of the participle form. In order to understand fully the use of the participle, it must be emphasized that verbal aspect and not time is the major semantic component of its verbal status. Therefore, the verbal aspect grammaticalized by the tense-form must be understood as a major semantic feature, regardless of whether this is brought forward in translation.

By using the language of slot and filler, an important distinction between form and function of the participle can be made. The flexibility of the participle makes it suitable for use in environments where other words are often found in Greek (e.g. nouns, verbs, adjectives and adverbs). For example, in a place where a noun might occur, such as the subject or complement (object) of a clause, the participle may occur instead. Thus the participle may fill the subject or complement slot, and take the kinds of modifiers any substantive might (e.g. adjectives), as well as verbal elements (e.g. objects and modifiers such as adverbs). For example, in the English sentence 'Running hard to work every morning is my idea of fun', the participle 'running' is the governing (head) term of the subject, with several attached adverbial modifiers.

It is also possible for the Greek participle to perform a function similar to that of a finite verb, especially when the finite verb would occur in the indicative or imperative mood (these are the absolute and independent uses of the participle; see section 2 below). The most common independent construction is the so-called genitive absolute. Thus the participle may fill the predicate slot in a clause, and take the kinds of modifiers any word filling the predicate slot might take. English does not have an exact equivalent of the genitive absolute, so the translation uses normal finite verbs.

Within a larger structure—e.g. subject, complement or predicate structure—the governing (head) term of that structure may take modification. The participle often will fill the modifier slot of a noun or a verb phrase, and thus function similarly to an adjective or an adverb. It may also at the same time take its regular participle modifiers. For example, in the English phrases 'the gently floating wood' or 'the broken bottle', participles are used as modifiers of nouns, the first with its own modifier.

In a few instances, the use of the participle in place of a noun or other form may become so common that the participle is thought of as a noun form (e.g. ἄρχων, 'ruler'), but this is fairly infrequent. In the vast majority of instances, even though the participle may function similarly to a verb, noun, adjective or adverb, it never *becomes* these forms. It only *functions* in the way that these forms often (though not exclusively) function. The terminology regarding the participle varies widely from grammar to grammar. An attempt will be made to correlate the following outline with other frequently found terminology, although it must be remembered that the terms are rarely being used synonymously.

1. *Substantive*

As noted above, *a participle may serve in a variety of contexts in the same way as other substantives, including especially nouns.* This is called attributive usage in many grammars. The advantage that the participle has over these other forms is that it grammaticalizes verbal aspect, along with voice. In other words, the participle adds the semantic features of its respective verb tense-form, which must be considered in appreciating the full force of the phrase or clause. One of the distinguishing characteristics of the substantival use of the participle is the frequent syntactical accompaniment of the article (absence of the article does not guarantee that it is not substantival, however).

Lk. 10.37: ὁ ποιήσας τὸ ἔλεος (the one who practiced mercy).

Rom. 2.1: τὰ γὰρ αὐτὰ πράσσεις ὁ κρίνων (for you who judge [i.e. the one judging] do the same things).

Phil. 3.17: σκοπεῖτε τοὺς οὕτω περιπατοῦντας (watch out for those who walk [i.e. conduct themselves] in this way).

Acts 1.19: πᾶσι τοῖς κατοικοῦσιν Ἰερουσαλήμ (to all inhabiting Jerusalem).

Lk. 3.14: ἐπηρώτων...αὐτὸν καὶ στρατευόμενοι...(those serving as soldiers asked him...), a substantival usage without the article.

2. *Predicate*

A participle may function in a way similar to the function of a finite verb. This usage is not frequent, but certain syntactical patterns are worth noting.

2.1. *Genitive Absolute*

Along with a few other constructions, *a participle stands as an independent verb in a genitive absolute construction*. An absolute construction means that the participle is not formally dependent upon any other sentence or sentence element. In this construction the participle is found in the genitive case and normally has a noun or other substantive in the genitive case as well. In some instances, however, the noun may not be used.

Lk. 24.36: ταῦτα δὲ αὐτῶν λαλούντων αὐτὸς ἔστη ἐν μέσῳ αὐτῶν (but [while] they were speaking these things, he stood in their midst). In this use of the genitive absolute (αὐτῶν λαλούντων), an item in the absolute clause (first αὐτῶν) is referred to in the finite verb clause (second αὐτῶν). This connection between the clauses is more usual in Hellenistic Greek than in earlier classical Greek, although it was far from unknown then.

Rom. 2.15: συμμαρτυρούσης αὐτῶν τῆς συνειδήσεως καὶ μεταξὺ ἀλλήλων τῶν λογισμῶν κατηγορούντων ἢ καὶ ἀπολογουμένων (their conscience bears witness and among each other their thoughts condemn or give excuse).

Lk. 2.42-43: ἀναβαινόντων αὐτῶν κατὰ τὸ ἔθος τῆς ἑορτῆς καὶ τελειωσάντων τὰς ἡμέρας (and they went up according to the custom of the feast and they completed the days [i.e. stayed to the end of it]). This double use of the genitive absolute well illustrates that verbal aspect is not time-bound. The present participle is used to refer to an action which occurred before the action referred to using the aorist participle.

Mt. 17.14, 26: ἐλθόντων πρὸς τὸν ὄχλον...εἰπόντος δέ ([they] came to the crowd...and [Peter] said), examples where the subject of the participle is not included in the construction.

It is debated by grammarians whether there are examples of the dative or accusative absolute in the Greek of the NT.[1]

Mt. 14.6: γενεσίοις δὲ γενομένοις τοῦ Ἡρῴδου (and when the birthday of Herod came about), a possible example of the dative absolute.

Acts 26.3: μάλιστα γνώστην ὄντα σε (you are exceedingly knowledgeable), a possible example of the accusative absolute.

2.2. *Independent Participle*

The independent or hanging nominative participle (see under cases, Chapter 4 section 2.1.5) is an item of great dispute (see section 2.3 below for a particular use of the independent participle). The question is whether the independent participle (that is, a participle not directly dependent upon a finite verb or any other structure but clearly linked in some way) should be interpreted as simply a grammatical phenomenon whereby the author lost track of his or her syntax (anacoluthon) or whether the participle itself should be treated as the equivalent of a finite verb. Perhaps in a functional sense the result is the same, since the participle must do duty for the lacking finite verb.

Jn 7.38: ὁ πιστεύων εἰς ἐμέ (the one who believes in me), where

1. BDF, §200(3); Chapter 4 section 2.3.6 above.

this participle may stand on its own as an independent or hanging nominative, or, if the text is repunctuated, may serve as the subject of the previous finite verb (imperative) in v. 37.

2.3. *Commanding Participle*

There has been long-standing debate over whether the participle in NT Greek has a commanding sense (imperatival participle) when it is used independently (i.e. when it is not directly dependent upon a finite verb or any other structure, but is clearly linked in some way).

Rom. 12.9-19: ἀποστυγοῦντες τὸ πονηρόν, κολλώμενοι τῷ ἀγαθῷ...τῇ τιμῇ ἀλλήλους προηγούμενοι...τῷ πνεύματι ζέοντες, τῷ κυρίῳ δουλεύοντες, τῇ ἐλπίδι χαίροντες, τῇ θλίψει ὑπομένοντες, τῇ προσευχῇ προσκαρτεροῦντες, ταῖς χρείαις τῶν ἁγίων κοινωνοῦντες, τὴν φιλοξενίαν διώκοντες... τὸ αὐτὸ εἰς ἀλλήλους φρονοῦντες, μὴ τὰ ὑψηλὰ φρονοῦντες ἀλλὰ τοῖς ταπεινοῖς συναπαγόμενοι...μηδενὶ κακὸν ἀντὶ κακοῦ ἀποδιδόντες· προνοούμενοι καλὰ ἐνώπιον πάντων ἀνθρώπων· εἰ δυνατόν...μετὰ πάντων ἀνθρώπων εἰρηνεύοντες· μὴ ἑαυτοὺς ἐκδικοῦντες (hate evil, be united to good...be eager to honor one another...be zealous in spirit, serve the Lord, rejoice in hope, abide tribulation, be devoted to prayer, share the needs of the saints, pursue hospitality...think the same thing toward others, don't think on the loftiest things [i.e. don't have special regard for the privileged] but associate with the humble...pay back to no one evil for evil, observe good before all people; if possible...make peace with everyone, don't take vengeance for yourselves). This is the largest section of NT material where the independent participle might well occur. This passage has been explained in a number of ways.[1] Some say that it reflects a common Semitic idiom, in which the Semitic participle could substitute for an imperative.[2] Others believe that either there is some form of grammatical inconsistency or there is an understood form of εἰμί, making these examples periphrastic.[3] Others contend that the participles are adverbial, dependent upon another understood verb or

1. See Porter, *Verbal Aspect*, pp. 370-77.

2. E.g. D. Daube, 'Appended Note: Participle and Imperative in 1 Peter', in *The First Epistle of St Peter*, by E.G. Selwyn (London: Macmillan, 2nd edn, 1947), pp. 467-88, followed by many commentators, including Cranfield, Black, Michel, Wilckens.

3. E.g. Winer, *Treatise*, p. 442.

one more remotely placed.[1] Finally, some argue that these instances are intelligible examples of the independent use of the participle in Greek, in this case functioning as commands.[2] Moulton's support of the last proposal is compelling in light of the evidence he cites from contemporary papyri. This renders unnecessary any proposals regarding elided or understood finite verbs or regarding broken grammatical constructions.

1 Pet. 2.18: οἱ οἰκέται ὑποτασσόμενοι ἐν παντὶ φόβῳ τοῖς δεσπόταις (servants, be obedient in all fear to [your] masters).

1 Pet. 3.1: ὁμοίως [αἱ] γυναῖκες ὑποτασσόμεναι τοῖς ἰδίοις ἀνδράσιν (likewise women, be obedient to their husbands).

3. *Modifier*

A participle may serve as a modifier of verbal and substantival elements in a Greek clause.

3.1. *Substantives*

A participle, like an adjective, may modify substantives (adjectival, attributive, restrictive use). To use the analogy of slot and filler, there are instances where the participle may fill the slot occupied normally by modifying words such as adjectives. Linked with a substantive, the participle serves in much the same way as any other modifier, such as an adjective, except that it grammaticalizes verbal aspect and voice and can take its own objects and modifiers. In other words, it does not lose its verbal qualities.

Mt. 17.27: τὸν ἀναβάντα πρῶτον ἰχθύν (the fish coming up first).

Mk 3.22: οἱ γραμματεῖς οἱ ἀπὸ Ἱεροσολύμων καταβάντες ἔλεγον... (the scribes coming down from Jerusalem were saying...).

Rom. 3.5: μὴ ἄδικος ὁ θεὸς ὁ ἐπιφέρων τὴν ὀργήν; (the God who brings wrath is not unjust, is he?).

1 Tim. 1.18: τὰς προαγούσας ἐπὶ σὲ προφητείας (the prophecies previously made concerning you).

2 Tim. 2.6: τὸν κοπιῶντα γεωργόν (the hard-working farmer).

1. E.g. E. Mayser, *Grammatik der griechischen Papyri aus der Ptolemäerzeit* (2 vols.; Berlin: de Gruyter, 1906, 1934), II.1, pp. 196-97 n. 3, 340-41.

2. E.g. Moulton, *Prolegomena*, pp. 180-83, 223-25; Robertson, *Grammar*, pp. 944-46; Turner, *Syntax*, p. 343; Zerwick, *Biblical Greek*, pp. 129-30; BDF, §468.

3.2. *Verbs*

A participle may modify a finite verb (or another verb) in a sentence, a usage it has in common with, for example, adverbs (adverbial or circumstantial participle) (see sections 4 and 5 below for examples). Most grammarians treat this use of the participle as though the participle were modifying the verb alone. It must be remembered, however, that, although the participle in this construction is loosely dependent upon the main verb, it also retains its own relation to the subject of the construction, whether the subject is stated explicitly or simply understood.[1]

Lk. 21.1: ἀναβλέψας δὲ εἶδεν τοὺς βάλλοντας (and looking up, he saw those who were casting). In this example, the subject of the main, finite verb is also the one who is doing the looking.

Acts 21.36: ἠκολούθει...τὸ πλῆθος τοῦ λαοῦ κράζοντες... (the majority of the people were following, crying...), an *ad sensum* (according to sense) construction, with the plural modifying participle treating the singular subject and verb as collective.

The major issue in differentiating the use of the participle is its verbal aspect, as with finite verbs. Several of the implications of verbal aspect for use of the participle are brought out below.

4. *Issue of Time*

4.1. *Time and the Participle*

There is much confusion over the temporal sense of a participle. A persistent school of thought argues that the tense-forms even for participles convey past (aorist), present (present) or future (future) action.[2] This is despite a substantial current of thought by many grammarians that a participle conveys relative time only. In other words, *the temporal reference of a participle is established relative to its use in context.*[3] One might legitimately wonder what the contextual indicators are which might help to narrow the sphere of temporal reference. Two factors must be kept in mind. First, it is often the case that there is no need for determining 'when' an event referred to by a participle

1. Dana and Mantey, *Manual Grammar*, p. 226.

2. Winer, *Treatise*, pp. 427-32; Dana and Mantey, *Manual Grammar*, p. 230.

3. Robertson, *Grammar*, p. 1111; Moulton, *Prolegomena*, pp. 130-31; Zerwick, *Biblical Greek*, p. 129; Porter, *Verbal Aspect*, ch. 8.

occurred. This is frequently the case with substantival and modifying uses of the participle. Secondly, in contexts where issues of time are relevant, syntax seems to be important. This applies in particular to the verb-modifying (so-called adverbial) use of a participle (see section 3.2 above). *If a participle occurs before the finite verb on which it depends (or another verb which forms the governing or head term of the construction), the participle tends to refer to antecedent (preceding) action. If a participle occurs after the finite (or other) verb on which it depends, it tends to refer to concurrent (simultaneous) or subsequent (following) action.* This is only a generalization, but one which holds in a surprisingly large proportion of instances where temporal reference is at issue, and which includes usage of especially the aorist and present participles, as well as the perfect participle.[1]

This syntactical pattern is in conformity with use of verbal aspect in Greek. The aorist tense-form grammaticalizes the perfective aspect, which is often found in contexts—such as historical narratives—where action is looked upon as complete. Therefore, when an event is seen as preceding another action, or as already complete, the aorist is the natural form to use (though certainly not the only one available). When another aspect is used, note is to be taken of this usage. Likewise, when an event is seen as still taking place, especially as overlapping with a current action, or even still to come, the imperfective aspect grammaticalized by the present tense-form is the natural form to use.

Mt. 5.2: ἀνοίξας τὸ στόμα αὐτοῦ ἐδίδασκεν αὐτοὺς λέγων... (lit. having opened his mouth, he was teaching them, saying...). The opening of his mouth is seen as a necessary antecedent act. The teaching itself is the point of focus, warranting use of the present participle of concurrent action.

Jn 16.8: καὶ ἐλθὼν ἐκεῖνος ἐλέγξει τὸν κόσμον (and after he has come, that one will convict the world).

Jn 9.25: τυφλὸς ὢν ἄρτι βλέπω (having been blind, now I see), where the author clearly contrasts two temporal realms with the aid of an adverb.

Eph. 1.20: ἣν ἐνήργησεν ἐν τῷ Χριστῷ ἐγείρας αὐτὸν ἐκ νεκρῶν καὶ καθίσας ἐν δεξιᾷ αὐτοῦ ἐν τοῖς ἐπουρανίοις ([strength?] which he worked in Christ, raising him from the dead and

1. Moulton (*Prolegomena*, pp. 130-31) and Robertson (*Grammar*, p. 1113) seem to recognize this at least in part; it is developed more thoroughly in Porter, *Verbal Aspect*, pp. 380-85.

seating [him] at his right hand in the heavenlies), with aorist participles of concurrent and possibly subsequent action following the main verb.

Mt. 22.1: ἀποκριθεὶς ὁ Ἰησοῦς πάλιν εἶπεν ἐν παραβολαῖς αὐτοῖς λέγων...This example (a frequent pattern in the NT) appears to violate the general rule stated above. This is unless the author is seen as playing upon verbs of speaking, and the clause should be glossed: 'when he answered this time [answering seen as a complete process to introduce the section], Jesus again spoke in parables [complete process referring to the way in which he answered], saying [with the imperfective aspect forecasting the particular parable used]'.

4.2. *Subsequent Use of the Aorist Participle*

Many commentators minimize the subsequent (following) use of the aorist participle. Even such scholars as Robertson[1] and Moulton,[2] who recognize that the participle is not time-bound, resist this category of usage. But *there are a number of examples in biblical and extra-biblical Greek where an aorist participle is used to refer to an action occurring after the action of the main verb. In virtually all of these examples, the aorist participle is placed after the main verb in syntactical order.*[3] The future participle is not used in this way but is volitional[4] (see section 5.5 below).

Acts 23.27: ἐξειλάμην, μαθὼν ὅτι Ῥωμαῖός ἐστιν (I rescued him, learning [subsequently] that he was a Roman). In the sequence of events related in Acts 21, the Roman Lysias rescues Paul first, and then discovers that he is a Roman citizen, exactly what Acts 23.27 seems to say, according to the syntax. But commentators who hold to the traditional view of the tenses find this solution unacceptable, since the action of the aorist participle, they believe, should occur before the action of the main verb. For example, Marshall, in his commentary on Acts, states that the 'tribune twists the truth slightly in his own favour in the last phrase in the verse: it was not till after the arrest and the attempt to scourge him that the tribune learned that Paul was a Roman citizen'.[5] And Moule contends that it is an over-refinement to

1. Robertson, *Grammar*, pp. 861-63.
2. Moulton, *Prolegomena*, pp. 132-34.
3. See Porter, *Verbal Aspect*, pp. 385-87.
4. *Contra* Dana and Mantey, *Manual Grammar*, p. 230.
5. I.H. Marshall, *The Acts of the Apostles* (Grand Rapids: Eerdmans, 1980), p. 371.

analyze the aorist participle as subsequent.[1] But the syntactical rule regarding participles stated above provides an easy means of understanding this verse, legitimately harmonizing it with the earlier account in Acts.

Acts 25.13: κατήντησαν εἰς Καισάρειαν ἀσπασάμενοι τὸν Φῆστον (they went down into Caesaria, greeting [subsequently] Festus). A textual variant (in a few late texts) with the future participle perhaps indicates an understanding of the action of the aorist participle as subsequent to that of the main verb. The rule above accounts for this interpretation with the aorist, although many grammarians find it an odd construction.

Heb. 9.12: εἰσῆλθεν ἐφάπαξ εἰς τὰ ἅγια, αἰωνίαν λύτρωσιν εὑράμενος (he entered one time into the holy places, finding [subsequently] an eternal redemption).

4.3. *The Perfect Participle*

The perfect participle is less frequent than the other participles. It too seems to follow the syntactical pattern noted above, but this syntactical pattern is probably less important, since the stative aspect is more complex.

Jn 6.19: ἐληλακότες...θεωροῦσιν τὸν 'Ιησοῦν (having rowed ...they saw Jesus).

Mt. 6.5: φιλοῦσιν ἐν ταῖς συναγωγαῖς καὶ ἐν ταῖς γωνίαις τῶν πλατειῶν ἑστῶτες προσεύχεσθαι (they love standing to pray in the synagogues and on the corners of the streets).

5. *Relations between Events*

The verb-modifying participle enters into a number of syntactical relations which have semantic consequences. Some of these may be characterized as temporal relations between events (see section 4 above), *but others may be analyzed as indicating other sorts of circumstantial relations* (grammarians often label these the circumstantial or adverbial uses of the participle; see section 3.2 above). The following are some of the categories used by grammarians to indicate kinds of relations. These relations, however, are for the most part not grammaticalized but are inferred from context and tend to be subject to much discussion and debate. In English translation, even though a

1. Moule, *Idiom Book*, p. 100.

dependent clause may be used, the interpreter must resist the temptation to assume that a participle and a dependent clause are identical, since the participle is still a participle.[1] In some instances it may simply be better not to specify the relation between the participle and the other elements of the construction, since the context does not give specific indicators.

5.1. *Concessive*

A concessive relationship is one which concedes, grants or admits a point. Concessive use of a participle may be indicated by a concessive particle such as καίπερ (Heb. 7.5; 12.17); καί γε (Acts 17.27); καίτοι (Heb. 4.3).

Mt. 7.11: ὑμεῖς πονηροὶ ὄντες οἴδατε δόματα ἀγαθὰ διδόναι (you, although you are evil, know to give good gifts).

2 Cor. 10.3: ἐν σαρκὶ γὰρ περιπατοῦντες οὐ κατὰ σάρκα στρατευόμεθα (for although we are walking in the flesh, we are not fighting according to the flesh).

Heb. 5.8: καίπερ ὢν υἱὸς ἔμαθεν ἀφ' ὧν ἔπαθεν τὴν ὑπακοήν (in spite of being a son, he learned obedience from the things he suffered).

5.2. *Causal*

The cause of some other action or event can be indicated by use of a participle.

Mt. 1.19: Ἰωσὴφ...δίκαιος ὢν καὶ μὴ θέλων αὐτὴν δειγματίσαι, ἐβουλήθη λάθρᾳ ἀπολῦσαι αὐτήν (Joseph... because he was a just man and did not wish to disgrace her, determined to divorce her secretly).

Lk. 10.29: ὁ...θέλων δικαιῶσαι ἑαυτὸν εἶπεν πρὸς τὸν Ἰησοῦν (he...because he wished to justify himself, said to Jesus).

Acts 23.18: ὁ...παραλαβὼν αὐτὸν ἤγαγεν πρὸς τὸν χιλίαρχον (he...because he captured him, led [him] to the chiliarch).

1 Tim. 4.8: ἡ...εὐσέβεια πρὸς πάντα ὠφέλιμός ἐστιν, ἐπαγγελίαν ἔχουσα ζωῆς (godliness is profitable to all, because it has promise of life).

1. Dana and Mantey, *Manual Grammar*, p. 226.

5.3. *Conditional*
A participle may be used to indicate the protasis ('if') part of a conditional-like statement (see Chapter 16).

Lk. 9.25: τί γὰρ ὠφελεῖται ἄνθρωπος κερδήσας τὸν κόσμον ὅλον ἑαυτὸν δὲ ἀπολέσας ἢ ζημιωθείς; (for how does one benefit, if gaining the whole world but destroying or losing oneself?), where participles form the equivalent of the apodosis as well (ἀπολέσας, ζημιωθείς).

Acts 15.29: ἐξ ὧν διατηροῦντες ἑαυτοὺς εὖ πράξετε (if you keep yourselves from such things, you will do well).

Heb. 2.3: πῶς ἡμεῖς ἐκφευξόμεθα τηλικαύτης ἀμελήσαντες σωτηρίας; (how shall we escape, if we neglect so great a salvation?).

5.4. *Instrumental (Manner or Means)*
A participle can be used to indicate the instrument, manner or means by which another action takes place.

Mt. 6.27: τίς...ἐξ ὑμῶν μεριμνῶν δύναται προσθεῖναι ἐπὶ τὴν ἡλικίαν αὐτοῦ πῆχυν ἕνα; (who...among you, by fretting, is able to add one length to his age?).

Lk. 22.51: ἁψάμενος τοῦ ὠτίου ἰάσατο αὐτόν (by touching the ear, he healed him).

Phil. 2.7: ἑαυτὸν ἐκένωσεν μορφὴν δούλου λαβών (he emptied himself, by taking the form of a servant).

5.5. *Purpose (Final) or Resultive*
A participle may be used to indicate the purpose for an action or the result from some purposed act. A future participle is normally used in this way (volitional use).

Lk. 10.25: ἀνέστη ἐκπειράζων αὐτόν (he stood up, for the purpose of testing him).

Mt. 27.49: εἰ ἔρχεται Ἠλίας σώσων αὐτόν (if Elijah is coming, for the purpose of saving him), with a future participle.

Acts 8.27: ὃς ἐληλύθει προσκυνήσων εἰς Ἰερουσαλήμ (who came, for the purpose of worshiping in Jerusalem), with a future participle.

5.6. *Complementary (Supplementary)*
The complementary or supplementary use of a participle occurs when the idea of the finite verb is completed by the participle.

Eph. 1.16: οὐ παύομαι εὐχαριστῶν ὑπὲρ ὑμῶν (I do not cease praying for you).

Heb. 5.12: γεγόνατε χρείαν ἔχοντες γάλακτος (you have come to need milk).

Chapter 11

INFINITIVES

Introduction

The infinitive (often called a verbal noun), like the participle—a very important form in the Greek language—has similarities both to the noun and to the verb. Its similarity to the verb includes its grammaticalizing of verbal aspect (tense) and voice, as well as its ability to take objects and verbal modifiers. Its functional similarity to the noun is established by means of syntax, especially use of the article (always neuter singular), and thus it is given gender and case. If the subject of an infinitive is expressed, as it may be, it is often in the accusative case (see section 4 below).

There is a major formal distinction to make in uses of the infinitive: sometimes it occurs with the article (articular), and sometimes without the article (anarthrous). Most scholars are agreed that the difference between the two structures does not warrant a major distinction in meaning. The articular infinitive is marked by the article (see Chapter 5) either establishing a syntactical relation (such as case) or emphasizing the infinitive's substantival characteristics. The articular infinitive may be used as the object (completive) of a preposition as well. The prepositions help to specify the use of the infinitive (see Chapter 9 on prepositions). The anarthrous infinitive appears approximately six times as often as the articular infinitive, and most of the categories of interpretation rely upon the interpreter's evaluation of the context apart from specific syntactical indicators. See, for example, Lk. 2.22, 24: ἀνήγαγον αὐτὸν εἰς Ἱεροσόλυμα παραστῆσαι τῷ κυρίῳ...καὶ τοῦ δοῦναι θυσίαν. Even though there are no clear syntactical markers, the purpose use of the anarthrous infinitive parallel to the articular infinitive is a likely (but not the only) explanation: 'they brought him up into Jerusalem to present [for the purpose of presenting] him to the Lord...and to give a sacrifice'.

The functional similarities of the infinitive and participle raise a question about the semantic difference between the two. The participle apparently carries more semantic force than the infinitive. This may be related to the participle taking endings indicating gender, number and case. These are specifications which the infinitive does not offer without syntactical help, and even then in a limited way (only one gender is used). The infinitive, in many ways resembling an indeclinable form, is the closest the Greek language comes to simple representation of the verbal force. Like the participle, in the Greek of the NT the infinitive is negated by μή.

1. *Substantive*

An infinitive may function as a substantive in a variety of contexts; that is, it performs the same tasks as nouns and noun-substitutes such as pronouns. An important distinction between the form and function of the infinitive must be made. The flexibility of the infinitive makes it possible to use the infinitive in environments where other words are often used in Greek. In a place where a noun might be used, such as the subject of a clause, the infinitive may be used as well. To use the language of slot and filler, the infinitive may fill the subject slot, and take the appropriate modifiers of a noun as well as verbal elements (e.g. objects and modifiers such as adverbs).

1.1. *Subject*

An infinitive may serve as the subject (and so-called predicate nominative) of a clause. In the English sentence, 'To ask the right questions is to be a good student', the infinitive is both the subject and the so-called predicate nominative. The infinitive is frequently the subject of verbs which are often taken impersonally (see Chapter 3 section 2.2.4).

Mt. 3.15: πρέπον ἐστὶν ἡμῖν πληρῶσαι πᾶσαν δικαιοσύνην (to fulfil all righteousness is fitting for us).

Mt. 12.12: ἔξεστιν τοῖς σάββασιν καλῶς ποιεῖν (to do well on the Sabbath is lawful).

Phil. 1.21, 24: τὸ ζῆν Χριστὸς καὶ τὸ ἀποθανεῖν κέρδος...τὸ δὲ ἐπιμένειν [ἐν] τῇ σαρκὶ ἀναγκαιότερον δι' ὑμᾶς (to live [is] Christ and to die [is] gain...and to remain in the flesh [is] preferable because of you).

Mk 9.10: τί ἐστιν τὸ ἐκ νεκρῶν ἀναστῆναι; (what is 'to rise up from the dead'?), an instance of the predicate nominative in relation to the interrogative pronoun.

Moule contends that in a number of instances the infinitive following the genitive article is the subject of its clause: Lk. 17.1; Acts 10.25; 27.1; 1 Cor. 16.4.[1] The instances might also be construed as appositional uses of the genitive, restating or rephrasing the action being spoken of: e.g. Lk. 17.1: ἀνένδεκτόν ἐστιν τοῦ τὰ σκάνδαλα μὴ ἐλθεῖν (it is impossible for causes of stumbling not to come). See section 2.1 below.

1.2. *Complement (Object)*

An infinitive may appear in relation to the predicate or main verb of a clause as a complement or object (completive). This is similar to the way that an infinitive can be used as a complement or object in the English sentence, 'I like to drive'. There are several different contexts in which this usage appears.

1.2.1. *Complement or object. The infinitive may fill the slot of a substantival complement or object which receives the action of the predicate or main verb of the construction.*

Lk. 1.9: ἔλαχε τοῦ θυμιᾶσαι (he drew lots to offer sacrifices), where the object is found in the genitive case, not an unusual phenomenon in Greek (see Chapter 4 on cases).

Rom. 1.10: εὐοδωθήσομαι ἐν τῷ θελήματι τοῦ θεοῦ ἐλθεῖν πρὸς ὑμᾶς (I will have the way cleared by the will of God to come to you). Various interpretations of the relationship between the main verb and the infinitive may be postulated, but the syntax indicates the complement use as one of them.

2 Cor. 8.10-11: τὸ ποιῆσαι ἀλλὰ καὶ τὸ θέλειν προενήρξασθε ἀπὸ πέρυσι· νυνὶ δὲ καὶ τὸ ποιῆσαι ἐπιτελέσατε (from last year you started to do but also to desire [to do]—but now complete the doing). It is difficult in the second clause to translate the Greek infinitive into idiomatic English using 'to', illustrating that the English translation with 'to' may often be useful but is *not* necessary for understanding or translating the Greek infinitive.

Phil. 2.13: θεὸς...ἐστιν ὁ ἐνεργῶν ἐν ὑμῖν καὶ τὸ θέλειν καὶ τὸ

1. Moule, *Idiom Book*, p. 129.

ἐνεργεῖν ὑπὲρ τῆς εὐδοκίας (God is the one who works among you both to will and to accomplish for pleasure), where two infinitives are the objects of the participle (note repetition of ἐνεργέω).

1.2.2. *Indirect discourse* (see Chapter 17). *An infinitive can be used as an object of a verb of perception (speaking, thinking, and the like) to convey indirect speech.* If the subject of the infinitive is the same as that of the main verb (a) the subject need not be repeated but is usually in the nominative case if it is expressed. If the subject of the infinitive is different from that of the main verb (b) the accusative case is used to express the subject of the infinitive, as in normal use of the infinitive.

a. *Subject of infinitive same as subject of main verb.*

Acts 25.11: οὐ παραιτοῦμαι τὸ ἀποθανεῖν (I am not refusing to die).

Rom. 1.13: προεθέμην ἐλθεῖν πρὸς ὑμᾶς (I intended to come to you).

b. *Subject of infinitive different from subject of main verb.*

Mk 12.18: οἵτινες λέγουσιν ἀνάστασιν μὴ εἶναι (who were saying that there is no resurrection).

Phil. 2.6: οὐχ ἁρπαγμὸν ἡγήσατο τὸ εἶναι ἴσα θεῷ (he did not consider that equality with God was a thing to be grasped).

1.2.3. *Catenative constructions. Certain verbs in Greek—e.g.* μέλλω, θέλω, δύναμαι, δεῖ, *and a few others—appear frequently in conjunction with infinitives.* These instances could be construed as examples of the complement or object use of the infinitive (section 1.2.1 above). They are placed in their own category, however, because they form a definable, recurring construction. These are not properly called periphrastic verbal constructions, in which a participle is joined with a form of εἰμί (which is aspectually vague) to form a single verbal unit. *In catenative constructions the verbal aspects of the main verb and the infinitive are to be included in the semantics of the syntactical unit.*

Mt. 2.13: μέλλει... Ἡρῴδης ζητεῖν τὸ παιδίον (Herod is going to search for the child), cf. following final infinitive.

Mt. 7.18: οὐ δύναται δένδρον ἀγαθὸν καρποὺς πονηροὺς ποιεῖν (a good plant is not able to produce worthless fruit).

Lk. 13.14: δεῖ ἐργάζεσθαι (it is necessary to be at work).

Rom. 1.13: οὐ θέλω...ὑμᾶς ἀγνοεῖν (I do not want...you to be ignorant), a formulaic phrase used by Paul. Similar constructions are used frequently by other Hellenistic letter writers.

2. *Modifier*

There are a number of important modifying uses of the infinitive. Some of them appear with the article and some of them do not. Modifiers of substantives and verbs (or predicates) are included together, since the basic function is similar. It is not always easy to classify a given instance of the infinitive, since the contextual indicators may not be decisive. The infinitive often occurs without any modification or not within any tightly connected syntactical structure. When an infinitive is used as part of a prepositional phrase, this syntactical construction must be taken seriously, although even then it may not clarify every use. The infinitive after τοῦ may be placed in a number of the following categories.

2.1. *Epexegetic or Appositional*

Some grammarians distinguish between the appositive use for modifying substantives and the epexegetic use for modifying verbs.[1] The ability of the infinitive to serve as a modifier, specifying or defining the modified element (whether a word or a phrase), is the important factor.

Jn 1.12: ἔδωκεν αὐτοῖς ἐξουσίαν τέκνα θεοῦ γενέσθαι (he gave to them the authority to become children of God).

Acts 14.9: ἔχει πίστιν τοῦ σωθῆναι (he has the faith to be saved). This is one of only several possible understandings, another being result (see section 2.2 below).

Rom. 1.28: παρέδωκεν αὐτοὺς ὁ θεὸς εἰς ἀδόκιμον νοῦν, ποιεῖν τὰ μὴ καθήκοντα (God handed them over to a depraved mind, i.e. to the practice of things that are not appropriate).

Rom. 8.12: ὀφειλέται ἐσμὲν οὐ τῇ σαρκὶ τοῦ κατὰ σάρκα ζῆν (we are debtors not to the flesh, i.e. to living according to the flesh).

Jas 1.27: θρησκεία καθαρὰ καὶ ἀμίαντος παρὰ τῷ θεῷ καὶ πατρὶ αὕτη ἐστίν, ἐπισκέπτεσθαι ὀρφανοὺς καὶ χήρας ἐν τῇ θλίψει αὐτῶν, ἄσπιλον ἑαυτὸν τηρεῖν ἀπὸ τοῦ κόσμου (this is pure and undefiled religion from [our] God and father: to watch out for orphans and

1. E.g. Moule, *Idiom Book*, pp. 127, 129.

widows in their distress, to keep oneself spotless from the world); cf. Chapter 8 introduction and section 2.7.1.

Rev. 12.7: ἐγένετο πόλεμος ἐν τῷ οὐρανῷ, ὁ Μιχαὴλ καὶ οἱ ἄγγελοι αὐτοῦ τοῦ πολεμῆσαι μετὰ τοῦ δράκοντος (war came about in heaven, i.e. Michael and his angels fighting with the dragon). Note use of the nominative case for subject of the infinitive.

Moule notes several instances (Acts 15.10; Heb. 5.5; 1 Cor. 7.25) where it might be difficult to distinguish this use from result (section 2 below).[1]

2.2. Purpose or Resultive

It is often difficult to decide whether purpose or result is being expressed by use of the infinitive, even when it follows a preposition such as πρός or εἰς (see Chapter 14 section 1.1). This dilemma is caused in part by inherent difficulty in analyzing the preposition, and in part by the conceptual overlap of the categories of purpose and result. The difference in translation may often be reflected in phrasing like 'for the purpose of' versus 'with the result that'. Perhaps one of the most disputed uses is ὥστε with the infinitive. Many grammarians believe that in Hellenistic Greek ὥστε with the infinitive can have either a purpose or a result sense.[2] Other grammarians argue just as vociferously that the resultive sense is clearly predominant.[3] The words πρός, εἰς and ὡς are used to indicate the purpose or result relationship, with efiw (along with ἐν) the most frequent preposition with an infinitive in the Greek of the NT.

Mt. 5.17: ἦλθον καταλῦσαι τὸν νόμον (I came to destroy the law), where purpose seems most likely: 'I came for the purpose of...'

Lk. 8.5: ἐξῆλθεν ὁ σπείρων τοῦ σπεῖραι (the sower went out to sow), where purpose seems most likely; result is also a possibility.

Acts 5.3: διὰ τί ἐπλήρωσεν ὁ σατανᾶς τὴν καρδίαν σου ψεύσασθαί σε τὸ πνεῦμα τὸ ἅγιον καὶ νοσφίσασθαι ἀπὸ τῆς τιμῆς τοῦ χωρίου; (why did Satan fill your heart so that you lied to the Holy

1. Moule, *Idiom Book*, p. 127.
2. E.g. Moulton, *Prolegomena*, p. 207.
3. M.J. Higgins, 'NT Result Clauses with Infinitive', *CBQ* 23 (1961), pp. 233-41. Distinctions among kinds of result—actual, natural, conceived, intended—are not necessary to make here. In a given instance the differentiations might prove useful.

Spirit and withheld from the receipt for the land?), probably two instances of result.

Rom. 6.6: καταργηθῇ τὸ σῶμα τῆς ἁμαρτίας, τοῦ μηκέτι δουλεύειν ἡμᾶς τῇ ἁμαρτίᾳ (the body of sin might be destroyed, so that we are no longer [or, so that we might no longer be] slaves to sin), where purpose or result is possible, although here it may be that the sense of purpose is a necessary antecedent to any possible result.

Lk. 4.29: ὥστε κατακρημνίσαι αὐτόν (so that [they] might cast him down), where only purpose seems plausible, since the result was never accomplished.

1 Thess. 1.8: ὥστε μὴ χρείαν ἔχειν ἡμᾶς λαλεῖν τι (so that we might not have a need to say anything), an example of result; 1 Thess. 1.7: ὥστε γενέσθαι ὑμᾶς τύπον πᾶσιν τοῖς πιστεύουσιν (so that you might become a model for all who believe), another example of result.

Mt. 6.1: πρὸς τὸ θεαθῆναι αὐτοῖς (in order to be seen by them), with the infinitive following πρός.

Rom. 6.12: εἰς τὸ ὑπακούειν ταῖς ἐπιθυμίαις αὐτοῦ (so that [you] obey its desires), a familiar use of εἰς; Rom. 1.11: εἰς τὸ στηριχθῆναι ὑμᾶς (so that you might be established); Rom. 1.20: εἰς τὸ εἶναι αὐτοὺς ἀναπολογήτους (so that they are without excuse).

Lk. 9.52: ὡς ἑτοιμάσαι αὐτῷ (so as to prepare for him), a fairly rare use of ὡς and an infinitive to indicate purpose or result.

2.3. *Causal*

The infinitive may be used to indicate a causal connection. The prepositions διά and occasionally ἕνεκα (and its forms) are often used to indicate this relationship. ἐκ might have this sense as well.

2 Cor. 2.13: οὐκ ἔσχηκα ἄνεσιν τῷ πνεύματί μου τῷ μὴ εὑρεῖν με Τίτον τὸν ἀδελφόν μου (I did not have rest in my spirit because I did not find Titus my brother).

Jas 4.2: οὐκ ἔχετε διὰ τὸ μὴ αἰτεῖσθαι ὑμᾶς (you do not have because you do not ask); Mt. 13.5: ἐξανέτειλεν διὰ τὸ μὴ ἔχειν βάθος γῆς (it sprang up because it did not have [any] depth of earth).

2 Cor. 7.12: ἀλλ' ἕνεκεν τοῦ φανερωθῆναι τὴν σπουδὴν ὑμῶν (but on account of your desire being revealed).

2 Cor. 8.11: ἐκ τοῦ ἔχειν (because of having), the only instance in the Pauline writings with ἐκ.

2.4. *Temporal*

Temporal use of the infinitive is frequent, especially with prepositions. Use of the tenses with various temporal indicators shows that the tense-forms of the infinitive are not time-bound. The prepositions πρό, πρίν (ἤ) and ἕως are used with antecedent (previous) action; ἐν with concurrent (simultaneous) action; and μετά with subsequent (following) action.

Jn 1.48: πρὸ τοῦ σε Φίλιππον φωνῆσαι...εἶδόν σε (before Philip called you...I saw you).

Lk. 22.15: πρὸ τοῦ με παθεῖν (before I suffer).

Jn 4.49: κατάβηθι πρὶν ἀποθανεῖν τὸ παιδίον μου (come down before my child dies).

Acts 8.40: ἕως τοῦ ἐλθεῖν αὐτὸν εἰς Καισάρειαν (until [before] he came to Caesarea).

Lk. 8.5: ἐν τῷ σπείρειν αὐτόν (while he was sowing); Lk. 24.15: ἐν τῷ ὁμιλεῖν αὐτοὺς καὶ συζητεῖν (while they were talking and arguing).

Lk. 11.37: ἐν...τῷ λαλῆσαι ἐρωτᾷ αὐτὸν Φαρισαῖος (while... speaking, a Pharisee asked him).

Mk 1.14: μετὰ...τὸ παραδοθῆναι τὸν Ἰωάννην (after...John was arrested).

Mt. 26.32: μετὰ...τὸ ἐγερθῆναί με (after...I am raised).

2.5. *Substitutionary*

The infinitive may specify a relation in which substitution occurs (that is, one item is substituted for another). This use is very rare, but one example can be ascertained. Note that the preposition is important for establishing this semantic relationship.

Jas 4.15: ἀντὶ τοῦ λέγειν ὑμᾶς (instead of you saying), with something else endorsed.

3. *Predicate*

An infinitive may be used in a predicate structure, serving the function of a finite verb such as an imperative (commanding use). This is much more frequent in Greek outside of the NT (cf. e.g. Arrian, *Anabasis* 7.25; Epictetus). However, there are several noteworthy examples in the NT, especially in invocations of letters, reflecting wider Hellenistic Greek usage. Often an independent use of the infinitive functions in place of an imperative or in indirect discourse. These uses are very similar to the ones noted for the participle. To use the language of slot and filler, an infinitive can fill the verb slot in a predicate structure and take all of the appropriate modifiers or completives of a verb (e.g. objects and modifiers such as adverbs).

Acts 15.23; Jas 1.1: χαίρειν ('greetings'), a standard word of greeting widely used in the Hellenistic epistolary papyri discovered in Egypt. The first example quotes a letter sent by the Jerusalem council and the second occurs in the actual opening of James.

Lk. 9.3: μήτε [ἀνὰ] δύο χιτῶνας ἔχειν (neither have two garments), following an imperative. This may indicate a switch from direct discourse to indirect discourse with the infinitive (see Chapter 17).

Acts 23.24: κτήνη τε παραστῆσαι (and provide animals), following an imperative. This may indicate a switch from direct discourse to indirect discourse with the infinitive (see Chapter 17).

Phil. 3.16: εἰς ὃ ἐφθάσαμεν, τῷ αὐτῷ στοιχεῖν (to what we have attained, let us live to this level), with the commanding or exhorting sense of the infinitive.

Rom. 12.15: χαίρειν μετὰ χαιρόντων, κλαίειν μετὰ κλαιόντων (rejoice with the rejoicers, cry with the cryers). Note the use of infinitives and participles.

Heb. 7.9: καὶ ὡς ἔπος εἰπεῖν (so to speak), a classical Greek idiom found only here in the NT.

4. *Subject of the Infinitive*

The subject of an infinitive is usually the same as the subject of the main verb if there is no further specification. See, for example, Mt. 2.2: ἤλθομεν προσκυνῆσαι αὐτῷ (we have come to worship him). *In instances where the subject of an infinitive is different from the subject of the main verb, the subject of the infinitive is normally specified using an item in the accusative case*. See, for example, Jn 6.10: ποιήσατε τοὺς ἀνθρώπους ἀναπεσεῖν (make the men sit down). This is often called an accusative of respect, though it must be realized that it serves the function of the subject of the infinitive construction.

Determining the subject of an infinitive when two elements are found in the accusative case—and each stands as a plausible subject of the infinitive construction—can clearly present a problem. But recent research indicates that *in infinitive constructions in the NT where two items are found in the accusative, in the overwhelming majority of instances the subject precedes the object.*[1] 1 Cor. 7.10-11: γυναῖκα ἀπὸ ἀνδρὸς μὴ χωρισθῆναι—ἐὰν δὲ καὶ χωρισθῇ, μενέτω ἄγαμος ἢ τῷ ἀνδρὶ καταλλαγήτω—καὶ ἄνδρα γυναῖκα μὴ ἀφιέναι (a woman is not to be separated from [her] husband—but if she might be separated, let her remain unmarried or let her be reconciled to the husband—and a husband is not to send away a wife); 2 Cor. 2.13: μὴ εὑρεῖν με Τίτον τὸν ἀδελφόν μου (I did not find Titus my brother).

The few instances where the rule is not followed can be explained. In a few of these the subject is an interrogative pronoun (Mt. 16.13, 15; Mk 8.27, 29; Lk. 9.18, 20; Acts 2.12; 13.25; 17.20). More importantly, in a couple of instances it is clear that the author has altered the word order for the sake of emphasis (see Chapter 20 on word order and clause structure). For example, Jn 1.48: πρὸ τοῦ σε Φίλιππον φωνῆσαι (before Philip called you), where σε is displaced to the front because of emphasis placed upon Jesus' knowledge of Nathaniel, who has just asked Jesus, 'How do you know me?' This rule helps to establish the understanding of several potentially ambiguous clauses, such as Phil. 1.7: διὰ τὸ ἔχειν με ἐν τῇ καρδίᾳ ὑμᾶς (because I have you in my heart). Although several commentators opt for the Philippians having Paul in their heart,[2] Paul is probably the subject, as reflected in the translation above.[3]

1. See J.T. Reed, 'The Infinitive with Two Substantival Accusatives: An Ambiguous Construction?', *NovT* 33 (1991), pp. 1-27.

2. E.g. G.F. Hawthorne, *Philippians* (Waco, TX: Word Books, 1983), pp. 22-23, who thinks the Greek is almost unredeemably ambiguous.

3. See J.B. Lightfoot, *St Paul's Epistle to the Philippians* (London: Macmillan, 1913), p. 84, who recognizes a word-order rule; cf. M. Silva, *Philippians* (Chicago: Moody, 1988), pp. 56-57, who is right but for inadequate reasons.

Chapter 12

PARTICLES AND CONJUNCTIONS

Introduction

The Greek of the NT maintains a system of particles and conjunctions. There is the unfortunate tendency by some to see Hellenistic Greek (and the Greek of the NT) as deficient in comparison to classical Greek with respect to particles.[1] A more informed judgment recognizes that the languages are simply different. In other words, NT Greek has developed and changed in particular ways: reduction of combinations of certain particles, but new use and extended use of other particles.[2] When clauses are not connected by particles but are placed 'back to back' so to speak, they are said to be asyndetic, or to have asyndeton.[3]

1. *Definition*

For the sake of discussion in this chapter, *a particle is considered to be a word of set form (i.e. an indeclinable word) used for the purpose of introducing subjective semantic nuances (i.e. nuances of meaning) to a clause or to the relationship between clauses. Conjunctions are a sub-class of particles used to join various grammatical units, such as phrases, clauses, and so on.* Conjunctions and particles are treated together in alphabetical order, although reference will be made to

1. BDF, §438; on classical usage, see J.D. Denniston, *The Greek Particles* (Oxford: Clarendon Press, 2nd edn, 1954).

2. On Hellenistic and in particular NT Greek, see Thrall, *Greek Particles*; J. Blomquist, *Greek Particles in Hellenistic Prose* (Lund: Gleerup, 1969). For an attempt at applying modern linguistic principles, see V.S. Poythress, 'The Use of the Intersentence Conjunctions *De, Oun, Kai*, and Asyndeton in the Gospel of John', *NovT* 26 (1984), pp. 312-37.

3. See BDF, §§458-63.

other chapters where useful examples are presented in more detail. Semantic labels are employed for classificatory purposes; for example, adversative (contrasting things usually equal), causal, comparative, conditional, connective (linking things usually equal), consecutive, emphatic, explanatory, inferential (introducing a conclusion), and temporal. Each particle will be given one or more of these labels for ease of reference, but these should not be taken as categorical. The treatment is only meant to be suggestive, with examples often confined to a single useful instance. Not all particles and conjunctions are discussed, especially conjunctions that are used with dependent clauses (see Chapter 14).

Several particles are considered postpositive, and are so labeled. What it means to appear in postpositive position is difficult to describe. Postpositive words apparently can appear anywhere from right after the first word to after the first entire element (e.g. a phrase) or beyond (see Chapter 20 section 1.3.2, for placement of postpositive words).

2. *Particles and Conjunctions*

2.1. ἀλλά *(Conjunction, Adversative or Emphatic)*

This particle is frequent in the Pauline epistles. Its major usage is adversative.

Rom. 5.3: ἀλλὰ καὶ καυχώμεθα ἐν ταῖς θλίψεσιν (but let us also boast in tribulations), following οὐ μόνον δέ and retaining its adversative sense.[1]

It may also be used in an emphatic sense.

2 Cor. 7.11: πόσην κατειργάσατο ὑμῖν σπουδήν, ἀλλὰ ἀπολογίαν, ἀλλὰ ἀγανάκτησιν, ἀλλὰ φόβον, ἀλλὰ ἐπιπόθησιν, ἀλλὰ ζῆλον, ἀλλὰ ἐκδίκησιν (it accomplished such great earnestness in you, indeed self-vindication, indeed indignation, indeed fear, indeed desire, indeed zeal, indeed vengeance). These instances are characterized by various grammarians as confirmatory or continuative.[2]

Jn 8.26: ἀλλ' ὁ πέμψας με ἀληθής ἐστιν (indeed, the one who sent me is true), where the emphatic sense solves the problem of continuity with the first part of the verse: πολλὰ ἔχω περὶ ὑμῶν λαλεῖν καὶ κρίνειν (I have many things to say and judge concerning you); 2 Cor.

1. *Contra* Turner, *Syntax*, pp. 329-30.
2. Robertson, *Grammar*, p. 1185.

4.16: ἀλλ' ὁ ἔσω ἡμῶν ἀνακαινοῦται ἡμέρᾳ καὶ ἡμέρᾳ (but indeed our inner person is being renewed day by day), carrying an adversative and an emphatic sense.

ἀλλά γε (1 Cor. 9.2), ἀλλά γε καί (Lk. 24.21), ἀλλὰ μενοῦν γε καί (Phil. 3.8), unique instances where emphatic particles are added to ἀλλά.[1]

2.2. ἀμήν *(Particle, Emphatic)*

This particle is probably Semitic in origin.[2] The emphatic use (approximately 75 instances in the NT) always appears with λέγω.

Jn 1.51: ἀμὴν ἀμὴν λέγω ὑμῖν (truly, truly I say to you).

This particle is used substantivally as well (Rev. 3.14).

2.3. ἄν *(Particle, Conditional)*

This particle has been widely discussed in the grammars.[3] Some call it a 'modal particle', with the implication that it in some way alters the modal force of a verb with which it appears. This misconception must be abandoned. Recent research indicates that the particle is not a marker of 'verbal mood' but is a 'conditional' marker which implies an assumed general conditional clause. This is not to say that the language user would necessarily have had a conditional statement in mind but that it marks some kind of generality as would be indicated by a third class conditional statement (on conditional clauses, see Chapter 16). ἄν occurs with the indicative in the Greek of the NT, as well.

Mk 6.56: ὅσοι ἂν ἥψαντο αὐτοῦ (whoever touched it, i.e. if anyone touched it).

2.4. ἄρα, ἆρα *(Conjunction, Inferential)*

ἄρα was postpositive in classical Greek (see Acts 21.38; Rom. 8.1), but is widespread in first position in NT Greek.

Rom. 10.17: ἄρα ἡ πίστις ἐξ ἀκοῆς (therefore, faith [is] by hearing).

2 Cor. 5.14: ἄρα οἱ πάντες ἀπέθανον (therefore, all died).

ἆρα is simply another form of ἄρα and is also inferential, often being used in questions.

1. See Thrall, *Greek Particles*, pp. 36-37, 11-16.
2. See BAGD, *s.v.* ἀμήν.
3. See Porter, *Verbal Aspect*, p. 166; cf. Goodwin, *Greek Grammar*, pp. 277-80; Winer, *Treatise*, p. 378.

Lk. 18.8: ἆρα εὑρήσει τὴν πίστιν ἐπὶ τῆς γῆς; (will he, then, find faith upon the earth?).

Gal. 2.17. There is dispute whether this should be understood as (a) a question with ἆρα possibly implying a negative answer: ἆρα Χριστὸς ἁμαρτίας διάκονος; (Christ isn't a servant of sin, is he?), (b) a question with ἄρα: ἄρα Χριστὸς ἁμαρτίας διάκονος; (is Christ then a servant of sin?), or (c) simply inferential with ἄρα: ἄρα Χριστὸς ἁμαρτίας διάκονος (Christ then is a servant of sin).[1] The following μὴ γένοιτο makes (a) or (b) the most likely understandings.

ἄρα οὖν. This combination of particles is found in the NT exclusively in the Pauline writings (and is only attested a few times outside of the NT): Rom. 5.18; 7.3, 25; 8.12; 9.16, 18; 14.12, 19; Gal. 6.10; Eph. 2.19; 1 Thess. 5.6; 2 Thess. 2.15. According to Thrall, 'The purpose of the combination is presumably to provide an emphatically inferential connective'.[2]

Rom. 5.18: ἄρα οὖν ὡς δι' ἑνὸς παραπτώματος...(therefore, as through one man's transgression...), followed by οὕτως.

2.5. γάρ *(Conjunction, Inferential [Illative, Causal] or Explanatory, Postpositive)*[3]

The inferential sense is widespread.

Mt. 27.23: τί γὰρ κακὸν ἐποίησεν; (for what evil did he do?), occurring here in a question, a common pattern.

The explanatory sense is also found.

1 Cor. 11.7: ἀνὴρ μὲν γὰρ οὐκ ὀφείλει κατακαλύπτεσθαι τὴν κεφαλήν (for a man is not obligated to have [his] head covered).

Mk 16.8: ἐφοβοῦντο γάρ (for they were afraid). Some use this construction as an argument against the short ending of Mark because they believe that it is highly unlikely that a book would end with this

1. Position (a) is taken by N–A^{26} and *UBSGNT*^{3}; (b) by F.F. Bruce, *The Epistle to the Galatians: A Commentary on the Greek Text* (Grand Rapids: Eerdmans, 1982), p. 141; and (c) by Moule, *Idiom Book*, p. 196.

2. Thrall, *Greek Particles*, p. 10.

3. See C.H. Bird, 'Some gar Clauses in St Mark's Gospel', *JTS* NS 4 (1953), pp. 171-87; Thrall, *Greek Particles*, pp. 41-50; R.A. Edwards, 'Narrative Implications of *Gar* in Matthew', *CBQ* 52 (1990), pp. 636-55, who discusses and classifies the uses of γάρ in Matthew as predominantly 'reason' but also 'explanatory'.

connecting word. Recent research indicates that discourse units in Greek can end with this conjunction.[1]

2.6. γέ *(Particle, Emphatic, Postpositive)*
This enclitic particle emphasizes the word with which it occurs. It often occurs with other particles (e.g. ἀλλά, ἄρα, εἰ, καί).[2]

Rom. 8.32: ὅς γε τοῦ ἰδίου υἱοῦ οὐκ ἐφείσατο (who indeed did not spare his own son).

2.7. δέ *(Conjunction, Adversative or Connective or Emphatic, Postpositive)*
In NT Greek δέ rivals καί for the distinction of most common sentence conjunction.[3] The most common use of this widespread conjunction is adversative (it is not as strong an adversative as ἀλλά).

Mt. 5.22: ἐγὼ δὲ λέγω ὑμῖν (but I say to you), in the Matthaean antitheses.

Another significant usage, often neglected in analysis, is connective.

Rom. 2.8: τοῖς...ἐξ ἐριθείας καὶ ἀπειθοῦσι τῇ ἀληθείᾳ πειθομένοις δὲ τῇ ἀδικίᾳ (to those...who do not obey the truth out of strife, and who are persuaded to unrighteousness), with δέ connecting phrases.

Mt. 1.2-16, in the Matthaean genealogy.

A third use is for emphasis.

Rom. 3.22: δικαιοσύνη δὲ θεοῦ διὰ πίστεως (indeed the righteousness of God through faith), picking up reference to δικαιοσύνη in v. 21. (See also Chapter 5 section 2.8.2 on use of δέ with the article.)

2.8. δή *(Particle, Emphatic, Postpositive)*
δή and δέ are related (cf. Acts 6.3, where there are textual variants between the two). Most examples occur with the imperative (Acts 13.2; 1 Cor. 6.20) or hortatory subjunctive (Lk. 2.15; Acts 15.36), except Mt. 13.23: ὃς δὴ καρποφορεῖ (who indeed bears fruit).

δήπου. Heb. 2.16: οὐ γὰρ δήπου ἀγγέλων ἐπιλαμβάνεται (for indeed he does not help angels).

1. See P.W. van der Horst, 'Can a Book End with ΓΑΡ? A Note on Mk 16.8', *JTS* NS 23 (1972), pp. 121-24. This still may not have been Mark's original ending, however.

2. See Robertson, *Grammar*, pp. 1148-49.

3. See Turner, *Syntax*, p. 332, for proportions; cf. also S.H. Levinsohn, *Textual Connections in Acts* (Atlanta: Scholars Press, 1987), pp. 86-120.

2.9. διό *(Conjunction, Inferential)*
This particle is often considered a subordinator, although it is not clear that this is the way it is used in the NT.[1]

Mt. 27.8: διὸ ἐκλήθη ὁ ἀγρὸς ἐκεῖνος...(therefore, that field was called...).

2 Cor. 4.13: ἡμεῖς πιστεύομεν, διὸ καὶ λαλοῦμεν (we believe, therefore we also speak).

διόπερ. 1 Cor. 8.13: διόπερ εἰ βρῶμα σκανδαλίζει τὸν ἀδελφόν μου (therefore, if food offends my brother); 1 Cor. 10.14: διόπερ... φεύγετε ἀπὸ τῆς εἰδωλολατρίας (therefore...flee from idolatry).

διότι is treated as a subordinating conjunction: see section 2.26 below and Chapter 14 section 3.

2.10. ἐάν *(Conjunction, Conditional)*
See Chapter 16 on conditional statements, where ἐάν is commonly used to introduce protases with the subjunctive mood form.

2.11. εἰ *(Conjunction, Conditional)*
See Chapter 16 on conditional statements, where εἰ is commonly used to introduce protases with the indicative mood form.

εἰ μή (often translated 'except' or 'unless'; Rom. 13.8) is to be considered as a sub-category of the conditional conjunction (as is ἐὰν μή); εἰ καί (often translated 'although'; 2 Cor. 4.16) is to be considered as a sub-category of the conditional conjunction; εἴπερ (Rom. 3.30; 8.9, 17; 1 Cor. 8.5; 15.15; 2 Thess. 1.6) is an intensive form of εἰ.

εἰ δὲ μή γε. Lk. 10.6: εἰ δὲ μή γε ἐφ' ὑμᾶς ἀνακάμψει (but if indeed not, it will return to you). This is an expansion of classical εἰ δὲ μή with the emphatic particle γε.[2]

2.12. εἴτε *(Conjunction, Connective or Adversative)*
This conjunction (from εἰ) may be used to link phrases or clauses, most uses being adversative.

Linkage of phrases is illustrated by the following examples.

Rom. 12.6-8: εἴτε προφητείαν κατὰ τὴν ἀναλογίαν τῆς πίστεως, εἴτε διακονίαν ἐν τῇ διακονίᾳ, εἴτε ὁ διδάσκων ἐν τῇ διδασκαλίᾳ, εἴτε ὁ παρακαλῶν ἐν τῇ παρακλήσει (whether prophecy according to the proportion of faith, whether service in service, whether the one

1. Turner, *Syntax*, p. 333.
2. Thrall, *Greek Particles*, pp. 9-10.

teaching in teaching, whether the one comforting in comfort), a connective use.

Eph. 6.8: εἴτε δοῦλος εἴτε ἐλεύθερος (either slave or free), an adversative use.

Linkage of clauses is illustrated by the following example. Note the translations used to signal different uses of the conjunction.

2 Cor. 1.6: εἴτε δὲ θλιβόμεθα...εἴτε παρακαλούμεθα (but either we are afflicted...or we are comforted), an adversative use.

2.13. ἐπεί *(Conjunction, Causal)*
See Chapter 14 section 3.

2.14. ἕως *(Conjunction, Temporal)*
See Chapter 9 section 5, Chapter 11 section 2.4, and Chapter 14 section 6.2.

2.15. ἤ *(Conjunction, Adversative or Comparative)*
The adversative sense is found when phrases or clauses are joined.

Phrasal use may be seen in the following example.

Mk 3.4: ἔξεστιν τοῖς σάββασιν ἀγαθὸν ποιῆσαι ἢ κακοποιῆσαι, ψυχὴν σῶσαι ἢ ἀποκτεῖναι; (is it lawful on the Sabbath to do good or to do evil, to save a soul or to kill?).

Clausal use may be seen in the following example.

1 Cor. 11.27: ὃς ἂν ἐσθίῃ τὸν ἄρτον ἢ πίνῃ τὸ ποτήριον (whoever eats the bread or drinks the cup).

ἤ...ἤ (either...or) is also found.

Mk 13.35: ἢ ὀψὲ ἢ μεσονύκτιον ἢ ἀλεκτοροφωνίας ἢ πρωΐ (either in the evening or at midnight or at cockcrowing or early).

The comparative sense is often found with a comparative word.

Jn 3.19: ἠγάπησαν οἱ ἄνθρωποι μᾶλλον τὸ σκότος ἢ τὸ φῶς (people loved darkness rather than light).

On the use of ἤ with purpose clauses, see Chapter 14 section 1.2.

2.16. ἵνα *and* ὅπως *(Conjunction)*
The use of ἵνα is widespread, much more so than ὅπως. See Chapter 14 sections 2.2 and 4.1 on final and result clauses and content (objective) clauses, as well as Chapter 17 on indirect discourse. ἵνα and ὅπως are normally used in NT Greek to introduce clauses with verbs having the subjunctive mood form, although they are also found with the future form (e.g. 1 Cor. 9.18).

2.17. καθώς (καθά, καθό, καθάπερ) *(Conjunction, Comparative)*
This particle is usually considered an adverb (from καθ' ὡς), but it can conjoin clauses, and so is listed here as a conjunction. See Chapter 14 section 7 on comparative clauses.

2.18. καί *(Conjunction and Particle, Connective or Adversative or Emphatic)*
καί is the most widely used conjunction and particle in the Greek of the NT.[1] It is used to link items of equal status when it functions as a conjunction; it conjoins clauses, phrases or individual words.

2.18.1. *Adverbial.* Emphatic or adverbial uses of the particle καί are widespread.[2] Frequent translational equivalents are 'indeed', 'even' and 'also'.

Mt. 8.9: καὶ γὰρ ἐγὼ ἄνθρωπός εἰμι ὑπὸ ἐξουσίαν (for indeed I myself am a man under authority).

Col. 4.3: λαλῆσαι τὸ μυστήριον τοῦ Χριστοῦ, δι' ὃ καὶ δέδεμαι (to speak the mystery of Christ on account of which I also am a prisoner).

2.18.2. *Conjunctive.* Along with δέ, καί is the most common conjunction in Greek.[3] καί may be used in connective and adversative senses.

An example of the connective use includes the following.

Mk 10.1: καὶ ἐκεῖθεν ἀναστὰς ἔρχεται (and getting up from there he went), one of Mark's very frequent uses.

Examples of the adversative use are often overlooked.[4]

Mt. 11.19: καὶ ἐδικαιώθη ἡ σοφία ἀπὸ τῶν ἔργων αὐτῆς (but wisdom is justified by her works).

Rom. 1.13: καὶ ἐκωλύθην ἄχρι τοῦ δεῦρο (but I was hindered until now).

καί can connect items of various levels.

Jn 8.48: ἀπεκρίθησαν...καὶ εἶπαν (they answered...and said), connecting clauses.

Rom. 3.26: εἰς τὸ εἶναι αὐτὸν δίκαιον καὶ δικαιοῦντα τὸν ἐκ

1. See Levinsohn, *Textual Connections*, pp. 86-120.
2. Dana and Mantey, *Manual Grammar*, pp. 250-52.
3. See Turner, *Syntax*, p. 322.
4. Dana and Mantey, *Manual Grammar*, p. 250.

πίστεως (in order that he might be just and a justifier of the one of faith), connecting phrases.

καί...καί (both...and) is found often in the NT.

Mk 4.41: καὶ ὁ ἄνεμος καὶ ἡ θάλασσα (both the wind and the sea).

Note also καί γε (Acts 2.18; 17.27), καίτοι (Acts 14.17), καίτοιγε (Jn 4.2), with emphatic particles added to καί.[1]

2.19. μέν *(Conjunction, Adversative or Emphatic, Postpositive)*

This particle (related to μήν) is often used to contrast clauses or smaller units. It may appear in coordination with a number of other particles (e.g. δέ, τέ, καί),[2] but δέ is the most frequent.

Lk. 11.48: αὐτοὶ μὲν ἀπέκτειναν αὐτοὺς ὑμεῖς δὲ οἰκοδομεῖτε (they killed them but you built [their tombs]), although Robertson downplays the adversative force.[3]

1 Pet. 2.4: ὑπὸ ἀνθρώπων μὲν ἀποδεδοκιμασμένον παρὰ δὲ θεῷ ἐκλεκτόν (rejected by people but elect to God).

Mt. 3.11: ἐγὼ μὲν...ὁ δέ (on the one hand I...but he).

The particle occurs alone with emphatic value in many instances.

Rom. 1.8: πρῶτον μὲν εὐχαριστῶ (in fact, first, I give thanks).

See Chapter 5 section 2.8.2 for use with the article to form a conjunction (e.g. Acts 14.4).

Col. 2.23: ἅτινά ἐστιν, λόγον μὲν ἔχοντα σοφίας...πρὸς πλησμονὴν τῆς σαρκός (which things are—though having a reputation for wisdom...—for gratification of the flesh). The regularity of postpositive placement of this conjunction in the Pauline writings has led several scholars to posit that this construction has a dependent clause (introduced by μέν) embedded within its main clause (with δέ omitted for clarity).[4]

μὲν οὖν (conjunction, consecutive or adversative, postpositive). According to Moule this phrase has resumptive or transitional (consecutive) force in most instances.[5]

1. Thrall, *Greek Particles*, pp. 36-38.
2. See Robertson, *Grammar*, pp. 1152-53.
3. Robertson, *Grammar*, p. 1153.
4. B. Hollenbach, 'Col. 2.23: Which Things Lead to the Fulfilment of the Flesh', *NTS* 25 (1978–79), pp. 254-61.
5. Moule, *Idiom Book*, pp. 162-63; see also Levinsohn, *Textual Connections*, pp. 137-50.

Acts 5.41: οἱ μὲν οὖν ἐπορεύοντο (so they were going), continuing with those mentioned in the verses above.

There are a few examples of μὲν οὖν with adversative force.

1 Cor. 9.25: ἐκεῖνοι μὲν οὖν ἵνα φθαρτὸν στέφανον λάβωσιν, ἡμεῖς δὲ ἄφθαρτον (so that they might receive a perishable crown, but we an imperishable one), a use similar to simple μέν.

μενοῦν (Lk. 11.28); μενοῦνγε (Rom. 9.20; 10.18; Phil. 3.8). These words are written as one word in the texts of the NT. Whereas in most of the examples the consecutive use is clear, Thrall and Moule see an adversative force in Rom. 9.20 and 10.18.[1]

μέντοι. Jn 4.27; 7.13; 12.42; 20.5; 21.4; 2 Tim. 2.19; Jas 2.8; Jude 8. This is an intensive form of μέν.

2.20. μή *(μήτι, etc.) (Particle, Negative)*

In the Greek of the NT, μή usually negates the non-indicative moods. See Chapter 14 section 1.2 on use with the subjunctive and Chapter 19 on negation.

2.21. μήν *(Particle, Emphatic, Postpositive)*

Heb. 6.14: μὴν εὐλογῶν εὐλογήσω σε (indeed, I will in fact bless you).

2.22. ναί, νή *(Particle, Emphatic)*

These particles are used for corroboration and affirmation, often translated 'yes' or 'indeed'. ναί occurs in the NT in several instances.

Mt. 5.37: ἔστω δὲ ὁ λόγος ὑμῶν ναὶ ναί, οὒ οὔ (let your yes [be] yes, [your] no, no).

νή is used once, as it is in Greek oaths, in 1 Cor. 15.31: νὴ τὴν ὑμετέραν καύχησιν...ἣν ἔχω ἐν Χριστῷ Ἰησοῦ (indeed, by your boasting...which I have in Christ Jesus).

2.23. νῦν *(Particle, Inferential)*

This particle, and its strengthened form νυνί (e.g. Rom. 15.23, 25), is usually treated as a temporal adverb (see Chapter 7 on adverbs), but Thrall argues that there is an inferential use as well.[2]

1 Cor. 12.20: νῦν δὲ πολλὰ μὲν μέλη (therefore, [there are] many members).

1. Thrall, *Greek Particles*, pp. 34-36; Moule, *Idiom Book*, pp. 163-64.
2. Thrall, *Greek Particles*, pp. 30-34.

Acts 16.36: νῦν οὖν...πορεύεσθε ἐν εἰρήνῃ (therefore...go in peace).

2.24. ὅμως *(Conjunction, Adversative)*
This conjunction is used three times in the Greek of the NT.

Jn 12.42 (with μέντοι); 1 Cor. 14.7; Gal. 3.15. Although the usual understanding is as an adversative conjunction, BAGD (*s.v.*) suggests a connective sense ('likewise, also') for the Pauline examples.

2.25. ὅτε *and* ὅταν *(Conjunction, Temporal)*
The use of these conjunctions is widespread. See Chapter 14 section 6.1 on temporal clauses. ὅτε is normally used in the Greek of the NT with verbs in the indicative mood and ὅταν usually with verbs in the subjunctive mood.

2.26. ὅτι, διότι *(Conjunction)*
The use of ὅτι is widespread. See Chapter 14 sections 3 and 4.1 on causal and content clauses, and Chapter 17 on indirect discourse. ὅτι is normally used in the Greek of the NT to introduce clauses with verbs having the indicative mood form.

2.27. οὐ *(*οὐδέ, *etc.) (Particle, Negative)*
In the Greek of the NT, οὐ usually negates the indicative mood. This negative form occurs as οὐκ before smooth breathing and οὐχ before rough breathing. See Chapter 19 on negation.

2.28. οὖν *(Conjunction, Inferential or Consecutive or Emphatic or Adversative, Postpositive)*[1]
This is a widely used conjunction. The inferential sense is predominant.

Rom. 11.1: λέγω οὖν μὴ ἀπώσατο ὁ θεὸς τὸν λαὸν αὐτοῦ; (I say, therefore, God did not reject his people, did he?).

Dana and Mantey raise the question of whether there are other uses as well.[2] Although most grammarians do not mention such uses (apart from Robertson),[3] the following are worth considering. The first is consecutive.

1. See Levinsohn, *Textual Connections*, pp. 137-50.
2. Dana and Mantey, *Manual Grammar*, pp. 252-58. The 'responsive' category can probably be subsumed under the inferential.
3. Robertson, *Grammar*, pp. 1191-92.

Jn 3.25: ἐγένετο οὖν ζήτησις ἐκ τῶν μαθητῶν Ἰωάννου ('*Now* there was a controversy among the disciples of John');[1] see also Jn 4.6, 28; 9.17, 20; 12.1, 2, 3, 9, 17, 21, 29; 18.24; Acts 10.29, 32.

The second is emphatic.

Lk. 14.34: καλὸν οὖν τὸ ἅλας ('Salt *to be sure* is good').[2]

Rom. 5.9: πολλῷ οὖν μᾶλλον (much more).

The third is adversative.

1 Cor. 11.20: συνερχομένων οὖν ὑμῶν ('*However*, when ye assemble together');[3] Lk. 21.14; Jn 4.45; 11.6; 12.29; 18.11, 27.

οὐκοῦν. Jn 18.37: οὐκοῦν βασιλεὺς εἶ σύ. Moule debates the several different senses of this particle in this context:[4] resumptive ('Well, then...'), negative ('Art thou not a king, then?') or inferential ('So then, after all, thou art a king'), concurring with the last, suggested by Westcott.

2.29. οὕτω(ς) *(Particle, Inferential)*

This particle is an adverb, but it is also used to draw inferences, often following an introductory ὥσπερ in the conclusion to a comparison.

Rom. 5.19: ὥσπερ...οὕτως καὶ διὰ τῆς ὑπακοῆς τοῦ ἑνὸς δίκαιοι κατασταθήσονται οἱ πολλοί (just as...thus also through the obedience of the one man many will be constituted righteous).

2.30. πέρ *(Particle, Emphatic)*

This emphatic enclitic particle only occurs in the NT when linked to another word (εἰ, ἐάν, διό, ἐπειδή, καθώς, καί, ὡς).

2.31. πλήν *(Conjunction, Adversative)*

This particle is an adverb which seems to have taken on an adversative conjunctive sense.[5] It is used relatively frequently in Luke–Acts. In earlier Greek it was frequently used as a preposition, a function it continues in the Greek of the NT (see Chapter 9 section 5).

Lk. 6.35: πλὴν ἀγαπᾶτε τοὺς ἐχθροὺς ὑμῶν (but love your enemies).

1. Dana and Mantey, *Manual Grammar*, p. 254.
2. Dana and Mantey, *Manual Grammar*, p. 255.
3. Dana and Mantey, *Manual Grammar*, pp. 257-58.
4. Moule, *Idiom Book*, p. 165.
5. Turner, *Syntax*, p. 368.

2.32. ποτέ *(Particle, Temporal)*
This fairly frequent enclitic particle is used temporally to indicate a given or some specific time.

Heb. 1.5: τίνι γὰρ εἶπέν ποτε τῶν ἀγγέλων...; (for to whom of the angels did he at any time say...?).

Eph. 2.3: ἡμεῖς πάντες ἀνεστράφημέν ποτε ἐν ταῖς ἐπιθυμίαις τῆς σαρκὸς ἡμῶν (we all lived at that time in the desires of our flesh).

2.33. πού, πώς *(Particle, Emphatic)*
These enclitic particles are emphatic, with a sense of approximation.

Rom. 4.19: ἑκατονταετής που ὑπάρχων (being about 100 years).

Rom. 11.14: εἴ πως παραζηλώσω μου τὴν σάρκα (if I might somehow make my flesh [= Jews?] jealous).

2.34. τέ *(Conjunction and Particle, Connective, Postpositive)*
This enclitic particle and conjunction is rare in the NT except in Acts (and except for emphatic forms such as οὔτε, εἴτε and μήτε).[1]

As a particle, τέ is emphatic.

Acts 20.3: ποιήσας τε μῆνας τρεῖς (indeed doing for three months).

As a conjunction, τέ (or τέ...τέ) serves as a strong connective.

Acts 2.33: ὑψωθεὶς τήν τε ἐπαγγελίαν...λαβών (being elevated *and* receiving the promise).

Levinsohn contends[2] that τέ is not used to join items of equal significance, but either to join unequal items or to indicate a connection between them: Acts 12.17: εἶπέν τε (and he said), with the idea of 'in addition'.

τέ...τέ (both...and) only occurs a few times as well.

Acts 26.16: ὧν τε εἶδες ὧν τε ὀφθήσομαί σοι (both of the things you saw and of the things I will make appear to you).

Rom. 14.8: ἐάν τε οὖν ζῶμεν ἐάν τε ἀποθνῄσκωμεν (therefore, both if we might live and if we might die).

τέ...καί occurs a number of times.

Rom. 1.14: Ἕλλησίν τε καὶ βαρβάροις (both Greeks and barbarians).

Rom. 1.16: Ἰουδαίῳ τε πρῶτον καὶ Ἕλληνι (to the Jew first and also to the Greek).

1. See J.K. Elliott, 'τε in the NT', *TZ* 46 (1990), pp. 202-204.
2. Levinsohn, *Textual Connections*, pp. 121-36.

2.35. τοί *(Particle, Emphatic)*
This enclitic particle only occurs in the NT when linked to another word (καί, μέν, ἤ).

τοιγαροῦν (conjunction, inferential). 1 Thess. 4.8: τοιγαροῦν ὁ ἀθετῶν οὐκ ἄνθρωπον ἀθετεῖ (therefore, the one who rejects does not reject a human being); Heb. 12.1.

τοινῦν (conjunction, inferential). Lk. 20.25: τοίνυν ἀπόδοτε τὰ Καίσαρος Καίσαρι (therefore, give the things of Caesar to Caesar); Heb. 13.13; 1 Cor. 9.26 (postpositive).

2.36. τότε *(Conjunction, Consecutive)*
This particle is an adverb, but one which Turner believes is used in non-classical fashion as a conjunction because of Semitic influence.[1] It is widely used in the NT, especially in Matthew.

Mt. 4.11: τότε ἀφίησιν αὐτὸν ὁ διάβολος (then the devil left him).

2.37. ὡς *(ὥστε) (Conjunction, Comparative or Temporal or Purpose or Resultive)*
As a conjunction, ὡς (ὥστε) may be used in a wide variety of ways.

ὡς is used to connect phrases, often comparatively.

Mt. 6.10: ὡς ἐν οὐρανῷ καὶ ἐπὶ γῆς (as in heaven [so] also on earth).

1 Pet. 1.14: ὡς τέκνα ὑπακοῆς (as children of obedience).

ὡς (ὥστε) is used in a variety of contexts to connect clauses, including comparatively, temporally, and purposively or resultively, among others. See discussion of various uses in Chapter 11 section 2.2 and Chapter 14 sections 2.1, 6.3 and 7.

1. Turner, *Syntax*, p. 341.

Part II

CLAUSES AND LARGER UNITS

Chapter 13

COMMANDS AND PROHIBITIONS

Introduction

Commands and prohibitions are used to instigate, direct and thwart actions, often by others. Greek, like many languages, has a variety of means by which commands and prohibitions may be made. An important distinction to be kept in mind is the difference between the semantics of a given form and the uses of the form in a variety of contexts. This has two implications. The first is that one form may serve several different functions, depending upon context. The second is that the number and kind of syntactical constructions which can be made to accomplish a given linguistic task are almost innumerable, again depending upon context. An attempt to quantify and analyze all of these is impossible, because it would include any and all uses of language. For example, in a given context the statement 'it certainly is cold in here' could be construed as a command to close a window, although this statement would not be grammatically analyzed as an 'imperative form'. The treatment below and in subsequent chapters is designed to present constructions whose normal semantic features permit many different contextual applications. This chapter treats many of the different Greek constructions which may be used to convey commands and prohibitions.

1. *Commands and Prohibitions*

The discussion below includes the most common of many ways in which commands and prohibitions can be formed in Greek. To use the language of slot and filler, in contexts where a slot demanding a commanding word is required, the slot may be filled by one of several different Greek word-forms. This chapter assimilates and supplements material presented in other chapters above, to which the reader is referred.

1.1. *Imperatives, Subjunctives and Prohibitions*

1.1.1. *Imperatives. The most common means of forming commands is with an imperative mood form* (see Chapter 2 section 2.1). The imperative appears only in the second and third person singular and plural. The subject of the imperative, if expressed, adds emphasis and/or specification and occurs in the nominative case.

Mt. 6.6: εἴσελθε εἰς τὸ ταμεῖόν σου καὶ...πρόσευξαι τῷ πατρί σου (go into your private room and...pray to your father), with two second person singular aorist imperatives.

Lk. 9.60: σὺ...διάγγελλε τὴν βασιλείαν τοῦ θεοῦ (you... proclaim the kingdom of God), with a second person singular present imperative.

Jas 1.2: πᾶσαν χαρὰν ἡγήσασθε (consider [it] all joy), with a second person plural aorist imperative.

Mt. 5.44: ἀγαπᾶτε τοὺς ἐχθροὺς ὑμῶν (love your enemies), with a second person plural present imperative.

Mt. 6.9-10: ἁγιασθήτω τὸ ὄνομά σου, ἐλθέτω ἡ βασιλεία σου, γενηθήτω τὸ θέλημά σου (let your name be holy, let your kingdom come, let your will come about), with third person singular aorist imperatives.

Jas 1.6: αἰτείτω...ἐν πίστει (let [someone] ask...in faith), with a third person singular present imperative.

Lk. 16.29: ἀκουσάτωσαν αὐτῶν (let them hear them), with a third person plural aorist imperative.

1.1.2. *Prohibitions and subjunctives. For prohibitions the negative* μή *appears with the present imperative and normally with the third person aorist imperative. The negated aorist subjunctive is used in the second person.* The negated aorist imperative is only very rarely used for prohibitions (and does not occur in the NT) in the second person. There are also a few examples of the negated third person aorist subjunctive used as a prohibition in the NT (e.g. 1 Cor. 16.11; 2 Cor. 11.16; 2 Thess. 2.3; see Chapter 2 section 2.2.3). In most contexts, translations of negated imperatives and negated subjunctives used as prohibitions can be virtually identical.

Rom. 6.12: μὴ οὖν βασιλευέτω ἡ ἁμαρτία (therefore, sin is not to rule), with a negated third person singular present imperative.

Mt. 6.3: μὴ γνώτω ἡ ἀριστερά σου τί ποιεῖ ἡ δεξιά σου (your left hand is not to know what your right hand does), with a negated third person singular aorist imperative.

1 Tim. 4.14: μὴ ἀμέλει τοῦ ἐν σοὶ χαρίσματος (don't neglect the spiritual gift in you), with a negated second person singular present imperative.

Mt. 6.16: μὴ γίνεσθε ὡς οἱ ὑποκριταί (don't become as the hypocrites), with a negated second person plural present imperative.

Mt. 5.36: μήτε ἐν τῇ κεφαλῇ σου ὀμόσῃς (don't swear by your head), with a negated second person singular aorist subjunctive.

Mt. 5.17: μὴ νομίσητε ὅτι...(don't think that...), with a negated second person plural aorist subjunctive.

1.2. *Hortatory Commands and Prohibitions*

For first person commands and prohibitions (and similar directive statements), where no imperative form is available, the subjunctive (so-called hortatory subjunctive) is used for both the present and the aorist tense-forms (see Chapter 2 section 2.2.3).

Mt. 7.4 // Lk. 6.42: ἄφες ἐκβάλω τὸ κάρφος (permit me to remove the speck).

Lk. 15.23: φέρετε...θύσατε, καὶ φαγόντες εὐφρανθῶμεν (bring ...kill, and let us eat and rejoice), with the aorist participle being translated hortatorily as well.

Heb. 4.16: προσερχώμεθα...ἵνα λάβωμεν ἔλεος καὶ χάριν εὕρωμεν (let us come...so that we might receive mercy and find grace).

Jn 19.24: μὴ σχίσωμεν αὐτὸν ἀλλὰ λάχωμεν (let's not divide it but let's cast lots).

Rom. 14.13: μηκέτι...ἀλλήλους κρίνωμεν (no longer...should we judge each other), either a present or aorist tense-form.

1 Cor. 10.8, 9: μηδὲ πορνεύωμεν...μηδὲ ἐκπειράζωμεν τὸν Χριστόν (we should not commit sexual immorality...nor should we tempt Christ).

1.3. *Optative Form*

An optative, like a subjunctive, may be used in commanding (volitive) and prohibiting contexts (see Chapter 2 section 2.3). Most of the uses in the NT tend to be formulaic; that is, the optative is used with certain verb forms only. The most widely used verb is γίνομαι: Rom. 6.2: μὴ γένοιτο (may it never be). The optative is negated by μή in the Greek of the NT.

Mk 11.14: μηκέτι...μηδεὶς καρπὸν φάγοι (may no one ever eat fruit any more), with third person singular.

Phlm. 20: ναὶ ἀδελφέ, ἐγώ σου ὀναίμην ἐν κυρίῳ (yes, brother, may I benefit from you in the Lord), with first person singular.

1.4. *Participles, Infinitives and* ἵνα *Clauses*

A participle (see Chapter 10), infinitive (see Chapter 11) or ἵνα clause (see Chapter 14) may function as a command or prohibition. This usage must be determined on the basis of context. The context is often one where the participle, infinitive or ἵνα clause is used with content statements (occasionally in indirect discourse), although the independent use of the participle for commanding is also fairly well known.

Rom. 12.9-19. The participle functioning as a finite verb or as an imperative is heavily debated. Evidence of use of the participle as a command in the papyri, as well as in literary texts from the classical and Hellenistic periods, makes the commanding use of the participle plausible (see the discussion in Chapter 10 section 2.3 above).

Lk. 9.3: μηδὲν αἴρετε εἰς τὴν ὁδόν, μήτε ῥάβδον μήτε πήραν... ἔχειν (take nothing on the journey, have neither staff nor bag), where the commanding infinitive follows an imperative; Acts 23.24: κτήνη τε παραστῆσαι (prepare an animal), where the form could be an aorist middle imperative second person singular instead of an infinitive, except that the context is plural (ἑτοιμάσατε, v. 23).

Phil. 1.9: τοῦτο προσεύχομαι, ἵνα ἡ ἀγάπη ὑμῶν ἔτι μᾶλλον καὶ μᾶλλον περισσεύῃ (I pray this, that your love might grow still more and more). This usage with ἵνα has been widely debated in the secondary literature (see Chapter 14 section 4.2). One general guide to determining whether a ἵνα clause is functioning as a command or prohibition is to determine whether the word on which ἵνα depends is a verb of perception (thinking, saying, and the like). If it *is*, the commanding use is a possibility. If it is *not*, the commanding sense is less likely. But context must be the decisive factor. See also Mt. 4.3: εἰπὲ ἵνα οἱ λίθοι οὗτοι ἄρτοι γένωνται (say that these stones should become bread); Mk 5.23: ἵνα...ἐπιθῇς τὰς χεῖρας αὐτῇ (...place [his] hands on her); Jn 17.15: οὐκ ἐρωτῶ ἵνα ἄρῃς αὐτοὺς ἐκ τοῦ κόσμου ἀλλ' ἵνα τηρήσῃς αὐτοὺς ἐκ τοῦ πονηροῦ (I am not asking for you to take them out of the world, but for you to keep them from the evil one); 2 Cor. 8.7: ἵνα καὶ ἐν ταύτῃ τῇ χάριτι περισσεύητε (that you might multiply in this grace); Eph. 5.33: ἡ δὲ γυνὴ ἵνα φοβῆται τὸν ἄνδρα (let the wife fear [her] husband), following a third person singular imperative, ἀγαπάτω; Gal. 2.10: ἵνα μνημονεύωμεν (let us remember).[1]

1.5. *Future Form*

The future form can be used to make commands. The usage is ambiguous, since the frequent translation of the future with 'will' often makes good sense (see Chapter 1 section 2.4).

Mt. 27.4: σὺ ὄψῃ (you see to it).

1 Jn 5.16: αἰτήσει καὶ δώσει αὐτῷ ζωήν (let him ask and he will give life to him), the first verb a command in the apodosis of a conditional statement.

2. *Semantics of Imperatives and Subjunctives*

The semantic features of the imperative and subjunctive forms are very similar. *The imperative is used to direct someone's action (with no statement of whether the person will or will not actually perform the act), and the subjunctive projects a hypothetical action (again with no statement of whether it will ever come about).* Dana and Mantey say, 'The imperative is the mood of command or entreaty—the mood of *volition*...It expresses neither probability nor possibility, but only intention, and is therefore, the furthest removed from reality.'[2] Gonda says, 'The subjunctive...expresses visualization. A process in the subj. represents a mental image on the part of the speaker which, in his opinion is capable of realization, or even awaits realization.'[3]

2.1. *Verbal Aspect*

By means of their tense-forms, imperatives and subjunctives (limited here to discussion of subjunctives used in commands and prohibitions) *grammaticalize verbal aspect, not temporal reference.*[4] Some

1. See Moule, *Idiom Book*, p. 144.
2. Dana and Mantey, *Manual Grammar*, p. 174.
3. Gonda, *Character*, p. 70.
4. Porter, *Verbal Aspect*, esp. pp. 336-47, 351-60; Fanning, *Verbal Aspect*, ch. 5.

grammarians find this difficult to accept because they cannot capture in translation the difference in tense-forms. Some of this difficulty is caused by an incorrect understanding of verbal aspect.[1] For example, some interpreters maintain the traditional distinction that the present imperative refers to continual or habitual action or forbids ongoing action, while the aorist imperative refers to instantaneous or singular (once-for-all) action or forbids beginning an action (negated aorist subjunctive). If this framework is used, the interpreter is sure to be disappointed. Important research completed in the early part of this century[2] illustrates that the same aspectual distinctions maintained in all of the other moods are maintained in the imperative as well. Moule has supported this by citing examples which do not conform to the standard conception (see Chapter 2 section 2.1.1).[3] This is illustrated particularly well in instances where aorist and present imperatives are found in identical contexts, and are used of action which may be variously described (if one is seeking some sort of objective description).

Mt. 5.36: μήτε...ὀμόσῃς and Jas 5.12: μὴ ὀμνύετε (don't swear). Are interpreters to believe that the first is addressed to those anticipating but not yet swearing and the second to those already swearing? Rather the aorist subjunctive is used to exclude any swearing and the present the practice of swearing.

Lk. 19.13: πραγματεύσασθε ἐν ᾧ ἔρχομαι (carry on doing business until I come), where the servants are already engaged in the action commanded using the aorist imperative.

2 Cor. 13.11, 12: χαίρετε, καταρτίζεσθε, παρακαλεῖσθε, τὸ αὐτὸ φρονεῖτε, εἰρηνεύετε...ἀσπάσασθε ἀλλήλους ἐν ἁγίῳ φιλήματι (rejoice, be made complete, be comforted, think the same thing [= be unified], be at peace...greet each other with a holy kiss), where four present imperatives are then followed by an aorist imperative. Is Paul telling his readers to continue the actions of the first group, which they are then presumably already doing, and to begin the second, which they presumably are not? More likely Paul gives a list of particular and urgent commands to his audience (present imperatives),

1. See e.g. Thorley, 'Aktionsart in NT Greek: Infinitive and Imperative', pp. 290-313.

2. See Porter, *Verbal Aspect*, pp. 336-43, for citations.

3. Moule, *Idiom Book*, pp. 20-21; see also McKay, 'Syntax', p. 50.

and then concludes with a fairly routine closing formula using the aorist imperative.

Eph. 5.18: μὴ μεθύσκεσθε οἴνῳ...ἀλλὰ πληροῦσθε ἐν πνεύματι (don't get drunk with wine...but be filled with the Spirit), where the depiction of both actions as on-going is difficult.

Lk. 17.8: ἑτοίμασον τί δειπνήσω καὶ...διακόνει μοι ἕως φάγω καὶ πίω (prepare what I might eat and...serve me until I eat and drink), where a distinction between singular and repeated action breaks down in light of the temporal clause (ἕως) with two aorist subjunctives following the present imperative.

Jn 3.7: μὴ θαυμάσῃς ὅτι εἶπόν σοι (don't marvel [be shocked] that I said to you), where the crowd is already marveling.

Boyer in his recent study of the imperative has estimated that the negated present imperative in the NT calls for the cessation of something already being done in only 74 of 174 instances. In other words, in 100 of the 174 instances the negated present imperative is not to be interpreted as calling for cessation of ongoing activity. This is a far cry from the percentages needed to support the traditional 'rule'.[1]

2.2. *Conditional Imperatives*

Some scholars contend that in some instances the imperative is used as if it were a conditional ('if') or concessive ('although') clause.[2] This may be a legitimate understanding in some contexts, but such examples are perhaps better understood as normal variations within the commanding use of the imperative.[3]

Jn 2.19: λύσατε τὸν ναὸν τοῦτον καὶ ἐν τρισὶν ἡμέραις ἐγερῶ αὐτόν (destroy [if you destroy] this temple, and in three days I will raise it).

Lk. 6.37-38: καὶ μὴ κρίνετε, καὶ οὐ μὴ κριθῆτε· καὶ μὴ καταδικάζετε, καὶ οὐ μὴ καταδικασθῆτε. ἀπολύετε, καὶ ἀπολυθήσεσθε· δίδοτε, καὶ δοθήσεται ὑμῖν (don't judge [if you don't judge], and you won't be judged; don't condemn [if you don't condemn], and you won't be condemned. Destroy [if you destroy], and you will be destroyed; give [if you give], and it will be given to you).

1. See Boyer, 'Classification of Imperatives', pp. 40-45.

2. Winer, *Treatise*, pp. 391-92; Robertson, *Grammar*, pp. 948-49; BDF, §387(1, 2); see also Boyer, 'Classification of Imperatives', pp. 38-40.

3. Porter, *Verbal Aspect*, pp. 352-53.

Eph. 4.26: ὀργίζεσθε καὶ μὴ ἁμαρτάνετε (be angry [if you are angry], and don't sin).[1]

2.3. *Examples of Special Significance*
The following examples, among many others which could be cited, present various kinds of exegetical difficulties. They are selected to illustrate the relevance which grammatical study might have for exegesis.

Eph. 6.10-17: ἐνδυναμοῦσθε...ἐνδύσασθε...ἀναλάβετε... δέξασθε (empower...put on...take on...receive), with a present imperative followed by aorist imperatives simply listing what empowerment entails.

1 Pet. 2.17: πάντας τιμήσατε, τὴν ἀδελφότητα ἀγαπᾶτε, τὸν θεὸν φοβεῖσθε, τὸν βασιλέα τιμᾶτε (honor all, love the brotherhood, fear God, honor the king), following the NEB rendering: 'give due honour to everyone: love to the brotherhood, reverence to God, honour to the sovereign', with an aorist imperative used before three particular or specific items are selected using present imperatives.[2]

Jn 20.17: μή μου ἅπτου (don't touch me). The accepted interpretation of this clause is that Jesus says to Mary 'don't keep on touching me'.[3] This is probably dictated in part by reference to Mt. 28.9, which says that the women grasped Jesus' feet. The difficulty is that whereas in this verse Jesus says that Mary is not to touch him because he has not 'ascended' to the father, in Jn 20.27 Jesus instructs Thomas to put his finger in his hands and side, when he still does not appear to have ascended. This imperative probably refers to Jesus telling Mary not to begin to touch him, with no indication in the context that the women have touched him yet.[4]

1 Cor. 7.21b: ἀλλ' εἰ καὶ δύνασαι ἐλεύθερος γενέσθαι, μᾶλλον χρῆσαι (but if you are able to become free, make use of the

1. See D.L. Wallace, ''ΟΡΓ'ΙΖΕΣΘΕ [*sic*] in Eph. 4.26: Command or Condition?', *Criswell Theological Review* 3 (1989), pp. 353-72, for a treatment of the issues.

2. See S. Snyder, '1 Pet. 2.17: A Reconsideration', *FN* 4 (1991), pp. 211-15.

3. E.g. R.E. Brown, *The Gospel according to John* (2 vols.; Garden City, NY: Doubleday, 1966), II, p. 992; C.K. Barrett, *The Gospel according to St John* (London: SPCK, 2nd edn, 1978), pp. 565-66; L. Morris, *The Gospel according to John* (Grand Rapids: Eerdmans, 1971), p. 840.

4. Porter, *Verbal Aspect*, p. 356.

opportunity). This verse has been variously interpreted.[1] The two major opinions have traditionally been to translate the verse 'although you are able to become free, rather make use of your slavery', supplying a reference to slavery;[2] or to translate it 'if indeed you are able to become free, rather make use of your freedom', supplying a reference to freedom.[3] The use of the verb tenses alone will not prove which interpretation is to be preferred in this instance. Context is important, but several grammatical issues are also important.[4] The preceding present imperative, μελέτω (7.21a), must receive emphasis over the aorist imperative in this verse. Paul's overriding concern appears to be to 'stop being concerned about being a slave'. Paul also uses the present indicative, δύνασαι, which reinforces the connecting words as a strong adversative. Manumission did not reside with the slave but with the owner, and the use of the present tense-form seems to stress that the opportunity for freedom must be seized upon when it comes. Those who argue that the word 'in slavery' is to be supplied must not only take εἰ καί as concessive to the point of excluding the legitimate conditional sense, but must minimize the adversative force of ἀλλά. Thus 1 Cor. 7.21 should probably be rendered 'if, indeed, you become manumitted, by all means [as a freedman] live according to God's calling'.[5]

3. *The Aorist Imperative and Prayer to Gods*

Some scholars have argued that the aorist imperative is the only tense-form used in prayers to gods, with only a few exceptions. Investigation of usage by various Greek authors has shown that this is not strictly true, even if it may form a broad generalization.[6] Justification of the traditional explanation has revolved around formulating a reason for

1. See S.S. Bartchy, *First-Century Slavery and 1 Cor. 7.21* (N.p.: Society of Biblical Literature, 1973).

2. E.g. C.K. Barrett, *The First Epistle to the Corinthians* (New York: Harper & Row, 1968), p. 170.

3. Moulton, *Prolegomena*, p. 174; Turner, *Syntax*, p. 76; Moule, *Idiom Book*, p. 167 n. 3.

4. Porter, *Verbal Aspect*, pp. 357-58.

5. Bartchy, *Slavery*, p. 183.

6. See Porter, *Verbal Aspect*, pp. 347-50; *contra* Fanning, *Verbal Aspect*, pp. 380-82.

use of the aorist, rather than more appropriately citing aspectual factors, that is, appealing to the idea that use of the aorist imperative would be expected unless other factors call for use of the more emphatic present imperative form.

The classic NT example is Lk. 11.3. All of the commands in Matthew's version of the Lord's prayer (6.9-13) are forms of the aorist. In Luke's shorter version of the same prayer (11.2-4), four of the commands are aorist forms: ἁγιασθήτω (be holy); ἐλθέτω (come); ἄφες (forgive) and μὴ εἰσενέγκῃς (don't lead), as most grammars note. The middle command, in v. 3, uses the present tense-form: τὸν ἄρτον ἡμῶν τὸν ἐπιούσιον δίδου ἡμῖν τὸ καθ' ἡμέραν (give our daily bread to us each day). A standard explanation of Matthew's use of the aorist is that σήμερον (today) makes the request specific and thus warrants the aorist. The explanation of Luke's use of the present is that the following phrase—τὸ καθ' ἡμέραν—requires that the sense be iterative (repeated action). A more important contextual feature has been overlooked, however. The Lukan version is followed directly by the story of the man who implores his friend for bread at midnight (Lk. 11.5-8). The story concludes (v. 8), 'if he will not give to him...because he is his friend, because of his persistence ...he will give to him what he needs'. Then Jesus reportedly ties the prayer into the story (vv. 9-10; cf. Mt. 7.7-8): 'ask and it will be given to you; seek and you will find; knock and it will be opened to you. For everyone who asks receives, and the one who seeks finds, and to the one who knocks it will be opened.' The entire unit closes by saying that if those who are evil know how to give good gifts to their children (v. 13), 'how much more the father from heaven will give the Holy Spirit to those who ask him'. The present imperative in the Lord's prayer appears to be a self-conscious use by the author to signal a theme that is pursued in the following material (see Chapter 21 section 3.2).

Chapter 14

DEPENDENT CLAUSES

Introduction

This chapter, together with Chapters 15 and 16, analyzes a number of dependent clauses in Greek.[1] The treatment does not pretend to be complete, especially with reference to the numerous particles which may be used to introduce dependent clauses (see Chapter 12), but it does try to include most of the important ones. *A dependent clause is a clause with a finite verb*[2] *which cannot stand alone (i.e. it is not an independent clause), but it enters into a definable grammatical and semantic relationship (one of dependency) with another clause (often, though not always, an independent clause).* The connection is normally indicated by some form of connecting word (conjunction), which helps to define the relationship between the two clauses.

Two preliminary issues must be addressed before turning to specific examples. First, the same connecting word (e.g. ὅτι or ἵνα) may serve several different purposes or may connect several different kinds of clauses. The question naturally arises as to whether a significant distinction can be made between these clauses. On the one hand, many instances exist where such a distinction cannot be made, especially by non-native speakers looking at a passage centuries after it was written. On the other hand, in some contexts, even if only a few, such a distinction is demanded. It is best, therefore, to keep in mind the different sorts of clauses these connecting words may join and to understand the interpretative importance that attaches in some instances to

1. For useful statistics on a number of these clauses, see J.L. Boyer, 'Noun Clauses in the Greek NT: A Statistical Study', *GTJ* 10 (1989), esp. pp. 232-37.

2. To be correct, a clause with an independent participle or infinitive, as well as a verbless clause, can constitute a dependent clause, but the discussion here focuses for the most part upon clauses with finite verbs.

deciding between the meanings of the clauses. This arises in particular with purpose and result clauses.

Secondly, both indicative and non-indicative (in particular the subjunctive)[1] mood forms are used as the main verbs in dependent clauses, in all of the major tense-forms. The mood of a given verb form is an indicator of the attitude of the speaker toward reality (see Chapter 2). This extends to the proposition made by a particular clause. Since the dependent clause by definition is grammatically conjoined to another clause, one not necessarily using the same mood form, and since the entire unit is also found in a specific linguistic context, interpretation must take into account all of the mood forms, the relations among the involved clauses, and the larger context.

1. *Purpose Clauses*

A purpose clause (final or telic clause) specifies the intention of the agent with regard to the action described in the main clause. In other words, someone might perform an action and specify the intention for this action in the dependent clause. Purpose clauses may be constructed in a number of different ways, including equivalent (though not completely synonymous) constructions using participles and infinitives (see the discussion in Chapters 10 and 11 above for explanations; a few examples are cited below).

1.1. *Participles and Infinitives*

Structures using participles (Chapter 10 section 5.5) and infinitives (Chapter 11 section 2.2) are not dependent clauses (in Greek, not English translation). But they are included here because they often perform a similar function. The purpose function of an infinitive is often indicated by the prepositions πρός and εἰς.

Mk 10.45: οὐκ ἦλθεν διακονηθῆναι ἀλλὰ διακονῆσαι καὶ δοῦναι (he did not come to be served but to serve and to give), with anarthrous (without the article) infinitives.

Mt. 2.13: μέλλει... Ἡρῴδης ζητεῖν τὸ παιδίον τοῦ ἀπολέσαι αὐτό (Herod is going to search for the child to kill it), with an articular infinitive in a catenative construction (see Chapter 11 section 1.2.3) preceding the purpose use of an infinitive.

1. See J.L. Boyer, 'The Classification of Subjunctives: A Statistical Study', *GTJ* 7 (1986), pp. 3-19.

Mt. 6.1: πρὸς τὸ θεαθῆναι αὐτοῖς (to be seen by them), with an infinitive following πρός.

1 Thess. 3.5: ἔπεμψα εἰς τὸ γνῶναι (I sent in order to know), with an infinitive following εἰς.

Acts 20.24: οὐδενὸς λόγου ποιοῦμαι τὴν ψυχὴν τιμίαν ἐμαυτῷ ὡς τελειῶσαι τὸν δρόμον μου ('I do not consider my life of any account as dear to myself, in order that I may finish my course' [NASB]), with ὡς and an infinitive indicating purpose, a fairly rare use in the NT.

Acts 8.27: ὃς ἐληλύθει προσκυνήσων (he went to worship), with a future participle, a normal use of this relatively infrequent form.

1.2. *Subjunctive (and Future) Forms*

The most common method for forming a purpose clause is with the subjunctive mood form (and occasionally the future form), following either usually ἵνα or occasionally ὅπως, and negated by μή (μή or one of its compounded forms is used as the connective in some instances). ἄν occurs only a few times in these constructions: e.g. Mk 6.56; Lk. 2.35; Acts 3.20; 5.15; 15.17; Rom. 3.4. See section 2 below on the use of ἵνα in result constructions, a semantic overlap which makes it often quite difficult to decide on the exact function of a dependent clause. The examples below seem to be virtually certain as purpose clauses. There are many more which can be argued for as purpose clauses, but which are not as decidedly so as these. *A simple rule of thumb for deciding whether a clause conveys purpose is that if the main clause has a verb of intention, direction or purpose, or the action would not normally come about without some motivating force, then a purpose clause is probably being used.*

1 Cor. 1.27-29: τὰ μωρὰ τοῦ κόσμου ἐξελέξατο ὁ θεὸς ἵνα καταισχύνῃ τοὺς σοφούς...ἵνα καταισχύνῃ τὰ ἰσχυρά...ἵνα τὰ ὄντα καταργήσῃ ὅπως μὴ καυχήσηται πᾶσα σὰρξ ἐνώπιον τοῦ θεοῦ (God selected the foolish things of the world so that he might shame the wise...so that he might shame the things that are strong...so that he might condemn the things that are, so that all flesh might not boast before God), with several purpose clauses.

2 Cor. 8.14: ἵνα καὶ τὸ ἐκείνων περίσσευμα γένηται εἰς τὸ ὑμῶν ὑστέρημα ὅπως γένηται ἰσότης (so that their richness might come about for our poverty, so that equality might come about), with two purpose clauses.

Rom. 9.17: εἰς αὐτὸ τοῦτο ἐξήγειρά σε ὅπως ἐνδείξωμαι ἐν σοὶ τὴν δύναμίν μου (for this same purpose I raised you, so that I might show my power in you), with the dependent clause elucidating the prepositional phrase.

Mt. 17.27: ἵνα δὲ μὴ σκανδαλίσωμεν αὐτούς (but so that we might not offend them), in the context of paying the temple tax.

Acts 20.16: κεκρίκει γὰρ ὁ Παῦλος παραπλεῦσαι τὴν Ἔφεσον ὅπως μὴ γένηται αὐτῷ χρονοτριβῆσαι ἐν τῇ Ἀσίᾳ (for Paul decided to sail past Ephesus, so that he might not have to spend time in Asia).

Mk 13.35, 36: οὐκ οἴδατε γὰρ πότε ὁ κύριος τῆς οἰκίας ἔρχεται... μὴ ἐλθὼν ἐξαίφνης εὕρῃ ὑμᾶς καθεύδοντας (for you do not know when the lord of the house comes...so that he, coming immediately, might not find you sleeping), following μή alone as connective, sometimes translated 'lest'.

Lk. 20.10: ἀπέστειλεν πρὸς τοὺς γεωργοὺς δοῦλον ἵνα ἀπὸ τοῦ καρποῦ τοῦ ἀμπελῶνος δώσουσιν αὐτῷ (he sent to the farmers a servant, so that they will give to him from the fruit of the vine), with ·na and a future form.

Lk. 22.9: ποῦ θέλεις ἑτοιμάσωμεν; (where do you wish us to prepare [the Passover]?), with no connective between the independent and dependent clauses.

1.3. *Verbal Aspect*

The major semantic difference between the use of the tense-forms in purpose (as well as other) clauses is verbal aspect.[1] This is readily seen in constructions where the tenses are juxtaposed.

2 Cor. 13.7: οὐχ ἵνα ἡμεῖς δόκιμοι φανῶμεν ἀλλ' ἵνα ὑμεῖς τὸ καλὸν ποιῆτε (not so that we might appear proven but so that you might do good), with the present subjunctive indicating the item that is endorsed and the aorist subjunctive indicating the item rejected.

Jn 10.38: τοῖς ἔργοις πιστεύετε ἵνα γνῶτε καὶ γινώσκητε (believe the works, so that you might know and you might know), with aorist and present subjunctive forms of the same verb side by side. This poses a problem for any time-based view of the tense-forms, although one which depicts the action aspectually can explain it as inclusive reference.

1 Cor. 7.5: ἵνα σχολάσητε τῇ προσευχῇ καὶ πάλιν ἐπὶ τὸ αὐτὸ ἦτε ἵνα μὴ πειράζῃ ὑμᾶς ὁ σατανᾶς (so that you might devote yourself to

1. See Porter, *Verbal Aspect*, pp. 321-35; cf. Fanning, *Verbal Aspect*, pp. 390-404.

prayer and again might be together, so that Satan might not tempt you). The emphasis is upon escaping Satan's temptation, founded upon devotion to prayer. An *Aktionsart* view of the tenses (one-time prayer but continuing temptation) is clearly inadequate.

Eph. 6.21, 22: ἵνα...εἰδῆτε καὶ ὑμεῖς τὰ κατ' ἐμέ, τί πράσσω, πάντα γνωρίσει ὑμῖν Τύχικος...ἵνα γνῶτε τὰ περὶ ἡμῶν καὶ παρακαλέσῃ τὰς καρδίας ὑμῶν (so that...you might know the things related to me, what I am doing, Tychicus will make known all things to you...so that you might know the things concerning us and he might comfort your hearts), with one of the ten instances in the Greek NT of the perfect subjunctive, all forms of οἶδα.

2. *Result Clauses*

A result clause (consecutive or ecbatic clause) refers to an action which results from a previous action. There is an integral semantic relationship between purpose and result, which leads to significant connections between the two kinds of clauses.[1] In other words, in some contexts a dependent clause may refer to the result of an established purpose. *In contexts where the main clause does not have a verb of intention, direction or purpose, or the action would normally come about without some motivating force, a result clause is a distinct possibility.* The two major forms of result clauses in the Greek of the NT are formed with ὥστε and the infinitive or indicative and ἵνα and the subjunctive.

2.1. ὥστε *and Infinitive or Indicative*

The usual means in the Greek of the NT for forming a result clause is with ὥστε and the infinitive or even the indicative.[2] Distinctions in kind of result—actual, natural, conceived, intended—are not necessary to make here; in a given instance the differentiation may prove useful.

Mt. 15.30-31: ἐθεράπευσεν αὐτοὺς ὥστε τὸν ὄχλον θαυμάσαι (he healed them, so that the crowd marveled).

1 Pet. 1.21: τοὺς δι' αὐτοῦ πιστοὺς εἰς θεὸν τὸν ἐγείραντα αὐτὸν

1. Zerwick, *Biblical Greek*, p. 123.

2. Burton (*Syntax*, p. 100) posits that some ὥστε clauses are so disjointed from their contexts that they should be considered independent clauses: Mk 2.28; 1 Cor. 5.8; 1 Thess. 4.18.

ἐκ νεκρῶν καὶ δόξαν αὐτῷ δόντα ὥστε τὴν πίστιν ὑμῶν καὶ ἐλπίδα εἶναι εἰς θεόν (those faithful through him to the God who raised him from the dead and gave glory to him, so that your faith and hope are in God).

Gal. 2.13: ὥστε καὶ Βαρναβᾶς συναπήχθη αὐτῶν τῇ ὑποκρίσει (so that even Barnabas was led astray by their hypocrisy).

Jn 3.16: ἠγάπησεν ὁ θεὸς τὸν κόσμον ὥστε τὸν υἱὸν τὸν μονογενῆ ἔδωκεν ἵνα πᾶς ὁ πιστεύων εἰς αὐτὸν μὴ ἀπόληται ἀλλ' ἔχῃ ζωὴν αἰώνιον (God loved the world, so that he gave his only begotten son, so that all who believe in him might not perish but might have eternal life). The ἵνα clause is possibly a result clause as well, although a sense of purpose is certainly not beyond consideration.

2.2. ·na *and Subjunctive*

Whereas the purpose sense of ἵνα is still maintained in the Greek of the NT, it has long been recognized that this is not its only sense. ἵνα may also be used to convey a sense of result or consequence.[1] Examples of ἵνα and the subjunctive with the sense of result may well include the following examples.[2]

Jn 9.2: τίς ἥμαρτεν...ἵνα τυφλὸς γεννηθῇ; (who sinned...that he should be born blind?).

1 Cor. 7.29: ὁ καιρὸς συνεσταλμένος ἐστίν· τὸ λοιπὸν ἵνα καὶ οἱ ἔχοντες γυναῖκας ὡς μὴ ἔχοντες ὦσιν (the time stands shortened, with the result that those having wives might be as those not having [wives]).

1 Thess. 5.4: οὐκ ἐστὲ ἐν σκότει ἵνα ἡ ἡμέρα ὑμᾶς ὡς κλέπτης καταλάβῃ (you are not in darkness, so that the day should come upon you as a thief).

Phil. 1.25, 26: μενῶ καὶ παραμενῶ...ἵνα τὸ καύχημα ὑμῶν περισσεύῃ ἐν Χριστῷ Ἰησοῦ (I shall stay and remain...so that your boasting might multiply in Christ Jesus).

1 Jn 1.9: πιστός ἐστιν καὶ δίκαιος ἵνα ἀφῇ ἡμῖν τὰς ἁμαρτίας (he is faithful and just, so that he might forgive our sins).

1. See Moulton, *Prolegomena*, pp. 206-20.

2. Boyer ('Classification of Subjunctives', pp. 5-6) minimizes the result clause, contending that in the following list only the first four are *definitely* result, and the rest are *probably* result clauses: Mt. 23.26, 35; Lk. 9.45; 11.50; 12.36; 16.26; Jn 4.36; 6.5; Rom. 11.11 (see section 2.3 below); 2 Thess. 3.14; 2 Tim. 1.4.

2.3. *Passages with Exegetical Significance*
There are several passages where the issue of purpose or result may be especially relevant in terms of exegetical significance.

Mk 4.11-12: ἐκείνοις...τοῖς ἔξω ἐν παραβολαῖς τὰ πάντα γίνεται ἵνα βλέποντες βλέπωσιν καὶ μὴ ἴδωσιν, καὶ ἀκούοντες ἀκούωσιν καὶ μὴ συνιῶσιν μήποτε ἐπιστρέψωσιν καὶ ἀφεθῇ αὐτοῖς (to those outside all things come about in parables, so that seeing they might see and [yet] not see, and hearing they might hear and [yet] not understand, lest they should repent and it be forgiven them). Whereas Moule evades the grammatical issue by invoking theological criteria (i.e. the final or purpose sense, he believes, is out of keeping with the teaching in the rest of the NT),[1] a number of scholars have argued for a purpose sense rather than simply for result.[2] This would mean that Jesus is depicted as saying that parables are given for the purpose of keeping some outside.

Rom. 5.20-21: νόμος δὲ παρεισῆλθεν ἵνα πλεονάσῃ τὸ παράπτωμα· οὗ δὲ ἐπλεόνασεν ἡ ἁμαρτία, ὑπερεπερίσσευσεν ἡ χάρις ἵνα ὥσπερ ἐβασίλευσεν ἡ ἁμαρτία ἐν τῷ θανάτῳ οὕτως καὶ ἡ χάρις βασιλεύσῃ (but law entered, so that transgression might multiply; and where sin multiplied, grace overflowed, so that as sin reigned in death thus grace might reign). The law might be spoken of as introduced for the purpose of increasing sin[3] or more neutrally as introduced with the result that sin increased. Most commentators opt for the former on the basis of Paul's view of the law.

Rom. 11.11: μὴ ἔπταισαν ἵνα πέσωσιν; (they have not stumbled so that they might fall, have they?), where Paul asks whether Israel stumbled for the purpose of falling away, or with the result that they fell away.[4] Most commentators opt for the latter because of the plural subject of the main verb, implying that the question surrounds whether the Jews' 'stumbling' has resulted in their 'falling', not God's purpose. In context, however, the possibility that purpose is intended makes good sense: 'They have not stumbled [according to God's intention, vv. 7-10] in order that they might fall [altogether], have they? Absolutely not!' Paul goes on to insist that God's saving purpose for the Jews is being worked out even in the pre-ordination that some should resist.

1. Moule, *Idiom Book*, pp. 142-43.
2. E.g. BDF, §369(1); cf. Porter, *Verbal Aspect*, p. 325, for discussion.
3. Cranfield, *Romans*, I, pp. 292-93; Dunn, *Romans 1–8*, pp. 285-87.
4. Sanday and Headlam, *Romans*, p. 320.

3. *Causal Clauses*

A causal (or inferential) clause establishes a cause and effect relation between events. Causal clauses may be formed in a variety of ways, including use of the participle and infinitive (see Chapters 10 and 11). The usual and most common construction is with ὅτι and the indicative (or variations of ὅτι, such as διότι and καθότι), although other conjunctions may be used as well (e.g. ἐπεί and ἵνα). γάρ can be used to indicate a broad kind of causal or inferential connection, but it does not appear to create a dependent clause, and is therefore better treated elsewhere simply as a conjunction (see Chapter 12 section 2.5).

Mk 1.34: οὐκ ἤφιεν λαλεῖν τὰ δαιμόνια ὅτι ᾔδεισαν αὐτόν (he did not allow the demons to speak, because they knew him).

Jn 14.19: ὅτι ἐγὼ ζῶ καὶ ὑμεῖς ζήσετε (because I live you will live also).

Rom. 1.19: διότι τὸ γνωστὸν τοῦ θεοῦ φανερόν ἐστιν ἐν αὐτοῖς (because the knowledge of God is manifest in them).

Lk. 1.7: καθότι ἦν ἡ Ἐλισάβετ στεῖρα (because Elizabeth was infertile).

Mt. 18.32: πᾶσαν τὴν ὀφειλὴν ἐκείνην ἀφῆκά σοι ἐπεὶ παρεκάλεσάς με (I forgave you that entire debt, because you begged me).

1 Cor. 1.22: ἐπειδὴ καὶ Ἰουδαῖοι σημεῖα αἰτοῦσιν (because Jews ask for signs).

Lk. 1.1: ἐπειδήπερ πολλοὶ ἐπεχείρησαν ἀνατάξασθαι διήγησιν (because many have undertaken to compile a narrative), the only use of this emphatic connective word in the NT.

Jn 8.56: Ἀβραὰμ ὁ πατὴρ ὑμῶν ἠγαλλιάσατο ἵνα ἴδῃ τὴν ἡμέραν τὴν ἐμήν (Abraham your father rejoiced, since he might see my day).

4. *Content Clauses*

The clauses which are placed under this category are variously explained by grammarians. Some classify them as appositional, epexegetical or the like. They are placed together here, because they all have in common that *a content clause states the content of some other unit, such as a subject, complement, predicate, and so forth.* The conjunctions ὅτι and ἵνα are the most frequent for indicating a content clause.

4.1. ὅτι *and Indicative*

The most common form of content clause is with ὅτι *and the indicative mood form (the so-called recitative use of* ὅτι*).* This usage frequently occurs in instances of indirect discourse, in which the ὅτι clause marks the content of the cited utterance (see Chapter 17 on indirect discourse): Gal. 5.3: μαρτύρομαι...πάλιν παντὶ ἀνθρώπῳ περιτεμνομένῳ ὅτι ὀφειλέτης ἐστὶν ὅλον τὸν νόμον ποιῆσαι (I bear witness...again to every circumcised man that he is obligated to practice the whole law); Lk. 13.2: δοκεῖτε ὅτι οἱ Γαλιλαῖοι οὗτοι ἁμαρτωλοὶ παρὰ πάντας τοὺς Γαλιλαίους ἐγένοντο; (you think that these Galileans turned out to be worse sinners than [= sinners in distinction from] all Galileans? [for the comparative force of παρά, cf. Rom. 12.3]). Content clauses occur in a number of other instances as well.

Mk 4.38: οὐ μέλει σοι ὅτι ἀπολλύμεθα; (is it not a concern to you that we are perishing?), with the dependent clause stating the content of the subject, here used with a so-called impersonal verb.

Jn 8.17: ἐν τῷ νόμῳ...τῷ ὑμετέρῳ γέγραπται ὅτι δύο ἀνθρώπων ἡ μαρτυρία ἀληθής ἐστιν (in your law it is written that the testimony of two men is true), with the dependent clause stating the content of the subject.

1 Jn 1.5: καὶ ἔστιν αὕτη ἡ ἀγγελία...ὅτι ὁ θεὸς φῶς ἐστιν καὶ σκοτία ἐν αὐτῷ οὐκ ἔστιν οὐδεμία (and this is the message...that God is light and darkness is not in him at all); 1 Jn 5.9: αὕτη ἐστὶν ἡ μαρτυρία τοῦ θεοῦ ὅτι μεμαρτύρηκεν περὶ τοῦ υἱοῦ αὐτοῦ (this is the testimony of God, that he testified concerning his son).

4.2. ἵνα *and Subjunctive*

Less usual, but still significant, is the use of ἵνα to introduce a content clause. ἵνα is followed by the subjunctive mood form (see Chapter 13 section 1.4).

Mt. 18.14: οὐκ ἔστιν θέλημα ἔμπροσθεν τοῦ πατρὸς ὑμῶν τοῦ ἐν οὐρανοῖς ἵνα ἀπόληται ἓν τῶν μικρῶν τούτων (it is not the will of your father in heaven, that one of these small ones should perish).

Mk 9.12: πῶς γέγραπται ἐπὶ τὸν υἱὸν τοῦ ἀνθρώπου ἵνα πολλὰ πάθῃ καὶ ἐξουδενηθῇ; (how is it written about the son of man that he should suffer many things and be hated?), with the content clause serving as the subject of the main clause.

Mt. 5.29: συμφέρει...σοι ἵνα ἀπόληται ἓν τῶν μελῶν σου (it is advantageous... for you that one of your members should perish), with the content clause serving as the subject of the main clause.

Phil. 2.2: πληρώσατέ μου τὴν χαρὰν ἵνα τὸ αὐτὸ φρονῆτε (fulfil my joy, that is, think the same thing [= be unified]), where the content clause restates the content of the entire command.

Jn 1.27: οὐκ εἰμὶ [ἐγὼ] ἄξιος ἵνα λύσω αὐτοῦ τὸν ἱμάντα (I am not worthy that I should loose his strap), with the content clause modifying an adjective.

Jn 4.34: ἐμὸν βρῶμά ἐστιν ἵνα ποιήσω τὸ θέλημα τοῦ πέμψαντός με (my food is that I do [subjunctive] the will of the one who sent me), with the content clause serving as the predicate.

Jn 15.13: μείζονα ταύτης ἀγάπην οὐδεὶς ἔχει ἵνα τις τὴν ψυχὴν αὐτοῦ θῇ ὑπὲρ τῶν φίλων αὐτοῦ (no one has greater love than this, that someone should give his life for his friends), with the content clause defining ταύτης; Jn 15.12: αὕτη ἐστὶν ἡ ἐντολὴ ἡ ἐμὴ ἵνα ἀγαπᾶτε ἀλλήλους (this is my commandment, that you love each other).

5. *Locative Clauses*

A locative clause specifies where one action is located in relation to another. In the Greek of the NT, three different locative words (ὅπου, ὅθεν, οὗ[1]) are used to introduce dependent clauses of place. The indicative and occasionally the subjunctive (normally with a form of the conditional particle ἄν or ἐάν) mood forms are used, depending upon the writer's view of the action in relation to reality.[2]

Jn 4.20: ἐν Ἱεροσολύμοις ἐστὶν ὁ τόπος ὅπου προσκυνεῖν δεῖ (in Jerusalem is the place where one ought to worship); Jn 19.20: ἐγγὺς ἦν ὁ τόπος τῆς πόλεως ὅπου ἐσταυρώθη ὁ Ἰησοῦς (nearby was the place in the city where Jesus was crucified).

Mk 14.14: ὅπου ἐὰν εἰσέλθῃ εἴπατε τῷ οἰκοδεσπότῃ (wherever he comes in, say to the householder); Lk. 9.57: ἀκολουθήσω σοι ὅπου ἐὰν ἀπέρχῃ (I will follow you wherever you go). All examples with the subjunctive occur in the synoptic Gospels.

Mt. 12.44: εἰς τὸν οἶκόν μου ἐπιστρέψω ὅθεν ἐξῆλθον (I will return into my house, from where I came out). Only the indicative

1. ὅπου and ὅθεν are adverbs; οὗ is the neuter genitive singular form of the relative pronoun.

2. See Robertson, *Grammar*, pp. 969-70.

mood is found with this particle in the NT.

Mt. 2.9: ἐστάθη ἐπάνω οὗ ἦν τὸ παιδίον (it stood above where the child was). The indicative mood occurs with this particle in the NT, except for 1 Cor. 16.6: ὑμεῖς με προπέμψητε οὗ ἐὰν πορεύωμαι (you might send me on, wherever I go).

6. *Temporal Clauses*

A dependent temporal clause, which may be introduced by a variety of temporal particles, posits one action in temporal relation to another.[1] Finding appropriate labels for such temporal relationships is particularly difficult. Rather than simply categorizing them according to the temporal particle, a general conceptual scheme will be used in the sections below.

Like finite verb forms, the participle and infinitive may be used in dependent structures with reference to time as well. The temporal infinitive occurs in syntactical relation to a number of different prepositions (see Chapter 11 section 2.4). Temporal reference of the participle is determined according to syntactical criteria as well (see Chapter 10 section 4). Since these do not formally constitute dependent clauses in Greek, they are treated elsewhere.

6.1. *Time at Which*

Temporal clauses are often used to indicate the 'time at which' or 'when' some other event occurred. The most commonly used particles or conjunctions for introducing this kind of temporal clause are ὅτε and ὅταν. The difference is one of attitude grammaticalized by the mood form. ὅτε occurs with the indicative, and ὅταν (ὅτε + ἄν) normally (but not always) occurs with the subjunctive. The difference in attitude between the writer asserting (indicative) and merely projecting (subjunctive) is the major semantic distinction. Several other particles are used to designate time at which or when as well (see examples below).

Mt. 7.28: ἐγένετο ὅτε ἐτέλεσεν ὁ Ἰησοῦς τοὺς λόγους τούτους (it came about when Jesus finished these words).

Lk. 17.22: ἐλεύσονται ἡμέραι ὅτε ἐπιθυμήσετε μίαν τῶν ἡμερῶν τοῦ υἱοῦ τοῦ ἀνθρώπου ἰδεῖν (days will come when you will desire to see one of the days of the son of man).

1. See Chamberlain, *Exegetical Grammar*, pp. 165-70.

Mk 2.20: ἐλεύσονται...ἡμέραι ὅταν ἀπαρθῇ ἀπ' αὐτῶν ὁ νυμφίος (days will come when the bridegroom might be taken away from them).

Mt. 5.11: μακάριοί ἐστε ὅταν ὀνειδίσωσιν ὑμᾶς (you are blessed whenever they reproach [subjunctive] you).

Chamberlain notes several examples where ὅταν is not used with subjunctive mood forms, including: Rev. 4.9 with the future form; Mk 11.25 with the present indicative; Mk 3.11 with the imperfect; and Mk 11.19 with the aorist indicative.[1]

Lk. 7.1: ἐπειδὴ ἐπλήρωσεν πάντα τὰ ῥήματα αὐτοῦ (when he completed all his words [or, when he had finished all the things he had to say]), the only probable use of this conjunctive particle with temporal force in the NT.

Lk. 11.22: ἐπὰν...νικήσῃ αὐτόν (whenever...he conquers him); cf. also Mt. 2.8 and Lk. 11.34.

2 Cor. 3.15, 16: ἡνίκα ἂν ἀναγινώσκηται Μωϋσῆς...ἡνίκα δὲ ἐὰν ἐπιστρέψῃ πρὸς κύριον (whenever Moses is read...and whenever he turns to the Lord), with ἡνίκα aided by ἄν and ἐάν.

6.2. *Time up to Which*

A variety of temporal particles are used in Greek to introduce temporal clauses stating the 'time up to which' some event may have occurred (up to a given point or until another event is transpiring). Several of the most frequent of these particles are ἕως and its various forms (e.g. ἕως οὗ/ὅτου), πρίν, ἄχρι, and μέχρι (all normally used as prepositions), along with the indicative and subjunctive mood forms.[2] (Relative pronouns with prepositions used with temporal force are treated in Chapter 15.)

Mk 6.45: ἠνάγκασεν τοὺς μαθητὰς αὐτοῦ ἐμβῆναι εἰς τὸ πλοῖον...ἕως αὐτὸς ἀπολύει τὸν ὄχλον (he made his disciples get into the boat...until he released the crowd).

Mt. 24.39: οὐκ ἔγνωσαν ἕως ἦλθεν ὁ κατακλυσμός (they did not know until the flood came).

Lk. 9.27: οὐ μὴ γεύσωνται θανάτου ἕως ἂν ἴδωσιν τὴν βασιλείαν τοῦ θεοῦ (they might not taste death until they see the kingdom of God).

Acts 23.12: μήτε φαγεῖν μήτε πιεῖν ἕως οὗ ἀποκτείνωσιν τὸν

1. Chamberlain, *Exegetical Grammar*, p. 166.
2. See Robertson, *Grammar*, pp. 974-77.

Παῦλον (neither eat nor drink until they might kill Paul).

Lk. 22.16: οὐ μὴ φάγω αὐτὸ ἕως ὅτου πληρωθῇ ἐν τῇ βασιλείᾳ τοῦ θεοῦ (I will not eat it until it might be fulfilled in the kingdom of God).

Rev. 7.3: μὴ ἀδικήσητε...ἄχρι σφραγίσωμεν τοὺς δούλους τοῦ θεοῦ ἡμῶν ἐπὶ τῶν μετώπων αὐτῶν (don't injure...until we seal the servants of our God upon their foreheads).

Eph. 4.13: μέχρι καταντήσωμεν οἱ πάντες εἰς τὴν ἑνότητα (until we all attain to oneness).

Lk. 2.26: μὴ ἰδεῖν θάνατον πρὶν [ἢ] ἂν ἴδῃ τὸν χριστὸν κυρίου (not to see death before he might see the anointed of the Lord).

Acts 25.16: οὐκ ἔστιν ἔθος Ῥωμαίοις χαρίζεσθαί τινα ἄνθρωπον πρὶν ἢ ὁ κατηγορούμενος κατὰ πρόσωπον ἔχοι τοὺς κατηγόρους (it is not the Roman custom to hand over any man before the one who is being accused might have the accusers face to face), with the optative. This is possibly an instance of indirect speech in a mixed construction with ἔστιν, instead of ἦν.

6.3. *Temporal* ὡς

The particle ὡς is a general purpose particle which is used in temporal clauses but often with a slight comparative or causal sense; consequently, its meaning can be established only by context.

Jn 4.40: ὡς...ἦλθον πρὸς αὐτὸν οἱ Σαμαρῖται, ἠρώτων αὐτὸν μεῖναι παρ' αὐτοῖς (as/when/after...the Samaritans came to him, they were asking him to stay with them), or is this causal ('since')?

Lk. 5.4: ὡς...ἐπαύσατο λαλῶν, εἶπεν πρὸς τὸν Σίμωνα (when/after...he stopped talking, he said to Simon).

7. *Comparative Clauses*

A comparative clause describes items between which similarities are being drawn. Comparative clauses use a number of different connecting particles, often in conjunction with others, to establish the comparison, such as ὡς (ὥσπερ), καθώς (καθό, καθά, καθάπερ), and even the correlative pronoun ὅσος.[1]

Mk 4.26: οὕτως ἐστὶν ἡ βασιλεία τοῦ θεοῦ ὡς ἄνθρωπος βάλῃ τὸν

1. See J.K. Elliott, 'καθώς and ὥσπερ in the NT', *FN* 4 (1991), pp. 55-58. He notes that the tendency in the NT is for the clause with καθώς to follow its main clause.

σπόρον ἐπὶ τῆς γῆς (thus the kingdom of God is as though a man might cast seed on the ground), where the comparison is helped by οὕτως.

Rev. 10.3: ἔκραξεν φωνῇ μεγάλῃ ὥσπερ λέων μυκᾶται (he cried in a loud voice as a lion roars).

Rom. 1.17: καθὼς γέγραπται (as it is written), a fairly common comparative phrase, found over 20 times in the NT.

1 Pet. 4.13: καθὸ κοινωνεῖτε τοῖς τοῦ Χριστοῦ παθήμασιν χαίρετε (as you share in the sufferings of Christ, rejoice).

Mt. 27.10: καθὰ συνέταξέν μοι κύριος (as the Lord ordered me), the only occurrence of this word in the Greek NT, a quotation of Zech. 11.13.

1 Cor. 10.10: καθάπερ τινὲς αὐτῶν ἐγόγγυσαν (as some of them grumbled).

Chapter 15

RELATIVE CLAUSES

Introduction

The second major category of dependent clauses is the so-called relative clause (see also Chapters 14 and 16).[1] As the name implies, *a relative clause is linked to its main clause by a relative pronoun.* Although there are instances of unspecified referents (see sections 1 and 3.2 below) or of attraction (section 4 below), where the relative pronoun in the dependent clause is not the one 'required' by strict rules of grammar, *a general rule is that the relative pronoun agrees in gender and number with its referent (the thing to which it refers) and in case with its function in its own clause.* The relative pronoun *follows* its referent (antecedent) in over 80% of the instances in the NT. A variety of relative pronouns may be used. The usual one (appearing in over 80% of the instances) is the simple relative (ὅς, ἥ, ὅ). Occasionally the indefinite relative (ὅστις, ἥτις, ὅτι) and correlative relatives (ὅσος, οἷος) may be used as well, along with t¤w (in this last instance the interrogative pronoun functions like a relative pronoun). Grammarians debate whether there is a substantial difference between use of the simple relative and indefinite relative pronouns in NT Greek (in many instances the simple relative form will seem to be most naturally translated by an English indefinite relative such as 'whoever'). Moule[2] agrees with Moulton[3] that at least certain passages unavoidably illustrate the difference (Mt. 7.24; Acts 10.47; 17.11; Rom. 6.2; 9.4; 2 Cor. 8.10; Jas 4.14), despite NT use of the indefinite

1. For relevant statistics on relative clauses in the Greek of the NT, see J.L. Boyer, 'Relative Clauses in the Greek NT: A Statistical Study', *GTJ* 9 (1988), pp. 233-56.

2. Moule, *Idiom Book*, pp. 123-25.

3. Moulton, *Prolegomena*, pp. 91-92.

relative being restricted to the nominative case and ἕως ὅτου (see Chapter 8 section 2.6).

A relative clause may serve a number of functions. The two major uses are the so-called adjectival (modifying) and the substantival (filling the place of a substantive, e.g. noun, pronoun). To use the language of slot and filler, the substantival relative clause may fill a slot where a substantive may be used, such as a noun or pronoun. The adjectival relative clause may fill a slot where a modifier may be used, such as an adjective. To cite English examples, 'the man whom I saw at the store is my friend' contains an adjectival clause, since the relative 'whom' modifies 'the man', within the main clause 'the man is my friend'. In the sentence 'whoever gets the answer first will be rewarded', a substantival clause introduced by 'whoever' is the subject of the verb 'will be rewarded' in the clause 'x will be rewarded', where 'x' stands for the subject.

1. *The Substantival Relative Clause*

A relative clause may function as a substantive. A substantival relative clause—the most common form of relative clause in the NT—may take the indicative or the subjunctive mood form. The mood form indicates the language user's attitude toward reality grammaticalized in the clause. In many instances, the pronoun does not have a specific referent but it must be inferred from context (see section 3.2 below).

1.1. *Indicative Form*

The indicative mood form in a relative clause is used by the speaker to make an assertion about events. The indicative mood is used in the overwhelming majority of instances of the relative clause in the Greek NT (over 80%). The substantival clause can serve (1) as the subject or (2) as the object of its main clause; there are also several (3) independent constructions. (Several of the examples below have unspecified referents; see section 3.2 below.)

1.1.1. *Subject.* There are some similarities of this construction with the protasis of the so-called first class conditional (see Chapter 16 on conditional clauses), especially when the referent of the relative pronoun is unspecified.

Mt. 10.38: ὃς οὐ λαμβάνει τὸν σταυρὸν αὐτοῦ καὶ ἀκολουθεῖ ὀπίσω μου οὐκ ἔστιν μου ἄξιος (the one who [whoever] does not take his cross and follow after me is not worthy of me).

Mk 4.9 (cf. Mk 4.23): ὃς ἔχει ὦτα ἀκούειν ἀκουέτω (let the one who has ears to hear, hear), where a relative clause is the subject of the third person singular imperative.

Mk 6.56: ὅσοι ἂν ἥψαντο αὐτοῦ ἐσῴζοντο (whoever [= all who] touched it were saved), where an aorist indicative appears with ἄν.

Rom. 6.2: οἵτινες ἀπεθάνομεν τῇ ἁμαρτίᾳ, πῶς ἔτι ζήσομεν ἐν αὐτῇ; (any of us who die to sin, how shall [can] we still live in it?). Note how the indefinite relative pronoun is translated in relation to the first person plural verb.

1.1.2. *Object.*

Rev. 3.11: κράτει ὃ ἔχεις (grasp on to what you have), where the substantival relative clause is the object of the verb.

Lk. 11.6: οὐκ ἔχω ὃ παραθήσω αὐτῷ (I do not have what I will put before him), with the future form.

1.1.3. *Independent.*

Mt. 13.12: ὅστις γὰρ ἔχει, δοθήσεται αὐτῷ...ὅστις δὲ οὐκ ἔχει, καὶ ὃ ἔχει ἀρθήσεται ἀπ' αὐτοῦ (for whoever has, it will be given to him...and whoever does not have, even what he has will be taken from him). This verse contains two instances of the independent use of the substantival relative clause and one example of the 'properly' used substantival relative clause. In the first relative clause the grammatical relation is *not* between the one referred to by ὅστις and the subject of the main clause, but ὅστις and the object, αὐτῷ. The same is true of the second clause, which refers to the object of the prepositional phrase ἀπ' αὐτοῦ. The third relative clause functions as the subject of its clause.

Lk. 7.47: ᾧ...ὀλίγον ἀφίεται, ὀλίγον ἀγαπᾷ (the one to whom... little is forgiven, loves little), in an independent use of a substantival relative clause constructed to serve as the indirect object of the main verb, but whose referent is appropriated as the subject.

1.2. *Subjunctive Form*

The use of a subjunctive in a relative clause—the less frequent form (just under 10% of the instances)—projects a hypothetical realm of existence. It can be formed with a simple or an indefinite relative pronoun. In instances of the relative clause with the subjunctive, a form of ἄν or ἐάν normally appears in the clause as well. The similarity of this construction to the protasis of the so-called third class conditional (ἐάν + subjunctive)—especially when functioning as a subject with no specific referent of the relative pronoun—allows this construction to be called a conditional-like construction and warrants translation in some instances with the conditional 'if' (see Chapter 16 on conditional clauses). This construction is frequently called the indefinite relative clause.

Mt. 16.19 (cf. Mt. 18.18): ὃ ἐὰν δήσῃς ἐπὶ τῆς γῆς ἔσται δεδεμένον ἐν τοῖς οὐρανοῖς, καὶ ὃ ἐὰν λύσῃς ἐπὶ τῆς γῆς ἔσται λελυμένον ἐν τοῖς οὐρανοῖς (whatever you bind on the earth shall be bound in heaven, and whatever you loose on the earth shall be loosed in heaven). This clause has proved difficult to analyze for several reasons, including the use of the periphrastic perfect (see Chapter 1 section 3.2.2) and the conditional-like structure. In this example, the conditional-like clauses are the subjects of the periphrastic perfect verbal constructions.

Jn 4.14: ὃς...ἂν πίῃ ἐκ τοῦ ὕδατος οὗ ἐγὼ δώσω αὐτῷ οὐ μὴ διψήσει εἰς τὸν αἰῶνα (whoever drinks from the water which I will give to him will never thirst forever), a sentence which contains both a substantival relative clause and a modifying relative clause (οὗ ἐγὼ δώσω αὐτῷ).

Jas 2.10: ὅστις γὰρ ὅλον τὸν νόμον τηρήσῃ πταίσῃ δὲ ἐν ἑνὶ γέγονεν πάντων ἔνοχος (for whoever keeps the whole law but stumbles in one thing is guilty of all), an example of subjunctives without ἄν.

Mk 9.41, 42 (cf. Mk 9.40 with an indicative): ὃς...ἂν ποτίσῃ ὑμᾶς ποτήριον ὕδατος ἐν ὀνόματι...ὃς ἂν σκανδαλίσῃ ἕνα τῶν μικρῶν τούτων τῶν πιστευόντων καλόν ἐστιν αὐτῷ... (whoever gives you a cup of water to drink in my name...whoever causes one of the smallest of these believers to stumble, it is good for him...), where the substantival conditional-like relative clauses are independent, the first serving to identify the subject of a dependent content clause (not written above) and the second referred to in the following clause by αὐτῷ.

Lk. 12.8: πᾶς ὃς ἂν ὁμολογήσῃ ἐν ἐμοὶ ἔμπροσθεν τῶν ἀνθρώπων, καὶ ὁ υἱὸς τοῦ ἀνθρώπου ὁμολογήσει ἐν αὐτῷ ἔμπροσθεν τῶν ἀγγέλων τοῦ θεοῦ (everyone who confesses me before human beings, indeed the son of man will confess [that person] before the angels of God), with an independent clause referring to αὐτῷ in the main clause.

2. *The Modifying Relative Clause*

A modifying (or adjectival) relative clause is constructed much like a substantival relative clause, except that the clause modifies its referent by way of the relative pronoun as opposed to filling an entire substantival slot. In other words, the relative clause fills the slot which would have been filled by a modifier such as an adjective.

Mt. 24.21: ἔσται γὰρ τότε θλῖψις μεγάλη οἵα οὐ γέγονεν ἀπ' ἀρχῆς κόσμου (for then there shall be a great tribulation such as has not come about from the beginning of the world), where οἵα refers to θλῖψις μεγάλη.

Mk 3.14: καὶ ἐποίησεν δώδεκα οὓς καὶ ἀποστόλους ὠνόμασεν (and he appointed twelve, whom he indeed named apostles), with some textual uncertainty.

Jn 4.14: ὃς...ἂν πίῃ ἐκ τοῦ ὕδατος οὗ ἐγὼ δώσω αὐτῷ οὐ μὴ διψήσει εἰς τὸν αἰῶνα (whoever drinks from the water which I will give to him will never thirst forever), an example of attraction, where ὅν instead of οὗ would be expected; Jn 15.20: μνημονεύετε τοῦ λόγου οὗ ἐγὼ εἶπον (remember what [lit. the word which] I said) (see section 4 below on attraction).

Jn 4.39: εἶπέν μοι πάντα ἃ ἐποίησα (he told me all the things that I did).

Jn 12.1: ἦν Λάζαρος ὃν ἤγειρεν ἐκ νεκρῶν 'Ιησοῦς (there was Lazarus, whom Jesus raised from the dead).

Acts 10.45: ἐξέστησαν οἱ ἐκ περιτομῆς πιστοὶ ὅσοι συνῆλθαν τῷ Πέτρῳ (the 'Jewish believers' who accompanied Peter were astonished).

Rom. 2.5-6: τοῦ θεοῦ ὃς ἀποδώσει ἑκάστῳ κατὰ τὰ ἔργα αὐτοῦ (God, who will give to each according to his works).

Rom. 11.2: οὐκ ἀπώσατο ὁ θεὸς τὸν λαὸν αὐτοῦ ὃν προέγνω (God did not reject his people whom he foreknew).

Jas 1.12: μακάριος ἀνὴρ ὃς ὑπομένει πειρασμόν (blessed is the person who endures temptation).

1 Jn 2.7: γράφω ὑμῖν...ἐντολὴν παλαιὰν ἣν εἴχετε ἀπ' ἀρχῆς (I write to you...an old commandment which you had from the beginning).

In instances where the relative pronoun is referring to an extended phrase rather than to a particular word or a group of words, or where a group of items is referred to as a whole, the neuter pronoun is often used.

Acts 11.30: ὃ καὶ ἐποίησαν (which indeed they did), with a neuter singular pronoun referring to the procedures taken after the prophecy of Agabus.

Col. 1.29: εἰς ὃ καὶ κοπιῶ (toward which I am indeed working), with a neuter singular pronoun referring to Paul's work for the church; Col. 2.22: ἅ ἐστιν πάντα εἰς φθορὰν τῇ ἀποχρήσει (all of which are [destined] for corruption in their use), with a neuter plural pronoun referring to the three admonitions of v. 21 (this could also be considered an example of attraction to the predicate).

3. *Special Uses of the Relative Pronoun*

3.1. *The Relative Pronoun with Prepositions*

A relative pronoun with a preposition often establishes a more complex relationship than a relative pronoun alone establishes. The question that arises from this usage is whether there is a referent in the context for the relative pronoun or whether the pronoun and preposition together form their own grammatical unit, often requiring a different word for translation, such as 'when'. Some of these examples are difficult to resolve; several of them have theological significance. These are categorized into three groups: (1) external referent; (2) internal referent; and (3) connective.

3.1.1. *External referent.* The relative pronoun refers to an item external to the relative clause.

Mt. 1.16: Μαρίας ἐξ ἧς ἐγεννήθη Ἰησοῦς (Mary, from whom Jesus was born).

Lk. 7.47: οὗ χάριν λέγω σοι (on account of which [anointing] I say to you), with the neuter pronoun probably referring to the entire previous act of anointing (on χάριν, see Chapter 9 section 5 on improper prepositions).

1 Pet. 3.19: ἐν ᾧ καὶ τοῖς ἐν φυλακῇ πνεύμασιν πορευθεὶς ἐκήρυξεν (in which [or, 'by whom'], having gone also to the spirits in prison, he preached), where the antecedent is possibly πνεύματι in the previous verse; Acts 4.31: ὁ τόπος ἐν ᾧ ἦσαν συνηγμένοι (the place

in which they were gathered), where the relative pronoun refers to the preceding noun.

Jn 1.33: ἐφ' ὃν ἂν ἴδῃς τὸ πνεῦμα (upon whom you see the Spirit), referring to αὐτόν or ἐκεῖνος earlier in the verse.

3.1.2. *Internal referent.* The relative pronoun refers to a substantive occurring within the relative clause. These examples could be considered instances of 'incorporation' as well (see section 4.4 below).

Mt. 24.38: ἄχρι ἧς ἡμέρας εἰσῆλθεν Νῶε εἰς τὴν κιβωτόν (until which day Noah entered into the ark), with the phrase ἄχρι ἧς taking on a temporal value; Lk. 1.20: ἔσῃ...μὴ δυνάμενος λαλῆσαι ἄχρι ἧς ἡμέρας γένηται ταῦτα (you will be...unable to speak until which day these things come about).

Lk. 8.47: δι' ἣν αἰτίαν ἥψατο αὐτοῦ (because of which [cause] she touched him).

1 Pet. 1.10: περὶ ἧς σωτηρίας ἐξεζήτησαν (concerning which salvation they inquired).

3.1.3. *Connective.* The preposition and its relative pronoun may form a phrase which serves as a sentence connective.

Mt. 25.40: ἐφ' ὅσον ἐποιήσατε ἑνὶ τούτων (to the extent that [because] you did to one of these).

Lk. 13.7: ἀφ' οὗ ἔρχομαι (from which [since] I am coming), with no apparent referent for the pronoun οὗ.

Jn 5.7: ἐν ᾧ...ἔρχομαι ἐγώ (in which [while] I am coming), with the only possible external referent being the preceding τὸ ὕδωρ (the water), not a likely choice.

Rom. 8.3: ἐν ᾧ ἠσθένει διὰ τῆς σαρκός (in which [because] it was weak through the flesh).

Rom. 5.12 (cf. 2 Cor. 5.4; Phil. 3.12): ἐφ' ᾧ πάντες ἥμαρτον (upon which [because] all sinned). The explanations of this verse have been legion. Few verses with a relative clause have such important theological consequences. The following analyses have been suggested. (1) ἐφ' ᾧ meaning 'in which', with ᾧ, masculine, referring to an assumed antecedent, 'death' or 'law'. (2) ἐφ' ᾧ meaning 'in whom', with ᾧ, masculine, referring to 'one man', Adam (Augustine). (3) ᾧ, masculine, referring to 'one man', but ἐπί meaning 'because'. (4) ἐφ' ᾧ meaning 'because', possibly as an assimilation of classical ἐπὶ τούτῳ ὅτι. This still leaves open the (systematic-theological) question of who the sinners are: humans sinning independently but after Adam's example (Pelagius); humans actually sinning in Adam (realist view); or humans actually sinning because they were constituted sinners as a result of Adam (federalist view).[1]

3.2. *Unspecified Referent*

In nearly 500 instances in the Greek of the NT, *a relative pronoun standing alone (without an accompanying preposition) takes on a meaning apart from its normal relational usage (e.g. adverbial) or assumes an unspecified referent.* This usage is fairly common in substantival clauses, as noted above (section 1). Included here are several of the more unusual instances of this phenomenon.

Mt. 2.9: οὗ ἦν τὸ παιδίον (where the child was), a reasonably common use of the neuter genitive singular relative pronoun with locative sense (cf. Lk. 10.1; 1 Cor. 16.6) (see Chapter 14 section 5).

Jn 4.18: πέντε γὰρ ἄνδρας ἔσχες, καὶ νῦν ὃν ἔχεις οὐκ ἔστιν σου ἀνήρ (for you have had five husbands, and now [the one] whom you have is not your husband).

Rom. 6.10: ὃ γὰρ ἀπέθανεν, τῇ ἁμαρτίᾳ ἀπέθανεν ἐφάπαξ· ὃ δὲ ζῇ, ζῇ τῷ θεῷ (for what [= the death] he died, he died once to sin; but what [= the life] he lives, he lives to God). Moule entertains the adverbial use of the relative clause, and hence the translation 'whereas he died, he died to sin, once for all; and whereas he lives...', rather than the relative pronoun standing for τὸν θάνατον ὃν ἀπέθανεν.[2]

Gal. 2.20: ὃ δὲ νῦν ζῶ ἐν σαρκί, ἐν πίστει ζῶ τῇ τοῦ υἱοῦ τοῦ θεοῦ τοῦ ἀγαπήσαντός με (and what [= the life] I now live in the flesh, I live in faith in the son of the God who loved me).

4. *Attraction*

Attraction occurs when the 'required' case, number or gender agreement is not found between a referent and its relative pronoun. The attraction can work in two directions: the relative pronoun can be attracted to its referent or its referent attracted to the relative pronoun, the latter being called inverse attraction. Many reasons have been proposed for attraction. One possible reason is simply a colloquial flexibility in the Greek language which the Greek of the NT

1. See Porter, 'The Pauline Concept of Original Sin', pp. 22-24.
2. Moule, *Idiom Book*, p. 131.

reflects, perhaps something akin to English use of 'who' where 'whom' would be grammatically proper. Another possible reason is that there is theological or other significance which elicits the change. A third possibility revolves around the force of predicate structure, in which the relative pronoun serving as subject is attracted to its predicate.[1] The examples of attraction are categorized under the headings of case, gender, number and incorporation.

4.1. *Case*

In the majority of instances there is a change from the accusative case of the main clause to another of the oblique or non-nominative cases (there are other instances as well).

Lk. 19.37: περὶ πασῶν ὧν εἶδον δυνάμεων (about all the miracles which they saw), where the accusative case οὕς, not ὧν, is expected.

Acts 17.31: ἐν ἀνδρὶ ᾧ ὥρισεν (by a man whom he selected), where the accusative case, ὅν, is expected.

Mk 12.10 // Mt. 21.42: λίθον ὃν ἀπεδοκίμασαν οἱ οἰκοδομοῦντες (a stone which the builders rejected), where the nominative case, λίθος, is expected, an instance of inverse attraction.

4.2. *Gender*

Mk 15.16: τῆς αὐλῆς, ὅ ἐστιν πραιτώριον (the hall, which is the praetorium), an example of attraction to the predicate.

Jn 6.9: παιδάριον...ὃς ἔχει...(a small boy...who has...), where the attraction is to the natural gender (masculine) rather than the grammatical gender (neuter).

Eph. 5.5 (cf. Col. 3.5): πᾶς πόρνος ἢ ἀκάθαρτος ἢ πλεονέκτης, ὅ ἐστιν εἰδωλολάτρης (every fornicating or unclean or greedy [person], who is an idolater), where ὅς would be expected. The neuter relative pronoun seems to refer to each of the concepts in the abstract, rather than to the person performing the actions.

1 Jn 2.8: ἐντολὴν καινὴν γράφω ὑμῖν, ὅ ἐστιν ἀληθὲς ἐν αὐτῷ (I write to you a new commandment, which is true in him), where ἥ would be expected with reference to ἐντολήν. This is possibly an example of attraction to the predicate (see section 2 above on the modifying clause with neuter pronoun).

1 Cor. 15.10: χάριτι...θεοῦ εἰμι ὅ εἰμι (by the grace...of God I am what I am), where Paul uses the neuter rather than the masculine

1. See Green, *Handbook*, pp. 310-11.

relative pronoun (ὅς), perhaps emphasizing his qualitative character rather than his personal character (what I am as opposed to who I am).

1 Tim. 3.16: τὸ τῆς εὐσεβείας μυστήριον, ὃς ἐφανερώθη ἐν σαρκί (the mystery of piety, which was manifest in flesh), where the masculine rather than the neuter relative pronoun (ὅ) is used, probably referring to Christ as the mystery of piety. There is a textual variant with ὅ, although the masculine reading is very strong.

Eph. 1.13, 14: τῷ πνεύματι...ὅς ἐστιν ἀρραβών (the Spirit... who is the deposit), although there is a strong textual variant with the neuter ὅ. If the masculine relative pronoun is accepted, then there is grammatical evidence for the Holy Spirit being viewed here as personal rather than abstract.

4.3. *Number*

Several of the examples treated above with reference to prepositions with relative pronouns could be placed in this category as well.

Lk. 6.17, 18: πλῆθος πολὺ τοῦ λαοῦ...οἳ ἦλθον (a great crowd of people...who came), where the construction according to sense (i.e. taking the collective noun 'crowd' as plural) is understandable.

1 Cor. 3.17: ὁ γὰρ ναὸς τοῦ θεοῦ ἅγιός ἐστιν, οἵτινές ἐστε ὑμεῖς (for the temple of God is holy, which you [all] are), in which the members of the temple are specified, an example of attraction to the number of the predicate (ὑμεῖς) by the indefinite relative pronoun.

4.4. *Incorporation*

Incorporation occurs when the referent is part of its own relative clause. This is a sub-category of inverse attraction. Robertson counts 54 examples in the NT.[1]

Mt. 7.2: ἐν ᾧ γὰρ κρίματι κρίνετε κριθήσεσθε, καὶ ἐν ᾧ μέτρῳ μετρεῖτε μετρηθήσεται ὑμῖν (for by which [the] judgment you judge you will be judged, and by which [the] measure you measure it will be measured to you).

Mk 6.16: ὃν ἐγὼ ἀπεκεφάλισα Ἰωάννην (John whom I beheaded).

Lk. 24.1: φέρουσαι ἃ ἡτοίμασαν ἀρώματα (to bring which [the] spices they prepared).

Rom. 6.17: εἰς ὃν παρεδόθητε τύπον διδαχῆς (to which model of teaching you were entrusted).

1. Robertson, *Grammar*, pp. 718-19; see also Winer, *Treatise*, p. 205.

Chapter 16

CONDITIONAL CLAUSES

Introduction

Conditional constructions (or 'if–then' clauses) are interesting in virtually every language, and have been subject to much linguistic discussion.[1] As far as syntax is concerned, when discussion of conditional clauses begins, the terrain can often become quite rocky, since many different factors must be taken into account. It is necessary first to realize that *a conditional construction consists of two elements, the protasis, or the supposition of the condition (the 'if' part, which is a dependent clause), and the apodosis, or the consequence of the condition (the 'then' part, which is normally an independent clause).* In the Greek of the NT, the normal order is for the protasis to precede the apodosis, although either one may appear first. Some conditional constructions do not have both clauses (e.g. Lk. 13.9; 19.42), but the discussion here will for the most part be concerned about conditional statements with both clauses expressed.

1. *Classification of Conditional Clauses*

There have been several different systems devised for discussing the semantics of the various conditional constructions. For example, some grammarians classify them according to a temporal scheme, resulting in a mixed bag of categories such as 'simple', 'future more vivid', 'future less vivid', 'present general', 'past general', 'present contrary to fact', 'past contrary to fact', 'future most vivid'.[2] This classificatory scheme is not very helpful, because it is too dependent upon equating a tense-form with a fixed temporal value. It posits a temporal relation

1. See Porter, *Verbal Aspect*, ch. 6.

2. E.g. Goodwin, *Greek Grammar*, pp. 295-304; Smyth, *Greek Grammar*, pp. 512-37; Burton, *Syntax*, pp. 101-12; Zerwick, *Biblical Greek*, pp. 101-13.

between the protasis and the apodosis as well (see section 2.2 below). While this system may be useful in some cases, and has apparently been popular in various mutations among elementary Greek grammars, it is fundamentally misdirected because of its overreliance on temporal distinctions. A second system is to classify according to the mood form used in the protasis.[1] This scheme appears to be more satisfactory, since it pays close attention to the formal evidence of the language, without multiplying categories beyond necessity. It must be recognized that the so-called 'contrary to fact' conditional has some difficulty fitting into this system (see section 2.1.2 below). The scheme below introduces a two-part matrix for classification of conditional constructions. The first utilizes the protasis or 'if' clause as the basis for establishing the major categories of classification; the second analyzes some of the possible relationships between the protasis and apodosis clauses of a conditional construction. Each works independently, even though they are closely related.

On the basis of its syntax (the two clauses work together to form a unit larger than a single clause) and its dependence upon the mood of the verb, many grammarians classify the conditional construction as 'non-factive'. What this means is that the construction itself makes no necessary statement about the facts of the matter, about whether something is or is not true in reality. This is not the same as stating that what is posited through use of the construction is not true or cannot be true, but only that for the sake of the argument which uses this construction this question is held in abeyance. It must also be noted, however, that in a given context an author may use a conditional construction and wish to say something 'factive'. This will be indicated through other grammatical means besides use of the conditional, such as reference to known persons, places, and so on. As will be discussed below, *a conditional construction is used to posit a relationship between the hypothesis and its consequent, a relation which must be determined by appeal to context.*

2. *Greek Conditional Clauses*

2.1. *Protases*

There are two major categories of conditional protases. The first are

1. Winer, *Treatise*, pp. 363-70; Robertson, *Grammar*, pp. 1004-27; BDF, §§371-73; Schwyzer, *Griechische Grammatik*, II, pp. 682-88.

those with indicative verb forms in the protasis; the second are those with non-indicative verb forms in the protasis. Although in the popular literature of the Hellenistic period (papyri, even inscriptions) there seems to have been some loss of distinction between εἰ and ἐάν and the mood forms following,[1] this is not true of the Greek of the NT, as it is represented in the best manuscripts. (This is despite such verses as Acts 5.38, 39: ἐὰν ᾖ ἐξ ἀνθρώπων...εἰ δὲ ἐκ θεοῦ ἐστιν [if he is [subjunctive] from humanity...but if he is [indicative] from God].) Consequently, the use of the mood forms in protases should be differentiated, and the analysis according to 'classes' below follows a widely recognized scheme in doing this. One of the distinguishing features of the protasis of a conditional construction is some form of 'if' word—usually εἰ with the indicative, optative and future (or one of its variants, e.g. εἰπέρ, εἰ καί) and ἐάν (εἰ + ἄν, most scholars suppose) with the subjunctive.

1. εἰ + indicative, negated by οὐ
2. εἰ + imperfect or aorist, negated by μή (ἄν + imperfect or aorist in apodosis)
3. ἐάν + subjunctive, negated by μή
4. εἰ + optative, negated by μή (ἄν + optative, or imperfect in apodosis)
5. εἰ + future, negated by οὐ

Classification of Conditional Protases

2.1.1. *First class conditional* (simple condition): εἰ + indicative (negated by οὐ), with almost any verb form in the apodosis (see the classification list above). *A first class conditional makes an assertion for the sake of argument.* It is the most widely used conditional clause in the NT, with over 300 examples.[2]

a. *First class conditionals and reality.* It is sometimes posited (or assumed) that this kind of conditional can be translated with 'since' rather than 'if', on the basis that the first class conditional with the indicative states a true hypothesis.[3] There are some examples where this may be accurate.

Jn 11.12: εἰ κεκοίμηται σωθήσεται (if he is asleep, he will be

1. See Moulton, *Prolegomena*, p. 187.

2. For statistics and analysis, see J.L. Boyer, 'First Class Conditions: What do they Mean?', *GTJ* 2 (1981), pp. 75-114. Several conditional-like statements, noted above in discussion of the relative clause (Chapter 15 section 1.1), can be placed in this category for the sake of analysis, although they are not treated here.

3. Winer, *Treatise*, p. 364; BDF, §§371-72.

saved), in the sense that his being asleep allows there to be the expectation of his being saved: since he is asleep, he can expect to be saved. If he is dead, this expectation is removed.

Mk 4.23: εἴ τις ἔχει ὦτα ἀκούειν ἀκουέτω (if someone has ears to hear, let him hear), in the sense that having ears allows for hearing, although it does not guarantee it. (This protasis probably refers to someone having the capacity to understand, and could be translated 'since someone can understand...')

Use of 'since' in translating the protasis of a first class conditional cannot be made the rule, however. This is illustrated by the examples below.

Mt. 12.27: εἰ ἐγὼ ἐν Βεελζεβοὺλ ἐκβάλλω τὰ δαιμόνια, οἱ υἱοὶ ὑμῶν ἐν τίνι ἐκβάλλουσιν; (if I cast out the demons by Beelzebul, by whom do your sons cast [them] out?). Jesus is making this hypothesis not because he is casting out demons by Beelzebul's authority but because he is positing it for the sake of argument.

Jn 10.37: εἰ οὐ ποιῶ τὰ ἔργα τοῦ πατρός μου, μὴ πιστεύετέ μοι (if I am not doing the work of my father, don't believe me), where Jesus follows in v. 38 by saying εἰ δὲ ποιῶ (but if I do); cf. Jn 18.23; 20.15.

1 Cor. 15.13-14: εἰ δὲ ἀνάστασις νεκρῶν οὐκ ἔστιν, οὐδὲ Χριστὸς ἐγήγερται· εἰ δὲ Χριστὸς οὐκ ἐγήγερται, κενὸν ἄρα τὸ κήρυγμα ἡμῶν (but if there is not a resurrection from the dead, Christ was not raised; and if Christ was not raised, our preaching is empty).

Mt. 26.39, 42: πάτερ μου, εἰ δύνατόν ἐστιν, παρελθάτω ἀπ' ἐμοῦ τὸ ποτήριον τοῦτο...πάτερ μου, εἰ οὐ δύναται τοῦτο παρελθεῖν ἐὰν μὴ αὐτὸ πίω, γενηθήτω τὸ θέλημά σου (my father, if it is possible, let this cup pass from me...my father, if it is not possible for this to pass by unless I drink it, let your will come to pass), where positive and negative statements are used.

Boyer has estimated that, of the first class conditionals, 37% are obviously true, 12% are obviously false, and 51% are undetermined. If he is correct, then well over half *do not* show that the first class conditional is asserted as true ('since').

b. *First class conditionals and temporal reference*. A second distinction often made about the first class conditional is that the aorist and imperfect tense-forms are past-referring and the present tense-form is present-referring. There are many instances where this temporal equation may be accurate, but there are also many cases where it is not. A distinction of conditional clauses along temporal lines on the basis of tense-form (i.e. the present form means the conditional is present-referring, and the aorist past-referring, and so forth) cannot be sustained. Of course, just because an aorist is not past-referring does not mean that it is present-referring or future-referring, and the like, since temporal reference—if it is an issue with a given use of a conditional—must be determined by context.

Mt. 10.25: εἰ τὸν οἰκοδεσπότην Βεελζεβοὺλ ἐπεκάλεσαν, πόσῳ μᾶλλον τοὺς οἰκιακοὺς αὐτοῦ (if they call the householder Beelzebul, how much more the members of his household), with a timeless use of an aorist in the protasis of a conditional with a verbless apodosis.

Jn 15.20: εἰ ἐμὲ ἐδίωξαν, καὶ ὑμᾶς διώξουσιν· εἰ τὸν λόγον μου ἐτήρησαν, καὶ τὸν ὑμέτερον τηρήσουσιν (if they persecute me, indeed they will persecute you; if they keep my word, indeed they will keep yours). Embedded in a series of conditional constructions, these two conditionals with aorist verbs in the protasis illustrate that to press temporal distinctions on the basis of verb tense-forms is to run the risk of making nonsense. This is especially evident in light of v. 18 with εἰ and a present verb, since equating tense-form and time would create an unwarranted shift in temporal reference.

Gal. 2.17: εἰ...ζητοῦντες δικαιωθῆναι ἐν Χριστῷ εὑρέθημεν καὶ αὐτοὶ ἁμαρτωλοί, ἄρα Χριστὸς ἁμαρτίας διάκονος; (if...seeking to be justified in Christ we are found to be sinners, is Christ then a servant of sin?), with a timeless use of an aorist in the protasis of a conditional with a verbless apodosis (on interpretation of the apodosis see Chapter 12 section 2.4).

Mt. 8.31: εἰ ἐκβάλλεις ἡμᾶς, ἀπόστειλον ἡμᾶς εἰς τὴν ἀγέλην τῶν χοίρων (if you are going to cast us out, send us into the herd of swine), with future-referring use of a present tense.

Lk. 16.31: εἰ Μωϋσέως καὶ τῶν προφητῶν οὐκ ἀκούουσιν, οὐδ' ἐάν τις ἐκ νεκρῶν ἀναστῇ πεισθήσονται (if they did not hear Moses and the prophets, they will not be convinced if someone rises from the dead). The context indicates past reference of the present verb. (Note use of the subjunctive as well, part of the protasis of a third class conditional clause embedded within the larger conditional construction.)

In light of what has been said elsewhere about the priority of verbal aspect in Greek tense usage—that is, verbal aspect takes priority over temporal categories—the interpreter should not begin with preconceptions about temporal reference. This is further confirmed by the use of the conditional construction itself, which by its syntactical structure simply posits a hypothesis and its consequence.

c. *The perfect tense*. The perfect tense also appears in the first class conditional, although it is not often discussed in grammars. Its stative verbal aspect is clear.

Jn 11.12: εἰ κεκοίμηται σωθήσεται (if he is asleep, he will be saved).

Acts 16.15: εἰ κεκρίκατέ με πιστὴν τῷ κυρίῳ εἶναι...μένετε (if you judge me to be faithful to the Lord...stay).

d. *Verbal aspect*. The semantic difference in use of the present, the aorist and the perfect tense-forms in the protasis of the first class conditional (like all conditionals) is verbal aspect.

Jn 3.12: εἰ τὰ ἐπίγεια εἶπον ὑμῖν καὶ οὐ πιστεύετε, πῶς ἐὰν εἴπω ὑμῖν τὰ ἐπουράνια πιστεύσετε; (if I speak to you of earthly things and you do not believe, how will you believe if I speak to you of heavenly things?). Aorist and present tense-forms are parallel in the protasis. (Note also the use of the aorist subjunctive in the protasis of a parenthetical third class conditional clause.)

Rom. 2.17-19: εἰ δὲ σὺ Ἰουδαῖος ἐπονομάζῃ καὶ ἐπαναπαύῃ νόμῳ καὶ καυχᾶσαι ἐν θεῷ καὶ γινώσκεις τὸ θέλημα καὶ δοκιμάζεις τὰ διαφέροντα... πέποιθάς τε σεαυτὸν ὁδηγὸν εἶναι τυφλῶν...(and if you call yourself a Jew and rely on the law and boast in God and know [his] will and test the superior things...but you are confident that you yourself are a leader of the blind...).

e. *Exceptional structures*. Several instances of conditional clauses are not regular in their syntactical patterns (other examples could be cited as well).

1 Thess. 3.8: νῦν ζῶμεν ἐὰν ὑμεῖς στήκετε ἐν κυρίῳ (now we live if you stand in the Lord), with ἐάν in the protasis; cf. 1 Jn 5.15.

1 Tim. 6.3, 4: εἴ τις ἑτεροδιδασκαλεῖ καὶ μὴ προσέρχεται ὑγιαίνουσιν λόγοις...τετύφωται (if anyone teaches another doctrine and does not attend to healthy words...he is puffed up), with μή as the negative; cf. 1 Cor. 15.2; 2 Cor. 13.5; Gal. 1.7.

2.1.2. *Second class conditional* (contrary to fact): εἰ + indicative (negated by μή), with ἄν in the apodosis, usually with an aorist or imperfect tense-form (see the classification list on p. 256).[1] *The so-called 'contrary-to-fact' conditional (found less than 40 times in the NT) can be thought of as a sub-category of the first class conditional, since the protasis is formed in the same way (but negated by* μή*).* The major distinctive of this class is provided by the apodosis with the conditional particle (ἄν). However, there are several examples in which the apodosis of this conditional does not have ἄν: e.g. Jn 15.22: εἰ μὴ ἦλθον καὶ ἐλάλησα αὐτοῖς, ἁμαρτίαν οὐκ εἴχοσαν (if I had not come and spoken to them, they would not have sin), the negative in the protasis indicating that it is a second class conditional. The conditional particle in the apodosis is a grammatical indicator that the speaker is asserting for argument (but may not believe) that the protasis is contrary to fact. Whether it is *actually* to be considered contrary to fact must be determined by context.

a. *Imperfect and aorist tense-forms in the protasis.* The traditional distinction by many grammarians regarding this class of conditional is that the imperfect in the protasis is used for present reference, and the aorist in the protasis is used for past reference.[2] (The perfect and pluperfect tense-forms are also occasionally used in this class of conditional.) There are several conceptual problems with this scheme, besides a number of exceptions (see below). The first problem is the fact that this understanding goes contrary to a strict temporal understanding of the tense-forms, since the imperfect is normally understood as referring to past time. This formulation is tantamount to admitting that the conditional syntactical structure imposes patterns on tense usage which run contrary to the traditional temporal scheme. The second problem is related to the referential capabilities of the conditional statement. This conditional structure has been debated extensively by grammarians, but, on the basis of the information presented above, it is clear that the perceived relation of any conditional to the real world is based on context, not on its grammatical structure. Hence conditionals are referred to as non-factive constructions. See for example Lk. 7.39: οὗτος εἰ ἦν προφήτης, ἐγίνωσκεν ἂν τίς καὶ ποταπὴ ἡ γυνὴ ἥτις ἅπτεται αὐτοῦ (this one, if he were a prophet, would know who and what sort of woman it is who is touching him),

1. For statistics and analysis, see J.L. Boyer, 'Second Class Conditions in NT Greek', *GTJ* 3 (1982), pp. 81-88.

2. E.g. Dana and Mantey, *Manual Grammar*, pp. 289-90.

where even though the speaker is implying by the construction used that Jesus is not a prophet, the text makes clear that Jesus is capable of knowing these things. The second class conditional is a non-factive statement used contra-factively, making it even less likely or necessary that the structure have any temporal relation to the referential world.[1] The third problem is that the negative for the protasis of this conditional is μή. The use of the notional or ideal negative (rather than οὐ, the concrete negative) supports the concept that this conditional is contra-factive and non-referential.[2]

Mk 13.20: εἰ μὴ ἐκολόβωσεν κύριος τὰς ἡμέρας, οὐκ ἂν ἐσώθη πᾶσα σάρξ (if the Lord were not going to cut short the days, all flesh would not [= no flesh would] be saved), in which reference to tribulation with the aorist tense-form is quite possibly future.

Jn 5.46: εἰ γὰρ ἐπιστεύετε Μωϋσεῖ, ἐπιστεύετε ἂν ἐμοί (for if you had believed Moses, you would have believed me), with the imperfect used of past reference.

Mt. 12.7: εἰ...ἐγνώκειτε τί ἐστιν, ἔλεος θέλω καὶ οὐ θυσίαν, οὐκ ἂν κατεδικάσατε τοὺς ἀναιτίους (if...you knew what this is [= means], 'I want mercy and not sacrifice', you would not condemn those who are not guilty), where reference of the pluperfect is not to past time.

b. *Examples of the second class conditional.*

Jn 8.42: εἰ ὁ θεὸς πατὴρ ὑμῶν ἦν, ἠγαπᾶτε ἂν ἐμέ (if God were your father, you would love me), where Jesus is recorded as implying for the argument that his audience does not know God as father.

Acts 18.14: εἰ μὲν ἦν ἀδίκημά τι ἢ ῥᾳδιούργημα πονηρόν...κατὰ λόγον ἂν ἀνεσχόμην ὑμῶν (if there were some injustice or evil crime...I would have reason to be patient with you), where the speaker uses the conditional to say that he does not believe that there is.

2.1.3. *Third class conditional* (more probable, present general, future more vivid): ἐάν + subjunctive, with virtually any verb form in the apodosis (see the classification list on p. 256). Many grammarians recognize that the subjunctive, optative and even future forms in the protasis of a conditional should be analyzed together (as non-indicative forms), since their attitudinal characteristics are similar. Whereas

1. Porter, *Verbal Aspect*, p. 305.
2. See Chapter 19; Porter, *Verbal Aspect*, p. 296.

there is semantic overlap among these mood forms, there is not complete synonymy, so their individual semantic features should be preserved. *A third class conditional with ἐάν and the subjunctive, in distinction to a first class conditional, is more tentative and simply projects some action or event for hypothetical consideration.*

a. *Subjunctive mood form.* The protasis of this class of conditional is widespread, occurring approximately 277 times in the NT, with 107 present, 205 aorist and 6 perfect subjunctive verb forms used (the figures do not include use of forms of εἰμί).[1] Boyer has estimated that only 7% of third class conditional constructions are certain of fulfilment, 23% are probable, and 43% give no indication.[2] This reinforces the definition of mood used throughout this grammar, in which the non-indicative moods, such as the subjunctive, optative, and the related future, grammaticalize a projection or expectation, not an assertion, about reality. Note especially the following example where both sides of a proposition are stated using the conditional.

Mt. 6.14, 15: ἐὰν...ἀφῆτε τοῖς ἀνθρώποις τὰ παραπτώματα αὐτῶν...ἐὰν δὲ μὴ ἀφῆτε τοῖς ἀνθρώποις...(if...you forgive people their sins...but if you do not forgive people...).

Lk. 16.31: εἰ Μωϋσέως καὶ τῶν προφητῶν οὐκ ἀκούουσιν, οὐδ' ἐάν τις ἐκ νεκρῶν ἀναστῇ πεισθήσονται (if they did not hear Moses and the prophets, neither, if someone should rise from the dead, will they be convinced). The protasis with the subjunctive follows the protasis with the indicative, the former projecting what might come about and the latter being used assertively about a past event.

Mk 3.24-26: ἐὰν βασιλεία ἐφ' ἑαυτὴν μερισθῇ, οὐ δύναται σταθῆναι ἡ βασιλεία ἐκείνη· καὶ ἐὰν οἰκία ἐφ' ἑαυτὴν μερισθῇ, οὐ δυνήσεται ἡ οἰκία ἐκείνη σταθῆναι. καὶ εἰ ὁ σατανᾶς ἀνέστη ἐφ' ἑαυτὸν καὶ ἐμερίσθη, οὐ δύναται στῆναι ἀλλὰ τέλος ἔχει (if a kingdom is divided in relation to itself, that kingdom is not able to stand; and if a house is divided in relation to itself, that house will not be able to stand. And if Satan rebels in relation to himself and is

1. For statistics and analysis, see J.L. Boyer, 'Third (and Fourth) Class Conditions', *GTJ* 3 (1982), pp. 163-75, esp. 168-69. Many conditional-like statements, noted above in discussion of the relative clause (Chapter 15 section 1.2), can be placed in this category for sake of analysis, although they are not treated here.

2. The remaining categories (27%) he considers are those where fulfilment is doubtful, improbable, possible, conceivable or impossible.

divided, he is not able to stand but he has [his] end).

Lk. 9.13: εἰ μήτι πορευθέντες ἡμεῖς ἀγοράσωμεν εἰς πάντα τὸν λαὸν τοῦτον βρώματα (if we do not go and purchase food for all the people), where εἰ with the subjunctive occurs. This is a fairly common alteration in Hellenistic Greek, and is even found in earlier classical sources. It provides no difficulty since classification is based on the verb form, not the conditional conjunction.

b. *Verbal aspect.* Verbal aspect is the decisive factor for distinction among uses of the present, aorist and perfect subjunctive tense-forms. Most recent grammarians agree that the subjunctive is not present or past-referring on the basis of its tense form, but that any reference to time must be established by context. Therefore, some other rationale must be at work to explain the continued use of the tense-forms. Verbal aspect provides that explanation.

1 Cor. 13.2-3: ἐὰν ἔχω προφητείαν καὶ εἰδῶ τὰ μυστήρια πάντα καὶ πᾶσαν τὴν γνῶσιν καὶ ἐὰν ἔχω πᾶσαν τὴν πίστιν ὥστε ὄρη μεθιστάναι ἀγάπην δὲ μὴ ἔχω, οὐθέν εἰμι (if I should have prophecy and be knowledgeable of all the mysteries and all the knowledge and even if I should have all faith so as to remove mountains and I do not have love, I am nothing), where present and perfect tense-forms are contrasted.

1 Jn 1.6-10: ἐὰν εἴπωμεν (if we should say) that we are having fellowship with him and περιπατῶμεν (we should walk) in darkness, we are liars and not doing the truth. Note the continued opposition of present and aorist subjunctives throughout this section, with the aorist tense used with the verb of saying and the present tense used with the verb of doing. Emphasis rests upon 'doing'.

2.1.4. *Fourth class conditional* (future less vivid, past general): εἰ + optative in the protasis, with ἄν and an optative verb, or an imperfect verb in the apodosis (see the classification list on p. 256). *A fourth class conditional with* εἰ *and the optative, like the subjunctive, grammaticalizes the semantic feature of projection, with an element of doubt or contingency introduced.*

There is no example of a complete form of this conditional structure in the NT with ἄν + optative in the apodosis. There are several partial constructions, however, which are usually considered here.

1 Pet. 3.14: ἀλλ' εἰ καὶ πάσχοιτε διὰ δικαιοσύνην, μακάριοι (but

if you suffer because of righteousness, [you are] blessed), with a nominal clause in the apodosis.

1 Pet. 3.17: κρεῖττον γὰρ ἀγαθοποιοῦντας, εἰ θέλοι τὸ θέλημα τοῦ θεοῦ, πάσχειν ἢ κακοποιοῦντας (for [it is] better for those doing good—if the will of God wish it—to suffer than those doing evil), with a nominal clause in the apodosis.

Opinion is divided among scholars whether there are any complete examples of the fourth class conditional structure with the imperfect verb in the apodosis. Turner suggests that Acts 24.19 is the only example in the NT;[1] Winer also suggests Acts 27.39:[2] see Acts 20.16. Moulton explains all instances as indirect discourse, with the optative used instead of the subjunctive.[3]

Acts 24.19 ἔδει ἐπὶ σοῦ παρεῖναι καὶ κατηγορεῖν εἴ τι ἔχοιεν πρὸς ἐμέ (it was necessary to be present before you and to make accusation, if they might have anything against me).

On εἰ and the optative in indirect discourse, see Chapter 17 section 2.2.2.

1 Cor. 15.37: ἀλλὰ γυμνὸν κόκκον εἰ τύχοι σίτου ἤ τινος τῶν λοιπῶν (but a bare kernel, if it be of wheat or of something else); 1 Cor. 14.10, each with a parenthetical phrase using the optative.

2.1.5. εἰ + *future* (future most vivid), with several different verb forms in the apodosis (see the classification list on p. 256). Most grammarians include this construction under the first class conditional, because they construe the future as an indicative form. In discussion of the tenses and moods (Chapters 1 and 2), however, it is shown that the future form does not conform fully either to the indicative or to the non-indicative paradigm. In a scheme which distinguishes two major categories of conditional sentences, *a conditional protasis with a future form should be placed in a category close by the subjunctive, since it grammaticalizes the semantic feature of expectation.* This construction occurs approximately twelve times in the NT.

Lk. 11.8: εἰ καὶ οὐ δώσει αὐτῷ...διὰ τὸ εἶναι φίλον αὐτοῦ, διά γε τὴν ἀναίδειαν αὐτοῦ...δώσει αὐτῷ ὅσων χρῄζει (if he will not give to him...because he is his friend, indeed because of his shame-

1. Turner, *Syntax*, pp. 126-27.
2. Winer, *Treatise*, p. 367.
3. Moulton, *Prolegomena*, p. 196.

lessness...he will give to him what he needs), used in the timeless context of a parable.

2 Tim. 2.12: εἰ ἀρνησόμεθα, κἀκεῖνος ἀρνήσεται ἡμᾶς (if we shall deny [him], he also will deny us), in a context which includes a number of other conditionals, used in parallel fashion.

Lk. 19.40: ἐὰν οὗτοι σιωπήσουσιν, οἱ λίθοι κράξουσιν ('if the disciples keep silent, the stones will be forced to proclaim the mighty acts of God instead of them'),[1] where a future form occurs after ἐάν. This provides no serious problem, however, since classification is based on the verb form.

2 Cor. 5.2-3: καὶ γὰρ ἐν τούτῳ στενάζομεν, τὸ οἰκητήριον ἡμῶν τὸ ἐξ οὐρανοῦ ἐπενδύσασθαι ἐπιποθοῦντες, εἴ γε καὶ ἐνδυσάμενοι οὐ γυμνοὶ εὑρεθησόμεθα (for indeed we groan in this [body], longing to put on our heavenly habitation, if indeed we, being clothed, shall not be found naked), with the textual variant ἐνδυσάμενοι being accepted.

2.2. *Apodosis*

So far little has been said here about the apodosis or 'then' (consequence) part of the conditional construction. The secondary literature says relatively little about the relation of the protasis to the apodosis. Three major views have been developed, nevertheless. The major point of dispute regarding the apodosis is what temporal or other relation it enjoys with the protasis. For classificatory purposes, however, it does not usually enter into discussion (the major exception is the second class or contrary-to-fact conditional).

2.2.1. *Tense-form of apodosis.* The first view is that the action of the apodosis is present or past simply on the basis of the tense-form of the apodosis. In other words, present form means present time and aorist form means past time.[2] This absolutistic analysis of the tenses has not proved satisfactory, and has little application to any instances other than possibly the indicative mood form.

Mt. 18.15: ἐάν σου ἀκούσῃ, ἐκέρδησας τὸν ἀδελφόν σου (if he listens to you, you gain your brother), where use of the aorist indica-

1. I.H. Marshall, *The Gospel of Luke* (Exeter: Paternoster Press, 1978), p. 716, listed as one of four understandings.

2. Goodwin, *Greek Grammar*, pp. 298-300; Smyth, *Greek Grammar*, pp. 527-29.

tive is better explained as occurring concurrently or subsequently to the protasis (as the translation indicates), not before.

2.2.2. *Relative temporal usage*. The second scheme argues for a relative use of the tenses, and comes in two forms. One scholar argues that the tense-form of the protasis determines temporal relation.[1] That this will not work has already been shown in section 2.1 above.

Lk. 13.3, 5: ἐὰν μὴ μετανοῆτε πάντες ὁμοίως ἀπολεῖσθε...ἐὰν μὴ μετανοῆτε πάντες ὡσαύτως ἀπολεῖσθε (if all of you do not repent, you will likewise perish). If a temporal scheme is at work in this example, the action of the protasis would seem to be antecedent to the action of the apodosis, not concurrent, in defiance of the tense-form theory posited.

Another scholar argues that regarding third class conditionals the verb of the apodosis establishes a relative temporal relation to the protasis (e.g. the present tense is concurrent, the future form subsequent, and so forth).[2] This scheme is not satisfactory, since it is restricted to the third class conditional and does not take into account non-indicative verbs in the apodosis.

Jn 15.6: ἐὰν μή τις μένῃ ἐν ἐμοί, ἐβλήθη ἔξω ὡς τὸ κλῆμα καὶ ἐξηράνθη, καὶ συνάγουσιν αὐτὰ καὶ εἰς τὸ πῦρ βάλλουσιν καὶ καίεται (if someone does not remain in me, he is cast out like a branch and becomes dried up, and they gather them and throw them into the fire and they are burned), where the aorist verbs in the apodosis are not antecedent. Note also the aorist and present tense verbs used in parallel patterns.

2.2.3. *Logical relations*. A proposal first made by a scholar named Nutting and then applied to the NT by Kruger argues that different kinds of logical relations hold between the protases and apodoses of conditional constructions.[3] Some of these logical relations might include the following.

Cause and effect: Rev. 20.15: εἴ τις οὐχ εὑρέθη ἐν τῇ βίβλῳ τῆς ζωῆς γεγραμμένος ἐβλήθη εἰς τὴν λίμνην τοῦ πυρός (if someone

1. A. Rijksbaron, *The Syntax and Semantics of the Verb in Classical Greek: An Introduction* (Amsterdam: Gieben, 1984), pp. 68-74. He admits that first class conditionals are indeterminate.

2. Carson, *Exegetical Fallacies*, pp. 81-82.

3. See Porter, *Verbal Aspect*, pp. 319-20, for bibliography.

was not found written in the book of life, he was cast into the lake of fire).

Ground and inference: Heb. 9.13: εἰ...τὸ αἷμα τράγων καὶ ταύρων καὶ σποδὸς δαμάλεως ῥαντίζουσα τοὺς κεκοινωμένους ἁγιάζει πρὸς τὴν τῆς σαρκὸς καθαρότητα, πόσῳ μᾶλλον τὸ αἷμα τοῦ Χριστοῦ (if...the blood of goats and bulls and ashes of a heifer sprinkling those who are defiled purifies for the cleansing of the flesh, how much more the blood of Christ).

Equivalence: Jas 1.23: εἴ τις ἀκροατὴς λόγου ἐστὶν καὶ οὐ ποιητής, οὗτος ἔοικεν ἀνδρὶ κατανοοῦντι τὸ πρόσωπον τῆς γενέσεως αὐτοῦ ἐν ἐσόπτρῳ (if someone is a hearer of the word and not a doer, this person is like a man recognizing the face he was born with [lit. the face of his origin] in a mirror).

Adversative: 2 Cor. 4.16: εἰ καὶ ὁ ἔξω ἡμῶν ἄνθρωπος διαφθείρεται, ἀλλ' ὁ ἔσω ἡμῶν ἀνακαινοῦται ἡμέρᾳ καὶ ἡμέρᾳ (if even our outer person is being decayed, yet our inner person is being renewed day by day).

There are a number of examples which cannot be so easily classified, however. For example, Jn 21.22: ἐὰν αὐτὸν θέλω μένειν ἕως ἔρχομαι, τί πρὸς σέ; σύ μοι ἀκολούθει (if I want him to remain until I come, what [is that] to you? Follow me.), which may suggest a reason or justification for the action of the protasis. Nevertheless, the above scheme indicates that flexibility is required in assessing the relation of the protasis to the apodosis. It is better to say that *a conditional structure posits a relation between the protasis and the apodosis, one which the interpreter may attempt to define on the basis of context in any one of a number of logical or even temporal ways.*

Chapter 17

INDIRECT DISCOURSE

Introduction

The recording of direct speech in the form of indirect speech is much like what has been discussed elsewhere regarding dependent clauses. Preliminary to discussing indirect discourse, however, the recording of direct speech must be examined. The citing of direct speech begins with a main clause (often though not always an independent clause), with a verb of perception referring to speaking, thinking, and the like. These verbs readily take objects which convey the contents of their thoughts or words. The object slot may be filled by the clause of direct speech (dependent clause), in which in Greek no significant changes are made in the sentences apart from occasionally adding connectives rather than quotation marks (the connective frequently used in NT Greek, ὅτι, will be addressed below). For example, in English, if in direct speech the statement is 'I like pizza', when this sentence is filling the object slot of a first person sentence with a verb of saying, the following occurs: 'I often say "I like pizza"'. The same is true with second and third person as well (e.g. 'he often says "I like pizza"'). However, when this same sentence is put into indirect speech (that is, if it is not a direct quotation), certain changes are required on the basis of who made the original statement and who is reporting it (e.g. 'he often says that he likes pizza', but 'you often say that you like pizza' and many other variations). The use of indirect speech requires more detailed elucidation.

1. *Indirect Discourse in NT Greek*

In the Greek of the NT, a writer may use several different means to convey words and thoughts indirectly (indirect discourse). One constant factor, however, is *the Greek tense sequence rule: when one transfers the words of direct speech to indirect speech, despite several other changes which may be made (usually regarding person), the verbal aspect of direct speech is retained.* (If the verbal aspect is changed, then the example is no longer direct or indirect speech but paraphrase.) Normally the mood remains the same as well (unless an infinitive, a participle or—rarely—a subjunctive is used). For example, when a speaker's words using the imperfect form are recorded in indirect discourse, the imperfect indicative or present infinitive may be used. The Greek tense sequence rule reinforces analysis of the verb as aspectually and not temporally based. Aorist, present, and perfect tense-forms are all used to refer to words spoken before the words introducing the indirect speech (in other words, to refer to words spoken in the past). Indirect discourse in English is more difficult than in Greek, since in English a change in verb tense is often required. For example, if someone says 'I like pizza', indirect discourse could have in English 'he said that he liked pizza'. In Greek, the verbal aspect is retained; for example, if 'like' is a present tense in the original, the present tense is used in indirect discourse. One must make certain adjustments in the English translation of Greek indirect discourse as a consequence.

There are several ways to recognize instances of indirect and direct speech in Greek. They have in common that they are introduced by so-called verbs of perception (seeing, hearing, thinking, speaking and the like) in the main clause. In some printed editions of biblical texts, direct speech is introduced by capital letters, although this is not always true (it is an editor's decision). One of the major distinguishing factors of indirect speech is whether elements of the dependent clause (the words reported) are incorporated into the structure of the main clause (with the verb of speaking or thinking). If the grammatical structure is *not* incorporated, then it has a very good chance of being direct speech or quotation. If the grammatical structure *is* incorporated, then it is probably indirect speech. The major elements which are incorporated are personal references, including pronouns and the person of the verb. These must often be altered in light of how the direct speech was formulated and in light of how it is conveyed as indirect speech. For example, Mk 1.37, λέγουσιν αὐτῷ ὅτι πάντες ζητοῦσίν σε (they were saying to him, 'All people are seeking you'), is apparently direct speech, since the object has not been changed to αὐτόν, which would be required if this were indirect discourse. An example in which the person of the main verb agrees with the person of direct speech can be tricky, since one may not be able to determine if incorporation of the sentence has occurred and since the verb tenses will not help decipher the instance. Context must often prove the decisive factor in determining instances of indirect discourse. Even though in many examples the cited utterance could grammatically be either direct or indirect speech, the context may not allow direct quotation at that point. Some grammarians classify these instances as examples of indirect speech in which the tense of direct speech is retained.

2. *Forms of Indirect Discourse*

2.1. *Infinitive*

In Greek, one may report direct speech indirectly using the infinitive. Like all indirect discourse, indirect speech with the infinitive can be used not only to repeat words actually spoken but also to report words that could have been spoken or that have merely been thought. The verb that would have been used if someone had actually spoken the words is rewritten using the infinitive; it is not always clear what the exact wording would have been in the actual utterance.

2.1.1. *Subject retained.* If the subject of the infinitive is the same as that of the main verb, the subject need not be repeated. If the subject is expressed, it is normally in the nominative case.

Acts 25.11: οὐ παραιτοῦμαι τὸ ἀποθανεῖν (I am not refusing to die), where direct speech probably would require an aorist subjunctive.

Rom. 1.13: προεθέμην ἐλθεῖν πρὸς ὑμᾶς (I intended to come to you), where direct speech would require a statement in the first person with the aorist.

Rom. 2.19: πέποιθάς τε σεαυτὸν ὁδηγὸν εἶναι τυφλῶν (you are confident that you yourself are a leader of the blind), where direct speech would require first person ('I am a leader of the blind'). Note also that the nominative rather than the accusative case (as here) normally is expected in indirect speech, since the same subject is shared.

Jas 1.26: εἴ τις δοκεῖ θρησκὸς εἶναι (if someone thinks that he is religious).

2.1.2. *Subject shifted.* If the subject of the infinitive is different from that of the main verb, the accusative case is used for the subject of the infinitive.

Mk 12.18: οἵτινες λέγουσιν ἀνάστασιν μὴ εἶναι (who were saying that there is no resurrection), where the actual saying probably would have had ἔστιν, with the subject, ἀνάστασις, in the nominative case.

Lk. 20.6: πεπεισμένος γάρ ἐστιν Ἰωάννην προφήτην εἶναι (for it [the people] is persuaded that John was a prophet), where the actual saying probably had ἦν, although ἐστιν is also a possibility. The nouns will have been in the nominative case.

Lk. 24.23: ἦλθον λέγουσαι καὶ ὀπτασίαν ἀγγέλων ἑωρακέναι, οἳ λέγουσιν αὐτὸν ζῆν (they came saying that they had also seen a vision of angels, who were saying that he was alive), where the saying will have included ἑωράκαμεν and ζῇ. Note that the indicative λέγουσιν is used in the dependent relative clause, with an instance of indirect speech within indirect speech.

Acts 14.19: νομίζοντες αὐτὸν τεθνηκέναι (thinking that he was dead), where the quoted speech will have had τέθνηκε.

Acts 21.4: ἔλεγον διὰ τοῦ πνεύματος μὴ ἐπιβαίνειν εἰς Ἱεροσόλυμα (they were saying through the Spirit not to go up to Jerusalem), where the imperative ἐπιβαῖνε was probably found in the original utterance.

Acts 21.21: λέγων μὴ περιτέμνειν αὐτοὺς τὰ τέκνα μηδὲ τοῖς ἔθεσιν περιπατεῖν (saying for them not to circumcise their children nor to walk according to the customs), where the infinitives seem to represent the imperatives περιτέμνετε and περιπατεῖτε.

Acts 25.4: ὁ...Φῆστος ἀπεκρίθη τηρεῖσθαι τὸν Παῦλον εἰς Καισάρειαν, ἑαυτὸν...μέλλειν ἐν τάχει ἐκπορεύεσθαι (Festus said to keep Paul in Caesarea; he himself was going to go out immediately), with the first instance recording the imperative or possibly the indicative τηρεῖσθε, and the second μέλλω. The next verse uses direct speech.

2.2. *Finite Verb Forms with* ὅτι *and Other Conjunctions*

Very common in NT Greek indirect discourse is to use ὅτι, as well as εἰ, to introduce a clause of indirect speech (classical Greek also used ὡς). The connective is followed by a clause with a finite verb form recording the indirect speech.

2.2.1. *Standard examples*. It is not always possible to tell if the dependent clause with the finite verb preceded by ὅτι is recording direct or indirect speech, since ὅτι can be used with each (and with causal and other content clauses as well). Incorporation of the dependent clause into the main clause can frequently be decisive in determining instances of indirect discourse, although context must always be considered.

Mt. 20.10: οἱ πρῶτοι ἐνόμισαν ὅτι πλεῖον λήμψονται (they first thought that they would receive more), where the first person plural, λημψόμεθα, will have appeared in the quoted speech.

Jn 11.27: ἐγὼ πεπίστευκα ὅτι σὺ εἶ ὁ Χριστὸς ὁ υἱὸς τοῦ θεοῦ (I believe that you are the Christ the son of God), an instance of indirect speech within direct speech.

Jn 7.42: οὐχ ἡ γραφὴ εἶπεν ὅτι ἐκ τοῦ σπέρματος Δαυὶδ καὶ ἀπὸ Βηθλέεμ τῆς κώμης ὅπου ἦν Δαυὶδ ἔρχεται ὁ Χριστός; (doesn't the Scripture say that the Christ comes from the seed of David and from Bethlehem, the village David was from?), where indirect speech is contained within direct speech.

Acts 9.27: διηγήσατο αὐτοῖς πῶς ἐν τῇ ὁδῷ εἶδεν τὸν κύριον καὶ ὅτι ἐλάλησεν αὐτῷ καὶ πῶς ἐν Δαμασκῷ ἐπαρρησιάσατο ἐν τῷ ὀνόματι τοῦ Ἰησοῦ (he told them how along the way he had seen the Lord, and that he had spoken to him, and how in Damascus he had spoken freely in the name of Jesus), with πῶς introducing the first and third instances, examples of indirect questions (see section 2.4 below).

Gal. 2.14: εἶδον ὅτι οὐκ ὀρθοποδοῦσιν (I saw that they were not conducting themselves correctly).

Gal. 5.3: μαρτύρομαι...πάλιν παντὶ ἀνθρώπῳ περιτεμνομένῳ ὅτι ὀφειλέτης ἐστὶν ὅλον τὸν νόμον ποιῆσαι (I am bearing witness... again to every circumcised man that he is obligated to keep the whole law), where the direct statement probably would have been cast in the second person.

2.2.2. *Complex examples*. The following representative examples are to be categorized as instances of indirect speech, but they provide a variety of complexities for the interpreter. Context often proves decisive in determining indirect discourse, since the same statement could often be used as direct speech in another context.

Mk 8.31: ἤρξατο διδάσκειν αὐτοὺς ὅτι δεῖ τὸν υἱὸν τοῦ ἀνθρώπου πολλὰ παθεῖν (he began to teach them that it was necessary for the son of man to suffer many things), where this could represent Jesus' own use of third person language.

Mk 15.44: ὁ...Πιλᾶτος ἐθαύμασεν εἰ ἤδη τέθνηκεν (Pilate marveled that he was already dead), with efi probably introducing indirect speech.

Mt. 16.18: κἀγὼ δέ σοι λέγω ὅτι σὺ εἶ Πέτρος (and I say to you that you are Peter), where there is no change in person from direct speech. Jesus' words are not introduced by ὅτι in v. 17.

Jn 11.13: ἐκεῖνοι δὲ ἔδοξαν ὅτι περὶ τῆς κοιμήσεως τοῦ ὕπνου λέγει (but they thought that he was talking about ordinary sleep [lit. the sleep of sleep]), where there is no change from direct speech.

Jn 4.19: λέγει αὐτῷ ἡ γυνή, κύριε, θεωρῶ ὅτι προφήτης εἶ σύ (the woman said to him, 'Lord, I see that you are a prophet'), where indirect speech is contained within direct speech.

Lk. 5.14: παρήγγειλεν αὐτῷ μηδενὶ εἰπεῖν, ἀλλὰ...δεῖξον σεαυτὸν τῷ ἱερεῖ καὶ προσένεγκε...(he commanded him to say nothing, but...show yourself to the priest and offer...), where there is a combination of indirect speech with the infinitive and direct speech with the imperative. This pattern of combining direct and indirect speech is also found in classical Greek, giving further evidence of the consistent lack of precise distinction between the two discourse forms. See also Acts 1.4; 17.3; 23.22; 25.4-5 (see section 2.1.2 above).[1]

The general rule often learned regarding indirect discourse in classical Greek is that the mood form of the original statement is retained after a verb of saying or thinking with primary endings (i.e. present, perfect), but that after a verb of saying or thinking with secondary endings (i.e. imperfect, aorist, pluperfect) the mood form of the original statement *may* be changed to the same tense in the optative mood (if the original mood is not retained). In the Greek of the NT the optative is rarely used (see e.g. Acts 25.16, where the optative is probably used for the subjunctive; Chapter 2 section 2.3.3), and thus the mood form in most cases is retained, except if an infinitive, a participle or a ἵνα clause is used (see section 2.4 below).

1. Zerwick (*Biblical Greek*, p. 162) claims that the tendency to use direct instead of indirect speech is evidence of the tendency to greater simplicity in Hellenistic Greek.

2.3. *Participle*

A participle may introduce indirect speech in Greek, usually following verbs of perception, including knowing, remembering, and so on. This usage requires a fairly loose definition of what indirect discourse entails, as can be seen from the examples often cited as illustrating this.[1]

Lk. 10.18: ἐθεώρουν τὸν σατανᾶν ὡς ἀστραπὴν ἐκ τοῦ οὐρανοῦ πεσόντα (I saw Satan falling like a star from heaven), in which the modifying use of the participle makes adequate sense here.

Acts 7.12: ἀκούσας... Ἰακὼβ ὄντα σιτία εἰς Αἴγυπτον ἐξαπέστειλεν...(Jacob, hearing that there was grain in Egypt, sent...).

2 Thess. 3.11: ἀκούομεν γάρ τινας περιπατοῦντας ἐν ὑμῖν ἀτάκτως μηδὲν ἐργαζομένους ἀλλὰ περιεργαζομένους (for we hear certain people among you are conducting themselves irresponsibly and not working but fooling around [or, 'being busybodies']).

2.4. *Indirect Questions and Commands*

Questions and commands may be cited in indirect discourse. Many grammarians introduce this category under a separate heading reserved for citation of non-indicative forms. The essential grammatical factors are generally the same for all forms of indirect discourse, however.[2] *The distinguishing feature for indirect questions and commands is introduction of the indirect speech by means of certain words, in particular the interrogative pronoun for indirect questions and* ἵνα *(among others) for indirect commands.* Other introductory words that may be used include the relative pronoun (e.g. Lk. 11.6) and various interrogatives (e.g. Mt. 2.4; Jn 8.14), among others. The infinitive may be used for indirect questions and commands as well (see section 2.1 above).

Mk 9.6: οὐ γὰρ ᾔδει τί ἀποκριθῇ (for he did not know what to say [lit. 'what he might answer']), where the first person singular verb would have appeared in actual speech.

Jn 2.25: αὐτὸς γὰρ ἐγίνωσκεν τί ἦν ἐν τῷ ἀνθρώπῳ (for he knew what was in a person), where ἦν seems to stand for ἐστιν in direct speech, a fairly unusual change with a secondary tense in the dependent clause following a secondary tense in the main clause.

Mt. 6.25: μὴ μεριμνᾶτε τῇ ψυχῇ ὑμῶν τί φάγητε (don't trouble

1. See Chamberlain, *Exegetical Grammar*, p. 204.
2. See Dana and Mantey, *Manual Grammar*, pp. 298-99.

your soul [about] what you might eat), where the direct question probably would be τί φάγωμεν.

Mk 5.14: καὶ ἦλθον ἰδεῖν τί ἐστιν τὸ γεγονός (and they came to see what was happening), where this indirect question is the same as the direct question.

Mk 6.8: παρήγγειλεν αὐτοῖς ἵνα μηδὲν αἴρωσιν εἰς ὁδόν (he announced to them that they should not take anything on their journey), where the next verse switches back to direct speech with the imperative.

Acts 25.3: αἰτούμενοι χάριν κατ' αὐτοῦ ὅπως μεταπέμψηται αὐτὸν εἰς Ἰερουσαλήμ (requesting the favor from him that he might send him back to Jerusalem), for μετάπεμψον in direct speech.

Lk. 22.2: ἐζήτουν οἱ ἀρχιερεῖς καὶ οἱ γραμματεῖς τὸ πῶς ἀνέλωσιν αὐτόν (the chief priests and the scribes were looking for a way to kill him), where the article τό is used to distinguish the indirect question, which will have had first person in direct speech. Luke uses the article similarly elsewhere, including Lk. 1.62; 22.4, 23, 24.

Acts 10.18: ἐπυνθάνοντο εἰ Σίμων ὁ ἐπικαλούμενος Πέτρος ἐνθάδε ξενίζεται (they inquired whether Simon called Peter was staying there), where as Moule notes this may be direct speech, with introductory εἰ.[1]

Acts 17.19: ἤγαγον λέγοντες, δυνάμεθα γνῶναι τίς ἡ καινὴ αὕτη ἡ ὑπὸ σοῦ λαλουμένη διδαχή; (they led [Paul] saying, 'May we know what this new thing is, the teaching spoken by you?'), where the author includes indirect speech (τίς) within direct speech.

1. Moule, *Idiom Book*, p. 154.

Chapter 18

QUESTIONS

Introduction

To this point, statements have been the major concern of this book, with questions being treated incidentally. By far the majority of sentences in the text of the Greek NT are statements, but there are questions as well. Questions in Greek may be formed in a number of ways. Most of the ways are fairly straightforward, although a few of the more difficult constructions must be discussed. In contrast to English, there do not appear to be as many alterations in word order in forming Greek questions, and there are certainly not as many issues regarding helping verbs, despite their use in English translation.

1. *Open Questions*

An open question is one which gives no grammatical indication whether a positive or negative answer is expected. It is often difficult on the basis of how a sentence is constructed to determine whether it is in fact a question, since the only formally distinguishing feature is a Greek question mark (;) placed after the sentence by the editor. Context must provide the decisive information. Two of the most important contextual features are that, if the structure as a statement would contradict the clear statements of the text, or if it poses a set of alternatives, a question may well be indicated.

Mk 14.61: σὺ εἶ ὁ Χριστὸς ὁ υἱὸς τοῦ εὐλογητοῦ; (are you the Christ, the son of the Blessed One?).

Mt. 13.28: θέλεις οὖν ἀπελθόντες συλλέξωμεν αὐτά; (do you therefore want us to go away and collect these things?).

Gal. 3.2: ἐξ ἔργων νόμου τὸ πνεῦμα ἐλάβετε ἢ ἐξ ἀκοῆς πίστεως; (did you receive the Spirit by works of the law, or by hearing of faith?).

Since these questions are determined on the basis of context and are then indicated by the editor's placing a question mark at the end of the sentence, they are certainly subject to disagreement by other editors and interpreters. In some instances, the debate over whether a given sentence is a question or not has significant exegetical consequences.

1 Cor. 1.13: μεμέρισται ὁ Χριστός; (is Christ divided?). The words may well be a statement, 'Christ is divided', reflecting Paul's observation on the results of divisiveness in the Corinthian church.

Rom. 2.21-22: ὁ κηρύσσων μὴ κλέπτειν κλέπτεις; ὁ λέγων μὴ μοιχεύειν μοιχεύεις; ὁ βδελυσσόμενος τὰ εἴδωλα ἱεροσυλεῖς; (do you, who preach not to steal, steal? Do you, who say not to commit adultery, commit adultery? Do you, who abhor idols, commit sacrilege?), where most recent editors take these as questions, reflecting the diatribal (dialogical) style of Romans (see section 2.2 below as well).

2. *Questions with Negative Particles*

In Greek, questions formulated by the author to expect negative and positive answers can be indicated by the use of negative particles. The negative particle tends to be placed near the beginning of the question or proximate to the main verb.

2.1. *Questions Expecting a Negative Answer*

A question expecting a negative answer normally is negated by μή. In translating such questions, one way to indicate this understanding is with a phrase similar to 'not...is it?', since the use of the negation is a discourse marker for the interpreter. The one who formulates the question decides whether the question expects a negative answer, not the objective facts in and of themselves.

Jn 7.31: ὁ Χριστὸς ὅταν ἔλθῃ μὴ πλείονα σημεῖα ποιήσει ὧν οὗτος ἐποίησεν; (the Christ, whenever he comes, won't do greater signs than this person does, will he?).

Rom. 11.1: μὴ ἀπώσατο ὁ θεὸς τὸν λαὸν αὐτοῦ; (God did not reject his people, did he?). Paul's response in vv. 1, 2 is μὴ γένοιτο ...οὐκ ἀπώσατο ὁ θεὸς τὸν λαὸν αὐτοῦ ὃν προέγνω (may it never be...God did not reject his people whom he foreknew).

Jn 4.29: μήτι οὗτός ἐστιν ὁ Χριστός; (is this possibly the Christ?), where Chamberlain believes that μήτι leaves doubt about the answer.[1]

1. Chamberlain, *Exegetical Grammar*, p. 208.

Cf. the translations: NASB: 'This is not the Christ is it?'; NIV: 'Could this be the Christ?'; RSV: 'Can this be the Christ?' See also Mt. 12.23: μήτι οὗτός ἐστιν ὁ υἱὸς Δαυίδ; (this isn't the son of David, is it?), where the translations are inclined toward the question implying a clearly negative answer.

2.2. *Questions Expecting a Positive Answer*

A question expecting a positive answer normally is negated by οὐ. Although the negation is included in the English translations given below, the negative is not required in the translation so long as the interpreter understands that the question implies a positive answer from the standpoint of the one formulating it. In other words, the negative is a discourse marker to indicate how the entire sentence is to be taken; it does not require a literal word-for-word rendering. As noted above regarding questions expecting a negative answer, the one who formulates the question decides whether the question expects a positive answer, not the objective facts in and of themselves.

Mt. 6.25: οὐχὶ ἡ ψυχὴ πλεῖόν ἐστιν τῆς τροφῆς καὶ τὸ σῶμα τοῦ ἐνδύματος; (isn't the soul more than food and the body [more] than clothing?), where Chamberlain contends that οὐχί is emphatic, to be answered 'most assuredly, it is'.[1]

Rom. 2.21: ὁ οὖν διδάσκων ἕτερον σεαυτὸν οὐ διδάσκεις; (therefore, do you, who teach another, not teach yourself?), an ironic question expecting a positive answer, preceding three more open questions (see section 1 above).

Rom. 5.15, 16: ἀλλ' οὐχ ὡς τὸ παράπτωμα, οὕτως καὶ τὸ χάρισμα; ...καὶ οὐχ ὡς δι' ἑνὸς ἁμαρτήσαντος τὸ δώρημα; ('But does not the free gift operate just as the trespass did?...And is not the free gift transmitted in the same way as sin was transmitted by the one who sinned?').[2]

1 Cor. 9.1: οὐκ εἰμὶ ἐλεύθερος; οὐκ εἰμὶ ἀπόστολος; οὐχὶ Ἰησοῦν τὸν κύριον ἡμῶν ἑώρακα; (Am I not free? Am I not an apostle? Did I not see Jesus our Lord?), or 'I am free, right? I am an apostle, right? I saw Jesus our Lord, right?'

Jas 2.5: οὐχ ὁ θεὸς ἐξελέξατο τοὺς πτωχοὺς τῷ κόσμῳ πλουσίους

1. Chamberlain, *Exegetical Grammar*, p. 207.

2. This repunctuation as questions was recently proposed by C.C. Caragounis, 'Rom. 5.15-16 in the Context of 5.12-21: Contrast or Comparison?', *NTS* 31 (1985), pp. 142-48. His translation is used.

ἐν πίστει καὶ κληρονόμους τῆς βασιλείας ἧς ἐπηγγείλατο τοῖς ἀγαπῶσιν αὐτόν; (didn't God elect the poor in the world [to be] rich in faith and heirs of the kingdom which he promised to those who love him?).

Lk. 6.39: μήτι δύναται τυφλὸς τυφλὸν ὁδηγεῖν; οὐχὶ ἀμφότεροι εἰς βόθυνον ἐμπεσοῦνται; (surely a blind person is not able to lead a blind person—won't both fall into a ditch?), with examples of questions expecting negative and positive answers.

2.3. *Multiple Negation*

In some tricky examples more than one negative word appears in a question. The grammatical task is to sort out whether the negatives are to be taken as working together or separately, and whether they are negating individual words or the entire clause (see Chapter 19 on negation). *A good rule of thumb is that* μὴ οὐ, *a compound negative, results in a question expecting a negative answer, with the clause and the verb negated.* οὐ μή *is simply an emphatic single negative* (see Chapter 19 section 2.1).

Rom. 10.18, 19: μὴ οὐκ ἤκουσαν;...μὴ Ἰσραὴλ οὐκ ἔγνω; (it is not that they have not heard, is it?...It is not that Israel does not know, is it?), where a negative answer is expected for each question (no, it is not that they have not heard, i.e., they have heard).

1 Cor. 9.4-5: μὴ οὐκ ἔχομεν ἐξουσίαν φαγεῖν καὶ πεῖν; μὴ οὐκ ἔχομεν ἐξουσίαν ἀδελφὴν γυναῖκα περιάγειν; (it is not that we do not have authority to eat and drink, is it? It is not that we do not have authority to take along a sister as wife, is it?), where Moule argues that the negative οὐκ with ἔχομεν forms a unit, within the question expecting a negative answer.[1]

Jn 18.11: τὸ ποτήριον ὃ δέδωκέν μοι ὁ πατὴρ οὐ μὴ πίω αὐτό; (the cup which the father has given me, won't I drink it?), a question expecting a positive answer.

3. *Questions with Interrogative Words*

In Greek, questions can be introduced by a number of words, including especially pronouns such as the interrogative pronoun (see Chapter 8), *and various particles* (see Chapter 12) *and adverbs* (see Chapter 7). The question word or the phrase it appears in virtually

1. Moule, *Idiom Book*, p. 156.

always appears first in the clause. The following gives examples—but by no means all—of the words which can be used to introduce questions.

Mt. 3.7: τίς ὑπέδειξεν ὑμῖν φυγεῖν ἀπὸ τῆς μελλούσης ὀργῆς; (who warned you to flee from the coming wrath?), with an interrogative pronoun.

Mt. 8.27: ποταπός ἐστιν οὗτος; (what sort of a person is this?), with ποταπός, a qualitative interrogative pronoun.

Mt. 13.10: διὰ τί ἐν παραβολαῖς λαλεῖς αὐτοῖς; (why [on account of what] do you speak to them in parables?).

Mt. 21.23: ἐν ποίᾳ ἐξουσίᾳ ταῦτα ποιεῖς; (by what sort of authority do you do these things?), with ποῖος, a qualitative interrogative pronoun.

Mk 6.38: πόσους ἄρτους ἔχετε; (how many loaves do you have?), with πόσος, a quantitative interrogative pronoun.

Mk 9.11: ὅτι λέγουσιν οἱ γραμματεῖς ὅτι Ἠλίαν δεῖ ἐλθεῖν πρῶτον; (why do the scribes say that it is necessary for Elijah to come first?), with an infrequent use of ὅτι as an interrogative particle.

Mk 14.4: εἰς τί ἡ ἀπώλεια αὕτη τοῦ μύρου γέγονεν; (for what purpose did this loss of the myrrh come about?).

Lk. 22.49: κύριε, εἰ πατάξομεν ἐν μαχαίρῃ; (Lord, shall we strike with a sword?), with interrogative use of εἰ. As Winer suggests,[1] this use of the conditional conjunction may once have implied an apodosis (e.g. 'I should like to know'), although by this time it is unlikely that any user of the language had this in mind.

Acts 8.30: ἆρά γε γινώσκεις ἃ ἀναγινώσκεις; (do you know what you are reading?).

1. Winer, *Treatise*, p. 639.

Chapter 19

NEGATION

Introduction

A very simple and yet very useful rule for use of negative particles in the Greek of the NT is that οὐ *(and its forms) appears with the indicative mood form and* μή *(and its forms) appears with the non-indicative mood forms (i.e. the subjunctive, optative and imperative, as well as infinitive and participle).*[1] There are several exceptions to this rule (e.g. questions expecting a negative answer and second class or contra-factual conditionals), but this rule has a surprisingly high degree of consistency. This correlates well with the characterization by Moorhouse that οὐ is the negation of the 'concrete or actual', and μή is the negation of the 'notional or ideal'.[2] The use of the negatives in the NT represents a growing strength of the negative μή, as it encroaches on areas previously reserved for οὐ (e.g. optative, participles except for conditional use, and certain uses of the infinitive).

1. *Word versus Clause Negation*

In Greek, as in other languages such as English, a negative may be used to negate an entire clause (which usually means the verb in the clause) or a smaller group within a clause, such as a phrase or an individual word. Most of the examples of negation which are commonly cited (e.g. in Chapter 18 on questions) contain examples of clause negation.

1. This is referred to by Moulton (*Prolegomena*, p. 170) as Blass's canon, found in F. Blass, *Grammatik des Neutestamentlichen Griechisch* (Göttingen: Vandenhoeck & Ruprecht, 1896), p. 248(1).

2. A.C. Moorhouse, *Studies in the Greek Negatives* (Cardiff: University of Wales Press, 1959), p. 40 n. 1. This is not to be taken to mean that the indicative is the mood of actuality (see Chapter 2).

The most common word negation occurs with the negative pronouns οὐδείς and μηδείς. It is often possible to determine which kind of negation is at play on the basis of whether the negative is οὐ or μή. Clause negation often but not alway appears at the beginning of a clause or proximate to the verb. See section 2.2 below, also.

Rom. 2.21-22: ὁ οὖν διδάσκων ἕτερον σεαυτὸν οὐ διδάσκεις; ὁ κηρύσσων μὴ κλέπτειν κλέπτεις; ὁ λέγων μὴ μοιχεύειν μοιχεύεις; ὁ βδελυσσόμενος τὰ εἴδωλα ἱεροσυλεῖς; (therefore, do you, who teach another, not teach yourself? Do you, who preach not to steal, steal? Do you, who say not to commit adultery, commit adultery? Do you, who abhor idols, commit sacrilege?). In this series of four questions, the first has clause or verb negation, and consequently expects a positive answer to the question. The next two questions have word negation.[1]

Rom. 2.28: οὐ γὰρ ὁ ἐν τῷ φανερῷ Ἰουδαῖός ἐστιν, οὐδὲ ἡ ἐν τῷ φανερῷ ἐν σαρκὶ περιτομή ('For he is not a real Jew who is one outwardly, nor is true circumcision something external and physical' [RSV]), examples of clause negation, as is indicated by the contrast in Rom. 2.29 introduced with ἀλλά (but) and a verbless clause.

1 Pet. 3.3: ἔστω οὐχ ὁ ἔξωθεν...κόσμος (let not the external be [your] adornment), an example of phrase (word) negation, as indicated by the contrasting subject phrase in 1 Pet. 3.4 introduced by ἀλλά.

Many examples are much more difficult.

1 Cor. 12.15, 16: οὐ παρὰ τοῦτο οὐκ ἔστιν ἐκ τοῦ σώματος ('it is not for this reason any the less *a part* of the body' [NASB]), with a footnote indicating the negation of the verb. Both phrase and clause negation are used. One would err by taking the two negatives as identical in function or by simply taking the statement as a positive one.

Phil. 1.29: οὐ μόνον τὸ εἰς αὐτὸν πιστεύειν ἀλλὰ καὶ τὸ ὑπὲρ αὐτοῦ πάσχειν (not only to believe in him but to suffer for him), where the negative οὐ does not negate the infinitive directly, but the verbal phrase introduced by adverbial μόνον in the μόνον...ἀλλά opposition.

Phil. 2.4: μὴ τὰ ἑαυτῶν ἕκαστος σκοποῦντες ἀλλὰ τὰ ἑτέρων ἕκαστοι (each one not observing one's own interests, but each the interests of others), where the negative μή negates the participle and

1. One could argue that the second and third questions have clause negation as well, since the negative is with an infinitive in indirect speech, but the point is that only this word (or phrase) is negated and not the major clause in which it appears.

hence the entire verbal phrase, not its object alone. This disruption of the parallelism is remedied by analyzing the second half of the opposition as eliding (omitting) the participle.[1]

Col. 3.2: τὰ ἄνω φρονεῖτε, μὴ τὰ ἐπὶ τῆς γῆς (think on the things above, not [i.e. don't think on] the things on the earth), where the negative μή indicates that the elided (omitted) imperative and hence the entire clause are negated.

1 Pet. 3.6: ἀγαθοποιοῦσαι καὶ μὴ φοβούμεναι μηδεμίαν πτόησιν (doing good and not giving in to [lit. fearing] any fear), where there may be clause and word negation, or two instances of word negation.

2. *Special Instances of Negation*

2.1. οὐ μή *as Emphatic Negative*

There has been much debate whether an aorist subjunctive or future form with οὐ μή *is emphatically negated.* Some argue that, since most instances in the NT are in either quotations from the OT or records of the words of Jesus, this negative is a peculiar stylistic feature reserved for decisive language and containing no more negative force than a simple negative particle.[2] Most grammarians believe that οὐ μή is in some way emphatically negative, however.[3]

Mt. 24.2: οὐ μὴ ἀφεθῇ ὧδε λίθος ἐπὶ λίθον (no stone here will be left on [another] stone), with an aorist subjuntive.

Mt. 16.22: οὐ μὴ ἔσται σοι τοῦτο (no way will this happen to you), with a future form.

2.2. *Multiple Negatives*

Of English it is often (quite inaccurately) said that 'two negatives make a positive'. Besides the fact that this rule does not work in English ('I am *not un*concerned' does not mean 'I am concerned'), Greek often uses multiple negatives which cannot simply be counted to see if the number is odd (implying negativity) or even (implying positivity). One must observe how the negatives are used, including determining whether clause or word negation occurs.

1. Note the shift from singular ἕκαστος to plural ἕκαστοι, although there are textual variants.

2. Moulton, *Prolegomena*, pp. 187-92.

3. E.g. Goodwin, *Greek Grammar*, p. 289; Winer, *Treatise*, p. 642; Moule, *Idiom Book*, pp. 156-57.

Mk 5.3: οὐδὲ ἁλύσει οὐκέτι οὐδεὶς ἐδύνατο αὐτὸν δῆσαι (no one was able any longer to bind him with a chain), where a literalistic rendering might be, 'no, no one no longer was able to bind him with a chain', conveying a sense of how emphatically negative this statement is. There are examples of clause and word negation.

Lk. 4.2: οὐκ ἔφαγεν οὐδὲν ἐν ταῖς ἡμέραις ἐκείναις (he ate nothing in those days), where colloquial English could have the literal 'he didn't eat nothing'. The first negates the clause and the second the object.

Jn 15.5: χωρὶς ἐμοῦ οὐ δύνασθε ποιεῖν οὐδέν (apart from me you are not able to do anything), literally 'you can't do nothing', a natural construction in certain forms of informal spoken English.

2 Cor. 11.9: οὐ κατενάρκησα οὐθενός (I did not burden anyone).

2.3. *The Negated Future Form*

A negated future verb form is often used as a form of prohibition. Several of these appear in quotations of the OT (e.g. Mt. 5.21, 27).

Mt. 5.33: οὐκ ἐπιορκήσεις (you will not swear an oath).

2.4. *'Exceptions' to the Rule*

There are more than a few instances where Blass's canon regarding negation is not followed in the Greek of the NT. As a consequence, in some instances μή occurs with the indicative and οὐ with the participle, two relatively common patterns. Grammarians have attempted various explanations for these occurrences. They may simply be grammatical slips.

Jn 3.18: ὅτι μὴ πεπίστευκεν εἰς τὸ ὄνομα (because he has not believed in the name). Moulton argues that the classical notional distinction is to be found,[1] and Chamberlain says that μή is used because 'this is a supposed case'.[2] Other grammarians do not find this convincing.[3]

1 Jn 4.3: πᾶν πνεῦμα ὃ μὴ ὁμολογεῖ τὸν Ἰησοῦν (every spirit which does not confess Jesus). Is this just a supposed case? Cf. 1 Jn 5.10 with οὐ and the indicative.

Jn 10.12: ὁ μισθωτὸς καὶ οὐκ ὢν ποιμήν (the hired servant and not the one being a shepherd), an obvious exception to Blass's rule?

Col. 2.19: οὐ κρατῶν τὴν κεφαλήν (not holding fast to the head),

1. Moulton, *Prolegomena*, p. 171.
2. Chamberlain, *Exegetical Grammar*, p. 159.
3. E.g. Moule, *Idiom Book*, p. 155.

which Zerwick contends is equivalent to the affirmative 'he is letting go of, or rejecting', but with the negative οὐ instead of μή.[1]

1 Cor. 2.2: οὐ γὰρ ἔκρινά τι εἰδέναι ἐν ὑμῖν (for I did not determine to know anything among you), where Moule believes the negative was displaced and should be translated as if it read μηδὲν εἰδέναι (to know nothing).[2]

Heb. 11.1: πραγμάτων ἔλεγχος οὐ βλεπομένων (conviction of things not seen), where οὐ must negate the participle.

1. Zerwick, *Biblical Greek*, p. 148.
2. Moule, *Idiom Book*, p. 156.

Chapter 20

WORD ORDER AND CLAUSE STRUCTURE

Introduction

Syntax is the analysis of the meaningful order of various structural elements, such as words, phrases, and so forth, as they are part of larger units. With regard to NT Greek, this is an area which has not been studied nearly so much as many other areas. Units larger than individual words—for example, various prepositional phrases and various kinds of clauses (treated in previous chapters)—have often been examined in this book in significant detail. But the analysis has often focused more on what these units mean in their entirety (e.g. is this a purpose clause or a result clause?) than on the syntax or the arrangements of the individual elements. The brief discussion in this chapter presents the results of initial studies into word order and clause structure in the Greek of the NT. It is meant to be suggestive rather than definitive.

1. *Essential Features of Greek Word Order and Clause Structure*

Greek syntax has several important features, and these are in part determined by the nature of the Greek language.

1.1. *Greek as an Inflected Language*

Greek is an inflected language (or, to use the language of some linguists, a fusional language, in which various parts of a word are fused together). *To be more precise, nouns, verbs, adjectives, and the like, take various endings which place them into particular grammatical categories*. These grammatical categories are essential for specifying their semantics and their syntactical functions. For example, a noun occurring with a particular ending may be identified as in the nominative case; a verb occurring with a particular set of endings may be identified as an aorist tense-form. Because Greek is an inflected language, its syntax has a certain kind of flexibility not present in non-inflected languages. For example, in the English sentence 'I gave him the book', an English speaker will know that the item being given is 'the book' and not 'him' because of the syntax or order of the elements. When the order of the objects is switched, a preposition is normally used to indicate the same relationship ('I gave the book to him'). In Greek, however, one could switch the two elements without adding any words and retain roughly the same meaning, since each noun or pronoun would be marked with its own case. On the one hand, it must not be supposed that English has invariable word order. In the example 'He took his hat off'/'He took off his hat', English displays a flexibility in word order. On the other hand, it must not be supposed that Greek has completely free word order. As seen below, there are well-established patterns of Greek word order and clause structure. Rather than play English off against Greek, therefore, it is better to see fixed and flexible word order languages as arranged on a continuum. They differ in degrees of flexibility (rather than in kind) and with regard to which particular elements of each language can be moved.

1.2. *The Greek Clause*

The clause in Greek does not necessarily consist of a subject and predicate, as students of other languages are often taught. For example, there is nothing un-Greek or unnatural about the following Greek clauses: Mt. 5.3: μακάριοι οἱ πτωχοὶ τῷ πνεύματι (the poor in spirit [are] blessed), a verbless clause with a subject (adjective) and a predicate complement, a fairly common sentence type; Rom. 7.16: καλός ([it is] good), with a simple adjective serving as the entire clause; Rom. 12.9-19, with participles functioning like finite verbs (imperatives); and a simple finite verb which does not have a separate word for its subject, a very frequent occurrence. It is often said that several of these constructions have elided items (e.g. omission of a form of the verb εἰμί), but this kind of analysis is not necessary. It is sufficient to say that what constitutes a 'clause' in Greek may be different from what constitutes a clause in other languages. For Greek, a subject word (noun, adjective) and a predicate word (verb) are not required to constitute a clause, no matter what elements may appear in English translation.

1.3. *Established Word-Order Patterns*
In Greek, certain words or kinds of words normally appear in established places (or slots) in the Greek clause.[1] For example, certain words in Greek cannot (or only exceptionally) occur at the beginning of a clause. Other words in Greek normally do not end a clause. Still other words do tend to occur at the beginning of a clause.

1.3.1. *The Greek article.* In Greek if a substantive appears with its article, the article is placed before the substantive: e.g. ὁ θεός, *not* θεὸς ὁ.

1.3.2. *Postpositive words. The following words tend not to begin a clause (or phrase) in NT Greek, but usually appear in the second structural position*: ἄν, γάρ, δέ, γέ, μέν, οὖν, and enclitics such as ποτέ, πώς, τέ, as well as a number of pronouns (με, μου, μοι). These are often called postpositive words. Postpositive means that the word occurs anywhere from right after the first word in a syntactical unit (Mk 15.6: κατὰ δὲ ἑορτὴν [and at the feast]) to after the first entire element (such as a phrase; e.g. 1 Cor. 1.18: ὁ λόγος γὰρ ὁ τοῦ σταυροῦ [for the word of the cross]), or beyond (Rom. 9.19: ἐρεῖς μοι οὖν [therefore, you will say to me]), and anywhere in between (2 Cor. 1.19: ὁ τοῦ θεοῦ γὰρ υἱός [for the son of God]). To use the language of slot and filler, the slot for a postpositive word is a large one, extending from right after the first word to and including the next place after the first entire phrase, and all points in between (and sometimes even beyond).

a. In NT Greek, some words which in classical Greek are postpositive occur first in clauses.

Lk. 11.28: μενοῦν μακάριοι οἱ ἀκούοντες τὸν λόγον (therefore, blessed are those who hear the word), where μενοῦν appears at the beginning of the clause.

1 Thess. 4.8: τοιγαροῦν ὁ ἀθετῶν οὐκ ἄνθρωπον ἀθετεῖ (therefore, the one who rejects does not reject a human being), where the connective consists of three words which are usually postpositive; Heb. 12.1: τοιγαροῦν καὶ ἡμεῖς τοσοῦτον ἔχοντες...(therefore, we indeed having such...).

1. See K.J. Dover, *Greek Word Order* (Cambridge: Cambridge University Press, 1960), esp. ch. 2, whose work is drawn upon for sections 1.3.1–1.3.4.

b. In NT Greek, some words which in classical Greek are not postpositive are occasionally used as if they were.

2 Cor. 2.4: τὴν ἀγάπην ἵνα γνῶτε (so that you might know the love); cf. Gal. 2.10; Col. 4.16; Acts 19.4.

Rom. 11.2: ἐν Ἠλίᾳ τί λέγει ἡ γραφή; (in [the case of] Elijah, what does the Scripture say?), where the interrogative pronoun normally occurs first.

1.3.3. *Non-final words. A number of words are not normally used to end a clause in NT Greek*: e.g. ἀλλά, ἤ, καί, οὐδέ/μηδέ, οὔτε/μήτε, εἴτε, μή (lest), relative pronouns, a number of indeclinable words (εἰ, ἐπεί, ἵνα, ὁ [the]), and most prepositions.[1]

1.3.4. *Fronted elements. A number of words tend to be placed near the beginning of a clause in NT Greek*: interrogatives, clause negatives, words of succession (πρῶτον, ἔπειτα, εἶτα), most pronouns including demonstratives in the nominative case, νῦν, τότε, αὐτός (self), ἄλλος and ἕτερος, ἀμφότεροι, πολύς, πολλάκις, εἷς.

Rom. 1.8: πρῶτον μὲν εὐχαριστῶ τῷ θεῷ μου (first, I give thanks to my God).

Lk. 16.7: ἔπειτα ἑτέρῳ εἶπεν (then he said to someone else).

Rom. 1.13: ὅτι πολλάκις προεθέμην (that many times I planned).

Rom. 4.1: τί οὖν ἐροῦμεν; (what therefore shall we say?).

Rom. 4.13: οὐ γὰρ διὰ νόμου ἡ ἐπαγγελία (for the promise was not through the law); Rom. 6.12: μὴ οὖν βασιλευέτω ἡ ἁμαρτία (therefore, sin is not to rule).

2. *Patterns in NT Greek Word Order and Clause Structure*

The flexibility of Greek syntax because of its inflected endings and its various ways of forming clauses does not mean that the order of various elements makes no difference. This can be seen from the use of postpositives and other words and elements discussed above (section 1.3). Greek has several well-established structural patterns. There are two problems with arriving at a formulation of these, however. The first is that grammarians are not agreed on a proper method and terminology to determine and discuss word order and clause structure,[2] and

1. There is dispute regarding γάρ. See Chapter 12 section 2.5 on Mk 16.8.
2. There are at least three different methodologies at play. Some start with a pre-

the second is that grammarians fail to make necessary distinctions regarding clause structure. To aid in discussion below, a differentiation will be made between word order (e.g. the relation of a noun and an adjective, and the placement of individual words within clauses), clause structure (e.g. the order of subjects, predicates and complements), and sentence structure (the relation of independent and dependent clauses). At the level of word order there is much more regularity in several NT Greek writers than many grammarians have been willing to recognize, even though individual authors may reflect differing patterns. Although these conflicting data present problems for arriving at meaningful patterns for all Greek usage (even for all of the Greek of the NT), they do set useful parameters for discussion of individual NT writers.

2.1. *Word Order*

Word order includes the order of individual words usually within such groupings as prepositional phrases, noun phrases, verb phrases, and even clause structure. Many of the word-order patterns noted here have been mentioned elsewhere in this book, without their significance being drawn out. The results listed here are preliminary but reflect recent thought regarding the Greek of the NT, and to a very limited extent extra-biblical writers of Greek.[1]

2.1.1. *Adjectival modifier.* In the Greek of the NT, the adjectival modifier follows its noun approximately 75% of the time in Luke and Mark, whether it is in attributive or predicate structure. It precedes its noun approximately 65% of the time in Paul. Thus the normal Lukan structure occurs in Lk. 15.13: χώραν μακράν (a distant land), the normal Markan structure in Mk 4.41: φόβον μέγαν (great fear),[2] and

conceived 'natural' (Winer, *Treatise*, pp. 684-85) or 'stylistic' order (BDF, §472); others calculate statistical patterns (Dover, *Greek Word Order*); and still others begin with language typologies, i.e. a classificatory scheme based on recurring orders of constituent elements in languages (M.E. Davison, 'NT Greek Word Order', *Literary and Linguistic Computing* 4 [1989], pp. 19-28).

1. The results of Davison ('NT Greek Word Order', pp. 22-24) are drawn upon for sections 2.1.1–2.1.5. He formulates statistics for Luke (Luke–Acts), Paul (primarily Romans, but including other writings), and Epictetus (Book 1).

2. On Mark, see E.C. Maloney, *Semitic Interference in Marcan Syntax* (Chico, CA: Scholars Press, 1981), p. 54.

the normal Pauline structure in Rom. 1.13: ἐν τοῖς λοιποῖς ἔθνεσιν (among the remaining nations).[1]

2.1.2. *Demonstrative pronoun*. In the Greek of the NT, the demonstrative follows its noun (or substantive) far more frequently than it precedes it, approximately 85% in Paul and 78% in Luke.[2] Thus the normal structure occurs in Lk. 4.2: ἐν ταῖς ἡμέραις ἐκείναις (in those days), and Rom. 12.2: τῷ αἰῶνι τούτῳ (this age), as opposed to 2 Cor. 7.1: ταύτας... ἔχοντες τὰς ἐπαγγελίας (having these promises).

2.1.3. *Genitival modifier*. In the Greek of the NT, the genitival modifier follows its noun in Paul in 96% and in Luke in 99% of all instances. Thus the normal structure occurs in Rom. 5.5: ἡ ἀγάπη τοῦ θεοῦ (the love of God), and Lk. 1.44: ἡ φωνὴ τοῦ ἀσπασμοῦ σου (the sound of your greeting), as opposed to Rom. 11.13: ἐθνῶν ἀπόστολος (apostle of the nations).[3]

2.1.4. *Object of preposition*. In the Greek of the NT, the object of a preposition virtually always follows its preposition, except for the use of such words as χάριν, χωρίς (at Heb. 12.14), and ἕνεκα (and its

1. In extra-biblical Greek, according to Davison, Epictetus (Book 1) evidences the adjective preceding its noun in 77% of the instances. But in the Tebtunis papyri, according to Mayser, the overwhelming majority of examples have the adjective following its noun (Mayser, *Grammatik der griechischen Papyri*, II.2, pp. 53-54). The noun–adjective pattern is purportedly the predominant one in small selections taken from Polybius Books 1 and 2 (approximately 85%), Josephus, *Contra Apionem* and *Antiquities* (approximately 85%), Epictetus Books 3 and 4 (approximately 77%), and Plutarch's Lives (approximately 56%) (these figures are extrapolated from R.A. Martin, *Syntactical Evidence of Semitic Sources in Greek Documents* [Missoula, MT: Scholars Press, 1974], p. 30). Martin claims that the adjective tends to precede its noun (approximately 58%) in the select number of papyri he examines.

2. The same pattern (75%) is found in the papyri surveyed by Mayser, *Grammatik der griechischen Papyri*, II.2, p. 80, but is reversed for Epictetus (69% of demonstratives precede their noun), according to Davison.

3. Epictetus Book 1 (Davison) maintains the same pattern of the genitive modifier following its noun, although at a lower percentage (63%) than in the Greek of the NT. The tendency for the genitive modifier to follow its substantive appears to be the clearly dominant pattern in various collections of papyri, with percentages according to presence of the article ranging from approximately 65% to 90% in those roughly contemporaneous with the New Testament (see Mayser, *Grammatik der griechischen Papyri*, II.2, p. 143; Maloney, *Semitic Interference*, p. 199 n. 27).

various forms). These appear rarely in the NT. (The phenomenon of the object preceding its preposition [postposition] does occur with some regularity in Hellenistic Greek poetical texts outside of the NT, such as Cleanthes' Hymn to Zeus.)

2.1.5. *Sentence structure.*[1] In the Greek of the NT, the relative clause follows its referent in Paul in approximately 93% and in Luke in approximately 96% of the instances. Thus Rom. 5.2: δι' οὗ (referring to Jesus Christ, above)...ἐν ᾗ (referring to grace, above), and Acts 20.18: ἡμέρας ἀφ' ἧς ἐπέβην εἰς τὴν 'Ασίαν (day from which I went up into Asia) follow the pattern. The same pattern holds for other dependent clauses, in which the vast majority follow their main clause, except for conditional constructions, where the tendency is for the protasis to precede the apodosis.

On the basis of the statistics and examples cited above, it can be asserted with some plausibility that *the Greek of the NT is best described as a linear language, certainly for word order, but also probably for sentence structure.* This means that in any given construction the governing (head) or main term has a definite tendency to precede its modifier.[2]

2.2. *Clause Structure*

When discussing the order of clausal elements (subject, predicate, complement), there is still a great deal of disagreement among grammarians. Discussion of participles in Chapter 10 shows that syntax makes a significant difference in understanding the temporal relations of verb-modifying participles to their main verbs; and discussion of substantives with infinitives in Chapter 11 shows that syntax makes a

1. The discussion of sentence structure properly belongs in its own section, but is included in terms of the relative pronoun and its referent as an extension of the kinds of patterns discussed under word order.

2. As distinct as this tendency is, however, it must be noted that Greek allows for interruption of a given phrase by word(s) of another phrase, making matters of generalization and computation more difficult.

Rom. 11.24: σὺ ἐκ τῆς κατὰ φύσιν ἐξεκόπης ἀγριελαίου; Rom. 12.4: τὰ δὲ μέλη πάντα οὐ τὴν αὐτὴν ἔχει πρᾶξιν, where a finite verb intervenes in a noun phrase.

Heb. 6.11: τὴν αὐτὴν ἐνδείκνυσθαι σπουδήν, where the infinitive intervenes in its object phrase.

significant difference in establishing the subject and complement of an infinitive structure. Many of the reference grammars of the Greek of the NT are convinced that standard NT Greek 'word order' is verb-subject-object.[1] One of the major problems with such analyses is caused by the failure to recognize that the majority of Greek clauses do not express all of the elements used in the formulation. For example, there are many clauses in Greek which consist of simply a verb *or* a noun (or noun phrase with predicate), or of a verb and an object. Greek verbs are monolectic; that is, the one form contains information regarding the verbal action (aspect, mood, voice), as well as information about the subject (even though it does not explicitly specify or express that subject). It can only skew the results for determining clause structure if one presupposes some idea of where the non-expressed subject would fall in the clause, as some grammarians seem to do. The second major problem with most formulations of clause structure is that to base one's formulation of standard order on instances where all three elements are present misrepresents the evidence and the results. The minimal forms necessary for a Greek clause (e.g. subject or predicate, consisting of noun, adjective, verb) should also be used to formulate generalities regarding clause structure.

Although the following results are still very tentative,[2] there is good reason to analyze clause structure in NT Greek in the following way. In independent *and* dependent clauses (so far the results do not warrant differentiating structural patterns of these clauses), the two most frequent patterns (in no designated order) are simply predicate and predicate–complement structures. These are followed (again in no designated order) by complement–predicate and subject–predicate structures. In other words, the most common patterns are when a verb or a verb and its object (with their accompanying modifiers) are used. Monolectic verbs in Greek make it understandable that predicate and

1. Winer, *Treatise*, pp. 684-702; Robertson, *Grammar*, pp. 417-25; BDF, §§472-78; Turner, *Syntax*, pp. 344-50; Moule, *Idiom Book*, pp. 166-70; cf. Schwyzer, *Griechische Grammatik*, II, p. 693. The categories of subject, verb and object are used by most grammarians, and they are enshrined by language typology. The categories used in this chapter, however, are more useful, with subject, predicate and complement (direct and indirect objects), including any and all elements which might fill these functional categories.

2. The results are based upon analysis of major passages throughout the NT, including continuous passages such as Philippians, 1 and 2 Timothy, Mt. 5–7, Acts 21–23, Rom. 5–6, 1 Cor. 12–14, and 2 Cor. 10–13.

complement elements form the basic necessary units, since the verb cannot supply information about the object as it can about the subject. Depending upon the passages, the predicate–complement and complement–predicate structures are often quite close in ratio of usage.

2.2.1. *Predicate structure.*[1]

1 Cor. 13.8:...καταργηθήσονται...παύσονται...καταργηθήσεται (...they will be eliminated...they will cease...they will be eliminated), in predicate structures; their subjects are all expressed in preceding verbless protases.

2 Cor. 11.4: καλῶς ἀνέχεσθε (you bear [it] well).

Phil. 2.17: χαίρω καὶ συγχαίρω πᾶσιν ὑμῖν (I rejoice and I rejoice with you all), two examples of predicate structure.

2.2.2. *Predicate–complement structure.*

Mt. 5.17: μὴ νομίσητε ὅτι...(don't think that...).

Rom. 6.13: μηδὲ παριστάνετε τὰ μέλη ὑμῶν ὅπλα ἀδικίας τῇ ἁμαρτίᾳ, ἀλλὰ παραστήσατε ἑαυτοὺς τῷ θεῷ (don't offer your members as instruments of unrighteousness to sin, but offer yourselves to God).

Phil. 2.2: πληρώσατέ μου τὴν χαράν (fulfil my joy).

2.2.3. *Complement–predicate structure.*

Mt. 6.11: τὸν ἄρτον ἡμῶν τὸν ἐπιούσιον δὸς ἡμῖν σήμερον (give our daily bread to us today).

1 Cor. 13.1: ἀγάπην δὲ μὴ ἔχω (but I do not have love).

Phil. 1.9: καὶ τοῦτο προσεύχομαι (I am praying this).

2.2.4. *Subject–predicate structure.*

1 Cor. 13.4a: ἡ ἀγάπη μακροθυμεῖ (love is patient), but cf. v. 4b with reverse order (and punctuation variants); 1 Cor. 13.8: ἡ ἀγάπη οὐδέποτε πίπτει (love never fails).

1 Tim. 2.11: γυνὴ ἐν ἡσυχίᾳ μανθανέτω ἐν πάσῃ ὑποταγῇ (let a woman learn in quietness in total obedience); 1 Tim. 2.13: Ἀδὰμ γὰρ πρῶτος ἐπλάσθη (for Adam was formed first); 1 Tim. 2.14: καὶ

1. This is to be distinguished from predicate structure as defined in Chapter 6 section 1.2. Predicate structure here means that the clause consists of a verb phrase with its modifiers (predicate) excluding complements (necessary noun phrases).

Ἀδὰμ οὐκ ἠπατήθη, ἡ δὲ γυνὴ...ἐν παραβάσει γέγονεν (and Adam was not deceived, but the woman...was in sin).

2.3. *Conclusions*

If these are the normal patterns in NT Greek word order, clause structure and sentence structure, there are several noteworthy consequences. With regard to word order, the patterns noted above tend to occur with high frequencies. These must be considered the normal or non-descript ('unmarked') word-order patterns. *In analysis of a given biblical writer, it is not incumbent upon the exegete to explain the normal patterns of usage, but to explain the instances which depart from these patterns* (that is, the 'marked' instances).

With regard to clause structure, the most important observation is that Greek bases its structure upon the predicate as its minimal unit. One of the emphases of this grammar book has been to appreciate the significance of Greek verbal usage. The importance of the verb for Greek is confirmed by the central place occupied by the predicate in clause structure. The second-most-basic element of structure is the complement, which may occur either before or after the predicate in roughly equal proportions, although apparently with a slightly higher proportion of complements following rather than preceding the predicate. When the subject is expressed, the most common pattern for the Greek of the NT is for the subject to occur first, especially in subject–predicate structure but also in such structures as subject–predicate–complement and subject–complement–predicate. Thus, according to these findings, the frequent analysis of NT Greek clause structure as verb–subject–object is probably inaccurate. In dependent clauses, which tend to have a greater number of expressed subjects, the subject definitely tends to occur first because the expressed subject is often a relative pronoun.

These findings point to the expressed subject as an important element of Greek clause structure. The expressed subject is often used as a form of topic marker or shifter (in a 'topic and comment sequence'), and is appropriately placed first to signal this semantic function.[1] What this means is that when the subject is expressed it is often used either to draw attention to the subject of discussion or to

1. Several grammarians have recognized subject–predicate order as the basic order for NT Greek, as well as for other Hellenistic Greek. See Maloney, *Semitic Interference*, p. 197 n. 1, and the studies he cites.

mark a shift in the topic, perhaps signalling that a new person or event is the center of focus. Then comment is made upon this topic by means of the predicate. The subject gives new or emphatic information and the predicate elucidates it. For example, in 1 Tim. 2.13-14, Adam and Eve are both introduced as subjects of discussion. When statements are made about each, Adam is the expressed subject in v. 14a, then 'the woman' is mentioned in v. 14b. In each clause of v. 14 the subject is placed in initial position apparently to mark this emphasis or shift from the outset of the clause, minimizing any potential ambiguity. The rest of the clause (centered upon the predicate) then comments upon this marked or shifted topic. In Phil. 2.6 (part of a supposed hymn) the relative pronoun (ὅς) refers to Jesus Christ in v. 5, and this subject is maintained in all of the clauses until v. 9, where ὁ θεός is used in a subject–complement–predicate structure. As Hawthorne says of v. 9, 'there is a radical change in the hymn. Whereas the first half spoke of Christ as the acting subject of all the verbs, now in the last half "it is God who acts and Christ is the object of the divine action" (Beare).'[1] Hawthorne's statement can be confirmed by analysis of clause structure.

When the subject is placed in the second or third position in the clause (i.e. after the predicate and/or complement), its markedness or emphasis apparently decreases. The reason for this is related to the linear structure of NT Greek, in which the first position is reserved for the most important element.[2] Moving the subject to a subsidiary position, however, does not necessarily elevate another element in the clause to a position of prominence. Placing, for example, the predicate (the basic structural element) first or the complement first does not necessarily draw attention to either element, since the resulting pattern is very similar to the two basic clause structure patterns. This movement of clause elements does decrease the importance of the subject, however, relegating it to a secondary position as a topic marker. Further examples with the expressed subject include the following.

Phil. 4.5: τὸ ἐπιεικὲς ὑμῶν γνωσθήτω πᾶσιν ἀνθρώποις (let your patience be known to all people), with subject–predicate–complement structure, and the imperative in second position.

Phil. 1.15: τινὲς...τὸν Χριστὸν κηρύσσουσιν (some...are preaching Christ), with subject–complement–predicate structure.

1. Hawthorne, *Philippians*, p. 90. See also Phil. 2.27.
2. BDF, §472(2).

Jn 17.4: ἐγώ σε ἐδόξασα ἐπὶ τῆς γῆς (I glorify you on the earth), with subject–complement–predicate structure; cf. Jn 17.5: καὶ νῦν δόξασόν με σύ (and now, glorify me), with predicate–complement–subject structure. There is a distinct tendency in clauses with imperatives for the predicate to be fronted.

Rom. 11.17, 23: σὺ δὲ ἀγριέλαιος ὢν ἐνεκεντρίσθης...κἀκεῖνοι δέ, ἐὰν μὴ...ἐγκεντρισθήσονται (but you, being a wild olive, were grafted...but they, unless...will be grafted), subject–predicate structure, with intervening elements such as the participle structure and the conditional clause.

Mt. 3.2: ἤγγικεν...ἡ βασιλεία τῶν οὐρανῶν (the kingdom of heaven is near), with predicate–subject structure.

Mt. 10.5: τούτους τοὺς δώδεκα ἀπέστειλεν ὁ Ἰησοῦς (these twelve Jesus sent), with complement–predicate–subject structure.

Chapter 21

DISCOURSE ANALYSIS

Introduction

Discourse analysis (or text linguistics as it is occasionally labeled) is an area of language investigation which cannot be ignored in any thorough treatment of the Greek language. *The fundamental starting point of discourse analysis is that language is not used in isolated words or even sentences, but occurs in larger units called discourses.* These discourses may range from a single word, to a one-page letter, to a heated argument, to a multi-volume work, or even to a biblical book.[1] In fact, this entire grammar has been written with principles of discourse analysis firmly in mind. This chapter brings much of the previous discussion of individual discourse features together, with focus upon the grammatical indicators treated in previous chapters. Other discourse features could also be analyzed (e.g. lexical or vocabulary patterns), but fall outside the purview of this book.

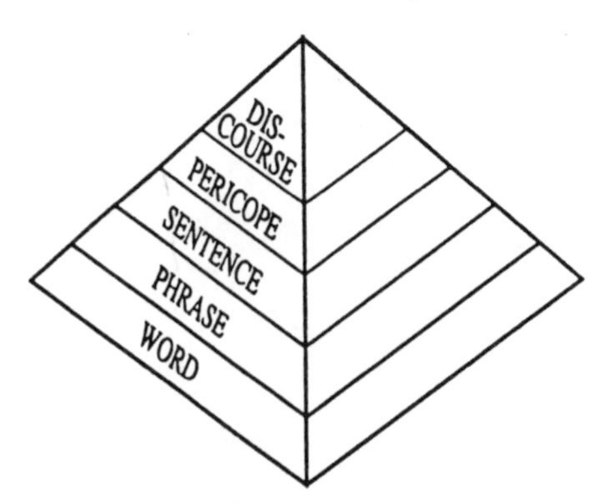

Figure 21. *Discourse Pyramid*

1. This paraphrases Z.S. Harris, 'Discourse Analysis', *Language* 28 (1952), p. 3.

A useful model of discourse analysis works from the analogy of a pyramid (fig. 21).[1] The pyramid is composed of various layers, including word, phrase (or group), sentence (clause), pericope (or paragraph) and discourse. The pinnacle of the pyramid represents the entire discourse, since it is at this level that singular topics or thematic structures can be stated and analyzed. The discourse is then broken down into an increasingly larger number of smaller units, its constituent elements. At the base of the pyramid are the formal units of language which comprise the larger structural and conceptual units. In discourse analysis one can begin at the top (the pinnacle of the pyramid) or the bottom (the base), but one must work through all of the stages, from both directions, to provide a full analysis. For example, starting at the bottom, Rom. 6.15 begins with the terse phrase τί οὖν (what therefore), composed of two words, an interrogative pronoun and an inferential particle. Together they form an expression common in philosophical discourse (diatribe) of the Hellenistic period to signal the words of a hypothetical discussion. At a larger level than the word or phrase, this question begins a coherent section in Rom. 6.15–7.6 which consists of the false conclusion of the discussion partner and then a two-fold response from Paul (6.15b-16). This is followed by a two-part development of his response (6.17-18 and 19-23), and another false conclusion (7.1), again followed by a two-part development (7.2-6). At a larger level, this dialogue is a development from 6.14 in the preceding author–interlocutor debate which all together forms part of the argument of chs. 6–8 regarding the life of the believer in light of justification. Even larger still, chs. 6–8 close the Pauline discussion of the universal human plight and God's solution, begun in 1.16, and precede an argument regarding God's faithfulness with respect to Israel in chs. 9–11, before turning to an ethical (parenetic) section in chs. 12–14. All of this takes place in the epistolary

1. Much of what is said here synthesizes a wide range of material new to NT studies. Secondary literature worth considering includes: J.P. Louw, 'Discourse Analysis and the Greek NT', *BT* 24 (1973), pp. 101-18; E.A. Nida *et al.*, *Style and Discourse, with Special Reference to the Text of the Greek NT* (Roggebai, South Africa: Bible Society, 1983); P. Cotterell and M. Turner, *Linguistics and Biblical Interpretation* (Downers Grove, IL: Inter-Varsity Press, 1989), pp. 238-92; G. Brown and G. Yule, *Discourse Analysis* (Cambridge: Cambridge University Press, 1983); K. Callow, *Discourse Considerations in Translating the Word of God* (Grand Rapids: Zondervan, 1974); and S.E. Porter and J.T. Reed, 'Greek Grammar since BDF: A Retrospective and Prospective Analysis', *FN* 4 (1991), pp. 143-64.

framework of Romans, indicated primarily in ch. 1 and 15.14–16.27. Starting from the top of the pyramid, one could move in the opposite direction, from the entire discourse as a diatribal epistle, down through the major sub-units, to the individual phrases and even words. The entire structure constitutes what might be referred to as 'context' in a fairly expansive sense.

Another way of formulating an approach to discourse analysis is in terms of micro- and macro-structures. The micro-structures are the smaller units (such as words, phrases, clauses, sentences and even pericopes and paragraphs) which make up macro-structures. The macro-structures are the units of discourse which convey the large thematic ideas which help to govern the interpretation of the micro-structures. Macro-structures serve two vital functions. On the one hand, they are the highest level of interpretation of a given text. On the other hand, they are the points at which larger extra-textual issues such as time, place, audience, authorship and purpose (more traditional questions of biblical backgrounds) must be considered. A complete discourse analysis must also treat this issue of extra-textual context from a discourse analysis perspective. Unfortunately this chapter must confine itself to issues more readily apparent within the written text.

Knowledge of the language system of Greek (in particular of the Greek of the NT, for the purposes of this book) should prove adequate to perform a good bit of the most important language-centered discourse analysis of NT Greek texts. There is of course much more that can and must be done, but this book has provided sufficient information to enable grammatical analysis of the major categories at the word, phrase, clause and sentence levels. Along the way, relevant comments have been included to aid in grasping the significance of the categories under discussion. For example, on issues of time and tense it was pointed out that discourse factors play a major interpretative role, especially with respect to deictic indicators (on deictic indicators, see Chapter 1 section 1.2); on use of cases and prepositions, the threefold framework of formal meaning, syntax and context was employed (Chapters 4 and 9); on particles and conjunctions, analysis was frequently presented in light of their common function of connecting units such as phrases and clauses (Chapter 12); and on various types of clauses, their syntactical and semantic relations were indicated.

In this chapter, in an effort to unify a number of discourse factors more explicitly, several further categories are discussed. These categories bring together many of the concepts treated in the chapters above and extend them through application to larger discourse units.

1. *Discourse Boundaries*

A discourse boundary is a linguistic means of indicating when a unit of a discourse, such as a pericope or paragraph, concludes and when a new unit begins. Smaller units, such as clauses and sentences, have their own particular boundary markers, such as marks of punctuation and various connecting words (such as καί or δέ).[1] The concern here is with boundaries of larger units, such as pericopes and paragraphs. The question of the conventions of various literary genres could be included here, if one were to extend discussion to complete discourses. Boundaries of discourse in Greek may be indicated by a variety of means, several of which are discussed below.

1.1. *Shift in Grammatical Person*

Shifts in grammatical person (e.g. first to third person, and so forth) are often useful indicators of the closing of one discourse unit and the beginning of another.

Rom. 1.18-32; 2.1-29. The first discourse unit (1.18-32) is a discussion in third person of the universal human plight. At 2.1 there is a shift to second person when Paul focuses his attention more clearly on the one who judges. This shift provides a closing boundary to 1.18-32 and signals the beginning of a new unit (2.1-29) dominated by use of the second person.

1.2. *Shift in Verb Tense-Forms*

Verb tense-forms are frequently shifted (e.g. aorist to present, and so forth) to indicate the boundaries of a discourse. Particularly useful is the switch to or from the narrative tense-form (aorist) to signal the opening or closing of a discourse unit.

Mk 7.1. The historic present (συνάγονται) introduces a new pericope, the previous one (which goes back at least as far as Mk 6.53) having ended with a series of aorist and imperfect tense-forms. Furthermore, Mark frequently uses καί and a verb, often of speaking

1. See Levinsohn, *Textual Connections*, pp. 83-120.

or location, occasionally in the historic present, to mark a new pericope.[1]

2. *Prominence*

Prominent features in a discourse may be selected for grammatical as well as conceptual emphasis. As Longacre humorously remarks, 'Discourse without prominence would be like pointing to a piece of black cardboard and insisting that it was a picture of black camels crossing black sands at midnight'.[2] Greek contains a number of linguistic means to indicate prominence.

2.1. *Verbal Aspect*

Verbal aspect does not need to be defined here, since it was treated at length in Chapter 1. *The planes of discourse as indicated by use of the verbal aspects are a means by which the points of emphasis or peaks of a discourse may be indicated* (see Chapter 1 section 1.1.2). Items which are placed in the background tense (aorist) comprise either the backbone (in narrative) or supporting illustrative material (in exposition) against which more prominent items are set. The foreground (present) and frontground (perfect) tense-forms are used to mark prominent features. The planes of discourse apply both to narrative and to expositional material.

Mk 11.1-11. This new pericope is introduced by several historic presents (vv. 1-2). The backbone of the narrative is carried by aorist tense-forms (vv. 4, 6, 7, 8, 11), occasionally heightened by imperfects (vv. 5, 9). The most significant action is described by the foreground and frontground tense-forms. The foreground (present) tense-form is used of the content of Jesus' instructions (vv. 2-3), the response to Jesus' commands (v. 7), and the introduction of the OT quotation (v. 9). The frontground (perfect) tense-form is reserved for two key items. The first instance uses the perfect tense-form of the colt the

1. See e.g. Mk 1.9, 16, 21, 39, 40; 2.1, 13, 15, 18, 23; 3.1, 13, 20, 31; 4.13, 21, 24, 26, 30, 35; 5.1, 21, 24; 6.1, 14, 21, 30; 7.1, 14; 8.11, 14, 22, 27, 31, 34; 9.1, 9, 14, 33; 10.2, 13, 17, 23, 35, 41, 46; 11.11, 15, 20, 27; 12.1, 13, 18, 28, 35, 41; 13.1, 3; 14.3, 22, 26, 27, 32, 53, 65, 66; 15.21, 33; 16.1.

2. R.E. Longacre, 'Discourse Peak as Zone of Turbulence', in *Beyond the Sentence: Discourse and Sentential Form* (ed. J.R. Wirth; Ann Arbor, MI: Karoma, 1985), p. 83.

disciples are instructed to find—it is to be bound (vv. 2, 4)—and of the people who observe the disciples taking it (v. 5). The second frontground focus is reserved for the people's response to Jesus' entry, with the perfect participle (vv. 9, 10) highlighting their praise of the coming one. The two words of praise occur in quotations of the OT (Ps. 118.25), linking the OT to messianic fulfilment with the aid of verbal aspect.

Rom. 5.1-5. Paul lays down his assumption regarding justification with the background (aorist participle) tense-form (v. 1a) before giving his exhortation with the foreground (present subjunctive) tense-form (v. 1b). He draws special attention to the status which enables this word of encouragement by means of two frontground (perfect) tense-forms, concerning having access and standing (v. 2). Paul uses a similar pattern in the next two sections: the exhortation to boast using the foreground (present) tense-form (v. 3a) is followed by the ground of boasting, stated by the frontground (perfect participle) tense-form (v. 3b); hope is said not to cause shame, using the foreground (present) tense-form (v. 5a), because of the love of God poured out in Christians' hearts, using the frontground (perfect) tense-form (v. 5b).

2.2. *Word Order and Clause Structure*

Several chapters above have drawn attention to the fact that in Greek there is unmarked and marked word order and clause structure. *When the marked order is found the interpreter is free to ask whether prominence is being established.* Chapter 20 on word order and clause structure gives more detail regarding this factor in textual prominence.

Rom. 7.15-16, 19-20. Paul places the relative clauses which are serving as objects of their verbs before the verbs themselves. This gives prominence to the relative clauses, which normally follow their main clauses.

2.3. *Redundant Pronouns*

The use of pronouns as subjects, which are by strict rules of grammar usually unnecessary, indicates the establishment of prominence in discourse. The classic example might be the Johannine ἐγώ εἰμι phrase, in which the personal pronoun is not strictly required but is used to draw attention to the metaphors Jesus reportedly uses (e.g. Jn 6.48, 51).

Since Greek verbs are monolectic, whenever the subject is expressed (if it is not necessary to eliminate ambiguity), prominence is indicated.

1 Thess. 2.1-2. Paul uses the initial intensive pronoun αὐτοί and the term ἀδελφοί (nominative plural of direct address), along with the verbal shift from first person to second person plural, to establish prominence in his contrast between 'us' and 'you'. Cf. Jn 11.1-2, where the specification of the participants is necessary.

3. *Cohesion*

Cohesion refers to grammatical, semantic and contextual factors which hold a discourse together. Discourse analysis begins with the assumption that texts cohere or hold together in a unified way. Various linguistic elements can be seen to form systems of signs used to establish textual cohesion, with the result that often apparently diffuse and diverse textual phenomena can be brought into meaningful relations. A number of factors help to establish the cohesion of a text.

3.1. *Person Reference*

Reference to person is established through a variety of means, including direct address, grammatical person of a verb, and pronoun reference.[1]

1 Timothy. In 1 Timothy, all grammatical instances of first person singular have Paul, the purported author, as their referent. Use of second person, including especially use of the pronoun, is entirely in the singular, with reference to the epistle's addressee, Timothy,[2] except for the last words of 1 Tim. 6.21, where the plural pronoun is used (note that there are textual variants with the singular). Regardless of whether one argues for pseudepigraphical authorship or for address of the epistle to the early church concerning how to govern its affairs,[3] one must begin with the cohesive factor that the letter purports to be a personal letter from 'Paul' to 'Timothy'.

3.2. *Verbal Aspect*

Verbal aspect not only can be used as a means to mark prominent and

1. See C.E.B. Cranfield, 'Changes in Person and Number in Paul's Epistles', in *Paul and Paulinism* (ed. M.D. Hooker and S.G. Wilson; London: SPCK, 1982), pp. 280-89.

2. See e.g. 1 Tim. 1.3, 18; 3.14; 4.6, 7, 11, 12, 13, 14, 15, 16; 5.1, 3, 7, 11, 19, 20, 21, 22, 23; 6.2, 11, 12, 17, 20.

3. See e.g. M. Dibelius and H. Conzelmann, *The Pastoral Epistles* (Philadelphia: Fortress Press, 1972), p. 1.

significant discourse features, but it can serve an important cohesive function. This is often done by employing patterns of verbal aspectual usage that do not draw undue attention to themselves. These include the use of the aorist and (to a lesser extent) imperfect tense-forms in narrative, and the present tense-form in exposition (see Chapter 1 section 1). Furthermore, there are examples where marked instances of verbal aspect are used to link pericopes (or paragraphs) into coherent units.

Lk. 11.3 and 5-13. Luke records Jesus' prayer to God in 11.2-4. The middle petition (v. 3) contains a present imperative rather than an aorist, the verb form used elsewhere in this version of the prayer, as well as in Matthew's (6.11). This tense usage is perplexing, until it is realized that the parable of the friend who begs for food at midnight (Lk. 11.5-13) follows upon the prayer. The use of the present imperative in Lk. 11.3 anticipates the subsequent episode and gives coherence to the two pericopes (see Chapter 13 section 3).

3.3. *Connectives*

Various connectives are used by various authors to give cohesion to their discourse (see Chapter 12).

Mark, for example, often uses εὐθύς, an adjective functioning adverbially (often preceded by καί), to signal significant turning points in his narrative (e.g. 1.23, 29; 6.45; 8.10; 14.43; 15.1). Significant events within narratives are signalled by εὐθύς in, for example, Mk 9.15, 24.

In Paul the connective οὖν is used to link various segments together (in this sense it may serve as a discourse boundary marker as well). It is used in conjunction with γάρ, which can likewise serve as a cohesive device. For example, οὖν links rhetorical questions or statements to previous discussion in Rom. 3.1, 9; 4.1; 5.1; 6.1, 12, 15; 7.7, 13; 8.12, 31; 9.14; 11.1, 11; 12.1. Instances of γάρ are much too frequent to note here with any completeness. Significant instances of cohesive use include Rom. 1.11, 16, and 18 (two fairly significant structural junctures); 4.13, where the argument about Abraham turns to more general statements regarding promise; 7.14, 18; 8.18; 11.25, where a disclosure formula occurs; and 12.3.

3.4. *Informational Structure*

The informational structure of a passage—the order and manner in which information is presented in a discourse—serves as a vital item to establish coherence. Informational structure is very much related to the 'topic and comment sequence', in which an author often establishes a theme and then develops ideas concerning it. The issue of introduction of topics and subsequent comments upon them was considered briefly in Chapter 20 on word order and clause structure. At this point the categories can be expanded.

In the epistles, topic and comment work in a coordinated fashion when the author selects particular topics for discussion and elucidation (see Chapter 20 section 2.3). In Paul's use of diatribe, for example, he introduces rhetorical questions to raise issues he wishes to probe more fully. His answers to the hypothetical questions then propel the inquiry forward.

Rom. 1.16–3.20. In 1.16-17 Paul states the theme of the book of Romans, that the just by faith shall live. Before he can establish this theme, he must document the human condition. Paul chronicles the universal sinful plight of humans, with some reference to distinctives of Judaism, in 1.18–2.29. Then Paul's imaginary discussion partner asks in Rom. 3.1: τί οὖν τὸ περισσὸν τοῦ Ἰουδαίου ἢ τίς ἡ ὠφέλεια τῆς περιτομῆς; (what therefore is the advantage of the Jew, or what is the profit of circumcision?). Paul then answers this question in 3.2-20. The result is a coordinated discourse which moves from general humanity to the particular case of the Jew. At that point he is ready to define justification.

Rom. 13.1-7. In Rom. 13.1-7 Paul presents his information by means of a structured outline. The information structure proceeds from a command for obedience to just authorities (13.1a) to two reasons, one theological reason stating that the commands are given by God (13.1b-2) and one practical reason regarding the reward of good and punishment of evil (13.3-5). Paul concludes with a practical example (13.67).[1]

In the records of the historical books, the information structure may well proceed in the same way. But at several places there are noticeable deviations from the expected pattern.

Jn 3.1-21. Regarding the encounter between Jesus and Nicodemus, Cotterell's excellent analysis argues that Nicodemus initiates conversation and suggests several topics to Jesus for discussion: his claim to being a rabbi, his function as teacher, his origin from God, and

1. See S.E. Porter, 'Rom. 13.1-7 as Pauline Political Rhetoric', *FN* 3 (1990), pp. 115-39.

the signs he has performed (3.2). But Jesus refuses all of these topics and instead pursues the topic of what it means in Jn 3.3 that τις γεννηθῇ ἄνωθεν (someone might be born again [or from above]). Nicodemus then follows Jesus' lead and responds.[1]

Acts 21.18-26. In Jerusalem Paul reports to James and the other elders. Paul initiates the topic of the things God had been doing among the Gentiles (21.19). Although the elders briefly acknowledge Paul's work, they immediately shift the flow of the discourse to the topic of the Jews, abandoning the topic of the Gentiles and introducing accusations made regarding Paul's teaching on the law (21.20-21). Paul is then compelled to follow their advice to perform a temple rite in order to alleviate fears regarding his ministry.

4. *Conclusion*

By way of conclusion to how discourse analysis is performed, an analogy can be introduced from a common practice in map-drawing. This well illustrates the relationship between a text's macro-structure and its micro-structures. When presenting a map of a certain locale it is often beneficial to show how the smaller locale fits into its larger regional sphere. The smaller locale is superimposed to the side of its larger area, being significantly enlarged to reveal details otherwise unseen in the larger scaled map. Micro-structures too can be analyzed in detail, somewhat out of proportion to their larger framework. The micro-structures are part of something larger, the 'global map', so to speak, and must be understood within that framework. Conversely, the larger macro-structures are composed of micro-structures and thus the 'global map' would be incomplete without its smaller, individual regions. Discourse analysis provides a means of analyzing how these various linguistic items—including the word, phrase, clause or sentence, pericope or paragraph—work together to form entire discourses, and it opens the door to seeing how the discourse as a linguistic structure can inform analysis of its smaller components.

1. F.P. Cotterell, 'The Nicodemus Conversation: A Fresh Appraisal', *ExpTim* 96 (1984–85), p. 239.

GLOSSARY

The following glossary defines a number of terms which are used in this book and which may be unfamiliar to some students and teachers of Greek. A brief definition is given in order to aid the reader with new terminology, although the chapter in which related topics are discussed will need to be consulted for a fuller understanding. Many of the definitions draw upon the *Dictionary of Language and Linguistics*, by R.R.K. Hartmann and F.C. Stork (New York: Wiley, 1972), with adaptations for this work.

Adjectival: performing or functioning like an adjective or similar modifier, that is, to modify a noun or other substantive.

Adverbial: performing or functioning like an adverb or similar modifier, that is, to modify a verb or other modifier such as an adjective. An example is the adverbial (circumstantial) use of the participle, when a participle is dependent upon and modifies a finite verb.

Agent (agency): the individual (or thing) responsible for performing an action. With an active voice verb, the agent is usually the grammatical subject of the verb. In English, with a passive voice verb the agent is often the one referred to with the word 'by', as in 'The ball was thrown by Bill' (Bill is the agent). Greek has three levels of agency: primary or personal (often with ὑπό), secondary or intermediate (often with διά), and instrumental or impersonal (often with ἐν or the simple dative case).

Aktionsart: a German grammatical term devised late in the nineteenth century to describe an approach toward verbal action. The advocates of *Aktionsart* theory held that events could be objectively characterized by a limited number of descriptive labels—punctiliar or momentary, iterative, linear, and so on. The verb tenses of Greek, as well as the individual lexical items, were equated with these labels.

Anaphora (anaphoric): reference by grammatical means to a person or thing mentioned previously in the text. It is an important category when discussing pronoun usage. In the previous sentence, 'it' was an anaphora for the word 'anaphora'.

Anarthrous: without the article.

Apodosis: the 'then' or consequence clause of a conditional ('if–then') construction, or the independent clause in a sentence which has a conditional-like clause (e.g. 'whoever...'). See protasis.

Apposition: a semantic relationship whereby one item (a word, phrase or even clause) defines another. Apposition in Greek may be established through a variety of means, including an appositional genitive, appositional nominative, appositional accusative, and the use of the infinitive. An *appositional* relationship is sometimes distinguished from an *epexegetical* one, with apposition expressing a relationship for nouns and epexegesis for verbs.

Arthrous: with the article.

Articular: with the article.

Aspect (verbal): a semantic category which governs verb tense-form usage in Greek. A language user chooses to view an action as occurring in a particular way and then selects one of the established verb tense-forms of Greek to convey that meaning. For example, if the speaker sees the action as complete (perfective aspect), the aorist verb tense-form is used.

Asyndeton: a construction in which clauses are joined without the use of connecting particles or conjunctions.

Attitude: a semantic category which is grammaticalized by the Greek mood forms. A language user states his or her view of an action's relationship to reality by selecting one of the verb mood forms of Greek to convey that meaning. For example, if the speaker wishes to assert that an action occurred (assertive attitude), the indicative mood form is used.

Attributive: refers to a syntactical structure whereby a quality or attribute is considered part of what another item is by nature. This is normally reflected syntactically by the attribute (frequently an adjective or participle) falling within the range of the substantive and its article, whether preceding or following. See Chapter 6.

Auxiliary (verb): a verb such as εἰμί which helps another verb, such as a participle, to form a complete verbal unit. Auxiliary verbs are necessary in periphrastic and catenative verbal constructions.

Catenative construction: a small group of constructions consisting of an auxiliary verb with verbal aspect (i.e. not εἰμί) and an infinitive, which form a single unit used regularly together. Catenative constructions are to be distinguished from periphrastic verbal constructions in Greek.

Circumstantial: a word or phrase is considered *circumstantial* if it is concerned with the way in which an action occurs. For example, a circumstantial use of the participle describes how the action occurred (cause, manner, means, and so forth).

Clause: a complete grammatical construction consisting of one or more phrases. In Greek a clause may consist of anything from a single verb, noun or adjective (one-word phrase), to an intricate complex of phrases. Clauses may be independent (free-standing) or dependent (subordinate). Dependent clauses may be linked in a variety of syntactical and semantic relations to their independent clauses (e.g. time, cause, inference, and the like). The term 'main clause' is used of any clause (whether dependent or independent) in relation to which other clauses are dependent.

Collocation: a regular or standard combination of words. For example, English speakers usually say 'toasted bread' but 'grilled steak' to refer to the same cooking process.

Complement: the element which completes (or complements) a predicate. The complement is often equated with the object of a verb (either direct or indirect). In clause structure, the complement is one of the three major components (the others being subject and predicate), and consists of at least one phrase.

Completive: any element which can complete another element. For example, an object (direct or indirect) is the completive of a verb; objects of prepositions are completives.

Consequential: describing an action that comes about as a consequence of another; or as an expected result.

Constative: a label given to particular verbs or uses of verb tenses (often the aorist) which are said to treat a given action in its entirety or as a whole, from start to finish.

Deixis: means used by a language to place events in their relational (especially temporal) contexts, including reference to person, place, time and discourse features. 'Deictic indicators' are the particular linguistic items that establish these relationships, such as the words 'now', 'then' and 'tomorrow', among many others.

Deliberative: referring to thought, consideration or intention. See volitive, hortatory.

Demonstrative: words such as (in English) 'this', 'that', 'these' and 'those'. They are particular words used to point out or indicate persons or things. In NT Greek, the most common demonstratives are οὗτος and ἐκεῖνος.

Desiderative: expressing desire, usually in the form of a mild command.

Ecbatic: see resultive.

Effective: concerning the endpoint of an action.

Enclitic: this term is descriptive of a small group of words that rely upon the preceding word for their accent. Among enclitic words (or 'enclitics') are the indefinite pronoun, forms of the verb εἰμί, and various particles.

Epexegetic: a semantic relationship whereby one item (a word, phrase or even clause) defines another (also known as apposition). An epexegetic relation in Greek may be established through a variety of means, including an epexegetical genitive, epexegetical nominative, epexegetical accusative, and the use of the infinitive. This use is often distinguished from apposition, with epexegesis expressing a relationship for verbs and apposition for nouns.

Etymology: the reconstruction and study of a word's history and origin, including changes in form and meaning. The etymological fallacy is the belief that the history of a word is determinative for its meaning.

Factive (non-factive) statements: statements which (do not) assert facts.

Filler (slot and filler): in a particular grammatical model (tagmemics), this term refers to the items which are placed in the available slots in a construction. For example, in a noun phrase in Greek, a filler might be a participle which fills the substantive slot or a modifier slot.

Final: see purpose.

Finite verb: a verb that grammaticalizes person, such as those used in the indicative, subjunctive, optative and imperative mood forms. The infinitive and the participle are not finite forms, since they do not grammaticalize person.

Gnomic: this term characterizes an event as continuous or as recurring over the course of time, and normally relates to processes of nature. Also known as omnitemporal.

Grammaticalize: to express semantic information by means of a particular structure (often the form of an individual word) in a language. For example, the aorist verb tense grammaticalizes perfective verbal aspect.

Head-term: the syntactically dominant or governing term in a construction, often the noun in a noun phrase or the verb in a verb phrase. The head-term has the same function as the entire construction in which it stands.

Hortatory: characterized by language designed to direct, incite or encourage.

Illative: inferential.

Imperfective: this term refers to the semantic value of the verbal aspect grammaticalized by the present and imperfect verb tenses in Greek. It is used to describe an action as in progress.

Inceptive: expressing the beginning of an action.

Inchoative: expressing the beginning of an action.

Inferential: pointing to a logical conclusion to be drawn from another action.

Inflection: the sets of endings which some languages (inflected or fusional languages such as Greek) attach to their words to distinguish various semantic and syntactical categories and relations.

Ingressive: expressing the beginning of an action.

Instrumental: expressing or indicating the means or agent by which an action is accomplished.

Intermediate agency: see secondary agency.

Intransitive: Intransitive verbs make complete sense without requiring an object (complement). In English the verb 'run' (like most verbs of motion) is considered intransitive: 'I run every Tuesday'. Some verbs in Greek (and English) may be intransitive and transitive. See transitive.

Iterative: expressing repetition of an action.

Lexical: related to the vocabulary items of a language, susceptible to semantic analysis. Lexical meaning is often associated with the 'dictionary' meaning of a word.

Linear language: a language where the subject precedes the verb, modifier precedes its governing or head-term, referent precedes its relative pronoun, and so forth.

Marked and unmarked: labels given to various constructions to imply their relative semantic weights. The unmarked structure is often more frequently found, more diverse in form, less regular in structure, of less formal substance, less emphatic and of minimum essential meaning. The marked structure is often less frequent in appearance, more stable in form, more regular in structure, of greater formal substance, more emphatic, and of greater significance in meaning.

Modal: related to mood.

Monolectic: a descriptive term for Greek finite verbs, which refers to their ability to contain sufficient information, in particular indication of grammatical subject, aspect, mood and voice, to constitute complete clauses.

Mood: the label given to the forms used to indicate the speaker's view of an action's relation to reality. Greek has four recognized mood forms: indicative, subjunctive, optative, imperative. The future form has characteristics of the indicative and non-indicative (in particular, subjunctive) mood forms. The participle and infinitive are often considered non-indicative moods for the sake of discussion.

Morphology: a grammatical category describing the analysis and discussion of the function, use and classification of the smallest units of meaningful structure in a language (morphemes). In the word 'boys', there are two meaningful units of structure: 'boy' and the plural indicator 's'.

Omnitemporal: occurring at any and all times. See gnomic.

Paradigm: model or pattern, often used to refer to the list of various inflected forms of a given morphological category. For example, there are certain regular formal features of the aorist paradigm.

Particle: an indeclinable word with grammatical and relational meaning. Prepositions, conjunctions and adverbs are all particles.

Partitive: describing the function of a word or phrase which refers to a part of a larger whole. For example, the phrase 'some of the people' uses 'some' partitively.

Perfective: this term refers to the semantic value of the verbal aspect grammaticalized by the aorist verb tense in Greek. It is used to describe an action as whole or complete.

Periphrastic: (1) describing a verbal construction consisting of the auxiliary verb εἰμί in its various forms and a participle in appropriate grammatical relation, separated by nothing other than elements which complete the participle. If any modifiers of the auxiliary, including an expressed subject, intervene between the two elements, the construction is not periphrastic. Periphrastic verbal constructions are to be distinguished from catenative constructions in Greek; (2) describing any means by which one statement may be used as a substitute for another.

Personal agency: see primary agency.

Phrase: a group of words forming a syntactical unit which may constitute a subject, predicate, complement, and the like. Phrases are labeled as noun/nominal, verb/verbal, prepositional, and so forth, depending upon the construction of the unit. A phrase may consist of only one word.

Postpositive: not occurring in first position in a sentence or phrase.

Predicate: (1) a structure whereby a quality or attribute is given to another item, syntactically indicated normally by the predicated item not falling within the range of the substantive and its article (see Chapter 6); (2) the functional name for the verbal part of a clause, consisting of a verb phrase (verb and its modifiers). These categories, although similar in some ways, are not to be confused with predicate structure, as discussed in Chapter 20 on word order and clause structure.

Preposition: a word belonging to a group of particles often used to aid the cases in their function by joining a noun phrase to other words in a clause. Prepositions are often described as 'taking' objects or 'governing' particular cases. Prepositions may also be prefixed to verbs and other words.

Primary agency: the primary cause of an action, often a personal agent. In Greek, primary or personal agency is often indicated with ὑπό and the genitive case.

Proleptic: future-referring or looking to the future.

Protasis: the 'if' or supposition clause of a conditional ('if–then') construction, or the dependent clause in a sentence which has a conditional-like clause (e.g. 'whoever...'). See apodosis.

Punctiliar: expressing momentary or point-like action.

Purpose: the intention behind or reason for another action. Purpose often overlaps with result, because to intend an action can mean that something comes about as a result.

Result: the results or consequences of another action. Result often overlaps with purpose, because to bring about a result can mean that an action was intended.

Secondary agency: an agent that contributes to an action's occurrence but does not instigate it, often specifying a channel or means for a primary or personal agent. In Greek, secondary agency is often indicated with διά and the genitive case.

Semantics: the study or analysis of meaning as it is conveyed by language, specifically by the particular forms of the language, such as the cases, the verbal aspects, the prepositions, and so forth.

Sentence: a syntactical unit consisting of one or more clauses, at least one of them an independent clause.

Slot (slot and filler): in a particular grammatical model (tagmemics), the definable spaces (environments) in a construction into which items may fit. For example, in a noun phrase in Greek, there are slots for a substantive, modifiers before and after, and the article.

Stative: this term refers to the semantic value of the verbal aspect grammaticalized by the perfect and pluperfect verb tenses in Greek. It is used to describe an action as being in a particular complex state.

Subordination: the grammatical means by which dependent relations especially between clauses are indicated. See clause.

Substantive: a term given to any word which may be used like a noun. For example, in Greek, participles, infinitives, and especially adjectives, besides nouns, are often used as substantives.

Syntax: a grammatical category concerned with the order of words, phrases and other elements, and the meaning relationships they enter into. For example, the attributive structure in Greek normally has a syntax in which the modifying word may be covered by the article either before or after the substantive.

Telic: describing the intention behind or reason for another action; see purpose.

Timeless: not restricted to any temporal sphere of reference. Mathematical and many theological propositions are considered timeless in their formulation.

Transitive: transitive verbs require direct objects to make complete sense. In English the verb 'buy' is transitive: 'I buy my clothes at the thrift store'. Some verbs in Greek (and English) may be transitive and intransitive. See intransitive.

Unmarked: see marked.

Verbal aspect: see aspect (verbal).

Voice: a semantic category used to describe the relation of the agent to its action. Greek has three voices: active, in which (to speak generally) the subject or agent performs the action; middle, in which the subject participates in or benefits from the action; and passive, in which the action is done to the grammatical subject by another agent.

Volitive: describes a wish; a volitive is a mild form of command.

BIBLIOGRAPHY

Not all of the works listed below are cited frequently in the text above, but their importance warrants inclusion in this list, which attempts to give those works worthy of a place in a library of Greek grammar.

Bauer, W., *A Greek–English Lexicon of the NT and Other Early Christian Literature* (trans. W.F. Arndt and F.W. Gingrich; rev. F.W. Gingrich and F.W. Danker; Chicago: University of Chicago Press, 2nd edn, 1979).

Blass, F., and A. Debrunner, *A Greek Grammar of the NT and Other Early Christian Literature* (trans. R.W. Funk; Chicago: University of Chicago Press, 1961).

Brooks, J.A., and C.L. Winbery, *Syntax of NT Greek* (Washington, DC: University Press of America, 1979).

Burton, E.D.W., *Syntax of the Moods and Tenses in NT Greek* (repr. Grand Rapids: Kregel, 1976 [3rd edn, 1898]).

Chamberlain, W.D., *An Exegetical Grammar of the Greek NT* (repr. Grand Rapids: Baker, 1979).

Dana, H.E., and J.R. Mantey, *A Manual Grammar of the Greek NT* (N.p.: Macmillan, 1955).

Fanning, B.M., *Verbal Aspect in NT Greek* (Oxford: Clarendon Press, 1990).

Goodwin, W.W., *A Greek Grammar* (London: St Martin's, 1894).

Green, S.G., *Handbook to the Grammar of the Greek Testament* (London: Religious Tract Society, n.d.).

McKay, K.L., *Greek Grammar for Students: A Concise Grammar of Classical Attic with Special Reference to Aspect in the Verb* (Canberra: Australian National University, 1974).

Mandilaras, B.G., *The Verb in the Greek Non-Literary Papyri* (Athens: Hellenic Ministry of Culture and Sciences, 1973).

Moule, C.F.D., *An Idiom Book of NT Greek* (Cambridge: Cambridge University Press, 2nd edn, 1959).

Moulton, J.H., *A Grammar of NT Greek*. I. *Prolegomena* (Edinburgh: T. & T. Clark, 3rd edn, 1908).

Moulton, J.H., and W.F. Howard, *A Grammar of NT Greek*. II. *Accidence and Word-Formation* (Edinburgh: T. & T. Clark, 1929).

Porter, S.E., *Verbal Aspect in the Greek of the NT, with Reference to Tense and Mood* (New York: Peter Lang, 1989).

Robertson, A.T., *A Grammar of the Greek NT in the Light of Historical Research* (Nashville: Broadman, 4th edn, 1934).

Schwyzer, E., *Griechische Grammatik* (2 vols.; Munich: Beck, 1939, 1950).

Smyth, H.W., *Greek Grammar* (rev. G.M. Messing; Cambridge, MA: Harvard University Press, 1956).
Turner, N., *A Grammar of NT Greek*. III. *Syntax* (Edinburgh: T. & T. Clark, 1963).
Winer, G.B., *A Treatise on the Grammar of NT Greek* (trans. W.F. Moulton; Edinburgh: T. & T. Clark, 1882).
Zerwick, M., *Biblical Greek* (Rome: Pontifical Biblical Institute, 1963).

INDEXES

INDEX OF NEW TESTAMENT REFERENCES

INDEX OF SUBJECTS